# INNOVATION, POLICY AND LAW

# INNOVATION, POLICY AND LAW

*Australia and the International High Technology Economy*

CHRISTOPHER ARUP

*Department of Legal Studies, La Trobe University, Melbourne*

CAMBRIDGE
UNIVERSITY PRESS

CAMBRIDGE UNIVERSITY PRESS
Cambridge, New York, Melbourne, Madrid, Cape Town,
Singapore, São Paulo, Delhi, Mexico City

Cambridge University Press
The Edinburgh Building, Cambridge CB2 8RU, UK

Published in the United States of America by Cambridge University Press, New York

www.cambridge.org
Information on this title: www.cambridge.org/9780521430036

© Cambridge University Press 1993

This publication is in copyright. Subject to statutory exception
and to the provisions of relevant collective licensing agreements,
no reproduction of any part may take place without the written
permission of Cambridge University Press.

First published 1993

*A catalogue record for this publication is available from the British Library*

*Library of Congress Cataloguing in Publication Data*
Arup, Christopher, 1949- .
Innovation, policy and law: Australia and the international
high technology economy/Christopher Arup.
Includes bibliographical references and index.
ISBN 0 521 43003 8.
1. High technology industries – Law and legislation – Australia.
2. Foreign trade promotion – Law and legislation – Australia.
3. Intellectual property – Australia. I. Title.
KU1018.H54A88 1993
346.9404'8—dc20
[349.40648]
92-34686
CIP

ISBN 978-0-521-43003-6 Hardback
ISBN 978-0-521-11052-5 Paperback

Cambridge University Press has no responsibility for the persistence or
accuracy of URLs for external or third-party internet websites referred to in
this publication, and does not guarantee that any content on such websites is,
or will remain, accurate or appropriate. Information regarding prices, travel
timetables, and other factual information given in this work is correct at
the time of first printing but Cambridge University Press does not guarantee
the accuracy of such information thereafter.

# Contents

| | |
|---|---|
| *Acronyms* | vi |
| *Acknowledgements* | vii |
| PART I: THE FRAMEWORK FOR THE STUDY | 1 |
| 1  Innovation and policy | 3 |
| 2  Policy and law | 34 |
| PART II: INTELLECTUAL PROPERTY | 61 |
| 3  Patents and living organisms | 63 |
| 4  Copyright and computer software | 96 |
| 5  Information and appropriation | 123 |
| PART III: COMPETITION AND TRADE | 155 |
| 6  Competition law | 157 |
| 7  Foreign trade and investment | 194 |
| PART IV: GOVERNMENT SPONSORSHIP AND ENTREPRENEURSHIP | 221 |
| 8  Direct grants and tax concessions | 223 |
| 9  Procurement preference and offsets | 244 |
| 10  Telecommunications licensing | 260 |
| 11  The positive adjustment measures in the courts and legislatures | 278 |
| CONCLUSIONS | 300 |
| *Bibliography* | 308 |
| *Index* | 338 |

# Acronyms

| | |
|---|---|
| AIRDIS | Australian Industrial Research and Development Incentives Scheme |
| ASTEC | Australian Science and Technology Council |
| AUSTEL | Australian Telecommunications Authority |
| CIRCIT | Centre for International Research into Communications and Information Technologies |
| CLRC | Commonwealth Copyright Review Committee |
| DITC | Department of Industry, Technology and Commerce (Australia) |
| EC | European Community |
| EFTA | European Free Trade Association |
| FIRB | Foreign Investment Review Board |
| GATT | General Agreement on Tariffs and Trade |
| GIRD | Grants for Industrial Research and Development |
| IPAC | Industrial Property Advisory Committee |
| IRDB | Industrial Research and Development Board |
| MITI | Ministry for International Trade and Industry |
| OECD | Organization for Economic Cooperation and Development |
| TPC | Trade Practices Commission |
| TRIMs | Trade Related Investment Measures |
| TRIPs | Trade Related Intellectual Property |
| UCC | Universal Copyright Convention |
| UNCTAD | United Nations Conference on Trade and Development |
| UNESCO | United Nations Educational, Scientific and Cultural Organization |
| WIPO | World Intellectual Property Organization |

# *Acknowledgements*

This book has had a long gestation. I should like to thank my University, La Trobe, and my Department, Legal Studies, for providing me with the environment in which such a work could be completed and in particular with study leave. I'd like to thank the Department of Law at the University of Warwick and the Science Policy Research Unit at the University of Sussex for accommodating me during periods of leave; also the Organization for Economic Cooperation and Development and the Centre for Commercial Law Studies at Queen Mary College for briefer visits. My School, Social Sciences, generously made grants available to help with the expense of collecting material for the book. I am grateful to academic colleagues, David Doyle, David Brereton, Pat O'Malley, Martin Chanock, Don Lamberton, Peter Drahos and Sam Ricketson, for the helpful suggestions they have made along the way. For secretarial assistance beyond the call of duty, I am indebted to Kelly Pyers, Denise Lumsden, Sue Stoikos, Brigitte Carevic, Nola Andrew, Sandra Stone and Jean Crowther. The editorial staff at Cambridge University Press, Robin Derricourt and Phillipa McGuinness, have shown me considerable patience and professionalism in rendering the work publishable. Finally, I should like to thank my family, and particularly my wife Jennifer, for their support and forbearance. This book is dedicated to the concern that Australia does not slide directly, to recall the words of Michael Porter (1990), from a country that lives off natural resources to a country that lives off rents, and also to the idea that we can avoid this fate by aiming for higher standards all round and especially by respecting and fostering the talents of all the people of Australia.

*For Jennifer, Thomas, Henrietta and Janet Arup*

# PART I
*The Framework for the Study*

CHAPTER 1

## *Innovation and Policy*

This opening chapter begins by outlining the interests of the book. It then sets the scene for the studies of the law, first by recounting recent insights into the nature of innovation. It next considers the implications of these insights for the fashioning of policy measures in the Western economies. It raises particularly the question whether a market-oriented approach to innovation promotion has been supplanted by closer, more selective, relations between government and industry.

## OUTLINE OF THE BOOK

### THE FIELD OF STUDY

This book is the result of a study of the responses in the law to recent policies to promote innovation in high technology industries. I have become interested in innovation as a theme for a study because it is so often advanced these days as the key element in the transformation of the economy, influencing the distribution of power and wealth, and perhaps altering the nature of our relations as members of society – even our definition of ourselves as human beings. Certainly, the concern with competitiveness in a rapidly changing, often internationally drawn economy explains much of the experience with government policy in the field of economic law during the eighties.

In return, I hope to make some valuable connections between innovation, policy and the arcane world of law for the benefit of non-lawyers and lawyers alike. For some, law is an esoteric interest to pursue in the round of innovation policy, but in fact it is represented in a broad spectrum of policy measures. I suggest that even non-specialists will find its consideration rewarding. Accordingly, the book attempts to bring together developments in the economically interdependent areas of intellectual property law, the law of contract and economic association; competition, foreign investment and trade law, the legal supports for government assistance to industry, and the legal frameworks for the participation of public enterprises in industry. The focus is upon the law most directly relevant to the origination of new high technology products and processes, and the organizing theme is that this law might no longer be confined in its approach to the classic liberal law of property and trade, but is now also associated with a range of administrative styles of mediation, patronage and organization. Connections can be made between these two competing legal approaches and the more familiar rivalries of free market and free trade policies on the one hand and neo-corporatist and neo-mercantilist industrial policies on the other. The book is especially concerned with the space found for these closer collaborations between state and industry in their complex relationship with the very resilient, yet itself evolving, liberal approach.

The field of study is of course a large and complex one. The bulk of the book therefore comprises a set of case studies of the legal experience with particular policy interventions in the last decade. Their ultimate focus lies with recent Australian developments but, because the high technology industries operate today on a world scale, the studies also consider legal developments elsewhere in the advanced Western economies, such as the United States, the European Community and Japan. It should thus be of interest beyond the shores of the Australian outpost. The particular case studies chosen concern the patenting of living organisms; the copyright of computer software; the confidentiality of industrial know-how; trade practices regulation of intellectual property licensing and research and development consortia; foreign investment review and technology transfer; grants and tax concessions for research and development; procurement preferences and offset arrangements; and the licensing of telecommunications carriers. These case studies commence in chapter 3.

Naturally, the process of innovation also involves the application of these new products and processes to established industries. I have endeavoured elsewhere to evaluate the roles of labour, health, safety and environmental law in smoothing the path for the application of new technology and ameliorating its deleterious impacts (e.g. Arup, 1983; 1991). There is of course a wider literature on the complex relationship between regulatory standards and innovative activity (e.g. Rothwell and Zegveld, 1981; Stewart, 1981). The focus here on economic law does not mean to belittle the questions associated with the social regulation of new technology. But it does work on the premise that, because new technology is a social construct, it can be treated as a resource with potentially many beneficial uses, at least in comparison with aspects of the old, 'dirty' technology characteristic of the industrial revolution (Mathews, 1989). If it is at all evidence of a beneficial use, it should be remembered that this manuscript was produced on a computer. Certainly, the study holds to the view that the law of property and other elements of economic law structure the innovation process, sending messages about areas in which to invest and creating commitments to distinctive versions of the technology. By the time we try to apply social regulation, powerful forces have already formed around the technology, making it difficult for that regulation to have much effect (Collingridge, 1980). Concern with social justice and environmental balance starts with the supply side of the system, by which we meet our various needs.

## SOCIO-LEGAL ASPECTS

As an interdisciplinary work, the book's primary concern is to place this law in its social context and in particular to study the ways in which the law is implicated as high technology producers and their government sponsors try to step up the pace of innovation. If its treatment of the law is to be 'socio-legal', it must look not only at recent developments in the content of the 'law in the books', but also at the practical significance of the different kinds of law to the strategies of the innovating firms and the promotional activities of their governments. It should endeavour to draw upon schematic analyses and empirical findings regarding the experience with the take-up of the different kinds of legal facilities by the corporate and public sectors. As much as innovation policy is concerned with the objective of capturing the benefits of innovation as with the generation of innovation *per se*, a study of this nature should also consider the place of the law in efforts to ensure the success of particular firms and nations within the technological revolution which is taking place in world markets.

Yet, if one of the characteristics of the legal experience in the eighties has been attempts to gear it to the objectives of innovation interests, it remains the case that the law does not prove to be a wholly pliable or effective instrument. We should be mindful of the fact that in many respects the law responds on its own terms to the policy demands which are placed upon it. We need not go as far as the recent notion of 'autopoietic law' to suggest that law is a totally closed normative system (Teubner, 1989), but the engagement of the law as a prospective instrument of policy does have its own impact on the producers and governments who turn to it for aid (Daintith, 1988). To some extent, as we know, its inflexibilities and impositions encourage them to bypass the law, but we shall hold to the view that it is difficult to do entirely without the law in this field. Rather, the characteristics of the different competing legal approaches help to explain the choices made in matching policy functions to government structures in the field of innovation. Accordingly, even for non-lawyers, I argue that it is worth investing some time in the study of the law.

## APPROACHES TO INNOVATION POLICY

This section explores recent insights into the nature of successful innovation. It considers how these insights might bear on the formation of government policy. It commences with their impact on the liberal approach by which the state provides industry with a clear, general framework for investment in innovation. Doubts are raised about the continuing relevance of property to investment decisions, but the section also suggests how interest in the appropriability of innovations can be broadened. The section next looks for evidence in recent policy measures for the proposition that the state has moved beyond the liberal approach into corporatist and administrative arrangements with industry. It notes, for instance, ways in which liberal regimes might be qualified to provide advantage to favoured producers. It also identifies the tendency to deploy positive measures of assistance to improve the prospects of targeted activities.

## INSIGHTS INTO INNOVATION

### *The Process of Innovation*

Before we turn to the law, it is important we set the scene by recounting some insights into the nature of innovation that have premised recent policy interventions. We should start by acknowledging the fact that innovation has become a central concern of policy as governments (or at least elements within them) subscribe to the view that a country's economic success now depends not so much on the comparative advantage of natural resource endowments as on the comparative advantage of technological and organizational superiority (Porter, 1990). And this means in part that innovation is anti-establishment. It has the potential to undermine existing monopolies of thought and interest within the economy. Of course, it can on occasions be used to confirm the strength of established producers; one of the impacts of the new technology is the way in which it extends the reach of existing products by offering new media for their expression and diffusion. But it also provides opportunities for fresh rivals to enter and capture burgeoning markets by capitalizing on freedoms and flexibilities which the incumbents may no longer enjoy. Indeed, the technology may provide a direct means to bypass the existing monopolies by offering cheap ways to copy their products or to achieve the same result by alternative routes. These opportunities may provide scope for whole countries to participate for the first time in the high technology industries.

Even so, it is well appreciated that innovation is not driven by some autonomous, irresistible logic (Winner, 1977). New technology needs the right social conditions in which to flourish, and its progress may falter if these conditions are not present (Heilbroner, 1970). Its actual course will be mediated by the nature of existing economic, political and cultural conditions. Accordingly, one of the most crucial developments in policy circles has been the acceptance that innovation is not confined to bright ideas and original inventions (Rothwell and Zegveld, 1981). Of course, innovation still depends in part on the contribution of rare and abnormal qualities of curiosity and creativity. But, despite the notorious success of certain individuals, it would be wrong to think that innovation is a singular endeavour. Many of the basic innovations of recent years are the products of big science and planned research and development, shaped by the signals received from major sponsors, large producers and key users (Cicciotti, Cini and De Maria, 1975). We know that this insight has had an influence upon the practice of science itself. There has been a shift in emphasis from the descriptive to the instrumental disciplines of science and a growing industrialization of the practice of scientific research (Yoxen, 1981).

Generally, this process favours the capacity to invest on the scale required for big science: to provide, for example, the critical mass of equipment, materials and researchers, or to carry the risks of failure and survive the long lead times, and see the inventions through to successful production and sale (Freeman, 1983). One consequence of this is that innovation becomes less of a serial activity, progressing from research to development, manufacturing and marketing. If it is in fact technology-driven, it is less likely on the whole to be a success. Successful innovations are designed, refined and applied in an interactive loop of collaborative problem-solving that involves researchers, producers, financiers, distributors and customers (Gardner and Rothwell, 1986).

The collective, cumulative nature of contemporary innovation is further illustrated by events in the second phase of the latest technological revolution we are experiencing (Hill, 1983). The basic or breakthrough innovations are followed by what Joseph Schumpeter (e.g. 1954) characterized as a swarming of imitators who are attracted to the opportunities arising in the newly emergent industry. As the technology matures, firms turn their attention to product refinements and applications, and to processing efficiencies and marketing capabilities. Only some of the initial designs survive, and standardization sets in with the exploitation by producers of economies of scale and scope. An important insight into successful innovation, then, is its dependence, not only on the development and appropriation of particular inventions, but also on the control and exploitation of less discrete and transferable resources, such as research, development and processing know-how, and firm-specific cumulative learning or 'learning by doing'. It also depends upon the command of complementary assets, such as access to finance, production facilities and marketing networks, and organizational flexibility and general capability (Pavitt, 1984).

## *The Structure of the Industries*

Such conditions tend to favour large organizations (Commonwealth of Australia. Bureau of Industry Economics, 1989). Evident in the computer and converging information and communications industries is the dominance of a small number of large companies, originating in the United States and Japan, but now operating on a transnational basis (Smith, 1982). So too in biotechnology, while many of its inventions remain to be commercialized, drug and other multinational companies in such fields as medicine, agriculture, food processing and materials refining are already assuming control (Elkington, 1985). These companies can exploit the advantages of internalization, performing much of their research and development in-house, raising their own finances internally, organizing their own manufacturing, and marketing their products through their own networks (Mercer, 1987).

Yet, even the large corporations sometimes see the need to go outside their own organizations, so that industry relations are also characterized by a variety of semi-market connections, such as specialized subcontracting and sales to the large producers by small firms, and collaboration through joint ventures, strategic partnerships and technology consortia between the large producers themselves, sometimes with the participation of major users and sponsors. To the extent, then, that there is still reliance on external circulation, much of it involves relations between firms of similar technological sophistication, notably in the high technology industries, possibly as part of loosely knit, international oligopolies (Chesnais, 1986). Large corporations perceive the advantages of pooling resources and limiting competition by forming consortia, cartels and blocs – for example, in the semiconductor and superconductor markets. These connections tend to be formed within the larger producer nations and regions such as the United States, Japan and Western Europe, carrying the danger of the exclusion of firms from the smaller, peripheral countries such as Australia (Commonwealth of Australia. Australian Science and Technology Council, 1986a).

At the same time, small firms often represent the most creative and enterprising side of these industries, especially in the early years of an innovation, where barriers to entry are low. Their presence has been felt, for example, within computer technology (in microcomputers, software and specialist information services) and within biotechnology (in diagnostic techniques and new plant varieties). But they are often daunted by the high investment thresholds in the core of the markets and discouraged by the aggressive practices of the large companies (OECD, 1985a). The large companies seek not only to consolidate their traditional bases by vertical integration with smaller suppliers (Soma, 1976), but also to move horizontally into converging fields by buying into smaller firms which hold specialized assets. Thus, IBM has acquired interests in companies making private digital telephone exchanges, operating communications satellites, and providing commercial information services (Barr, 1985).

Large firms also tap into specialized expertise and externalize the risks of innovation by contracting out work to the smaller firms, often in exclusive agreements, patronizing these suppliers and distributors selectively, or buying up inventions for production and sale. Small firms tend not to compete directly with the corporate producers. Instead, they gear their activities to fit in with the strategies of the large companies, for example by providing specialized chips, software and peripherals which are compatible with the core technology (MacDonald, 1983).

Thus, the high technology industries reflect a pecking order with a division of cultural labour and a layering of markets on an international scale (Smith, 1982). Some manufacture and assembly work is moved offshore to foreign subsidiaries and local licensees, notably in the low wage countries. Design and management functions are often concentrated in the home countries, technology transfer to foreign subsidiaries and local licensees being delayed and subjected to restrictive conditions (Long, 1981). Small firms, especially those based in the peripheral industrialized countries, seek to find niches and develop specialities, participating marginally in new product markets and adapting the core technologies to local uses.

*Public Sector Participation*

A further feature of note is the connections in the high technology industries between the private sector and the public sector performers and sponsors of research. These connections go back a long way (Noble, 1979), but are receiving renewed attention now (Kenney, 1986). Such connections have been notable in the biotechnology area, where much of the original breakthrough research is performed in universities, public hospitals and research institutes. Scientists from these institutions have moved out to set up their own firms, feeding off and finding applications for the basic research and subsequently selling their businesses to large companies (Etzkowitz, 1983). The larger companies have also established direct connections with public institutions, most commonly by taking on an invention at the prototype stage to scale up for production and marketing, but also by commissioning applied research and sponsoring generic research in these institutions (Clarke, 1986).

In the computer field too, the early innovators often started in public research institutions and moved out to private companies (Pugh, 1984). The contribution of public sponsors (notably the military agencies in the United States) has been influential in establishing connections between professionals, bureaucrats and industry representatives, in conditioning the kind of technology which was developed, and in insulating the work from economic pressures (Noble, 1979). Such public agencies have also been major consumers of high technology products and their facilities have been used as a means to trial, refine and implement innovations, for example in the field of telecommunications.

Thus, recent innovation studies stress the importance to success of the presence of clusters of firms, often cutting across traditional industry and sector demarcations in chains or *filières* of effective economic networks (Porter, 1990). Marceau (1990) cites such exotic examples of the linkages as integrated hierarchy, semi-hierarchy, coordinated contracting, coordinated revenue links, joint ventures, co-making and spot-networking – all organizational responses to the new economic challenges. These linkages are often greatly aided by advances in the information and communications technologies themselves, so that the networks can transcend physical boundaries, even on a transnational scale (Rosegger, 1991). Accordingly, a country's chances of success benefit greatly from its development of superior transport and communications infrastructures. Yet, interestingly, recent studies detect a residual hankering for physical proximity and face-to-face contact, so clusters may take on a spatial, often regional, dimension (Jevons and Saupin, 1991), and transnational corporations still have identifiable home bases (Thurow, 1992). Obviously, this insight provides lessons for policy formation, partly of a land-use planning nature.

## THE LIBERAL APPROACH

Perhaps this is a good point to begin to discuss the impact such insights have had on government policy generally. The discussion will help to map out the areas which require detailed analysis in subsequent chapters. Of course, in some schools of thought, notably free market economics, the place for government policy is minimal. The recurring advice from free market economists is for government to abstain from policy interventions, as the firms of each country will find their own natural place in an increasingly international market. This prescription often takes for granted the important role the state plays in providing a clear framework for the conduct of private innovation undertakings in the economy. At the very least, government has a role in constructing the sympathetic formative context and institutional structure for sustained and successful innovation. This support can be manifested in several ways. The provision of skilled personnel through public education and training systems has recently been highlighted as a vital contribution. More directly, as we have already noted, much of the basic scientific and economic research is performed in public institutions. The examples can be multiplied, but, for our purposes, a key point is that the infrastructure includes the legal institutions of property protection and related rights.

### Legal Infrastructure

We might term the approach represented by those legal institutions the liberal approach. The legal dimension to this approach is concerned with establishing and upholding a set of rules which will govern in general or categorical terms the process by which resources (such as resources for innovation) are allocated in the economy. The approach is usually associated with a market supportive or deferential policy, where the law provides at arm's length the conditions of formal equality for participation in economic activity in the private sector and 'civil society'. In this approach, the law is properly confined to a limited role, concerned with facilitating the processes of resource development, exchange and utilization, and in particular with overcoming the imperfections of the market where these present obstacles to the efficient workings of such processes. This approach is typified by the backing the state provides in the form of fully blown property rights over economic resources and its non-judgemental support for their transfer and application through the complementary legal institutions of private contract and business association. Such guarantees are said to provide reassurance to those who are planning to invest in innovation or release its products onto the market. Evaluation of the importance of this approach requires any study of the law relevant to innovation to examine closely the extension of property rights to new technologies and the prescription and regulation of the conditions on which they may be used in contracts and associations between producers.

## The Importance of Appropriability

One of the perennial debates in the policy literature concerns the importance of appropriability to ultimate success with innovation. For example, it is sometimes alleged that innovators are motivated by other than economic considerations to invest their talents and energies in innovation. More to the point, where competition is concerned with economic returns, it is argued that efforts by one producer to appropriate benefits can often be circumvented by rivals. It is far more important to rely on being first into the market with a new product or on obtaining access to know-how about manufacture and marketing than it is to acquire the property rights in an invention. The experience with innovation lends some support to this contention. We have already noted the significance of the command of less discrete and transferable assets, such as know-how, and the control over complementary assets, such as production facilities. Because so many of the essential capacities for successful innovation can be regarded as person- or firm-specific, the 'owners' must depend on the expertise and cooperation of managers, scientists, engineers and others, if they are to obtain a return on their investments. This dependence means that these investors are separated from the effective control of their assets.

This is one version of the theory of separation of ownership and control in the modern economy. Effective control – control over access, use and disposition – no longer necessarily coincides with legal ownership. In particular, the right of the shareholder and other financiers who receive rent and income from the corporation has been divorced from the effective disposition and use of its productive forces. This development is said to indicate how a legal relation of ownership can have varying social meanings, depending upon the social order of which it is part (Scott, 1979). The fragmentation of property rights, their distribution amongst a large number of holders, the limited interest of investors, and the assumption of control by those without property interests all signify the declining importance of ownership as a social institution. In some accounts, this becomes an effective socialization of production.

The differentiation of property rights and the complexity of industrial undertakings may not mean, however, that property has lost all social significance. Much of the literature about the separation of ownership and control was produced before the phenomenon of corporate buy-outs and takeovers burgeoned, spurred by the increasingly sophisticated creation and deployment of financing instruments. With the aid of loans from financial institutions, entrepreneurs have strategically used shareholdings to capture important high technology producers. More directly, property rights over high technology innovations, notably in the biotechnology area, have been used by entrepreneurs to float companies and attract debt and equity investment, even, in some cases, when they had very little resolve ever to work those rights and arrive at a finished product (Teitelman, 1989).

Speculative interest in the trade of companies and their assets as commodities in their own right, rather than as organizational bases to pool resources and administer productive undertakings, caused a re-evaluation of the role of the individual capitalist in the control of corporate life. This trade encouraged a reorientation of corporate strategy towards realizing a short-term financial return from the assets of the corporation. Some policy analysis suggests that this orientation has been at the expense of the long-range planning and commitment necessary to see through major innovative undertakings in high technology industries (Storey and Sissons, 1990). On this score, an unfavourable contrast has been made between the economies of the English-speaking countries (the United States, the United Kingdom and Australia) and countries such as Japan, West Germany and Sweden. This is said to be part of a bigger cultural problem which these societies face in engendering a preference, an aspiration, amongst managers, shareholders, banks, workers, politicians, bureaucrats and so on to devote their resources to rebuilding production bases (Thurow, 1992). In part, this concern directs attention to the (partly legal) climate in which corporate financing decisions are taken.

## The Uses of Property

In addition, the differentiation of holdings and functions in the modern corporation does not necessarily mean that ownership cannot be used as a means to control access to the use of productive forces. Legal ownership of these productive forces is now often vested in the corporation itself. For some, this corporate holding does not tell us very much about the social relations of ownership. The corporation is discounted as a mere legal device (Scott, 1979). Others, however, regard the corporation as a factual social institution rather than a fiction, a locus for economic decisions which are driven by the imperatives of capital. The presence of the impersonal, multifaceted corporation at the core of the high technology industries might suggest that capital itself has replaced the individual owner and interpolated itself as a legal subject, holding property and exercising its powers to deny access, conduct exchanges and organize production (Edelman, 1979). In particular, the liberal approach has been able to accommodate the idea of the corporation as the owner of intellectual property, enabled to exercise this power to order relations – both to bar outsiders and to regulate insiders (Gamon, 1983).

Though the corporation must act through individual persons, these persons are in turn dependent upon the facilities of capital to realize their own creative and productive capacities and earn a livelihood – the inventor, for example, must obtain access to the resources necessary to gear up, manufacture and distribute a promising innovation or even, as science industrializes, obtain use of the essential laboratory and related facilities to invent in the first place. As a consequence, the managerial, scientific and engineering personnel become the employees of and subcontractors for the corporate patrons and organizers of science (Noble, 1979). Corporations seek to exploit this dependence in order to capture the person- and firm-specific assets vital for successful innovation by using restrictive arrangements in employment, licensing, joint venture and merger relations.

Rather than our losing interest in appropriability, these developments suggest we should broaden our horizons. In part, we can do this by treating property not as a means to stand alone and exclude others from access to a resource, but as a base from which to reach out and link up with other complementary researchers, workers, subcontractors and partners through contracts, consortia and incorporation. Instead of concentrating exclusively on the appropriability of particular inventions (through the intellectual property of patents and copyright), we should look to legal opportunities for the capture of such important assets as intangible know-how, the expertise of skilled workers and the learning of specialist firms. We can broaden our appraisal of the ways in which the facilities of the liberal approach accommodate strategies to capture important resources by seeing how the process of innovation drives producers in search of relational or organizational structures of command.

A feature of such arrangements is the restrictions they place on competition. It is a paradox of the liberal approach that its use can lead to concentrations of economic power. An increasingly common response of the state to this use of property and its related trading and associational powers is the regulation of competition policy schemes. Indeed, in some countries, with the roll-back of regulation in other guises, including public ownership, competition policy is regarded as the linchpin of controls on the abuses of private power. Yet controversy surrounds the question of the best competition policy approach to enhance the prospects of a country's innovation industries. Some prescriptions for innovation stress the need to ensure vigorous conditions of competition between domestic producers (Porter, 1990). However we should note that the generalized regimes of competition policy have not entirely won the day. As we shall see in chapter 6, the virtues of interlinkages and integrations have led others to advocate softening hardline provisions against anti-competitive practices and even compromising the even-handed treatment of contraventions. Purist competition policy can also run counter to the kinds of restrictions some nation states wish to place upon the operations of foreign suppliers and investors in order to bolster their local firms. A more discriminating regulatory approach is the continuing concern of review schemes with the importing practices and direct investment of foreign corporations. Indeed, competition policy demands can clash with a whole range of positive measures of government support to give preferment and assurance to favoured firms, by way of, for example, exclusive licences and procurement contracts.

The presence of these measures begins to raise the possibility that the involvement of the state with industry is much closer and more concerted than that inherent in the liberal approach. We must consider the contention that the scale, sophistication and uncertainty of the innovation process in high technology industries leads individual producers to seek direct assurances against business failure and social opposition, drawing them into collaborative relations with the agencies of the state (Hirsch, 1978).

## THE CORPORATIST APPROACH

What is said to be driving the partners together? In the broadest terms, the modern corporation is characterized by an urge to reduce the sources of uncertainty and competition to the administrative logic of centralized control, whether the problems lie with capital requirements, the supply of labour or materials, or product markets (Keenoy, 1980). It seeks that stability immediately through the ordering of its own internal processes, extending the reach of this domain by collaboration and merger with other firms and the incorporation of labour unions. But the search for stability progresses to the level of the state and to reliance upon the state for overall rationalization and management of the corporations' economic environment. The state becomes involved in technically organizing society into a manageable administrative process. This organizational goal is reflected not only in the policies of the state but, as we shall suggest in chapter 2, in the legal style of implementation adopted by the state agencies.

## Features of the Corporatist Approach

The interpenetration of state and society is associated with administrative and corporatist approaches to economic management that compromise or circumvent the liberal form. This development is the theme of several accounts. Problems of functional coordination, from a functionalist point of view (Teubner, 1983), of crisis management in the capitalist economy and its superstructure, from a Marxist point of view (Hirsch, 1978), and of competition and coordination between centres of corporate power, from a corporatist point of view (Winkler, 1977), are all seen as provoking official demands for forms of regulation both more precise in effect and more flexible in use than those encompassed by the idea of the rule of law (Cotterell, 1984).

A variety of factors seem to point in the direction of the adoption of closer forms of government–industry relationships – for example, the destabilization of long-standing economic patterns; the high resource demands of major innovation undertakings; the internationalization of the economy; the concentration of power in large industrial organizations and state agencies; the unease felt by small businesses, labour unions and other dependent groups in a period of rapid change; and the growth of an instrumental and technocratic approach to economic questions and social problems generally.

So, for example, in the realm of innovation policy, it is suggested that successful innovation today depends not only on the size, scope and reach of individual firms but also on the quality of production relationships between producer firms and sectors. It is also promoted by the strength of domestic markets and the feedback of sophisticated users, as well as support from non-market provisions such as public sector services, trade assistance and regulatory schemes (Chesnais, 1986). In these respects, the state can play an important role by co-ordinating economic actors, affording them competitive advantages and socializing risks.

## Policy Functions

What shape does this new approach to policy implementation take? In contemporary Western economies, it seems evident that governments often reach the view that the liberal approach is too indirect, obtuse or uncertain a means to satisfy the economic demands which have been placed upon them. Governments are under pressure not only to support the processes of the market through the liberal approach but also to intervene more actively and selectively in order to compensate for deficiencies and gaps in private production in the overall long-term interests of the economy and to correct for the market's adverse effects upon a variety of business, labour and other groups (Offe, 1984). These demands are likely to intensify when the economy is going through a period of major structural change.

Concerned that their traditional approach will not guarantee the benefits of innovation through the necessary mix between invention and imitation, competition and concentration, indigenous activity and foreign investment, governments are moving to more direct and discriminating measures for the support of key sectors, firms and ventures. Routinized involvement with industry is now perhaps unavoidable. Notwithstanding the inhibitions of governments' various political traditions and core ideologies, close, practical working relations are forged with industry sectors in most economies (Wilks and Wright, 1987).

### POLICY MEASURES

Today, then, in the realm of innovation policy, the state not only provides general support to industry by way of infrastructure, including the legal infrastructure of property and trading entitlements, but also alters the general conditions of the market in selective and discriminating ways, through the use, for example, of regulatory clearances, tax concessions and tariff barriers. It also allocates favours directly to particular economic agents – for example, by way of grants, purchases and exclusive licences (Jessop, 1982). The state not only discriminates between producers through the allocation of resources but also engages directly in production itself, in the process gearing its own agencies and instrumentalities to develop working partnerships with private firms and, indeed, using its offices to organize linkages between the different kinds of producers. In the practice of economic policy, a contrast can thus be drawn with a second approach, one which is both more purposeful and particularistic but at the same time more informal and inflexible than the liberal approach. This approach works through administrative discretion (Prosser, 1982). Here, the main role of the law becomes the provision of a space in which policy can be developed progressively, fashioning working standards and individual decisions to promote innovation objectives under fluctuating conditions.

So, have the governments of the home states of these various firms responded with a relaxation or circumvention of the liberal approach? Of course, any generalized observations about the trends in government structures will have to be extremely reserved. We should of course keep in mind the fact that the countries which participate in the high technology industries vary in many ways – in their core ideologies, political systems, administrative traditions, industry structures and financial markets (Hills, 1984). Their legal practices also display differences. In many ways, each country is a prisoner of its history and culture. Still, there is perhaps enough in the way of general tendencies or currents throughout these countries to make the question worth exploring further.

One consequence of the approach is that we might expect government to make more deliberate, strategic use of the liberal approach. For example, government recognition of the urge to build links, pool resources and order markets might lead to a relaxation and manipulation of the regulatory standards observed in competition, foreign investment and import control schemes. For instance, the object might be to afford local firms an opportunity to organize so as to match the strength of foreign rivals. Indeed, governments might even threaten to qualify or withdraw the basic liberal facilities of property protection, trade freedom and business association. For example, foreign nationals might be denied these facilities if indigenous companies do not receive access to partnerships in the local economy and parity of treatment in the export economies. In such ways, the state's provision of the facilities of the liberal approach is conditioned by a more explicitly policy-oriented and critical stance.

## GOVERNMENT PATRONAGE

This organizational policy is furthered by the deployment of the government resources of patronage and participation. The style of policy implementation shifts from the use of defensive regulatory measures designed to shore up local industry and insulate it from the rigours of international exposure. The new approach to tariffs is evidence of this trend, though it should be noted that tariffs have not disappeared entirely and other non-tariff barriers to trade, such as quotas, voluntary restraints, differential technical and safety standards and abstruse screening procedures, have emerged to fulfil a similar function. Still, the emphasis has shifted some way towards the use of such 'positive' adjustment measures as grants, bounties, tax concessions, purchases and licences. The aim of these measures may be to make investment in local innovation attractive to both foreign and indigenous producers (Commonwealth of Australia. Bureau of Industry Economics, 1987). As part of an outward-oriented, neo-mercantilist approach, these measures may be designed to strengthen the position of local firms seeking to export to overseas markets.

In some instances, these various instruments of industry support are integrated into a concerted strategy to build high technology industries. As we have noted, government involvement is extending further than these positive incentives for private sector investment into a variety of active and direct measures to influence the organization of industry. Thus governments take on the roles of industrial entrepreneur and broker, organizing linkages and mergers between various economic actors – large and small firms, foreign and local companies, producers and users, private and public organizations. Powers of patronage, loans, grants and tax concessions, procurement, trade and diplomatic services, good offices and administrative guidance are all manipulated to motivate the desired connections. Governments indeed become involved as parties to productive and commercial undertakings, taking up equity investment, licensing public inventions, forming collaborative ventures with private companies and providing trialling and applications facilities.

## THE MAJOR ECONOMIES

There are signs that the 'home' states of the largest transnational corporations have conditioned and supplemented their support for the liberal approach. The best recognized case is Japan. Japan's technological successes are often attributed to the government's role in identifying major emerging technologies and coordinating public, industry and finance sectors to develop national capacity (Freeman, 1987). Much has been made of the Japanese government's use of a range of incentives and pressures to promote industry policy through the process of administrative guidance. Notable in this approach is its use of the threat to withdraw such favours as regulatory exemptions, licences, subsidies, import protections, credit provision or government services as a means to induce compliance with government development and rationalization plans (Upham, 1987). Examples in the high technology industries include corporate commitment to innovation programs in computer technology, such as the fifth-generation computer project and the parallel processing software project (Arnold and Guy, 1986). In part, this approach may be favoured because explicit legal controls now appear too crude (Wakiyama, 1987). This strategy has been assisted by the operation of differential intellectual property recognition, the waiving or bypassing of competition requirements and the deployment of foreign investment reviews. Japan's approach is not one of public ownership and provision but rather the deployment of government inducements to gain industry consent to indicative planning.

If the United States disclaims any interest in coherent industry planning, the spending of its government agencies on technology development and procurement still exceeds the commitment of any public program in the other Western countries. A good illustration is the role of the Defense Advanced Research Projects Agency in nominating, funding, organizing and assuring innovative ventures in computer technology such as the strategic computing initiative. The National Science Foundation and the National Institute of Health also put large amounts of resources into areas such as medical technology. Faced with the rivalry of Japan, the US government is now giving financial and organizational support to domestic producers in civil technology sectors such as semiconductors and superconductors. This approach extends to local, state and regional levels (Eisinger, 1989). Material support is provided both through the contribution of massive funds for research and development in university and industry laboratories and through the support of government demand in its procurement of products for military, healthcare and other purposes. The role of the government agencies in this regard is not simply to finance the conduct of private ventures but also to initiate and organize collaborative associations in the name of advancing national security through technological superiority (Dickson, 1984). In these realms, close corporate ties between government and industry are the norm rather than the exception, yet the privileged position enjoyed particularly by the defence sector has rarely been the subject of serious political challenge (Vogel, 1987). National security and regional assistance provide a means of legitimating the selective support and guidance of high technology industries (Hills, 1984). This approach has been bolstered by the relaxation of anti-trust requirements, the institution of foreign investment reviews, and the deployment of selective trade and aid sanctions.

The expansion of the European Community (EC) and the success of some of its members are now making it a world force, possibly on a par with the Japanese and American economies (Thurow, 1992). To match the power of the American and Japanese producers, the smaller industrialized nations of Western Europe have also felt the need actively to encourage the development of local high technology industries, at both the national and regional levels (Jasanoff, 1985). The EC has a history of high profile collaborative projects (Williams, 1973). While the Treaty of Rome places some controls on state aid by individual member countries, the EC itself has provided funds through its framework programs for the advancement of technical progress. A recent example is the ESPRIT program, incorporating representatives of the member countries and a round table of major European countries, which funds pre-competitive research and development by public universities and private firms (Arnold and Guy, 1986). More recently, the Eureka program has provided support for innovation activity closer to the market (Peterson, 1991). Anti-trust provisions have been modified to accommodate regional consortia and, in some quarters, to deter foreign takeovers.

## PERIPHERAL ECONOMIES

Such developments in these key locations, the 'triad' economies, have widespread implications (Commonwealth of Australia. Bureau of

Industry Economics, 1989). The drive to order supply and product markets in their large domestic economies and on an international scale puts pressure on dependent groups such as small firms and labour unions. For the smaller industrialized and developing nations, without the advantages of their own multinational corporations, the nature of relations with the major corporate producers from the United States, Japan and Europe is a significant factor in their economic performance. Despite their specialized assets, this dependent status is likely to place small firms in a weak bargaining position. It makes them vulnerable to cutbacks in any global rationalization of their industry. They may only be given access to opportunities on conditions that restrict their capacity to develop self-sufficiency. Chesnais (1986) suggests that unless they possess some very specialized unique technical assets, smaller firms experience great difficulty in becoming parties to consortia or gaining access to licences. This difficulty is experienced against a backdrop in which monopolization is said to be closing up markets and encouraging capital intensive methods that displace smaller businesses and workers.

These smaller producers and other dependent groups may seek the aid of their own governments in order to negotiate the pressures they experience from the larger companies. In the rare case, such governments might seek to support a local producer to compete squarely with the foreign companies at home and in export markets, hoping to build a multinational of its own. More often, governments seek ways to put the indigenous producers in touch with the opportunities the large foreign producers can provide. Such a strategy may direct governments' attention to the legal conditions on which foreign suppliers are prepared to transfer their technology, whether by way of local investment and in-house transfer, licensing to outsiders, or the release of finished products. In focus also are the conditions on which multinationals provide access to export markets to local producers, through joint ventures, outward licensing, production facilities and marketing networks. Therefore, the returns which local industry might obtain from such market-related legal policies as intellectual property, competition, foreign investment and trade policy become relevant to the privileges which are to be afforded to foreign companies.

Increasingly, these governments are coming to the view that the development of local capability and opportunity does not come solely on the strength of favourable transfers from overseas. Technology transfer must be supported by a program to establish a local foundation of essential knowledge, skills and networks so that indigenous firms are in a position to appraise and exploit the opportunities the worldwide technological revolution is providing (Freeman and Lundvall, 1988). In pursuit of a suitable climate for local research, design and product development, many national governments have striven in recent years to gear a range of traditionally distanced activities – such as their education and training, research and development, public utilities, taxation, grants, procurement, and labour and social regulation activities – to their innovation objectives. Australia is a case in point. As a small country, Australia may not readily enjoy some of the advantages experienced by the large Western nations, such as the reach of its own multinationals, but it might be able to exploit certain local strengths, such as its relatively high education levels, the presence of consensus-seeking institutions, and sound public and welfare sectors.

## A CHANGED WORLDVIEW?

Are these developments anything more than an addition to the inventory of policy measures? To move the analysis up a level of generality, to the possible worldview which informs such a concerted approach, some interesting connections might be drawn between the nature of the new technology itself and the developing organizational modes of industry and government. At its grandest, this reading of events might suggest a compatibility in the drive to harness natural, human and social forces alike to the technocratic discipline of an instrumental process. The developments also represent a revolution in cultural conventions and attitudes. The restructuring of the industrial base associated with biotechnology is changing the concept of life itself. Biotechnology is the projection onto an industrial scale of a new view of nature as programmed matter. And, so it seems with the development of genetic engineering, nature here clearly extends to human life. The cultural revolution entails new information technology too, for the notion of programming connects biotechnology with information technology in parallel forms of programmed labour and programmed intelligence, thus weakening distinctions between the natural and non-natural, the material and non-material (Sprowl and Myrick, 1982).

For lawyers, the most direct manifestation of this worldview is the application of high technology to the processes of the law itself. A prosaic illustration is provided by the technification of the measure of certain criminal offences (such as the use of breathalysers) (Cotterell, 1984). More subtly, its influence is felt in the judicial system through the curtailment of due process, the reliance on expert solutions, and the removal of the human factor from legal disposition (Tribe, 1973). Yet, as we have been suggesting more generally, the approach is represented in the urge to circumvent the restrictions and limitations of a purely liberal approach. Structures are sought which facilitate the application of the techniques of scientific-administrative control, to plan rationally, to incorporate the necessary functional interests, and to eliminate the wastefulness, volatility and divisiveness associated with the market form of resource allocation and interest mediation (Collins, 1982). Instrumental engineering emphasizes the fully rational employment of resources, while the rule-oriented liberal approach introduces inflexibilities through defined spheres of competence, systematic lines of delegation and authority, and adjudication of conflict on the basis of rights (Selznick, 1969).

Thus, the state enlists the support of large corporations, peak producer councils, trade associations and, in some economies, the labour unions, to organize and discipline industrial activity towards modernizing production and renewing growth (Simiditis, 1986). The economy becomes dominated by industrial corporations and government agencies which are run by technocrats dedicated to the steady and responsible illustration of productive capacity. Control is exercised more through the power of information and 'insideration' than through the force of ownership and exclusion; and private property loses its pre-eminent place to organizational and scientific power, which become the organizing principles of economic and political operation (Galbraith, 1974).

## THE INTERPLAY OF LIBERAL AND CORPORATIST APPROACHES

This section endeavours to temper the arguments for the strongest sense of a corporatist approach by identifying the problems it encounters both in being effective instrumentally and in securing legitimacy. The continuing presence and pull of the liberal approach can be seen to contribute to corporatism's incompleteness and fragility. The section suggests that the effectiveness of a corporatist state strategy is limited by the international mobility of private capital, the idiosyncratic and elusive nature of much successful innovation, and the fragmented nature of the high technology sectors. The strategy also experiences legitimacy problems, especially in the Anglo-American economies, as those disadvantaged by selective government support lobby in both national politics and international forums for liberal property, trade and investment regimes, and equal treatment in the allocation of state favours.

## INSTRUMENTAL LIMITATIONS

The picture of policy formation as an uncontroversial, technical process taking place within an accepted political framework does seem overdrawn. What cannot be assumed are the needs of the producers for state support, the capacity of the state to coordinate the innovation process, and the political acceptability of such a government structure. Perhaps the strongest writing on the emergence of corporatism was based on the experience with the provision of government assistance to failing industries and depressed regions during the seventies, a time when governments were in a relatively strong position to insist on their own conditions. In the high technology industries of the eighties and nineties, governments are often seeking to induce a wealthy and mobile private sector to choose, over its other investment options, innovative and productive activity in local economies. The approach is likely to face problems, both in proving effective instrumentally and in obtaining legitimacy (Newman, 1981).

## THE MOBILITY OF CAPITAL

The nation state's own support for property and trading rights provides part of the basis for this private control over investment decisions. But the individual government cannot freely choose to withhold the power which these rights afford. The transnational corporations' mobility affords them the power to play off competing nation states and regional provinces in the world economy for the legal support they desire. Peripheral nations may be tempted to overbid each other for the favours of the large producers. Even the bigger countries can be threatened with retaliation in lucrative export markets if they do not give reciprocal backing to the liberal form. Thus, the liberal approach provides a source of independence from the ministrations of the government of the day. It does so not only in the form of the property and trading rights directly associated with innovation but also, and maybe more importantly, by contributing to the general international framework for investment decisions, notably through the liberal rules for financial markets. Firms make locational decisions which are based upon their overall advantages in the world economy. Operating increasingly on an international scale (the scale incidentally enhanced by the new technology itself, which permits communication and organization to take place in a mobile, disembodied way, transcending national boundaries), capital interests cannot be readily disciplined or coopted by the nation state to a concerted innovation policy (Krommenacker, 1986). In addition, the rapidity and reach of technological changes render existing institutional structures irrelevant or provide the means for them to be bypassed. A good example is the pressure being applied to national telecommunications monopolies and regulatory systems as a result of the facilities presented by the convergence of computers and communications (Howse, Prichard and Trebilcock, 1990). We shall need to trace the experience with the liberalization and privatization of these markets.

## THE NATURE OF INNOVATION

So the nature of innovation itself inclines government to concede autonomy to the private sector in its choice of innovation activity. Invention of a truly radical and creative nature depends, at least in part, upon the presence of idiosyncratic and elusive qualities of ingenuity and dedication. Commercialization in turn depends upon the investment of cumulative and tacit assets of technical know-how, production and market capability as well as general organizational ability. Under these conditions, it becomes difficult cognitively to specify in a regulatory mode precisely the kinds of responses which lead to the desired outcome of successful innovation (Jarass, 1988). For government, the promotion of innovation in the private sector often becomes a question of selecting the most likely group of candidates, making the conditions favourable to their success, and then placing its faith in their willingness and ability to produce the outcome. One of the consequences of this uncertainty is that some state-supported ventures fail, while in other instances state assistance is siphoned off into unproductive activities. Indeed, the offer of state assistance does not necessarily guarantee that the support will be taken up at all and the desired innovation pursued. Governments may become involved in ventures which the market has decided not to support, not so much because of market imperfections (such as the inability to capture the benefits of the innovation) but because of their commercial unviability (Pavitt, 1979). Government involvement socializes the losses associated with unsuccessful innovations and becomes a target for sectional interests more concerned with the benefits of public patronage than with genuine innovation.

## INDUSTRY FRAGMENTATION

The concerted strategy is also a fragile one because of the high degree of cohesiveness it requires. Business interests in the high technology industries are by no means unified, and, where divisions occur, their representatives at peak council level are unlikely to be able to control their members because their power continues to reside essentially at the level of the individual enterprise (Panitch, 1980). For instance, large producers may find it uncomfortable to collaborate with competitors, thus sharing research results and limiting market share. In several cases, high technology consortia have collapsed when key players saw an opportunity to capture benefits for themselves (Wakiyama, 1987; Rosegger, 1991). In the case of international collaborations, this distrust may be compounded by national rivalries. Such suspicions have fuelled the controversy over collaboration by the United States with Japan on the giant FSX fighter plane project (Wallerstein, 1991). The Eureka program has also been marred by national jealousies (Peterson, 1991). Furthermore, where the industry is not dominated by a small key group of oligopolist producers, but fragmented among a large number of diverse firms, it proves even more difficult to organize. For example, the computer software production industry has presented difficulties to government strategists in this regard. So too, governments have encountered some resistance from their own institutions, such as the research universities, to the idea of industry collaboration (Jasanoff, 1985).

The fragmentation is also reflected in the economic environment for the conduct of high technology industries. The notion of 'disorganized capitalism' stresses not simply the limited capacity of the nation state to control transnational corporations but also the lack of coordination and commonality between economic sectors, the most marked being the detachment of the financial system from the system of production, with its growing internationalization (Lash and Urry, 1987). This impact seems strongest in the Anglo-American economies, including Australia, where deregulation of the financial sector in the eighties had profound and often unanticipated effects on the environment for investment decisions. One of Japan's traditional advantages is said to be the *keiretsu* form of coordination between government departments, industrial corporations and central banks (Hills, 1984). Yet, even in Japan, money was diverted in the eighties into less productive activities such as real estate speculation. In addition, after the long span of post-war prosperity, many economies have suffered several periods of recession (including the current one), indicating that the cycle of boom and bust has not been broken. Under such conditions, the prospects of obtaining investment for production (patient money), especially venture capital for new product ventures, are diminished (Thurow, 1992).

## LEGITIMACY PROBLEMS

If there are instrumental problems associated with this approach to policy implementation – that is, technical problems in producing the desired outcome – then there are also problems concerning the legitimacy of the government structure with which it is associated. Resort by the state to market correcting and replacing activities may be regarded in some quarters as a threat to the processes of private accumulation (Offe, 1984). This kind of state activity can, of course, involve the direct displacement of attractive markets, as it has done in some countries in the core of the telecommunications network services market. We see now the counter pressure to break down public monopolies and open up private commercial opportunities.

Such state activity can also be regarded as a less direct challenge, providing political opportunities for various interests, such as those associated with small business and labour, to influence the conditions of private resource allocations. At the same time, such activities shift a considerable financial burden onto the state, which it may endeavour to meet by the imposition of further taxes and charges on the private sector. Those sections which are not advantaged by the support may resent the discrimination against their interests and be sensitive to the costs of providing that support. Thus, criticism is generated among those who also wish to have economic favours conferred upon them. Resistance develops among those whose interests are prejudiced by the competitive advantage given to the favoured firms, for example by allowing them to reduce their prices or boast of their reliability.

## FREE MARKET THOUGHT

The debate readily translates into a contrast between the free market and selective intervention approaches to industry policy (Grant, 1982). Interests associated with the free transfer of technology from overseas, such as foreign suppliers, local distributors and major users, may assert the merits of maintaining the so-called level playing field of the market (Joseph, 1984). The selective intervention approach meets opposition on the basis that it distorts market forces, diverts resources away from the more efficient sectors of the economy, involves the government in the business of 'picking winners', and engenders dependence on government support among the target firms (Commonwealth of Australia. Industries Assistance Commission, 1987).

Such a debate taps general ideological and symbolic concerns as well as narrow material interests. While it is true that in some countries state intervention is customary and goes largely unremarked, in others it is routinely contested and commonly the subject of controversy. The particular formative context not only helps determine where the burden of persuasion between the two approaches is likely to lie, but also influences the scope of the terms of the debate about legitimate government action. There will always be material interests favoured by the outcome of these ideological battles. But, as Pusey (1991) suggests, an approach may also enjoy a certain intellectual appeal. The free market approach may provide relief to overloaded politicians and administrators from the kind of cognitive and political demands that the fashioning of selective interventions imposes. By deferring to the processes of the market, it permits policy-makers to free themselves of the burdens of particularized decision-making about the outcomes they prefer and the measures needed to achieve them. (Specifically, this divesting of responsibilities for decision-making may entail the privatization of previously publicly-held innovation undertakings.) Certainly, the literature on what makes for international success is now both voluminous and contradictory. The free market economists display a very strong scepticism about the validity of the nostrums of their business school counterparts, let alone the policy analysts who speak from other disciplines.

As we shall see in the next chapter, in the realm of law the strategy gives rise to concerns about the cognitive and political stresses placed on the law by its involvement in particularized economic management. Constitutionalist lobbies seek to confine public agencies to their traditional roles in providing the basic infrastructure and guaranteeing the 'rules of the game' for private sector activity. They seek to render the new fields of policy implementation accountable by the standards of the courts and the legislatures.

## INTERNATIONAL CONTEXT

At the same time, no national debate is likely to be immune from the pressures on the world stage for liberalization. In the high technology areas, the formative context is also influenced by the lobbying activities of private interests and national governments in the international forums of the OECD, GATT, United Nations agencies and the like. Arguments for regulation of the transnationals and for discrimination in favour of local industries meet strong lobbies for the pursuit of liberal property, trade and investment regimes within the world economy from leading producer nations such as the United States. The leading technology nations are said to give the strongest external support to these approaches where their citizens are often the best placed to take advantage of their facilities (Raghavan, 1990). Certainly, the greatest reservations have been raised by the less developed nations, such as the countries which form the coalition known as the Group of 77 (Nixson, 1983). In fact, all governments would appear to operate barriers to trade to a greater or lesser extent. Yet, the free trade rhetoric often seems to have a particularly strong appeal to representatives of government in some of the smaller Western countries which share a similar intellectual tradition, even if their industry is not always well placed to take advantage of such open markets. Perhaps they think that they have even less prospect of achieving advantage by negotiating on a bilateral basis. Australia is a case in point.

In such forums, such countries are pressured to institute full intellectual property protection, lower tariff and non-tariff trade barriers, make regulatory requirements transparent, and treat foreign and local producers even-handedly in the award of state favours. Particularly notable has been the move to have many of these measures considered as issues of free trade in the Uruguay round of GATT. These forums are also used to put pressure on those larger producer nations which have tended to close economies to foreign participation and to sponsor local industry. They have been complemented by various bilateral initiatives, such as the United States' 'structural impediments initiative' against Japan. Under this initiative, the United States has attempted to exert pressure upon Japan to open its economy by strengthing its intellectual property protection, applying its anti-monopoly laws, and reducing government subsidies and controls. The United States has also threatened trade sanctions against a number of smaller nations.

The resurgence during the eighties of free market thought in some of the Western nations also had international implications. This resurgence was most manifest in the tax relief afforded to business, the roll-back of controls on financial transactions and various kinds of social regulation, and the exposure of public enterprise to competition or privatization. At home in these countries, the goals of industry assistance and organization policies have often had to compete with the effects of the 'deregulatory', market-oriented policies of the same governments, especially in the realm of fiscal and monetary policies. With the increasingly international mobility of capital and production, these policies have also created pressures for governments in other economies to follow suit and offer similar facilities. In Australia, with conservative parties positioned to win government, these forces have by no means run their course.

## SOCIAL OPPOSITION

Finally, though it is not the focus of this study, we should note the existence of broader questioning of the direction of innovation. Here, we have tended to concentrate on the conditions of uncertainty and resistance which pertain within the sphere of the producer interests which governments seek to harness. We should also note the presence of lobbies in the political arena which reflect disillusionment with the qualities of the high technology products. The concerns of environmentalists and philosophers about the ambitions of genetic engineering are perhaps the most intense, though concerns are also expressed about the impact of computerization (Rifkin, 1985; Weeramantry, 1983; Roszak, 1986). At their most sophisticated, these critiques question the fundamental nature of the technologies themselves (Hill, 1988).

At this general level, we might also associate this inclination to question the modernist project and its claims to rationality, coherence and enlightenment with the influence of recent postmodern movements in intellectual circles (see Callinicos, 1989; Smart, 1991). It is not suprising that these movements have also called into question the capacity of government or law to provide answers to the challenges the new technology presents.

CHAPTER 2

# Policy and Law

In this second chapter we aim to develop the broad theme concerning the tension between the claims of the resilient liberal legal approach and the drive to construct closer, more flexible forms of collaboration between government and industry. I hope that this theme helps provide a coherent structure to the inquiry in the case studies and even offers a guide to further legal developments beyond the life of this work. In broad terms, it offers a socio-legal study of economic law, an area of law perhaps somewhat under-treated in comparison with criminal law and social regulation, at least in Australia, and yet arguably still at the core of an understanding of the role of law in society (Lowe and McQueen, 1985; see also Bankowski and Mugham, 1974). Using the contrast developed in the first chapter, this second chapter examines the ways in which the liberal approach's property and trading rights take form in the high technology industries today. It then identifies the role of law in an administrative or corporatist approach. It subsequently considers why this new putative form runs into checks from liberal legality. Accordingly, it suggests a way in which the experimentation with this form of government inducement and collaboration can be reconciled with the continuing presence of the liberal form.

The first chapter has shown us that the discussion cannot proceed on the assumption that it is easy to determine how and to what extent innovation should be promoted. Nonetheless, the study also appreciates that policy implementation does not reduce itself to a mere technical exercise once the objectives are settled enough for action to be taken. Policy formation also presents a problem of finding a workable procedure or mode of operation for the state itself. The difficulties involved in settling objectives interact with the problem of finding workable strategies (Ezrahi, 1980). This 'structure-function' problem is one of establishing and institutionalizing a method of policy production that strikes a balance between the activities required of the state in the modern economy and the instrumental and ideological demands on the internal structure of the state itself (Offe, 1975). Government structures have internal characteristics and external associations that limit their availability and deployability in the performance of policy functions.

Law is a case in point. This insight provides a way of according the law (one kind of government structure) due respect as a social phenomenon and of studying its complex interrelations with the other subsystems of society, such as the economic and political spheres. In this way, the shortcomings of a unilinear determinist account of the relationship between law and other parts of society can be avoided. In keeping with this idea of the structure-function problem, the study can work with the notion that the law is multifaceted. In particular, law is to be regarded both as a means of policy definition and implementation and as an opportunity to check policy-making and administration. In short, law appears as both a social medium and a social institution (Habermas, 1985). Let us now develop this theme by considering the contrast between the two legal approaches. For the time being, we shall concentrate on the liberal approach, for, while its role may have changed with society, it shows little sign of demise.

## LIBERAL LAW TODAY

This section examines the characteristics of the liberal approach today with a view to anticipating the likely content and significance of responses to claims to appropriate and trade in innovations in industrial techniques. The section then notes the intrusion into the liberal approach of various qualifications and conditions motivated by substantive policy considerations. Concern to maximize innovation might be represented among those considerations. If the body of liberal law reveals some modification, then we must also consider the possibility of an erosion of the practical significance of that law as a means of ordering access to the benefits of innovation. The section concludes, however, by suggesting that property and contract remain significant, not simply as a means to exclude and ration access to resources through market relations, but as a basis on which to internalize and organize the complementary assets needed for successful innovation.

## THE CHARACTERISTICS OF MODERN PROPERTY LAW

### Property and the State

We have said that the liberal legal approach is concerned with establishing and upholding a set of rules which will govern in general or categorical terms the process by which resources (such as resources for innovation) are allocated in the economy. This support for the private sector comes in the nature of both a declaration of rights and an enforcement of rights. This latter coercive role of the law is usually a backup rather than a first strike role (Sugarman, 1983). Yet the threat of the ultimate application of its coercive sanctions often provides an important deterrent to rivals of various kinds and thus a security for investment in research and production, and the exposure of products to the market. In the last resort, the coercive power of the law may be used to counteract the anti-competitive practices of certain producers who wish to create barriers to the introduction of innovative products. For this reason, incumbent monopolies and cartels have occasionally experienced the full force of the law. More to the point, perhaps, this power may be used to protect producers against 'excessive' competition, such as the competition they encounter from unauthorized derivation and imitation – the weight placed behind the enforcement procedures of the copyright laws in Australia, particularly in relation to imports, provides an example.

More routinely, the apparatus of the law is committed to devising, clarifying and extending the conditions which govern resource allocation so that uncertainty and conflict among producers are minimized. The agencies of the state make an extensive commitment of public resources to the processes of establishing intellectual property rights, constituting contracts and registering companies, for example, so that the liberal approach can serve effectively as a means to arrange in an orderly fashion the appropriation of, trade in, combination and private administration of the resources associated with innovation. The support these facilities give to private economic activity provides a major facility for producers to manage in advance the risks, attract the investment, and organize the undertakings involved in innovative activity (Commons, 1924). We understand that these facilities do not simply work in a mechanical or instrumental way, they also engender commitment and discourage interference by legitimating this way of structuring the process of innovation and capturing its benefits (Arnold, 1937).

The state does not play this part simply by providing an empty shell to be invested with whatever content the individual producers see fit. The liberal legal approach can also be associated with a state role in prescribing a set of general regulatory standards, through either the civil or the criminal law, whereby conditions are placed upon the exercise of economic power whenever the facilities of the form are taken up. We shall see this illustrated in the case of intellectual property. Often these conditions are not directive, but are designed instead to give the parties information about contingencies and to provide terms for their convenience, so as to minimize potential breakdowns in the process of accumulation and exchange (Posner, 1970). Determining the location and extent of legal liability for computer malfunction is an example.

## Property and Policy

Sometimes, of course, these conditions may become categorical and mandatory, so that the law substitutes a public policy for that of the producers. Nevertheless, within the liberal legal approach, it does so through the imposition of standards which are cast in the form of rules and applied at arm's length from the parties themselves. In this approach, governments can then be held accountable in the legislatures and the courts if they fail to adhere and confine themselves to these conditions. This prescriptive role is not necessarily a move away from the liberal form of law to other forms of law, for example from contract to status. As Kahn-Freund (1967) observed, such law still leaves it to the private parties to enter and sever the relations which attract these conditions. The conditions are superimposed upon a relation that remains fundamentally constituted in the liberal form.

As an ideal, the liberal legal approach is linked with a set of constitutional standards bound up in the concept of 'the rule of law'. These standards include the maintenance of a distinction between the public and private sectors, a limited and detached role for the public sector, the supremacy of the legislature over the executive and the administration, and the independence of the judiciary as a source of review and check on the legality of government action. This legal approach is said to reach its highest point with the development of competitive market economies and liberal democratic political systems. By offering a calculability and predicability to social relations, this formally rational legal approach was said to be particularly complementary to the purposive-rational conduct of economic activity in a capitalist industrial economy (Weber, 1954). Thus it came to be typified in Western societies by the law of private property and its complementary institution, the law of contract. The approach is closely associated with the modernization of Western societies, indeed to Parsons (1964), a society could not really be modern until it achieved such a form of law: a set of positive laws which are logically derived and consistently applied by separate and specialized personnel. This form of legal thought had to be clearly differentiated from, and indeed to exercise supremacy over, other sources of normative ordering or social control.

Yet, in receiving this picture of law as distanced from economics and politics, it should not be thought that such a legal framework is necessarily abstentionist or neutral in the position it takes regarding the order which economic and other social relations assume within modern society. While one which is often taken for granted, this state-backed legal framework promotes a distinctive pattern of capacities and entitlements. This pattern is settled in many parts of the economy, but innovation raises afresh the questions surrounding the virtues of commodification and the command it supports. Innovation creates opportunities for the reach of the traditional liberal form to be significantly extended. Copyright in an artistic performance can, for example, be translated into so many different mass media (Ricketson, 1991). Part of any assessment of the place of law in innovation is the effect of conferring property rights over various intellectual resources and supporting their exercise through exclusion, trade and association. Such a liberal approach expresses fundamental preferences for private and individual holdings over public or common resources, the active exploitation of resources over the passive enjoyment of natural and reflective states, and economic value over moral concerns (Horwitz, 1977). The liberal legal approach represents decisions about the reach of the market – what is to be appropriable and tradeable in our society. Then, within this basic economic structure, it supports the disposition and application of the commodities according to the preferences of those stakeholders with market and industrial power (Sugarman, 1983).

## Property and Appropriation

Nowhere, indeed, is the essential role of the state in structuring economic relations better illustrated than by the extensions of property and trading rights to intangible resources such as intellectual creations. Once created, the products of intellectual activity are often easy to share or reproduce, so that the legal power to withhold and ration them can become very important to the prospect of capturing their benefits (Adelstein and Peretz, 1985). Paradoxically, new technology can itself be a source of the means to expropriate innovations. For example, photocopiers and tape recorders have dramatically undermined the capacity of producers to control access to original literary and artistic works. It is often said that the protection of intellectual property rights is a necessary security for those who contemplate the often sizeable investment of effort and capital needed for innovation. The property right gives the investor time to recoup the investment before competitors are allowed in to the market for the product.

The extension of property to intangibles highlights the fact that property has become significant as a legal relation between persons rather than as the ownership of a physical thing (Vandevelde, 1980). This is not to say, of course, that the producers never have other strategies available by which to exert control over access to resources, nor is it to say that the legal strategy of asserting proprietary and contractual rights is necessarily a convenient or effective one. Empirical work indicates that producers do not always find the process of identifying and asserting these rights an easy one to negotiate, and that they turn to other strategies to secure their interests as an alternative or supplement to taking up the facilities of the law (Teece, 1987). In relation to investment in innovation, these strategies include attempts to engineer protection in the technologies themselves or to exploit economic advantages in order to bar others from access. The producers make pragmatic choices between the different strategies for capturing the benefits of innovation. These are possibilities we must explore when making an appraisal of the social significance of the relevant law.

Nevertheless, the legal response to claims that fundamental, possibly life-saving or life-altering techniques be appropriable and tradeable can have important consequences. It can greatly influence the distribution of the benefits of the new techniques. Indeed, the prospects of appropriation can influence the kind of innovation in which producers are prepared to invest. Yet, if the broad historical thrust of the liberal approach seems to be support for the creation and operation of new markets, by its nature it is not an automatic, reflexive response to such economic pressures. Eras of radical innovation turn up new resources which do not readily fit the existing property and contract categories. As competing interests seek to capture the benefits of these innovations, they generate claims which may be translated into questions both of appropriability *per se* and of the rights over the distribution of any property entitlements which ensue. In other words, the role of property is a very live issue in the field of innovation. The process of extension of the liberal approach is not necessarily an untroubled one. This lack of responsiveness to policy objectives lies partly in the nature of law as an institution. A rule-oriented and somewhat institutionally distanced legal approach does not necessarily respond directly and automatically to the emergent claims. The responses of the courts to claims for the application of intellectual property categories to innovations in biotechnology and computer technology may point this up. The variety of perspectives represented in legislatures and bureaucracies may also complicate policy formation.

## Property and Innovation

The partiality of response lies also in the competition between objectives. The fact that its support is needed might lead the state to entertain the claims of other interests and consider a policy concerned with exacting conditions or applying qualifications when it does grant property rights. The 'relativization' of property indicates how much the question of the nature of rights over any new resource has become a matter of the appropriate policy for the particular situation. Perhaps this is especially true where the concerted intervention of the legislature is required to settle the property right on an innovation. For some, the demise of the necessary physicalist and absolutist qualities of property already signifies the end of the rule of law in its strongest sense (Vandevelde, 1980).

Accordingly, the state might withhold the full weight of its support from the interests which seek property rights. Some limits and exceptions to the coverage of property rights might be installed because of distributional or moral concerns about the consequences of placing crucial resources in private hands (Calabresi and Melamed, 1972). Exceptions in the patent law of some countries regarding therapeutic processes and higher life forms reflect these concerns, though, as we shall see, the economic pressures to extend appropriability can be very strong. One study (chapter 3) is concerned with the pressure worldwide, especially from the United States, to override restrictions on the appropriation of biotechnologies and extend property to higher life forms that promise economic value. It is interested in the responses of administrators, legislators and judges in countries such as Australia.

Perhaps, less fundamentally, the state might advance its protection in return for the observance of certain safeguards. These safeguards might of course reflect a range of concerns, but pertinent to this study is the preparedness of the state to extend its support only on the basis that access to the innovation remains open to other potential producers who may wish to learn from and build upon the original innovation. The partial concern of intellectual property with innovation is of course represented in the threshold requirements for recognition: that the intellectual creations exhibit qualities of novelty, originality or inventiveness. To nominate the most familiar provisos placed on recognition, the conditions might entail requirements that the intellectual creations be registered and revealed to others, that they be licensed to others for purposes of research and education, or more generally (if they are not being worked, for instance), that they be monopolized for only a limited period of time, or that they not be protected against independent invention or discovery through reverse engineering.

The study must therefore consider the reservations with which property right is conferred over emerging intellectual creations such as computer software or genetically engineered organisms. For instance, one case study (chapter 4) notes that, in the past ten years or so, most Western countries have afforded the protection of copyright to original computer programs. Piracy is a serious problem for producers, but subsequent litigation has highlighted questions about the level of protection copyright holders enjoy against genuine industrial competitors. Has a way been found to reconcile this concern with the desire for a clear property right? Legal responses in other areas might have gone further. Ultimately we need to consider whether conditions have developed which go so far as to compromise the attributes of the liberal approach. What is to be said, for example, about a scheme that confers title on audiovisual performances but licenses the copying of those performances for certain purposes and then raises income for the producers by means of a levy administered by the state on blank tapes?

## Property and Trade

At the same time, it is clear that the bundle of rights clustered around the concept of property is capable of differentiation between rights, for instance, to title, possession, control, use, disposition, security, rent and royalty. In turn, the exercise of these rights might be qualified by other legally recognized claims on the resource. The resulting complex of rights is increasingly refined and fragmented. Perhaps the most graphic illustration in recent years is the explosion in the range of legal securities – that is, the 'securitization' of various commodities and the creation of secondary markets. With this diversification comes the opportunity to apportion the various rights between different holders. Rights over intellectual creations may be distributed among, for example, authors, industrialists, financiers, shareholders, distributors, users, consumers and public agencies.

In some cases, the pattern of distribution is ordered in the body of the law. The public disclosure and compulsory licensing provisions of some intellectual property regimes provide an example; as does the reservation to authors of certain moral rights over subsequent uses of their work in foreign jurisdictions. The law may also play a facilitative role by offering principles by which uncertainties surrounding the apportionment of rights in the private economy can be resolved. An example is the provisions which ascribe to employers intellectual property rights over their employees' work (in the absence of agreements to the contrary). But generally the policy of liberal law is to leave the ultimate destination of the rights to be determined by the market. The rights it affords are freely tradeable in the market. The level of actual access to these rights for any one group then depends largely upon the capacity to acquire and retain them on the strength of associated technical, economic and other extra-legal power.

## PROPERTY'S SOCIAL SIGNIFICANCE

The developments we noted in the opening chapter – the fragmentation of property interests, the growth of other interests, and the general bias towards the active exploitation and exchange of resources – have led some to suggest that contract has surpassed property as a functionally significant social institution (Renner, 1949). Where the organization of innovation moves from the market, the corporate legal form of economic association has also provided a means for the rights over resources to be distinguished and apportioned. When the differentiation of property rights is combined with the functional complexity of contemporary industrial production, it causes some to suggest that nominal title says little as a matter of social fact about the control of resources (Edgeworth, 1988).

## Property and Know-How

Yet the lesson we derived from the consideration of innovation in chapter 1 was the need to broaden the scope of our survey rather than turn away from liberal law. Acknowledgement of the role in successful innovation of command over complementary assets, such as research and development infrastructure, production facilities and marketing networks, reminds us that the command of property over the more familiar tangible resources is still important to the prospects of capturing the benefits of innovation (Teece, 1987). Yet, at the same time, we should acknowledge the increasing importance of information as a strategic resource, an importance enhanced by the processing and transmitting capacities of the new computer and communications technology. Indeed, some analysts go so far as to suggest that the centrality of information renders beside the point many of the old competitive distinctions between firms along managerial and legal lines (Lamberton, 1984). The flow of information breaks down institutional barriers and draws producers into new networks. It also tends to drive producers in the direction of cooperative relationships (Rosegger, 1991). This is not to say that the process does not meet with obstacles, but these obstacles are likely to lie in the costs of using and applying the information rather than in its acquisition. These developments challenge law's relevance (as we shall see, another such development is the growth of clusters or *filières* of enterprises through functional linkages), yet it is probably too early to say that such a transformation is complete. Pertinently, lawyers will note that the concept of intellectual property has by no means run its course, and we can observe the drive to render appropriable in some apt legal form such intangible resources as know-how and goodwill, which do not readily translate into the conventional categories of patent and copyright (Weinrib, 1988).

Therefore, we need to examine the development of the idea of information as property, by looking at the policy expressed in the law of confidential information and the protection of trade secrets, as well as the criminalization of unauthorized access to information, especially information which is stored in the technology itself. As one of the case studies (chapter 5) points up, the potential value of confidential information, trade secrets and industrial know-how is creating an argument for strengthening rights in civil law. The support of the criminal law, particularly to render inviolate information held on computers, is also being sought. But freedom to use the know-how can also be vital for others to practise their trade, and in some cases it is difficult to separate that know-how from the persons themselves. A good example of the issue is provided by the response to the employer's claim to restrain the competitive work of its employees through obligations of confidence, fidelity and fair competition.

*Property and Internalization*

It might remain the case that legal control over information is most likely to be maintained in those close working relationships in which the information is kept in-house and the parties with access to it are limited. Nor might property rights readily afford command over the kind of accumulative, inchoate know-how which is difficult to isolate as the subject of a discrete, identifiable holding. Unless the legal interest becomes one which is truly maintainable against the world, perhaps it is best portrayed as a contractual or otherwise relational rather than a property form of assurance. It assumes its greatest significance when it is combined with efforts to internalize potential competitors and imitators through the media of employment, joint venture or merger arrangements.

As Karl Renner (1949) might have predicted, contract and its like forms become a means to condition access by outsiders to vital intellectual resources and their complementary assets of production and distribution capabilities. They also become the legal basis on which to bring inside the suppliers of specialized assets and to regulate the internal innovation process. In doing so, they provide a framework for the organization and direction of innovative endeavour. Thus, the power over innovative activity is a mixture of both exclusion and exchange, expressed in market relations with outsiders and the internalization and integration of insiders developing into domestic workplace and other administrative relations. The power to withhold and dispense economic benefits such as employment, goods and services, goodwill and membership can be used to regulate 'privately' (Bercusson, 1988). As Nelken (1982) has suggested, the liberal form can lend itself to a managerial, directive approach to the regulation of human affairs. In the contemporary economy, the liberal form may effectively endow an agency with the authority to legislate internal rules or exercise discretionary decision-making about the conduct of economic undertakings (Collins, 1986).

While these regulatory practices largely occur in the private sector, they have the ultimate backing of the state in its support for the liberal form. Indeed, the picture is complicated today by the operation of public agencies through the medium of the liberal form, making exchanges and organizing undertakings, while presenting themselves as ordinary players in the economy and attributing their decisions to commercial considerations not susceptible to conventional public law scrutiny (Aubert, 1985). We can say that the backing of the state involves the delegation of a legal mechanism of social power to the economic agencies; some operating on a very small, local scale, but others regulating 'domestic' domains on a large, possibly international, scale (De Sousa Santos, 1985). IBM, a high technology corporation, is an example of the latter – a vast regulatory system and a government structure which has many parallels with the modern state itself (Nora and Minc, 1980). The public telecommunications instrumentalities are another example.

## *Property and Regulation*

The liberal form is not used directly to embody these relations. Something more is needed to turn it into an organizational and managerial power. It proves too abstract, inflexible and obtuse a form to order and adjust the ensuing relationship when the combination of resources takes place over an extended time, the actual performance of innovative work is a complicated and tacit activity, and the circumstances in which it is conducted are liable to fluctuate. But the presence of the liberal rights may still act as an indirect discipline on these internal processes. The internal strategies interact with the market or external strategies which control entry to and exit from the organization (Edwards, 1979). Such a characterization allows us to acknowledge the continuing significance of the liberal facilities of property and contract in the ordering of economic relations. If property and contract are not the media in which the ongoing administrative relationships of large innovation undertakings are elaborated, they might still constitute the means of entry and exit to these relationships, and might have an indirect influence upon the conduct of their internal processes (Collins 1986). Liberal law might be simultaneously dominant and recessive (Offe, 1984).

Property rights are still used to exclude potential competitors from access to innovations as producers employ aggressive strategies of intellectual property acquisition, consolidation and assertion in order to tie up key techniques (Noble, 1977). We shall see that property rights are employed in this fashion in the high technology industries today to keep resources close, inhibit market entry by competitors and lock in customers. Yet, at the same time, a property entitlement is increasingly regarded as a bargaining chip by these producers, to be used as part of a broader strategy to negotiate and build the relationships necessary to combine the specialized resources required for production and to order developing markets (Bertin and Wyatt, 1988). Property rights are brought in-house and pooled and licensed out selectively, rather than used to stand alone. So too, contract is still used to conduct a large number of routine exchanges on the market: acquiring standard materials, hiring temporary labour, and selling discrete finished products. But the need for vital person- and firm-specific assets drives producers to form ongoing working relations where contractual relations are often characterized by hierarchy and solidarity (Gordon, 1985). Contract becomes a means to plan and adjust continuing relationships, a means not only to anticipate the key issues in the relationships but also to locate authority for the formulation and alteration of ongoing working rules (Atiyah, 1979). Furthermore, where contract proves inadequate or unreliable as an ongoing form of regulation, producers use it to move by collaboration and integration into the closer, non-market forms of government structure and internal regulation (Williamson, 1981).

## LIMITS TO THE LIBERAL APPROACH

Yet, if liberal law often seems to be extremely accommodating of a variety of social relations, it might still be the case that radical or rapid changes in economic conditions give rise to problems of fit with social realities. For example, Selznick (1969) has suggested that, while contract retained its force as the dominant legal idea in the realm of labour relations, difficulties of fit would arise if the parties were to seek to reorganize the enterprise in a fundamental way and move to a different government structure. As an institution, the liberal legal form seems to be encountering difficulties in coming to grips with the implications of modern production relations and finding satisfactory alternative conceptual and normative equipment to deal with them. A common criticism of the traditional analyses of contract and company law is that they are out of touch with the realities of industrial practice. In contract, the disparity between the consensual ideal and the frequently collective, hierarchical and bureaucratic nature of economic relations is well recognized. So too company law, with its notion of separate, self-governing entities, needs to grapple with the presence of complex configurations of associated companies and the hierarchical structures of parent and subsidiary companies within the corporate empires (Sugarman and Teubner, 1990). Consequently, contract and company law often seem to rest on the margins of major systems of private government that operate through institutionalized social structures and less formal social fields, affected but seldom controlled by the formal legal system (Macaulay, 1985). The commercial world is a 'social world of semi-autonomous contracting cultures, governed by relations of cooperative organic solidarity and of pervasive hierarchical domination' (Gordon, 1985: 575).

### Adjustment of Doctrine

Despite these developments, the liberal approach might continue to have an impact, but now in its capacity as a distinctive way of construing and representing the nature of these relationships. The rhetoric or imagery of property and contract is often enlisted in the support of competing claims on resources. To give some examples, not only industrialists but other groups, such as artists, employees and claimants for social assistance, employ the language of property to give strength to their causes. It can prove advantageous to large producers to cast their strategies in the form of contract in order to gain the benefits of the symbolism of the freely bargained agreement. The language of contract can be used in the privatization of decisions of public significance, such as the conferral of public benefits on private interests (Cameron and Midgeley, 1982). Contract may at times be an instrument of government regulatory policy, such as the expression of conditions on which state assistance is made available to the private sector (Daintith, 1979). As we shall note below, governments may barter regulation and support to obtain the cooperation of producers (Daintith, 1985).

If there seems to be a widening gap between the legal imagery and the reality of economic practice, this is not to say that these bodies of law have remained static. Within contract law, there is a lively exploration of the boundaries of the category and its connections with principles of tort and equity law (Hedley, 1988). Atiyah (1979) charts the move away from bargaining and free choice conceptualizations of interpersonal obligations to non-voluntary rights and liabilities; from promise-based liabilities to benefit-based and reliance-based liabilities; and from the use of contract as an instrument for planning future exchanges in relationships in which exchanges are made on terms open to continuous adjustment. In the terms of Kamenka and Tay (1975), this move reflects a greater concern for policies than principles, consequences than intentions, and future relations rather than past actions. On a similar theme, Macaulay (1985) notes a trend for the courts to uphold claims of administrative rationality and organizational flexibility at the expense of strict contractual rights and duties. In company law, commentators are interested in the partial attempts to 'pierce the veil' of incorporation and the development for regulatory purposes of notions of associated or related companies (Collins, 1990).

These tendencies seem to excite a great deal of interest among legal commentators, possibly because they represent activism on the part of the makers of the base law in the Anglo-law tradition, the common law of the courts. Yet these may only represent developments at the margins. It is difficult for a tradition-bound legal authority like the courts to invent overnight a new jurisprudence to deal with changes in social relations. Rather, the old concepts are likely to remain the reference point, albeit with adjustments and extensions which permit their use in a way somewhat responsive to the new demands on law (Daintith and Teubner, 1986). For example, only gradually do organizational concepts such as hierarchical authority enter contract law, or do theories of the firm inform company law. The public law or collective interest criteria which have been applied to decisions in the government sector are still to find much purchase in the realm of private transacting and administration, despite the marked similarities between the larger organizations in the two sectors (Bercusson, 1988). At the same time, as we shall see below, there is some ambivalence about the appropriate legal response to the new 'managerialism' in the public sector and the shift of public functions out to hybrid commercial agencies (Allars, 1990). Should private or public law standards of decision-making and accountability apply to these practices?

## Transcendence of the Liberal Approach

Such skirmishes in the body of liberal law may in any case be overshadowed by legislative restrictions on the freedom to exercise property and contract powers, a movement away from direct reliance upon the market and thus upon external relations of exclusion, competition and exchange, and a preference for closer administrative and corporatist relationships. Today, expositions of the law of property and contract readily acknowledge the inroads made into open and uninhibited use of their power by legislation representing a variety of competing claims, such as land-use planning, consumer protection and environmental quality. We have foreshadowed these possibilities within our scheme for the study of developments in the law governing the granting of intellectual property rights and their alienation and trade. We should also look at these possibilities in the now well established fields of trade practices and foreign investment regulation.

Yet, far more important in practice might be the tendency to engage the powerful, non-market structures directly and work from inside or around these legislative frameworks through administrative and corporatist processes (Hancher and Ruete, 1987). It is to this possibility that we now turn. What legal form do these closer relations assume? Do, in fact, they find a position in the law's conceptual framework? And how do these relations fit in with the liberal form which, as we have already acknowledged, remains a resilient, if adaptable force? Atiyah (1979: 717) suggests, for instance, that 'the distinction between market and non-market relationships ends in a murky grey area where contractual and administrative-law ideas struggle for paramountcy'.

## A CORPORATIST APPROACH?

This section takes up the idea that a new legal approach might be emerging with this concern to ensure the conditions for successful innovation. It begins by outlining the possible legal features of this corporatist approach and in particular its flexible and particularistic use in the implementation of policy. Its contrasts with liberal law are drawn out in its movement away from the 'rule of law' into the construction of spheres or spaces for purposive executive and administrative action, often with the incorporation of representatives of the key producer interests. It notes both the purposive use of regulatory powers and the recent deployment of government powers of patronage and subsidy. However, it concludes by acknowledging the specifically legal problems the approach encounters with effectiveness and legitimacy on the reassertion of liberal legality.

### THE CHARACTERISTICS OF CORPORATIST LAW

What shape does this new approach to policy implementation take? In the practice of economic policy, a contrast can thus be drawn with a second legal approach, one which is both more purposeful and particularistic but at the same time more informal and inflexible than the liberal legal approach. In this approach, the main role of the law becomes the provision of a space in which government can progressively develop policy, fashioning working standards and individual decisions to further innovation objectives under fluctuating conditions, including the feedback they receive from the targeted groups (Hancher and Moran, 1989). The law provides a shell to negotiate for collaborative arrangements between government and industry by removing policy from rule-based review through the use of statutory privileges, flexible regulation, administrative proceedings and collaborative decision-making (Winkler, 1975).

This 'purposive action' approach is associated with a shift in the locus of legal power away from the legislatures and the courts to executive and administrative bodies and further to hybrid bodies such as industry councils and trading corporations. This generally means a shift away from the market-based, open and categorical liberal form and its 'rule of law' in the direction of administrative and corporatist relationships between the state and industry. It seeks the administrative regulation of social categories in accordance with technical norms. What has been the broad impact of these tendencies upon the law? The interpenetration of public and private law is said to have involved a decrease in the separate realm of private law (Slazidits, 1965). In property, contract and tort, for instance, the most important legal relations based on act or agreement have gradually ceded to regulation which in turn often shades off imperceptibly into public or private administration (Glendon, 1981). Distinctions between law and regulation, courts and tribunals, justice and administration all become less and less tenable (Kamenka and Tay, 1975).

## INFORMALITY AND COLLABORATION

One theoretical analysis to give real flesh to this possible transformation of the law was Winkler's notion of corporatist law (Winkler, 1975). This theory can be classed as corporatist because, unlike the theories which saw the approach as simply a response to the needs of capital in general (Holloway and Picciotto, 1978), or more directly to the needs of large monopolistic corporations (Jessop, 1982), Winkler saw the role of the state as harnessing capitalism to the interests of the nation. Corporatism was an economic system in which the state directed and controlled predominantly privately owned businesses to four national goals: unity, order, nationalism and success (Winkler, 1975).

The legal effect of these economic policies is said to be a culmination of more compulsion and increased discretion. The essential features of corporatism are a limited commitment to public ownership, detailed control over the internal decision-making of privately owned businesses, and a move away from explicit legal control. The corporatist state seeks mandatory control over private economic activity so that this activity cannot counteract national economic objectives, while it retains discretion for itself to adapt its policies to changing circumstances in pursuit of these objectives. Consequently, the approach of the traditional legal form of the market economy – permissiveness (as in freedom of contract) and stability (as in certainty of legal rules) – is no longer appropriate.

Accordingly, in the corporatist society, there can be no concept of the law either as separate from the state and capable of being used against it or as an autonomous body of rules that is neutral between interests and provides a framework within which private actors and the state each pursue their aims. All distinctions between law and policy disappear, and the law becomes an instrument which is used by the state for collective ends. The state resists codification of its operating principles and indeed there is a movement to reject law altogether. In the transition, controls are exercised through laws that target the sectors and subjects they aim to direct, while discretion to vary the controls is retained through the framework of an enabling statute model.

Indeed, to a large extent, the state exercises control by deploying its procurement, lending, subsidizing and other economic powers through the medium of administrative and quasi-contractual relationships with industry. Some of these powers like tariffs for instance, are inherently general and can only be used in relation to broad industrial groups; others, like price control and industrial assistance, are specific and may be manipulated to extract undertakings from individual companies. In this way control becomes strategic as the state attempts to regulate aggregate national economic performance through the direction of a few key, and often oligopolist, business entities. If the existing level of concentration is insufficient to make strategic control possible, the state will endeavour to foster industrial reorganization and establish cartels. The state may control without being seen to control: for example financial powers may be used for purposes which are not codified in law and the results need not be formalized in legally enforceable contracts.

Implementation is thus mediated and distanced. Controls are in part exercised through intermediary institutions which are nominally independent of the state. Some are quasi-governmental institutions such as telecommunications instrumentalities, and others are non-governmental institutions such as industry councils. By adopting this approach, the rigidity of formalized rules, whether statutory provisions, bureaucratic standards, or contractual obligations, can be avoided and potentially contentious state activities distanced and insulated from accountability. Private organizations are also enlisted to implement the policies of the state.

## *IMPERIUM* AND *DOMINIUM*

It has been widely appreciated that governments seek to manipulate conventional regulatory controls and directives in order to extract undertakings from industry. For example, they offer to refrain from instituting legislative controls in order to obtain cooperation with a preferred policy. More obviously, they offer to waive the enforcement of existing legislative provisions if compliance with policy objectives is obtained. Their flexibility to do so is not only developed informally as a matter of agency practice, increasing it may in fact be built into the structure of the regulatory scheme (Winter, 1985). The forms which competition and foreign investment law now take might prove to be a good illustration of this approach, their operation becoming a matter of corporatist consensus between state agencies and the leaders of financial and industrial capital (Picciotto, 1983). One case study (chapter 6) examines the ways in which legislators and administrators are managing this dilemma. The sheer complexity and dynamism of the industrial relationships which are to be regulated, coupled with ambivalence over the objectives to be achieved in the area, sends government in search of flexible bargaining relationships. So too, foreign investment both brings capital and promises access to overseas innovations and markets. Foreign corporations are likely, however, to impose conditions on technology transfer, competition by subsidiaries and licensees, and local participation. Another case study (chapter 7) considers by what processes and on what conditions the authorities screen foreign investment proposals. When government screens takeovers by local or foreign companies, it does not necessarily apply a set of firm rules. Negotiations might be conducted to extract the best return for administrative clearance.

At the same time, it is being suggested that governments may enjoy greater flexibility in the deployment of their considerable financial resources – their power of *dominium* rather than *imperium*. They seek to offer positive inducements and incentives for cooperation with government policy. Governments influence industry through the manipulation of their power to award advantages, say by way of the selective provision of financial subsidies to private companies, and indeed through their power to withdraw advantages which are presently enjoyed, say as a preferred supplier of the government's own procurement needs. This strategy has the most purchase when government seeks to influence the investment behaviour of a small number of key firms (Daintith, 1985). For example, tax concessions, cash grants and related financial assistance may be offered to encourage investment in innovation where the benefits seem hard to capture through the market. A case study (chapter 8) considers the experience with direct grant and tax concession schemes which seek to stimulate innovation while maintaining some distance from the decision-making of the private sector.

On the demand side, the procurement and purchasing powers of public authorities may be deployed to support innovators by guaranteeing demand and insulating them against the risks of failure. A case study (chapter 9) examines how a range of public purchasing programs – for defence, telecommunications, and health provision – have been enlisted to the cause of support for local innovation, sometimes at the expense of their original purposes. Executive officials have used discretionary powers of patronage to negotiate offsets from foreign suppliers for the benefit of local firms or to give preference directly to local suppliers. Governments may also provide support to key producers by rationing market entry through the use of selective licensing. Turning to the important telecommunications industry, a final case study (chapter 10) considers the extent to which the licensing of entry into both the core carrier and the peripheral value-added services and customer premises equipment markets has been employed to promote the development of the local equipment industry.

## LIMITS ON CORPORATIST LAW?

### *Overloading Law*

It is time again now to enter our reservations about the hold which the corporatist approach takes on policy implementation. We should recall how, in chapter 1, we noted that the corporatist approach encountered some difficulties in establishing both its effectiveness and its legitimacy. Given the focus in this chapter on the law, we should acknowledge the possibility that liberal legality is reasserted, both by circumscribing the scope of the space in which government is able to deploy the corporatist approach and in ordering the practice of policy implementation within the space it creates. We should note in particular how claims for the observance of liberal legality are translated into the exercise by the courts of a review jurisdiction over such administrative decision-making. We should also discern their expression in the processes to render administrators accountable to the legislature.

In keeping with this, one limitation on the purposive action approach is the possibility that it places the institutions of law under stress. For Teubner (1983) (in his distinctively Germanic way), the systematic rationality of autonomous liberal law is undermined as the system increasingly takes over responsibility for correcting market deficiencies, for global economic policy and for compensatory social policies. The law seeks a substantive rationality characterized by particularism, a result orientation, an instrumentalist social policy approach and the increasing legalization of formerly autonomous social processes. But the law is not effective in this rematerialization. Such a program of state intervention encounters a regulatory crisis because of 'the complexity of socio-economic processes, the contradictory imperatives of economic crisis management, and the cognitive limits of our mechanisms of political legal control' (Teubner, 1983: 268).

Thus, regulatory law, working with detailed directives and sophisticated implementation machinery, liquidates much of its socio-political power. The attempt to use the law intensively for the purpose of economic management both creates a cognitive overload for the law and erodes its normativity as it sends it in a futile search after a technocratic rationality (O'Malley, 1984). The law is placed under stress as it moves from the limited role of providing the basic general and formally equivalent conditions for participation in the private sector to a legitimacy which is contingent upon its success in the particularized management of the economy. With the development of substantive irrationality and ineffectiveness, the legitimacy of the law is undermined (Brand, 1982).

## The Rule of Law

Specifically, the purposive action approach gives rise to a concern about the state's commitment to guarantee the categorical and formally equivalent legal conditions for the conduct of private economic activity and to maintain the rule of law generally (Friedman, 1971). Criticism of the approach takes on a constitutional theme as it perceives a blurring of the line between the public and private sectors, a shift in power from legislatures and the courts to the executive and administrative agencies, a preference for discretionary programs and corporatist arrangements over rule-based and arm's length regimes; and the compromise of the detached and even-handed discharge of traditional public responsibilities. The involvement in commercial ventures of public agencies with private interests seems to attract particular concern. The collaboration is seen to risk a conflict of interest between the agencies' public responsibilities and their commercial interests.

## Legal Accountability

In acting in these ways, governments are often criticized for by-passing the usual rule-bound procedures of public decision-making and affording selected private interests a position inside the policy process, treating them on occasions as co-equal bargaining partners (Head, 1986). At the same time as this approach encounters a strong lobby to prevent further encroachment into the sphere of private economic autonomy and to privatize existing public assets, moves are being made to check government discretion and legalize the provision of state assistance, subjecting administrative decision-making to accountability in legislatures and the courts (Broekman, 1985). The agencies are pressed to articulate their policies, preferably in legislative form; restrict the factors they take into account; afford natural justice and due process; and act with consistency between individual cases. Such claims often translate into a desire to make the decision-making accessible to review in the courts and tribunals. Overall, there is a drive to render the award of government favours 'justiciable' (Commonwealth of Australia. Administrative Review Council, 1989). The legislatures may also be called on to assert greater accountability, both at the time of the formulation of the policies and periodically during their subsequent operation. Where such claims are unsuccessful at the national level, they are now being taken into the international arena. We shall explore these experiences with the courts and legislatures in chapter 11.

## SUMMATION

This section offers a tentative conclusion regarding the nature of the necessary interactive relationship between liberal and corporatist

Policy and law 57

legal approaches to policy implementation in contemporary society. Any study must recognize the push and pull between the contradictory claims of these approaches in the legal responses to innovation policy questions. Liberal law is not left untouched by this process, but closer government–industry relationships must be regarded as attempts, not to control and direct, but to construct a bargaining relationship that acknowledges the power of private producers and seeks to obtain the maximum cooperation possible with government objectives.

## TENSIONS BETWEEN THE APPROACHES

Summing up for now, we might say that, while technical problems of economic management seem to point the state in the direction of particularized and discretionary approaches, legitimation problems draw it back to a renewed emphasis on clearly defined rules (Cotterell, 1984: 187). The tensions between the two approaches are expressed not only in the activities which take place in the economic sphere but also surface in the political and legal spheres, that is in the government structures themselves. The tensions are not only reflected in the conflicting pressures placed upon government from such external sources as the producer groups but may also be represented within its own internal workings. Thus, the tensions create strains in the relations between the various legislative, executive, administrative and judicial elements of the state. Tensions may develop between the executive agencies, which wish to maintain discretion and flexibility in the promotion of innovation policy, the legislatures, which wish to impose standards of public accountability, or the courts, which wish to subject the agencies to the norms of judicial review. Strains indeed may develop between the various executive and administrative agencies as they hold to divergent missions. A common instance is the rivalry between Treasury and industry agencies. Consequently, the state itself may not be coherent or cohesive enough to follow a concerted strategy.

If the hallmark of modern Western societies has been the differentiation of functional subsystems and the separation of the law from political and economic subsystems, one might expect a legal culture to have developed which is not readily channelled into or subsumed by the other subsystems. It might not be so easy for the new administrative schemes to be immunized from this culture, and traditional legal standards may find their expression within the new agencies and tribunals themselves or impinge upon their operations through the review jurisdictions of the legislatures and ordinary courts. In his study of modern planning law, McAuslan (1983) found that limits were often built into the new schemes; assumptions were made about the legitimate reach of government intervention; and that these internal constraints were reinforced by external controls such as judicial reviews, which still operated on notions of the protection of private and individual rights rather than the promotion of the concerns of central coordination and collective consumption.

In such a climate, the law may experience some difficulty finding a suitable basis on which to conceptualize and order the new working modes of the state for the implementation of public policy. The singular reliance on the formalistic requirements of constitutional and other legal authority, insistence on a demarcation between public and private domains, and the curtailment of collective policies in defence of private rights seems an increasingly inadequate response. How can the dangers of arbitrariness and favouritism in government decision-making be checked without paralysing the prosecution of public policies in a complex and divided society? Some public law theorists have turned away from the courts and legislatures to the idea of suitable standards of internal administrative rationality and participatory democracy, so that decision-making can be informed, considered and reasonable, yet at the same time sufficiently uninhibited for public policies to be advanced (Stewart, 1988). This search is particularly important for theorists on the left of politics, who seem caught in a dilemma between their traditional suspicion of the rule of law and their desire to restrict the deployment of executive and administrative powers by the corporate or exceptional state (Harden and Lewis, 1986). A variation on this theme is the proposal that the law be confined to a role constituting 'reflexive' social subsystems through norms of organization and procedure (Teubner, 1984; Carney, 1991). But, as positive as these suggestions are, they are still to distinguish themselves thoroughly from the existing legal approaches (Blankenburg, 1984). Such tantalizing theories remain at the formative stage. We shall return to them in the final chapters of this book, and especially in chapter 12.

## ORDER BETWEEN THE APPROACHES

Whatever the answers to such jurisprudential questions, if there be answers, the questions do seem to indicate that the pressures for forms more responsive to economic management problems do not necessarily produce a crisis in liberal legal ideology (Nelken, 1982). The indeterminacy and lack of systematic coherence so often attributed to liberal legalism by its critics, might in fact be a source of its resilience and adaptability (Krygier, 1987). The tensions and shifts merely point up the existence of a multiplicity of social types. The development of welfarism and corporatism in modern society has not signified the end of the liberal type (Unger, 1986). While their new economic structures are yet to crystallize, the recent political upheaval in Eastern Europe is the most recent proof of the vitality of the liberal type as an ideological force.

How then are we to relate the resilience of the liberal approach to the emergence of these closer kinds of inducement and collaboration? We are left, perhaps, with the intellectually frustrating but most accurate picture of a matrix or layering of approaches. In other words, the new schemes of inducement and collaboration can be seen to operate in a complex interaction with the liberal facilities of property and contract. A 'map' for this complex world is offered by De Sousa Santos (1985). Law operates at any one time in a number of basic spheres or locations, some more oriented to the liberal approach, others to administrative and corporatist relations. The changing articulations between the laws of these different places can help explain the multi-layered regulation of innovation relations. In such a scheme, where property and contract retain an important role in the regulation of production relationships (for example in the workplace and in the world economy), we must view the forms of closer government–industrial collaboration as contingent and partial (Panitch, 1980). The new government strategies respect rather than transform the basic structures of the industries with which they are engaged (Loveday, 1982).

## CONNECTIONS BETWEEN THE APPROACHES

Acknowledging these structures, the role of these arrangements is to engage private interests in bargaining in order to obtain their cooperation with the objectives of public policy. In some realms, a two-way bargaining relationship develops between government and industry, a relationship that has been characterized as 'contradictory symbiosis' (Picciotto, 1983: 36). To some, these kinds of government strategies are designed to maximize the effectiveness of public programs rather than simply to serve the interests of private producers. Nevertheless, they do so by policies being negotiated and applied adaptively, legal powers used as instruments for bargaining with industry rather than for imposing directions. In other words, they are coping strategies, with limited expectations, which are meant to deal with the problem of making government objectives effective (Blankenburg, 1985). The interaction of the legal approaches with the political styles adopted at this level define the nature of the small 'space' created for policy implementation (Hancher and Moran, 1989).

At the same time as one of the thrusts of policy formation today is to reassert the exercise of economic prerogatives in the vast realms of industrial governance, another is the change in the state's own modes of operation (Considine, 1988). The state moves its own operations closer to the organizational structures and *modus operandi* of the modern corporation. As well as the greater freedom from legislative control and judicial review this style allows to executive and administrative heads, it provides private interests with positions in the policy-making process through the shifting of functions to executive bodies, government enterprises and hybrid industry councils, and through the participation of public agencies in joint ventures and commercial companies. These intermediate bodies vary in their constitutions and functions but they are often ambiguous in status, giving rise to concern because they blur the distinctions between the legal operating standards of public and private bodies and distance administration from the sites of conventional scrutiny (Lawrence, 1984). The practice of this approach exists in a state of tension with the continuing claims of the liberal form and the rule of law.

We should therefore use the case studies both to chart the limits which the liberal approach continues to set and to explore the use made of the surviving regulatory 'space' to pursue innovation policy options. For the studies to be useful, we must aim for precision in the reading of contributions made by legal policy, but I believe the effort will be worthwhile.

# PART II
*Intellectual Property*

CHAPTER 3

## *Patents and Living Organisms*

This chapter aims to assess the significance of the patents system for the process of innovation, especially in relation to biotechnology. It looks first at the essential features of the patent. Working on the basis that the patent is presently important to investment in biotechnology innovation, it then examines recent developments in patent policy with regard to that technology, focusing on the innovation of living organisms. Why is the case of living organisms chosen? The capacity to create living organisms (and especially higher life forms) will have a profound impact upon the course of scientific and industrial relations. Indeed, social relations generally are implicated: life itself is being redefined. These ramifications are not just a question for patents policy. But the appropriability of life is an exciting issue. When the infrastructure of property rights is so much taken for granted in Western societies, biotechnology presents a real question about the reach of the property form. It is no small question to ask how the administrators, courts and legislators are responding to this question.

### THE PATENTS SYSTEM GENERALLY

This section begins with a brief outline of the patents system. It identifies the justifications advanced for the provision by the state of a property right over certain kinds of innovations. It reviews the contention that patents are not regarded as an attractive strategy for capturing the benefits of innovation. The section goes on to identify concerns, in both industry and the wider society, about the command the patent power gives over the direction of innovation and access to its benefits. It suggests, however, that the patents systems are unlikely to be qualified in any fundamental way. It is necessary to look to the internal criteria of the systems for the policy regarding

## OUTLINE OF THE PATENTS SYSTEM

The patent is a form of intellectual property widespread and long-standing among the economies of the world (MacLeod, 1988). In Australia, the national legislation is based upon early British law. The *Patents Act 1990* (Commonwealth) specifies that an application for a patent may be in respect of a manner of new manufacture which would be a proper subject of letters patent and grant of privilege within the bounds of section 6 of the United Kingdom Statute of Monopolies. So, while Australian and British law have diverged somewhat in more recent years, the appropriate subject matter for the grant of a patent is indicated by a formula carried over from the early seventeenth century (Ricketson, 1984a). The legislation lays down the essential criteria and conditions for the grant of the patent. Accordingly, it sets the limits to the reach and facility of the property form. But the decision-making concerning the eligibility of individual applications involves complex considerations of law, science and economics, and the demands of this decision-making spawn an elaborate administrative and judicial system. The legislation is greatly elaborated and operationalized by the considerable body of patents office practice and a number of significant judicial decisions. A short description of the Australian system may be of some general use here.

In Australia, the Patents Office is the centrepiece of the administrative system. Both the Patents Office and the Commissioner of Patents enjoy statutory status. After examination within the office, the commissioner makes decisions on individual applications, which are published in an official journal. Hearings can be conducted by the commissioner if there is opposition to a grant. Official notices and statements of practice are also put out from time to time for the guidance of applicants. Of course, a professional body of patent attorneys has developed around the practice of the office and a number of sophisticated legal firms also specialize in patent law. Appeals from the commissioner's decisions go to the relevant state courts. The Federal Court and the High Court of Australia have review jurisdictions. In addition, the Commonwealth Administrative

Appeals Tribunal has jurisdiction over certain decisions. Patent entitlements also become the subject of litigation in infringement suits. In the field of biotechnology there have been some expansive decisions, making the courts, as we shall see, important contributors to the development of patents policy.

Being the subject of ordinary legislation, the Australian patents system is open to alteration by the government through the parliament. The legislation has been subject to revision on several occasions in recent years. Most fundamentally, in 1979 the Australian government charged its Industrial Property Advisory Committee (IPAC) to review the local patent system in order to make 'recommendations for practical measures to adapt patents to more effectively stimulate Australian technology development, looking to a more technologically progressive and export oriented future' (Commonwealth of Australia. IPAC, 1984). The government responded to the committee's recommendations at the end of 1986. The following year it transferred oversight of the system from the Department of Science to the Department of Industry, Technology and Commerce. After consultations with 'users', amendments to the legislation were finally made in 1990. Several of the recent changes have been relevant to the patenting of biotechnologies.

Realizing how international competitiveness is enhanced by the capture of the benefits of biotechnology, other countries have also been concerned with patents system promotion. The national systems operate today very much in an international context. Efforts by individual countries in the nineteenth century to secure reciprocal protection led in 1883 to a multilateral agreement, the Paris Convention for the Protection of Industrial Property (McKeogh and Stewart, 1991). The Paris Convention has been supplemented by various other treaties and conventions. Part of the international work is concerned with simplifying and harmonizing the administrative processes for obtaining worldwide recognition for an invention. The Patent Co-operation Treaty provides a means to avoid duplication of the processes of application and examination. This work is advanced by international organizations, the World Intellectual Property Organization (WIPO) being the most central. The internationalization of intellectual property extends to efforts to establish the same level of protection across the world. Yet the international forums reflect the tensions which develop between leading producer nations and the catch-up countries of the developing world over the appropriate strength of intellectual property rights regimes. A notable recent development has been the the increasing engagement of economic forums in promoting intellectual property protection. The OECD has been active in pursuing more effective property protection (de Miramon, 1990). As countries grow to appreciate the strategic trade role of intellectual property protection, protection has now been squarely characterized as a free trade question with its inclusion on the agenda of the Uruguay round of GATT (Slaughter, 1990).

## THE SIGNIFICANCE OF PATENTS FOR PRODUCERS

Several justifications can be advanced for the conferment by the state of a property right over these industrial innovations or manners of new manufacture. As in other fields, the argument for property is sometimes made in terms of the inventor's natural rights or just deserts. Increasingly, however, when we examine the language and the impact of patent law, we must say that its rationale is instrumental and economic. The patent right is supported on the basis that it provides a necessary encouragement to inventors, investors and industrialists to devote resources to the development and exposure of new processes and products. Patents provide an incentive to invest the major resources needed to invent and to put the results into circulation for practical use. This instrumental approach is said to be more deliberate and significant in the case of intellectual property because, unlike many physical goods, intellectual creations are not naturally scarce resources, requiring husbandry and rationing, but are often free and even easy to access and reproduce (Mandeville, 1982). Yet the ingenuity and effort which go into their creation can be rare and elusive commodities. Patents provide a protection against imitators and free riders.

Yet, why should the economic incentive of a property right be necessary to motivate innovation? Patent rights provide no guarantee to the state that inventions will be stimulated or to the holder that inventions will be successful. It remains an indirect means of promoting innovation (Taylor and Silberston, 1973). It does not do to assume the importance of the availability of the property entitlement to producers (Llewellyn, 1981). It is sometimes argued, for instance, that innovation is inspired, especially in its earlier stages, by motives other than economic gain. Much research in biotechnology is publicly pursued and governments also provide direct subsidies to private innovators. Some innovation might proceed in ignorance of the facilities which the patent system provides. Increasingly, however, innovation is a planned and organized activity, informed by and geared to identified opportunities for industrial production and commercial distribution. Increasingly, too, right back to the basic science, innovation is an activity conducted on a big scale of finance, manpower and infrastructure. One reflection of that reality is the group of patent legislation provisions designed to resolve the ownership question in the case of collective work. These provisions also permit the patent to be granted to an employer or a company. (It may also be granted to a foreign citizen.) The legislation further provides that patents may be assigned, even in advance of their grant. In such ways, the legislation indicates that patents may be treated as commodities for trade on the market or for integration within private industrial organizations. (This represents a significant policy preference and we shall refer to it again in chapter 5.)

## THE COST OF THE PATENT GRANT

More telling, perhaps, is the argument that patents are not regarded in practice as an especially useful strategy for protection against competitors. The establishment of the right to a patent can be an expensive and uncertain venture. Competitors may challenge the patent or find ways to work around it. Producers may place more stock in various other strategies (both technical and economic) to capture the benefits of innovation. Certainly, the take-up and deployment of patent rights depend upon the calculation of a number of practical factors. Patent rights are indeed assessed strategically by producers, and their delays, costs and conditions set against their returns in a comparison with the attractions of other strategies. In their survey, Bertin and Wyatt (1988) found that the appeal of patents to multinational companies varied with such factors as the scope of the property protection, the ease of fitting the innovation to the criteria of the law, the costs associated with the grant and defence of the right, the conditions on which the protection is extended, and the comparative efficacy of other available strategies.

One consideration is clearly the generosity and certainty with which the patent category acknowledges the emerging technology, and it is this fundamental feature we shall pursue when we look at the policy regarding living organisms. Another consideration is the transaction and administration costs of the system. For example, the evidential and procedural requirements for securing the patent right may be onerous. Complex administrative and judicial processes afford advantages to those with the experience and finance to exploit them (Van Zyl Smit, 1985). This point is underlined when we note some of the ways in which the system can be used aggressively against potential competitors, both in asserting patent claims and in challenging those of competitors. While the Patents Office provides a facility to applicants, it is meant to fund itself from its clients. More significantly, infringement questions have to be pursued privately or civilly through the courts and the state does not lend the support of the criminal law (McKeogh and Stewart, 1991). These features tend to drive the small or public inventor into the arms of the large industrial corporations and their advisers (Vaver, 1990).

Patent law reform may give attention to such procedural burdens (see Commonwealth of Australia. IPAC, 1992). The Australian government has, for example, recently eased transaction costs at the point of application with the institution of a petty patent category, which, while more limited in scope than the standard patent, involves less substantiation and examination. So, too, IPAC's proposals for the abolition of modified examination (in the case of applications concerning inventions already patented overseas) and pre-grant opposition to applications, were rejected on the basis that these procedures provided relatively inexpensive means to determine issues (Lamberton, 1987). The Commonwealth Administrative Review Council is reviewing the system of appeals from patent decisions. As we have noted, the work of the international bodies is also commonly concerned with easing procedural obstacles to the international recognition and enforcement of patents. Part of the concern is the cost of duplicating procedures. There is also a suggestion that some countries use opaque and abstruse procedures as a covert trade barrier to entry by foreign producers into their domestic markets (Wineberg, 1988).

## ALTERNATIVE STRATEGIES

The efficacy of alternative strategies is a related consideration. In the opening chapter I noted that other potential barriers to imitation and competition include command over know-how; the ability to exploit economies of scale and scope; the advantage of lead time; the availability of other factors of production; learning economies in processing, marketing and after-sales skills; and general organizational ability, including the ability to transcend outmoded firm and industry structures in response to radically changing technology (Pavitt, 1984).

For example, Teece's analysis of the way in which competing producers endeavour to capture the value from innovations stresses the importance of these complementary assets (Teece, 1987). 'Tight' conditions of appropriability (intellectual property) assist the original innovator to capture the benefits of the innovation. But in practice the conditions are often weak, because, for example, the coverage of the appropriability regime is limited or the appropriation can be circumvented by competitors. Especially, then, in situations where the conditions of appropriability are weak, firms have an advantage in the race to capitalize on inventions if they have access to complementary assets. Thus, a position as secondary producer may not necessarily be an unfavourable one. This interpretation receives support from the field of biotechnology, where the multinational pharmaceutical and chemical companies are now coming into their own (Kenney, 1986). Patent rights have often proved uncertain protections (Teitelman, 1989). The importance of command over complementary assets has meant that the place for public research institutions and small start-up firms seems largely confined to contract research, the sale of inventions, and buy-outs by the large corporations (Sharp, 1990).

## BIOTECHNOLOGY PATENTS

Yet, the field of biotechnology provides some exception to this general observation about the relevance of patents (OECD, 1985). Certainly the Australian Patents Office thinks that biotechnology is a significant source of applications (Commonwealth of Australia. Patents Office, 1989). Complementary assets perhaps assume their greatest significance as the shape of the new technology begins to settle and attention turns to product refinement, processing efficiencies and marketing techniques. Biotechnology is still at the stage where major breakthroughs are being made, the breakthroughs that set the foundations for the many commercial applications of the future. These broad, radical innovations may be worth securing through a property right against all the world: the Cohen-Boyer patent for recombinant DNA techniques serves as a good example.

More generally, biotechnology applications often involve large amounts of investment, high technical and commercial risk, and delay in implementation (because of the need, for example, to obtain regulatory approvals for products). The cost of obtaining the patent may in these circumstances seem small in comparison. Some of the products have a long commercial life and a large market potential, including export to other countries. Other economic barriers to entry might not prove sufficient in an oligopolistic industry where technological advances are vital to success and where imitators possess the necessary complementary assets to compete commercially. It is instructive to note that the pharmaceutical industry often lobbies to extend the term of the patent protection; it is also, in part because of the competition now from generic drugs, very much concerned with the trade-related apects of intellectual property rights at the GATT (Nogues, 1990).

The peculiar characteristics of this new technology also may make patents abnormally attractive. For example, the size and mobility of new micro-organisms makes them relatively easy to steal; and once engineered they are essentially self-replicating or propagating (Clark, 1981). While it may not be easy to reverse-engineer the techniques of creating the organisms, the organisms can be reproduced without fully understanding these techniques. There is also a risk that the organisms or at least organisms with the same functions might be independently created. In such circumstances, a strategy of technical control might not always be successful (Adelstein and Peretz, 1985). It might not be possible to maintain secrecy, as the technology is exposed to outsiders. Patent systems therefore provide some security against the consequences of disclosure.

In any case, there is no real need to contrast patents with other strategies as if they were mutually exclusive. The lesson of Bertin and Wyatt's survey (1988) is that patents are often used as part of an array of strategies to capture the benefits of innovation. In particular, they are used not only as a means to exclude others from access to the innovation but also as a bargaining chip in the negotiation of the collaborative agreements and licensing arrangements with other producers which are required to combine specialized assets and structure developing markets. In such a capacity, even the issue of patentability itself may be pursued strategically, say by licensing to avoid challenges or by instituting infringement suits to obtain other concessions (McKeogh and Stewart, 1991).

## CONCERNS ABOUT PATENT POWER

If it retains some significance, then the patent system as a whole, and certainly the extension of its facilities to new technologies, attracts criticism of various kinds. The patent confers an exclusive right over the exploitation of the technology (extending to making, hiring, selling or using the invention), which survives even in the case of its independent invention. In this way a patent excludes other producers and users from the technique, or at the least requires them to seek authorization from the holder in order to utilize it. Concern is expressed about the uses to which the patent power is put, especially in oligopolist industries.

### *Economic Concerns*

There is some argument about whether it is accurate to characterize the patent as a monopoly power, partly for the reasons we have identified above, such as the ease with which many patents can be circumvented or substitutes provided (Kitch, 1978). The 'Chicago School' of law and economics appears to have been influential in promoting a more benign view of the patent, especially in relation to its anti-trust implications (see OECD, 1989). Nonetheless, critics maintain that patents can be used in a number of anti-competitive ways. The property power can be used strategically to control both access to the use of the technology and the distribution of its benefits (Noble, 1977). For example, the strategy of patent consolidation may involve conscious attention not only to the development of patents through research, but also to the buying up of patents by means of contractual assignments or acquisition of the entities which hold them. Patents may be accumulated aggressively to 'ring-in' fields and cover associated lines. Would-be competitors may be threatened with infringement suits that divert their energies and discourage their patrons (Dunford, 1986).

In addition, patent pooling and cross licensing can be used to raise barriers to entry and to apportion markets. Conditions may be extracted from licensees: for example to restrict their competition with licensors in certain geographical or industrial markets or to tie them in to other goods and services. Research and development activity may also be affected where the price of the licence is that the licensee agrees not to research associated techniques or improvements, or agrees to assign such intellectual property back to the licensor. Licences to use the technique for research purposes may in fact be withheld if the researcher is a potential competitor (Eisenberg, 1989). The property power may thus permit its holders to influence the speed of technology transfer and to charge higher prices for access to the technology.

Such concerns place stress on the uses to which the patent facilities are put in practice and the structures of the industries in which they are deployed. The producers with the greatest power often end up reaping the benefits of the patent system and the patent power reinforces the influence they can exert over suppliers and users (Lawrence, 1989). The economic question is complicated by international differences. It is questionable whether the protection of the patent system is of benefit to a country in Australia's position, where around 90 per cent of all registered patents are held by foreigners (Commonwealth of Australia. Senate Standing Committee on Science, Technology and the Environment, 1987). Many of those patents may not be worked locally. The chemical and pharmaceutical industries are no exception: they are not only highly concentrated but the bulk of this ownership is in foreign hands (Johnston, 1983; Corones, 1990). On this basis, the benefits of the patent system lie in its contribution to inward technology transfer and export potential supported by reciprocal recognition overseas. As we shall see in Part III, there is evidence that foreign holders provide new technology to their local subsidiaries and licensees on restrictive conditions (Grant, 1983). But it cannot be assumed that the technology would become freely available in the absence of patent protection. Indeed, one of the claims for the patent system is, of course, that it encourages disclosure. Even if the disclosures in foreign patents systems remained available to Australians, the necessary attendant trade secrets and know-how might be less forthcoming. Regarding export prospects, we should note that much of the local research is of a basic and public nature. It is often taken up for commercialization by foreign rather than indigenous companies. But patenting might at least provide a means for local researchers to obtain some direct returns for their activity, for example by assigning or licensing their patents overseas (Lowe and

Atkins, 1991). Access to foreign markets (through either Australian or overseas companies) is often necessary if the outlay on investment in the innovation process is to be recouped.

## Moral and Social Concerns

The criticisms do not, however, end with such economic concerns. Apart from its tendency to contribute to the concentration of economic power among producers, it has been argued, the conferral of property rights promotes the commodification and commercialization of essential resources. This charge attracts particular interest in the field of biology because the technology appears to be subsuming or replacing fundamental natural processes, at the highest level through the production of living organisms, including human life. Critics have attributed not only health and environmental risks to the new technology but also, less tangibly, various moral and spiritual threats (Ricketson, 1984). For many, the concern extends to the pursuit and conduct of the research itself and the development of the technology *per se* (Rifkin, 1985). Attempts have been made to restrain such research through the courts, especially in the case of public research institutions (Kenney, 1986). In the United States, notably, scientists held a moratorium on much basic biotechnology research during the seventies (Goodfield, 1977). There is a view that such research should be restrained because the sort of reductionist, instrumental knowledge which is being obtained about the biological process diminishes our respect for the human being, indeed for life generally, and provides greater scope to manipulate it.

Supporters of patents for biotechnology often counter by claiming that the system does not have any effect on these issues. In the opinion of the Australian Minister for Industry, Technology and Commerce, the patent system has and should have a neutral role in moral and ethical questions concerning the technology (Commonwealth of Australia. Senate, 1988). He supported neutrality in the sense that the system should treat biotechnology in the same way it treats other technologies. But making property rights available at all may have an impact on the lines of research pursued, the availability of the research results and the distribution of the benefits of the research (Arup, 1982). It has been suggested, for example, that the availability of patents channels research into expensive appropriable technology and away from work on other socially beneficial innovations

(Phelps, 1990). Patents permit individuals (usually the holders of capital resources) to capture socially accumulated and significant knowledge (Biddle, 1984). This knowledge may, at least in the early stages of innovation, have been publicly funded and collectively produced. Applications of the knowledge are then driven by a concern with commercial gain. Patents may also provide a means to appropriate the properties of nature. The developing countries argue, for instance, that their natural genetic resources will be isolated, modified artificially, and then sold back to them as commercial products (Raghavan, 1990). Such concerns are also raised by the prospect of copyrighting a comprehensive map of the human gene: the human genome project (Labonze, 1988; Rosenfeld, 1988).

Why should this impact be of particular concern in the field of biotechnology? The effect of commodification on the maintenance of the natural resource base is one concern. The selective economic incentive of the property right is said to encourage concentration on artificial processes and products at the expense of the maintenance of natural genetic diversity and sufficiency (Acharya, 1991). For example, it raises the claims of the high technologies above the care and skill which traditional farming has applied to the land for many centuries. These large-scale and often chemical-dependent technologies may be too expensive for the ordinary farmer to use. The control of the resulting commodity is another issue. One concern is that the intellectual property right may be used to tie the user to the holder. Control over the offspring of genetically engineered animals is such an issue, as is control over the seeds of genetically engineered plants (Dresser, 1988). The technology has the potential to produce materials and procedures that are vital to human health and life (such as medical treatments and basic foodstuffs). Some take the view that such resources should not be rationed according to the measures of the market – that is, the capacity to pay rather than the extent of need – at least not without the back-up of public subsidies to indigent users and consumers (Lawrence, 1984). The technology may indeed lead to the production of life forms which should not be the subject of ownership and trade on any conditions: genetically engineered human life forms are the most obvious case. Critics argue that the treatment of living things as mere commodities has the effect of detaching them from their complex spiritual and ecological dimensions.

These are subtle arguments that cannot be afforded full justice here. Again, it is not easy to distinguish the contribution of the patent system to these undesired effects. It has been suggested that the nature of the technology lends itself to the appropriation and substitution of natural biological processes because it is such a mechanistic and interventionist approach (Yoxen, 1983). The trajectory of the technology seems very much an instrumental and industrializing one (see Yachinski, 1985; Elkington, 1985). Yet the patent is emerging as a symbol of the critics' concerns, a rallying point for opposition to the problems of biotechnology. Thus the commodification question is caught up in broader economic and moral issues concerning the treatment of living things (Scott, 1981). It is not intended here to rehearse the mighty arguments for and against property and trade on any normative basis but rather to document the trend of legal policy towards such innovation. It is possible that such concerns exert some actual influence upon the course of legal policy, but the law might just as well develop its responses according to a different momentum than a dialogue with distributional concerns and moral implications. Indeed, one of the current criticisms of the patent system and related trade systems (such as the GATT) is that they are forums that are far too narrow for such fundamental questions effectively to be determined (Acharya, 1991). Likewise, it appears the case that the courts eschew any role in weighing such policy considerations, claiming instead to merely 'interpret' the existing law to see whether its terms embrace the biotechnology innovations (Markey, 1989; Niers, 1990).

## THE RESILIENCE OF THE PATENTS SYSTEM

Despite these periodic criticisms, the general tendency in policy review is to reaffirm and indeed to extend the patent system. This state of affairs is sometimes attributed to lawyers' influence over intellectual property policy. With evident frustration, the economic advisers to the Australian Industrial Property Advisory Committee made the comment that:

> although the widely accepted rationale for the patent system is economic, much of patent law is drafted by those with a legalistic bent. Such people would appear to have great difficulty coming to grips with wider social cost and efficiency considerations, or equity issues across society as a whole. (Mandeville, 1982: 138)

It is certainly the case that legal detachment and gradualism, especially in the courts, can act to constrain the rapid and expedient adjustment of intellectual property policy. But this explanation perhaps exaggerates the singularity and omnipotence of lawyers. In fact, it seems difficult for anybody (including economists) to agree on the overall efficiency and equity implications of patents policy. Vaver recites the view that: 'If national patent laws did not exist, it would be difficult to make a conclusive case for introducing them: but the fact they do exist shifts the burden of proof and it is equally difficult to make a really conclusive case for abolishing them' (Vaver, 1990: 115).

In truth, the continued support of the system has been a strategic economic and political decision. While it expressed serious reservations about the benefit of patents to the Australian economy, the Industrial Property Advisory Committee itself was not prepared to recommend the elimination of patents because it took the view that it was both politically impossible and economically costly for the country to withdraw unilaterally from an international system (Commonwealth of Australia. IPAC, 1984). The government accepted the committee's view (Lamberton, 1987). This position was confirmed on the introduction of the revisions to the legislation in 1990. The minister's second reading speech again made the point that the patent system was a blunt instrument of industrial policy (Commonwealth of Australia. Senate, 1990b). He suggested there were other more direct ways in which innovation could be stimulated. A patent did not guarantee success, and entrepreneurial skills were needed to commercialize inventions. Yet Australia's patent policy could not operate in isolation from the international economy. It was true that patents owned by foreigners restricted imitation in Australia, but patents could also encourage the inward licensing of foreign technology. Reciprocal protection overseas for Australian inventions could make a tremendous difference to export markets.

## THE CRITERIA FOR THE PATENT GRANT

If the patents system seems here to stay, it is worth our while examining the limits to its accommodation of technology. In Australia, the coverage of the patent system, and hence the degree of protection it affords, is controlled in part by its concept of a 'manner of new manufacture'. Other national systems have a counterpart to this threshold requirement. In its 1990 revision of the legislation, the government accepted IPAC's recommendation that the concept be retained as the threshold test of patentability in preference to the adoption of a more inflexible codified definition. In the hands of the courts, the concept has proved to be quite flexible and accommodating. While unenthusiastic about any extension of the system's coverage, IPAC also recommended that no subject matter categories be specifically excluded from the legislation. (But this was not to be, as we shall soon see.)

The fundamental characteristics which a manner of new manufacture must display are novelty, inventiveness and utility. The manner of new manufacture is useful if it represents a contribution to the industrial art. That is, it must be a product or process of practical application and commercial value. There might seem to be some overlap between this requirement and the basic concept of the invention as a manner of manufacture, but, as the concept has lost its rigour, it seems that utility has become a more influential criterion. The other requirements of novelty and inventiveness reflect the system's concern with promoting innovation. These criteria are employed not only to control the categories of subject matter which are eligible for protection but also to fix the dividing line between the particular invention and the prior art, so determining the breadth or scope of the individual grant. Again, the Australian government chose in 1990 to reaffirm these requirements. However, the test of novelty and inventiveness in the case of a standard patent was widened in order to recognize the now rapid international transfer of knowledge and the higher requirements which applied in many of the countries with which Australia traded. In future, the invention would be tested against prior disclosures (in recorded form) anywhere in the world. In contrast, the prior art base for the assessment of the petty patent would include information only from prior disclosures that were published in Australia.

Broadly, the manner of manufacture is new or novel if it is something more than that which is already available and known publicly through publication or use to the point that a person skilled in the art could carry it out (Lahore, 1980). Resolution of this question involves a search through previous patent specifications and other sources of technical information to see whether the invention has been anticipated. Where the same invention is developed independently by two claimants, priority is given in most systems (including Australia) to the first to file an application, provided of course it has not by this time become public. By contrast, in the United States, priority is given to the first to invent.

Novelty has connections with inventiveness. The manner of manufacture is inventive if it is not obvious, having regard to what was published, used or otherwise known at the time of the application (Ricketson, 1984c). Thus, it cannot be part of the common stock of general knowledge of those versed and skilled in the art. A question relevant to biotechnology, given the organized, incremental practice of much science today, is whether a line of research might be obvious even though the applicant is the first to take it up (Szabo, 1990). It might still not be obvious if its successful definition and execution involve the exercise of ingenuity which is beyond the competence of the ordinary worker in the field. Its definition might not, for instance, be evidently worth trying, nor follow plainly from the prior art. Its execution might, leaving aside the effort and expense involved, entail making choices and overcoming difficulties which exceed the practice of routine science.

## THE CONDITIONS ON A PATENT GRANT

Innovation policy is also reflected in the conditions attached to a patent grant. The term of the patent protection is quite limited (in Australia it runs for sixteen years). The applicant must be prepared to disclose the invention in such a way that the specification adequately describes and characterizes the subject matter of the patent and enables the skilled worker in the field to repeat or reproduce it. Thus the patent system extracts the condition of making the implementation of the invention available to the rest of industry once the patent term expires, and allowing competitors to learn from it in the meantime. Supporters of the system often argue that this position is far preferable to producers keeping their inventions secret. Of course, as university scientists are learning, there is still great pressure to keep inventions secret before the application for the patent is made. The Australian legislation recognizes a few circumstances in which prior publication does not disqualify the application, such as where a presentation has been made to a learned society, but the constraint will remain unless countries adopt the idea of a period of 'grace' following publication before an application can still be made. The United States has such a provision.

Some provision to safeguard against 'abuses' of the patent power are also evident in the body of the law. A common provision (Australia is a case in point) is for the public assumption of patent rights or their compulsory licensing to other producers if the patent holder does not work the invention. The availability of essential foodstuffs and medicines is often a special concern (Nogues, 1990). In Australia, these provisions have generally not been taken up (Ricketson, 1991). They are, however, of considerable interest to certain developing countries, and one source of tension with the leading producer nations is the readiness with which they are invoked (Greif, 1982).

Concern with the restrictive uses of the patent power often finds expression not so much in the body of the patent law itself as in the country's competition and foreign investment laws. The Industrial Property Advisory Committee recommended that the anti-innovative uses of the patent power be countered by a stricter competition policy. We shall consider in chapter 6 the policy which is adopted towards practices relating, for instance, to the withholding of patent licences, the imposition of various conditions on licensees, and the cross-licensing of patents.

## PATENTABILITY OF LIVING ORGANISMS

This section examines the development of policy in the body of patent law towards the patenting of living organisms. It considers the extent to which the conventional criteria act to distinguish living organisms from patentable inventions. In particular, it considers the extent to which traditional distinctions against non-industrial processes, the products of nature, scientific discoveries, and the treatment of illness in human beings, prevent the patenting of living organisms. The section suggests that the course of the technology undermines the viability of these distinctions in the eyes of policy makers and encourages the extension of the patent form into new areas of economic endeavour and utility. The section investigates whether explicit public policy exceptions to patentability are being made for higher life forms. Throughout, the section recounts Australian developments within the international context and especially in the light of the United States experience.

We shall now be even more specific in our illustration by examining policies on the patentability of living organisms. Patents might be sought for the processes which produce such organisms, the organisms themselves, the uses of the organisms (for example in food production), and the end products of the organisms (for example in healthcare products). The West German Supreme Court employed an informative threefold classification of biological inventions (OECD, 1985). Its categories took in: inanimate agents or means which influence the course of biological events, such as cultivating procedures; biological agents or means which influence inanimate objects, such as the use of bacteria in fermentation processes or the production of antibiotics; and biological agents or means which cause biological effects, in other words in which the means as well as the final result lie within the field of biology. The use of genetic engineering techniques to produce new living organisms would fall into this last category.

THE APPLICATION OF THE CONVENTIONAL CRITERIA

## Non-Industrial Processes

Are living organisms patentable? In the first place, we should consider the restrictions created by the concept of a manner of manufacture. This concept acted as fundamental brake on the expansion of the patent form into many fields of economic endeavour so long as the courts read it to require the production of physical and vendible goods along the lines taken by traditional secondary manufacturing industry. Such a requirement restricted the eligibility of many biotechnology applications to the agricultural and service sectors of the economy where the commercial value of the innovations was nevertheless readily apparent.

An Australian case is credited with laying the ground for the relaxation of this requirement. The 1959 decision of the High Court in the case of the National Research Development Corporation v. The Commissioner of Patents (at [1959] 102 Commonwealth Law Reports 252) is often cited as the decision which opened up the Australian patent system to modern developments in biotechnology (Thomas, 1982). It has also received international recognition (Vossius, 1990). In this case, the commissioner had objected to the application of the corporation to patent a process involving the use of a herbicide which destroyed weeds but did not harm farmers' broad-leaf crops. In the development of the process, an interrelation between the enzyme structure of the plant crops and the chemical properties of the weed killer had been discovered. In short, chemical acids were able to interact with the tissues of the weeds so as to produce a substance which killed the weeds while not affecting broad-leaf crops. The chemical compounds were not new but their use as selective herbicides had not previously been appreciated.

One issue that arose was whether the process was a manner of manufacture. This horticultural process did not produce or enhance a vendible physical product but it did ensure a weed-free crop. It produced a useful result which was of commercial application; indeed, as the High Court remarked, it provided a remarkable economic advantage. The court upheld the application of the corporation. In doing so it took a liberal and dynamic approach to the interpretation of the patents legislation. The court's message was that the system should adapt not only to changes in technology but also to changes in economic practices. Valuable production was not to be confined to the realm of secondary industry turning out physical objects for sale.

The impact of this decision is reflected in an early Australian case concerning the patentability of a micro-organism; Rank Hovis McDougall Ltd's Application ([1976] 46 Australian Official Journal of Patents 3915). Rank Hovis had isolated a new strain of a micro-organism from a soil sample and then altered the strain by manipulating the composition of the culture in which it grew. The strain had a commercial application in the production of a protein food supplement. The Commissioner of Patents denied the claim to the isolated strain because the organism was found in nature. Thus, the subject matter of the application was not considered to be novel, nor was its isolation inventive, at best it was a discovery. The commissioner did not raise the same objections to the claims for the variants on the naturally occurring strain which the applicant had produced, saying (at p. 3968):

> On the other hand, I think the situation is quite different if, in producing the variant by some man controlled microbiological process, he has produced a new micro-organism which has improved or altered useful properties. To suggest that a patent should not be granted for such an invention would in my opinion hardly accord with the views clearly expressed in the decision in National Research Development Corp v. Commissioner of Patents. The objection that a claim to a new micro-organism, being something living, is not a manner of manufacture is based, in my opinion, on too restricted a view of the meaning of manufacture in section 6 of the Statute of Monopolies.

It should be noted that the commissioner raised objections to the claims for the variants on the basis that the applicant's specification had not met the description and enablement requirements of the legislation. In particular, the specification did not provide a method that would necessarily reproduce the particular variants which were claimed. We shall explore the significance of these requirements for biotechnology below. The commissioner also objected to claims concerning the culture in which the strains were produced and the methods of obtaining them. However, though the applicant was thus unsuccessful in the result of the application, the decision was subsequently regarded as a clear expression of opinion for the Patents Office that micro-organisms were patentable *per se*, and were not barred simply because they were living things (Thomas, 1982).

## Products of Nature

Instead, the case was evidence of another distinction which would come to have more significance for the patentability of living organisms. The case distinguished patentable inventions from those organisms found in nature. Claims to 'naturally occurring' organisms might be said to fail several of the conventional requirements for a patent. Such claims might be said to fail the test of novelty because the technology simply discovers and exploits a property that has always been in existence, albeit lying dormant in nature. Yet, in this respect, it cannot always be said that the technology is known and available to the public before the applicant for the patent reveals it.

More difficult perhaps is the need to show an inventive step, the ingenuity of human beings in intervening and altering the natural course of things, for example by removing genes from their natural habitat, cutting and joining DNA molecules into new gene sequences, and placing them in another bacterial culture. If the requirement is pressed, the question becomes whether the technology simply realizes the inevitable result of the inherent natural qualities of the subject matter – the powers and properties of nature – or whether it represents the artificial product of human ingenuity, an improved or altered product which differs markedly from the natural phenomenon.

This question has been a sticking point in the more established fields of agricultural and horticultural techniques. As a result, the breeding of new plant varieties has in recent years been given special recognition in plant variety rights legislation (Harding and Anderson, 1982). Australia enacted such a scheme in 1987 through the *Plant*

*Variety Rights Act* (Ellinson, 1987). Plant variety rights have of course raised policy controversies of their own (Poberezny, 1982). The conditions which have to be met to obtain such rights are generally less exacting than those laid down in the patents systems, but the coverage of rights is in some ways more limited (Commonwealth of Australia. Senate Standing Committee on National Resources, 1984). With genetic manipulation of plants increasingly supplementing the more conventional cross-breeding techniques, the patentability of the technology, including the plants themselves and their flowers and fruit, is likely to remain an issue. The policy in many countries (though not in Australia) is to make plant variety rights and patents mutually exclusive so that overlap and double protection are avoided.

## Chakrabarty

Living things may be patentable then if they are non-naturally occurring. This was the situation in the famous case of Diamond v. Chakrabarty (447 United States [Reports] 303 [1980]). While the decision was taken under the United States legislation, it was widely publicized and made an impact on the climate of opinion across the world. It was to be cited favourably by, for example, the Australian Minister for Science and Technology in introducing the *Patents (Amendment) Bill* in 1984 into the Commonwealth Parliament (Commonwealth of Australia. House of Representatives, 1984: 897).

A scientist working for the General Electric Company, Chakrabarty had produced a micro-organism strain that had the capacity to decompose crude oil. Chakrabarty engineered the strain by introducing compatible plasmids from three different bacteria into a fourth bacterium, in order to devise a new genetic structure. Chakrabarty applied on behalf of General Electric for patents to cover the method of producing the bacterial strain, the carrier material deployed when the strain was put into use in 'eating' oil slicks, and the strain itself. On appeal, the United States Supreme Court held that the subject matter met the standard requirements of novelty, inventiveness and industrial utility. The Court went on to say that the issue was not whether the organism was living but whether it was a product of nature. In the circumstances, the applicant had done enough to distinguish the subject matter from nature. The strain was a non-naturally occurring product, the outcome of human ingenuity, with markedly different characteristics from any strain found in nature and with the potential of significant utility.

The Supreme Court was presented with a number of public interest interveners who raised a range of arguments against patentability on grounds of public policy, including environmental risk, the loss of genetic diversity and the devaluation of human life. While doubting whether patentability made all that much difference to the progress of research on life forms, the majority finally declined to entertain the public policy considerations and confined itself to the task of statutory interpretation.

## *The Primacy of Economic Utility?*

Can the natural/non-natural distinction remain viable? Of course, genetic 'engineering' also employs natural materials and promotes natural functions. Science might modify the living thing, yet rely on the continuing life processes of that thing to give a beneficial effect to the modification (Clark, 1981). As a consequence, some officials have characterized the natural/non-natural distinction as being unhelpful because it requires the authorities to make judgements about causation or contribution that are difficult to make because of the complexity of the technology or the subjectivity of the criteria (Thomas, 1983). It has been argued, for instance, that the distinction is not helpful because it is difficult as a matter of fact to isolate the agents which cause the technology to work. In many cases the choice turns on the relative weight attributed to the contributions of humans and nature. At what point is the applicant for the patent no longer merely acting on nature with insight and skill to assist and enhance its way of developing inherent potential? A product might be said to be the applicant's creation in the sense that it does not occur naturally, at least not in that configuration, yet it might subsequently live and reproduce itself without further engineering.

The permeation of previously natural worlds by artificial, manipulative techniques adds fuel to arguments in policy circles that the distinguishing criterion should now be whether the product represents a valuable contribution to economic endeavour and forms part of the useful arts (OECD, 1985). It is so argued that it would be in keeping with the patent system to reward the applicant even if the organism is naturally occurring. As nature is researched purposefully and systematically, considerable expense, effort and insight are exhibited in the isolation, selection, purification and deployment of its properties. Accordingly, to interests associated with this work, it seems arbitrary to reward the production of artificial organisms but not the identification and harnessing of natural ones with commercial application (Wald, 1985). Requirements of expense, effort and insight could be employed to exclude those natural organisms which are the result of mere chance findings and conventional screening methods (see also Szabo, 1990).

## Scientific Discovery of the Principles of Nature

A related distinction between scientific discoveries and patentable inventions is also undermined by the course of biotechnology. Scientific discoveries regarding the principles of nature form the insights upon which intervention and manipulation are founded. As more inventions become science-based, and as science is geared to industrial uses, the results of basic research are increasingly hard to distinguish from the realm of applied innovation work. Certainly scientific research and development, including the investigation of nature, is increasingly costly and arduous. Though the results of the basic research may not directly yield useful techniques of commercial application, they are increasingly vital to the future development of industry. But in any case the discoveries may have direct applications in future scientific work (such as probes for use in genetic engineering) and it may often be possible to specify immediately a mode of carrying into effect a discovery in order to found an application for a patent.

It is a matter of concern in some quarters, however, that this merging of scientific research and industrial technique might allow patents to tie up the basic knowledge on which the technology is founded (Yoxen, 1983). An example is the concern raised by the Cohen-Boyer patent over broad gene splicing and cloning techniques, a concern ameliorated in that instance by their universities' policy to license the techniques non-exclusively at a fee of $10,000 and to license non-commercial basic research uses free of charge. As the science becomes more widespread and familiar, we might expect the patent grants to narrow. But the recent controversy over the sweep of the patent granted by the United States Office to Dr Czech

86  *Intellectual property*

(for the gene shears technology) suggests otherwise. Gene shears are a departure from the prior art in the sense that they act to eliminate rather than add genetic characteristics. In doubt as a result of the breadth of the grant are the Australian CSIRO's rights to patent a refinement and application of gene shears science (and the rights of its licensees, the French company Limograine, and Johnson and Johnson).

## *Methods of Treatment*

Another traditional distinction cast in doubt by developments in biotechnology is the distinction between patentable inventions and methods for the treatment of illness in human beings. The natural–non-natural criterion has relevance here but, as treatment methods increasingly manipulate and transform human bodily processes, again this criterion becomes less significant (Hausser, 1989). Possibly, such methods can continue to be excluded because they do not, unlike treatments for animals, represent a technology with commercial value. Whether methods of treating the human body are of commercial value depends very much on the particular system of funding and delivering health care (Koval, 1987). In a private system, they generate considerable direct value. It can also be argued that the effect of the use of the methods is indirectly valuable in the sense that it restores or safeguards the health of society, contributing, for example, to a more productive workforce (Lahore, 1980). If patent law moves away from earlier preoccupations with manufacturing and similiar industrial techniques, and the key criterion becomes the broad measure of commercial value, then the exception made for methods of treatment might also start to break down. Certainly, pharmaceutical drugs and surgical devices are already patentable in many countries. Methods of contraception have also been encompassed in recent years. In Joos v. The Commissioner of Patents (at [1972] 126 Commonwealth Law Reports 611) the High Court upheld a claim to a patent for a process for treating human hair and nails. The process enhanced the elasticity and strength of hair and nails by employing a preparation containing a fluid chemical composition. In doing so, the High Court, following the liberal approach adopted in the NRDC case, declined to exclude all methods for treating the human body from the protection of the legislation on the basis that they were not of economic significance. A process for improving the cosmetic appearance of the person can produce a result for which people are prepared to pay.

*Higher Life Forms*

The case law we have considered so far concerns applications to patent unicellular micro-organisms. Are higher life forms likely to be treated any differently? In 1980, after Chakrabarty, the Australian Patents Office published an official notice (at [1980] 50 Australian Official Journal of Patents 1162) informing applicants of its attitude to claims concerning living organisms generally. The notice read:

> Patent Applications concerned with Living Organisms
> The criteria to be met before an application concerning living organisms will be accepted are precisely the same as those for any other application i.e. no distinction is to be made solely on the basis that a claimed product or process is, or contains or uses, a living organism. Higher life forms will not be treated any differently from lower forms such as micro-organisms.
>
> The only criterion having particular significance in relation to living organisms is the requirement of S. 40 of the Patents Act concerning the full description of the best method of performing the invention. In this regard it should be noted the disclosure of the method of performing the invention that is producing the new organism, which by repetition will again produce the organism, is required.

At the time of this notice, the technology had not advanced sufficiently to present a genetically engineered animal for patenting. However in 1987 the United States Board of Patent Appeals and Interferences upheld a claim to a patent on the process for producing polyploid oysters (Markey, 1989). (The claim to the oyster itself was rejected because, as Lewis Carroll might have remarked, the oyster was obvious.) Four days later, the Commissioner of Patents and Trademarks held a press conference at which he announced the contents of a notice indicating that non-naturally-occurring animal life forms would be regarded as patentable (Niers, 1990). The following year, the commissioner issued a patent to Harvard University for a genetically engineered mouse (Eisenberg, 1989). Harvard's mouse had been invested with a human gene that made it susceptible to cancer, and this susceptibility made the transgenic mouse cheaper to use as a laboratory research tool in trialling new drugs and the like. Harvard was licensing the Du Pont corporation to produce and market the mouse.

## PUBLIC POLICY EXCEPTIONS

If, as it seems clear from these developments, the conventional requirements of patent law do not categorically rule out applications to patent higher life forms, would a line be drawn on the basis of competing public policy considerations? In some industrialized countries the legislature has made exceptions to the patentability of biotechnology. Perhaps forty-five countries worldwide exclude animals to some extent from patent protection (Crespi, 1986).

An important example is the European Patent Convention, which excludes plant or animal varieties or essentially biological processes for the production of plants or animals, except for microbiological processes or the products thereof. This exception was installed some years ago, before biotechnology had demonstrated its full promise (Moufang, 1989). The members of the European Community are obliged to adopt this convention – the United Kingdom patents legislation, for instance, essentially reproduces these exceptions (Lahore, 1980). In 1989 the European Patent Office decided that the Harvard mouse was unpatentable under the terms of this exception (Vossius, 1990). The decision caused a furore and, on appeal, a way was eventually found to overcome the exception.

In contrast, the United States legislation is much more accommodating and it contains no such categorical exceptions. The Japanese legislation is said to be similarly liberal, at least in regard to local inventions (OECD, 1985). The United States policy is an important reference point for all countries, given that so many of the biotechnology innovations are originating there and that it is also the largest potential market for the export of other countries' innovations. We should note that, in other areas, the United States has been prepared to use the provisions of its trade legislation to impose sanctions on imports from countries that engage in unfair trading practices by not providing adequate and effective intellectual property protection to United States products (McGovern, 1986). Brazil was sanctioned, for example, for its failure to provide patent protection to pharmaceuticals (Raghavan, 1990). We shall discuss these provisions in more detail in chapter 4.

Pressures are developing in international forums for the European countries in particular to remove their exceptions and, more generally for other countries to accommodate developments in biotechnology. The OECD has been an initiator in this regard (Wald,

1985). Sensitive to these concerns, the European Commission has issued a draft directive calling for more patent protection for biotechnological inventions, including genetically engineered plants and animals (Whaite and Jones, 1989). One fear is that European companies will move to the United States to exploit innovations caught by the exception (Acharya, 1991).

## GATT

The pressure has intensified in recent times with the inclusion of intellectual property protection on the agenda of the GATT. The *Punta del Este* Ministerial Declaration gave the Uruguay round a mandate to elaborate new rules and disciplines to reduce the distortions and impediments to international trade, taking into account the need to promote effective and adequate protection of intellectual property rights and to ensure that measures and procedures to enforce intellectual property rights do not themselves become barriers to legitimate trade (Golt, 1989). The promotion of this agenda item, especially by the United States, represents a major concern about the lack of enforcement against infringements of rights under existing laws. The United States has estimated losses as high as $61 billion per year from trade in counterfeit and pirated goods. GATT's dispute resolution mechanisms would facilitate quick effective action against countries that allowed violations of agreed intellectual property provisions (McKeogh and Stewart, 1991).

Is the trade question to extend beyond this concern? Perhaps the key point to note about the GATT round is that it does concern the scope, level and uses of intellectual property protection around the world (Slaughter, 1990). The leading producer nations mean to use the GATT for a substantive enhancement of intellectual property standards (Raghavan, 1990). The issues raised include the length of the patent term, disclosure requirements, the subject matter of protection, the rights of patent holders and the permissible scope for compulsory licensing and royalty ceilings (Turnbull, 1989). Some countries (for example Brazil and India) argue that the question of the level of protection is best left to traditional forums, such as the WIPO, and the GATT proceedings have stalled with the two contrasting proposals. Thus, the GATT strategy may create some tension with the traditional intellectual property bodies (Beier and Schricker, 1989). This is not so much an issue in the case of copyright because the main convention (the Berne Convention) has incorporated a 'mature' standard of protection. But the patents convention (the Paris Convention) makes minimal provision in regard to the level of protection. It is notable too that, in relation to biotechnology, WIPO issued an expert opinion in 1988 providing that any harmonization of patent laws exclude animal varieties from protection in the same terms as the European Convention (McKeogh and Stewart, 1991).

It remains to be seen whether countries like the United States will threaten unilateral sanctions against the goods and businesses of countries which do not meet their level of protection, if they are not successful at GATT. Dharjee and De Chazournes (1990) make the point that the Paris Convention (in particular) has left member states free to choose the terms of protection they feel appropriate to the needs of their own political, economic and cultural systems. The now developed countries took advantage of this freedom to decline protection for some goods when they were largely importing economies (Ricketson, 1991). Neither have they always been entirely diligent in the prosecution of patent infringement procedures. The United States did not even become a signatory to the Berne Convention until 1989. Several West European countries did not provide patent protection for chemicals or pharmaceuticals until very recently.

## THE AUSTRALIAN POSITION

In Australia, the policy issue seemed likely to come to a head sooner rather than later as Adelaide University scientists proceeded with an application to patent a transgenic breeding line of pigs. The pigs were said to grow more quickly and yield leaner meat than normal pigs. The Commonwealth Scientific and Industrial Research Organisation (CSIRO) was reported to be interested in patenting a genetically engineered sheep (the *Age*, 15 April, 1988). In November 1988, the Minister for Industry, Technology and Commerce informed the Senate that there had already been about a dozen applications for genetically engineered animals (Commonwealth of Australia. Senate, 1988). The minister added that it would be at least eighteen months to two years before any decisions would be made. However, he advised that the Patents Office would not refuse a patent for a new and non-human animal variety, provided of course that its invention satisfied the usual requirements of the legislation. In the event, a patent was granted in 1990 in respect of transgenic non-human animals produced by a method of introducing genetic material into a living cell through loaded sperm.

The Patents Office would, however, refuse a patent application for a human being as contrary to law. This position was presumably based on a reading of the legislation at the time. The Statute of Monopolies, which was imported into the Australian legislation, contained a provision for competing public policy considerations to be taken into account in deciding whether to grant a patent (Ricketson, 1984c). According to the statute, the grant of a patent should not be contrary to the law nor mischievous to the state by raising the prices of commodities at home, or hurting trade, or generally creating inconvenience. (It is worth noting also that opinion has it in the United States that the patenting of a human being would be contrary to its constitution.)

In September 1990, following debate on the Patents Bill, the Australian Democrats introduced an amendment that sought to exclude from patenting, subject to review by an ethics committee, any genes or genomes or the organisms so altered and their progeny (Commonwealth of Australia. Senate, 1990). This broad exclusion was opposed by the government (and the opposition parties), in part because the provision would destroy the degree of certainty the government was trying to introduce into the area. Instead, the government accepted another amendment, from the independent Senator Harradine, which provided: human beings, and the biological processes for their generation, are not patentable inventions (now section 18[2] of the Act).

So did that enactment put an end to the issue in Australia? We must certainly wait to see how inclusive the notions of 'biological processes' and 'for the generation' of human beings turn out to be. Senator Harradine was not concerned that his exception would embrace normal processes connected with the generation of human beings (such as different positions in sexual intercourse: Commonwealth of Australia. Senate, 1990a), but would the exception take in biotechnological processes (see Vossius, 1990)? At the same time, no definition of a 'human being' was attempted in the legislation. Senator Coulter, from the Australian Democrats, remembered that the biotechnology under discussion includes the transfer of genes from humans to animals (the Harvard mouse received such a gene to simulate human breast cancer). Perhaps animal genes will prove useful to people. Such a limit will eventually raise many conceptual difficulties. Technological developments may also blur the distinction between biotechnological creations and the more established industrial art of robotics (Tribe, 1973). The convergence of innovations in computer technology and biotechnology is permitting mechanical components to be mixed with organic materials. Certainly we now have mechnical parts transplanted into the human body; futurists envisage the attachment of biological organisms to machines. Much of this is still in the realm of science fiction, but the technology will ensure that these definitional issues will one day materialize.

## THE DEPOSIT PROCEDURE

Another development further indicates the challenges of biotechnology to the patent system and the ways it has responded accommodatingly. To obtain the patent, the applicant must be prepared to disclose the invention in such a way that the invention is adequately described and characterized, and the skilled worker in the field is enabled to repeat or reproduce it. This requirement clearly rules out the patentability of a chance finding of an organism, but even if the applicant has been inventive, it can prove difficult to repeat the process and produce afresh an organism with exactly the same characteristics. In many cases, until the technology becomes more systematic, it is difficult for the reader, and indeed the applicant, to repeat the process which produced the exact organism. And the organisms are often of such complex and dynamic constitutions that a description requires massive amounts of data. Access to the original organism and to its cell culture proves the best means of enablement because the organism can be reproduced from the culture deposit. A number of countries have now moved to a deposit requirement for the patentability of micro-organisms (Teso and Wald, 1984). In 1977, an international treaty was adopted to promote this facility. In 1984, the Australian federal government amended the local legislation to make possible Australia's accession to the Budapest Treaty on the international recognition of the deposit of micro-organisms for the purposes of patent procedure (Whalan and Kaney, 1986). The amendment provided the circumstances in which deposits would be required and the circumstances in which it would be sufficient compliance with the description requirement (Ellinson, 1987).

In the interests of innovation, other researchers and producers in the field may wish to use a sample of the deposited micro-organism for developmental work. An issue here is whether the deposit should be released for the purposes of improving or modifying the strain or producing another strain by mutation. Carrying out this developmental work is likely to involve reproduction of the organism itself and thus an infringement of the patent rights, even though the end result of the endeavour proves to be sufficiently novel and inventive to be eligible for a patent itself. The courts in the United States have explored the idea of an 'experimental use' defence to patent infringements but not yet with a great deal of success (Eisenberg, 1989). To avoid infringement, the use must not deprive the patent holder of the commercial benefit of the invention – in biotechnology today, even basic research can be geared to the development of a product. The example serves to illustrate the dilemma where innovation feeds off the pool of research and prior art in the discipline.

## THE BREADTH OF THE INDIVIDUAL GRANT

The deposit procedure is also relevant to the determination of the validity and scope of the patent application. In an area of such complexity and volatility, it can be difficult to determine just what contribution the particular applicant has made to the art and to distinguish it from inventions that precede and succeed it. Such a question also arises in infringement disputes. It is suggested, for example, that because the pathways to micro-organisms are not always unique and the behaviour of the organisms not always easy to predict, honest differences can arise over the novelty of competing inventions (Clark, 1981). Yet organisms can also be altered by mutation in order to conceal likenesses and still enjoy basically equivalent properties and functions.

Grants of protection could conceivably be confined to the particular strain of organism which is deposited. Much depends upon whether the applicant is claiming general process and use patents as well as particular organisms and their cell cultures (Szabo, 1990). Claims to related strains or mutants and other variants may also be entertained. Generally speaking, as the field becomes more competitive and the advances more incremental, we might expect

## 94  *Intellectual property*

broad claims to be viewed more sceptically and the applicant required to distinguish the invention more finely from closely related ones. The breadth of individual grants might well become the main concern for competitors in the field. Is a patent to extend to all mammals with a genetically engineered susceptibility to cancer, for instance, or just to mice (Eisenberg, 1989)? Is a patent to encompass any plasminogen activator of human tissue or just the activator as it is produced by a particular route (Slattery, 1989)? The fragmentation of rights in the field might also lead to complicated cross-licensing arrangements.

Indeed, over time, applications of the art may lose the necessary qualities of novelty and inventiveness (Szabo, 1990). It is already being suggested that many of the potential products are appreciated in advance and that the methods for actually arriving at them are being standardized. Patent lawyers seem particularly struck by Genentech's failure to protect its tissue plasminogen activator against Wellcome's intrusions in the British courts, despite the fact that it had taken Genentech considerable effort and expense to identify and engineer the elements needed for the enzyme (Sherman, 1990). It is on that note we conclude our examination of recent patents policy.

## CONCLUSIONS

The patents study shows that the property form is still relevant to the course of innovation. If there are real qualifications to be placed on the general significance of patents to producers, biotechnology presents some important exceptions. The patents system displays resilience in the ways in which it has accommodated developments in biotechnology. A notable characteristic has been the way that governments have been content to leave the accommodation to administrations and the courts. This has been the position very much in Australia, apart from the actions of a few rogue senators. And, except in certain specialist circles, the patenting biotechnology has not become a politically controversial issue in the way that direct financial assistance to industry has so become.

It could be argued that it has been possible to assume this position because of the law's capacity to adjust. The law has not proved so rigid that the extensions of the property form into the realms of biotechnology, indeed into the domain of life itself, have been

## Patents and living organisms 95

obstructed. One exception has been the existence of provisions expressly to exclude higher life forms from the coverage of some schemes: the European Convention is the most significant instance. We should be interested to see whether these exclusions will withstand the category-subverting and economically appealing innovations of the new biotechnology, especially now that intellectual property is squarely on the world trade agenda. Making higher life forms patentable is not really the same kind of unexceptional incremental adjustment to the system as previous extensions, whatever the strength of claims for continuity, reciprocity and certainty in intellectual property policy.

At the same time, the system's own criteria for recognizing invention show a real concern with innovation. Patents are probably the property form most closely attuned to a policy concern with industrial innovation. In some respects, that concern leads it to compromise the absolutist guarantees of a property right. The substantive criteria and the screening process for the support of individual claims do not fully fit the picture of the broadly cast, self-invoking rules of a classic property regime. At least in theory, the system extracts conditions from the applicants for its support in order to meet the needs of other innovators. The condition of public disclosure is the most significant of these concessions. Yet, in many ways, the system reaffirms the liberal form. The state still feels compelled to maintain and improve the facilities of the property form. Its impact merely reflects the subtle ways in which property rights are expressed in the contemporary economy, how property is used strategically by producers to soften up potential competitors and to bargain for the combination of complementary assets. The system is largely indifferent to the distributional and moral implications of the use of property power.

Nonetheless, before we become too firm in our conclusions, we should note that invention is not the end of innovation, and we must still consider how other bodies of law respond to the uses of patent power, along with other kinds of power, in the capture of the benefits of new technology.

CHAPTER 4

# Copyright and Computer Software

This chapter examines legislative responses to claims to copyright computer software products. It first considers the extent of the legal controls sought over software innovation and its subsequent uses, noting the economic stakes in the policy ultimately adopted towards appropriation. It then looks at the formation of the Australian legislative response in 1984, and goes on to note the subsequent international developments which have become part of the context for any further national legal responses.

## A POLICY OF APPROPRIATION?

This section begins by recognizing the stresses which come with the move of copyright into the industrial world. It identifies the various interests with an economic stake in the outcome of the property question, then examines the kinds of controls which are sought over the technology. These are controls not only over direct or literal copying but also over derivative development work by potential competitors. Here the significance of the idea/expression distinction is explored and the issue of licensing raised. The section notes the alternation between expansive and restrictive views of copyright protection, especially in the decisions of the courts which interpret the legislative enactments.

Moving copyright into the industrial area of software has tested the limits of appropriability. Conventionally, copyright is said to provide protection only for the original form of expression of a literary or other artistic work, however the nature of software makes it difficult to distinguish its form of expression from the underlying ideas, concepts and techniques on which the work is constructed (Allen *et al.*, 1972). Whether the traditional distinction is workable is important to the future of innovation in the software production industry. In particular, it influences the balance which is to be struck between the security provided to software producers for their investment and freedom of action for competitors who wish to build on the state of the art in industry and make conversions or develop enhancements to the existing software (Gesmer, 1986). A related issue is the reach of a copyright holder's rights over the software or, to express it in another way, the nature of the acts by others which will infringe the copyright. Several situations are problematic. What, for instance of the person who translates a software work into another form or adapts it as another version? What also of a person who decompiles or 'reverse engineers' a work and then produces another piece of software? What even of the person who invents another program independently but replicates some of the routines or formats which have been used in the earlier work? As copyright offers control over the reproduction and adaptation of the earlier work, the question of scope becomes a question of the level of abstraction at which any similarity between two rival products will be permitted by the law.

## FROM ARTISTIC TO INDUSTRIAL WORKS

Assimilating industrial technologies under the rubric of copyright protection might be difficult for a number of reasons. Books, especially fiction, are often valued for their appeal to human audiences as creative forms or modes of literary expression, while computer software is only of utility for the mechanical process it involves, the functions it performs and the effects it produces when it drives computer hardware. It distorts the traditional copyright concept of an artistic work to extend protection to the electronic impulses of a program and to control its uses (Lockhardt, 1984). Resistance to the extension of copyright may thus reflect a concern about the corruption of a venerable legal institution which has traditionally been associated with cultural endeavour in its various fields. The internal coherence of the legal doctrine is undermined as it is stretched and supplemented to encompass subject matter that is not truly analogous with its traditional concerns. For lawyers concerned with the spiritually uplifting activities of artistic creation and communication, it can be debasing to suggest that machine functions and operations should be afforded the same status (Hersey, 1979).

## THE ECONOMIC STAKES

While such sensitivities cannot be discounted, the debate over software copyright has been swept up in considerations of economic value and the capture of the benefits of industrial innovation. In economic terms, there is much at stake. Through lobbying for legislative change and litigation of enacted provisions, the firms which organize and finance software production have sought to settle protection on the technology. Governments, if not always the courts, have responded. The resources devoted to the development of software programs, especially to systems software and software packages, can run into many hundreds of thousands of dollars and consume many years of labour. Producers do not want to see the returns on their investment threatened by the appearance of cheap copies free-riding on their products.

Apart from maximizing sales, software rights are also regarded as a source of strategic advantage and market power (Gaze, 1989). Though (as we shall see below) certain forces do work against such an effect, proprietary software (and especially the key systems software) can be deployed as a means of tying in other products, creating barriers to entry for competitors, and locking in established customers (OECD, 1985a). Copyright can also act as a means of controlling the distribution of software through the use of exclusive dealerships and limited licensing. When a few countries (notably the United States) produce the bulk of software, the uses of these property rights can have different national impacts. One concern is the impact on prices and availability of a ban on parallel importing – that is, importing through other than the exclusive local dealers. On this basis, the Australian Prices Surveillance Authority instituted an inquiry into the price of computer software (the *Age*, 12 May 1992).

## CONTROL OVER COPYING

Like patents, copyright protection is a form of security against unauthorized imitation and derivation, so that the producer can capture the benefits of the innovation, sometimes by using the software exclusively, often by requiring a fee to be paid for purchasing or licensing the technology. Piracy of software, where firms make direct or literal copies to sell on the blackmarket, is a major problem for producers (Brazil, 1987). While software can be expensive to originate, it can be extremely cheap and simple to duplicate. Producers may endeavour to have technical protections against copying built into the software, but these protections are often circumvented by the application of other technologies. The pirates may not be inhibited by the need to maintain good relations with the core producers, so economic sanctions may not be a feasible deterrent. Much of the pirating has been done in Asian and South American countries, sometimes for domestic purposes and less often for import into the originating economies. The United States was estimated to be losing around one billion dollars per year in revenue from this source (Styrcula, 1991). In Australia, the Department of Foreign Affairs and Trade surveyed the local industry and detected a concern with the impact of practices in the South-east Asian region on the export trade in relation to microcomputer software (Commonwealth of Australia. Attorney-General's Department, 1988). Of course, free copying provides local consumers with cheaper versions of the software. Still, the genuine producers argue that consumers suffer in the long term because underground suppliers do not provide the necessary backup of debugging and maintenance services. The erosion of the producers' returns also undermines investment in further product innovation (Palmer, 1986). Local distributors and service companies also lose when the producers' trade is undermined.

Another concern for producers is the multiple use of single copies that have been legitimately acquired (Anon, 1985). A particular concern here is the reproduction of software by large organizations, such as financial and educational institutions, to make copies for use by branches or to disseminate along local area networks to personal substations. The Business Software Association, an industry group organized to combat piracy, recently estimated that 50 per cent of the software run in Australia had not been purchased (the *Age*, 10 April 1990). The enforcement of copyright entitlements now runs to court-authorized raids on public sector educational institutions in order to seize illegal copies.

CONSTRAINTS ON COMPETITION

Yet the producers' concerns do not rest with the direct or literal copying perpetrated by marginal pirating and bootlegging operations.

Producers are concerned that legitimate competitors do not develop and market a similar version of their product before they reap the benefits. With the advantage of their experience, competitors may be able to market a version that sells at a cheaper price, runs on rival technology, or offers enhanced performance. At stake here is the extent to which any one producer can capture and control advancements in the state of the art (Gesmer, 1986).

Again, producers may turn to extra-legal strategies as a means to exclude or inhibit potential competitors. With certain kinds of software, product replacement is extremely rapid, with producers relying on the advantage of being first into the market to gather their returns. Product differentiation and lack of standardization also discourage competition. Production of large-scale software packages and integrated systems may benefit from economies of scale and scope (OECD, 1985a). As the technology is complex, technical barriers may be placed in the way of those commercial rivals who wish to unlock its secrets. A notable practice has been the release of programs in object code only. Decompilation and reverse engineering are then needed to reconstruct the source code and reveal the concepts, logic and sequence of the program. Even a source code, without access to the diagrams, working notes and other explanations of the authors' methods, may not be altogether revealing. Producers also seek to control the uses of their software products by alternative legal means. Most prevalent here has been the pursuit of licensing conditions in contractual relations with customers. Users may be placed under obligations not to disclose trade secrets and confidential information associated with the software (Davis, 1985). Indeed, such contracts may seek to restrain the users' discovery of the technology by reverse engineering or modification for enhanced performance. Licences may also be employed to place restrictions on the number of copies a consumer can make (Pearson, 1984).

However, the efficacy of contractual obligations and sanctions diminishes as the number of consumers grows. These controls work best in the provision of applications programs which are tailor-made or customized for particular users' industrial needs. A sizeable proportion of operating systems and applications packages are aimed at the mass market. An endeavour may be made to engineer technical protections into the programs, but these devices seem only to provide a challenge to freelance operators and the producers may also meet with customer resistance if they make their software too inaccessible.

The source code needs to be released at least to the large-scale users and major distributors if maintenance work is to be effective. While the speed of innovation is somewhat of a barrier to entry by competitors, the time lag before programs can be reverse engineered is said to be dropping. And some of the successful software displays a long product life. In addition, industrial espionage is not unknown in the industry. Less dramatically, several of the copyright cases which have been litigated indicate the contested use of innovation by defendants who worked on the inside with the copyright claimant as employees or partners before a falling out.

So how far should copyright protection extend against 'exiting' employees, rival firms and potential competitors? From the very start of the debate, the prospect of settling copyright on the industrial technology of computer software has attracted critics. An abiding concern is whether the traditional distinction in copyright – between the ideas of a work and its form of expression – can be maintained. In the case of literary and other artistic works, it is often evident that the originality of the work lies in the particular expression which the author can give to it. This form is the true object of protection. And the aim of the author is to publish the work and reveal its contents for all to see, provided they are willing to pay a charge to meet the costs of the production of the work. The intention, with most books anyway, is to make the contents as accessible as possible. The purpose remains to disseminate the work. Indeed, as is often noted, developments in technology often provide a cheap and ready means to circumvent any control the copyright holders might wish to exercise over the diffusion of the work (Ricketson, 1991).

## THE IDEA-EXPRESSION DISTINCTION

In the case of software, these conditions cannot be assumed. For several reasons, the viability of the idea–expression distinction is a vital test of the suitability of copyright. We should use the experience with this distinction as a means to assess the extent to which legislation and case law have been attuned to innovation policy. Critics have argued that copyright is ill-suited to cope with the nature of software production: it runs the risk of providing too much protection (Breyer, 1970). On the one hand, it is observed that software programs are in many ways founded squarely on the prior art, which itself represents the incremental development of the technology throughout the industry. In particular, complex and substantial pieces of software often involve collections of subroutines and utility modules which have been developed in the past and become the stock in trade of the industry (Emerson, 1984). It would seem wasteful and inconvenient for subsequent programmers to be required to start from scratch and differentiate each component every time they sought to devise another program (Soltysinski, 1990). Access to subroutines, modules and other building blocks has facilitated the industrialization of programming, thus exploiting economies of scale and divisions of labour. Skill, time and labour still go into the deployment of these building blocks, but this effort is not the same as originality, and certainly not the same as the novelty and inventiveness required for the traditional category of protection for industrial techniques, the patent. Blanket protection might capture the unoriginal as well as the original elements of a program.

Rather, it is often argued that it is not so much the expression of the program which involves ingenuity and creativity as the perception and formulation of the problem to be solved and the function to be realized, followed by the selection and relation of components designed to achieve this aim (Kindermann, 1988). The real objects of protection are the non-expressive elements of the program: its logic, structure, architecture, layout and sequence of operations, and the functions and results which it effects. To what extent should these features be captured? Protection of the form may have the effect of locking up the ideas behind a program if, for functional reasons, there is only a limited number of ways of expressing those ideas (Waters and Leonard, 1991). To what extent ought efficiency and interoperability be impaired by insisting upon an artificial difference (Farrell, 1989)? For example, operating systems need common interfaces with recipient hardware and applications software if they are to be effective (Gaze, 1989). At the same time, programs can often be readily translated or adapted into another form, say from one code to another or one language to another. And while it is possible independently to create a program which resembles an existing program, it is also possible to alter an existing program so that it looks different but performs the same function. Protection would seem empty if such variations were enough to avoid infringement. So, at what level of abstraction will substantial similarity tell against the defendant? Should the form of expression be allowed to control ideas? On the other hand, should any recognizable derivation be enough to constitute infringement? Or should the law get away from the notion of similarity and apply more purposeful criteria, such as the level of inventiveness of the two programs, the reasons for any similarity, and the economic consequences for the competing producers (Karjala, 1987; Waters and Leonard, 1991)?

Such issues are addressed much more directly in patent law, where the successful applicant gains the power to prevent any unauthorized use of the technique itself, even if it has been arrived at independently or discovered by reverse engineering rather than simply mimicked. One American commentator (Styrcula, 1991) advances the proposition that the EC was at pains to promote copyright over patents as the appropriate form of protection for software because copyright would not protect the ideas of United States exporters. It is true that, where it applies, patent law ties up techniques more securely. Nevertheless, at the same time, the specialist patents offices make a purposeful inquiry into the novelty and inventiveness of a technique. Copyright does not demand satisfaction of the same process. The originality of a work is only tested in infringement proceedings through the ordinary courts. The courts would concede that they are only now only coming to grips with the nature of software production. In any case, the element of originality within copyright law has only been a minimal requirement (Gaze, 1989).

## LICENSING

In addition, it is to be remembered that the term of patent protection is limited to sixteen to twenty years, while copyright has traditionally extended to the life of the author plus another fifty years. Also, as we saw in chapter 3, a necessary condition of the patent grant is that the technique be placed on the record for public examination. We have suggested that this requirement would not be an issue in the case of artistic works, but that the different purposes of software brings it alive. Especially where the value of the software lies in an industrial application rather than in mass consumption, copyright may be combined with confidentiality to keep the technique exclusive (Hersey, 1979). Provision is made in patents law for compulsory licensing powers to be invoked if the patent holder tries to suppress the technique. Because copyright has not had the same industrial role, the same dangers have not been identified, and it is only now becoming a matter for scrutiny in competition policy (see chapter 6).

The one large exception to this innocent view of the world has been the response to the widespread unauthorized copying by consumers of books and recordings. Out of necessity, statutory licensing has been introduced, at least for the purpose of copying for personal use under defined circumstances. The producers have formed collective administration societies to negotiate and collect the fees chargeable for such licensing (O'Donnell, 1983). In some jurisdictions, government tribunals have been established to set fees and to examine the conditions where private agreement cannot be reached (Marks, 1987; Porter, 1989). The state has even lent its revenue collecting machinery to the cause of producers, for example by placing a levy on blank tapes for redistribution to copyright holders (Court, 1986). But this model has not been adopted for computer software.

Instead, a more conventional means has been explored to deal with the problems of enforcing copyright. The state has exhibited a willingness to weigh in with criminal sanctions. For example, the Australian government has made a series of legal and administrative reforms to strengthen the procedures for detecting, prosecuting and remedying copyright-infringing imports (Brazil, 1987). While the assertion of copyright is still in many respects a civil matter for the private litigant to pursue, it should be noted that the courts have been willing to make orders (called Anton Piller orders) which empower plaintiffs to seize transgressing copies if this course of action can assist in bringing the infringers to justice (Gaze, 1985).

## JUDICIAL POLICY

As software production increased, copyright began to be litigated in the courts, the first wave of cases concerning the applicability of the general provisions of copyright legislation and the second the strength of the specific enactments for software. One line of cases has explored the capacity of the legislation to describe and embrace the various manifestations of this rapidly developing technology, and in particular the different codes in which the programs are expressed – such as source code, object code, ROM and micro code

Copyright and computer software

(Stern, 1986). The major cases in the Australian jurisdiction, Apple Computer Inc. and another v. Computer Edge Pty Ltd and another (Gaze, 1989) and Autodesk Inc. v. Dyason (McKenna, 1991), play on this theme.

Another line of cases has tested the idea–expression distinction. Major software producers, such as Apple, have been ready to litigate around the world, not just to deter out-and-out software pirates but also to unsettle those competitors building on existing programs, for example to make versions compatible with other systems and to producer cheaper and perhaps functionally superior clones. A strand of these cases is the so called 'look and feel cases', where the defendants have produced programs that are similar in aspects of their audiovisual displays or screen formats – the important interfaces between computers and their users.

In the early decisions, commentators detected a tendency for the courts to take an expansive approach to the delineation of protectable expression (Gesmer, 1986). Even though the programs in question might have been rewritten by the defendant, similarities in their organizational structure and pattern, sequential flow of information and instructions, and processing methods were enough to indicate a breach of copyright (Karjala, 1987). Interestingly, Gaze (1989) suggests that judges in these cases were also influenced by the propriety of the defendants' behaviour, the defendants being employees or joint venturers who had broken away from the plaintiff and gone into competition. In more recent cases, greater reserve has been demonstrated. Mindful of the impact on competitors, the courts have asked whether the form of expression which the plaintiff seeks to protect is the only way of expressing the underlying ideas and purposes of the program (Pearson, 1987). In this event, the idea and the expression might be said to have merged (Polfanders, 1989). On the other hand, anything which is not necessary to the realization of the function of the program, but is merely a variation on the kinds of expressions available, should remain protectable. While this approach represents a check upon the expansion of copyright, Gaze (1989) argues that it still leaves the courts with some discretion as to how they characterize functions and options. She wonders if the courts are the most suitable forum for the reception and assessment of evidence on these questions. Certainly, the case law does not seem to be achieving the certainty of principle which is the hallmark of a secure property regime.

## THE AUSTRALIAN LEGISLATION

This section begins by noting the judicial decision which denied protection to software and moved the Australian government to promise legislation. It then analyses the nature of the debate over the options for legislation and in particular the interest group representations which the government received at a symposium in 1984. It describes the scope of the legislation subsequently enacted in 1984.

### THE APPLE CASE

In 1984 the Australian government enacted legislation specifically to settle copyright on computer software. The legislative changes were spurred by a Federal Court decision against Apple Computer Inc. which declared that the general provisions of the *Copyright Act 1968* (Commonwealth) did not extend to computer software. Apple had claimed infringement of its copyright by Computer Edge Pty Ltd. Computer Edge distributed Wombat computers in Australia. Imported from Taiwan, they embodied silicon chips derived from the circuitry of Apple 2 computers, probably as a result of reproducing the object code found in the Apple computers and burning this code into the Wombat chips (Taggart, 1987). Mr Justice Beaumont held that copyright did not subsist in Apple's object code as a literary work. While copyright subsisted in Apple's source code, the Wombat programs did not infringe that copyright as a reproduction or adaptation. (This decision was subsequently overturned by the Full Bench of the Federal Court, but, ultimately, a majority of the judges sitting in the High Court came to a similiar conclusion (see Computer Edge Pty. Ltd. and another v. Apple Computer, Inc. and another [1986] 65 Australian Law Reports 33).

Mr Justice Beaumont handed down the initial decision in favour of the Computer Edge Company on the 7th December 1983. On 21 December 1983, the Commonwealth Attorney-General, the Minister for Industry and Commerce, and the Minister for Science and Technology made a joint public announcement that the government intended promptly to undertake such legislative action as was necessary to ensure software was adequately protected (Commonwealth of Australia. Attorney-General's Department, 1984). They also stated that if necessary there would be some backdating of the remedial legislation. Consultations were initiated immediately with industry and user interests, and a national symposium was foreshadowed as a step towards developing a policy for the protection of software. The legislation was ultimately introduced into the commonwealth parliament in June 1984. In the interim, many public and private representations were received by the government. The enactment which eventuated was to be squarely in favour of comprehensive copyright protection.

Court (1986) remarks in another context that Australian debates over legal policy towards the new technologies take place in a pro-copyright culture. In her view,

> most of the expert writing on copyright in Australia is written by copyright specialists for other copyright specialists, legal practitioners and law students. It rarely, if at all, questions or criticises the copyright system, nor is that system considered from the perspective of the user or consumer. Indeed most of the expert writing in the subject is in defense of copyright, making a critical discussion difficult. (Court, 1986: 22)

This assessment is perhaps too strict. Certainly, some of the debate centres on copyright because it is a legal concept with a long tradition; some commentators, too, may be inclined towards copyright because they are comfortable with a legal policy that takes the form of individual rights. Nonetheless, the legal interests which are drawn to the concept of copyright, and which incidentally sometimes derive material comfort from the maintenance of the institution, do not totally explain the course of the debate over software copyright in 1984. Various supplier and user interests were active and vocal in the political process which led up to the legislative changes. Some sort of social accounting of the impact, across interests and society generally, of the choice of legal policy may be said to have taken place in the development of the legislation.

## THE COPYRIGHT SYMPOSIUM

The flavour of the representations can perhaps be obtained from the proceedings of the symposium which was held in Canberra in March 1984 (Commonwealth of Australia. Attorney-General's Department, 1984). We should examine those proceedings now, not in the expectation that they provide any definitive statement of the policy issues involved in the software question, but rather to identify the preoccupations at the time. According to the Attorney-General's

Department, the symposium was open to all interested persons. Around 120 attended, and they were drawn largely from government departments, computer firms, university law and science faculties, government scientific instrumentalities, computer interest groups, computer interest associations, intellectual property law firms, educational institutions, intellectual property groups, publishing houses and newspapers, together with some minority representation from consumer and welfare organizations.

The symposium took the form of an opening statement by the Attorney-General, followed by industry and user statements, then a session on policy suggestions presented by three lawyers from large legal firms, and finally a forum discussion involving a five-person panel, consisting of an academic economist who was previously a software developer, a partner in a large legal firm who was both a member of the government's Industrial Property Advisory Committee and its Copyright Law Review Committee, an engineer and director of Computer Power Group Holdings, a lecturer in computer science from the Royal Melbourne Institute of Technology who was also chairman of the Australian Computer Society's Software Industry Committee, and a spokesperson from Software Liberation.

## The Attorney-General's Statement

The Attorney-General, Senator Gareth Evans, made it clear in his opening statement to the symposium that the onus lay heavily on those who opposed legislative protection for software (Commonwealth of Australia. Attorney-General's Department, 1984). He suggested that the availability of software was critical to the efficiency and competitiveness of Australian industry, and that it was important to foster a strong local capability for systems development. Nonetheless, he recognized that a large share of computer software was imported. It might be that some overseas companies would be hesitant to market their most up-to-date packages in Australia if protection was in doubt. Software was a potential export growth industry and, if Australia was out of accord with the international consensus, it might find that its software products were inadequately protected in other countries. Nevertheless, the precise form of protection was open to consideration. Australia had an opportunity to seek to influence international discussions towards solutions which did not favour large industrialized countries at the expense

# Copyright and computer software

of smaller nations such as itself. Protection for other works had been balanced with mechanisms to ensure that the materials were available to certain classes of users, and he did not rule out the question of appropriate exceptions, for example in the fields of education and research. But, overall, the relative economic importance of the competing claims would probably depend on the particular nature of the protected material and the technology available to exploit it.

## Interest Group Representations

A number of industry associations presented summaries of their submissions. The Australian Equipment Suppliers Association (AESA), which represented the biggest economic interest in the local industry, was strongly of the view that copyright protection was appropriate. It cited technology transfer, local employment and the payment of taxes as some of the benefits of its activities in introducing foreign software to Australia. It opposed compulsory licensing provisions, which it considered would be a disincentive to development. It felt that the delay in the legislative action was intolerable. The AESA was backed by the Australian Software Houses Association, which said that copyright was apt in a property-owning democracy; by the Australian Computer Services Association, which considered the copyright was just and fair; and by the Australian Computer Retailers Association, which asserted that the opponents of property were seeking to destroy the fabric of our society.

The Australian Computer Users Association was concerned that in the absence of protection its members would be cut off from access to the latest products. The Australian Computer Equipment Manufacturers Association favoured short-term copyright cover but supported long-term *sui generis* protection if reciprocity were provided by other countries. The Australian Computer Society expressed some reservations about the implications of ownership of information in databases, heuristic programs, and expert decision-making systems. The Australian Copyright Council backed copyright protection for software and opposed a registration system, but was surprised at the government's speed and diligence in responding to the needs of industry.

The Australian Vice-Chancellors' Committee suggested special legislation was necessary and expressed its concern about exclusive rights where normal usage involved making copies of a program, where the common heritage or stock in trade might be tied up, and where the underlying ideas might be concealed in codes and not become available to users. The Australian Advisory Council of Bibliographical Services was concerned about copyright power to limit the use of software legally acquired, for example in transferring programs between libraries or downloading at workstations. It was also concerned about control over computerized databases. It submitted that fair dealing provisions were essential. The Australian Education Council accepted protection but was concerned whether programs would be made available to educational institutions and whether the conditions of access might be onerous – if, for example, limitations were placed on the permissible uses of the software. The Australian Federation of Consumer Organisations favoured protection against unauthorized commercial copying but was against limitation of copying for domestic or educational purposes. It suggested that such customers were lost to higher prices; on the other hand the availability of cheap programs was a stimulus to the hardware market.

It was left to Software Liberation and a radical computer scientist, best known for student activism in the sixties, to put the case against intellectual property. Albert Langer argued that legal protection would not be effective. It would be more effective to raise a levy, employing the hardware as a meter on use, and devoting the funds so raised to remunerate suppliers and sponsor local production. In Langer's view, software production was to be likened to infrastructural scientific research or public broadcasting rather than discrete product items for sale on the market. Local producers largely developed tailored software that could be protected by the law of confidential information – copyright protection would most benefit the importers and distributors of applications software packages, and royalties would flow largely to the United States. If necessary, a block payment could be made to these United States producers through their government (see further Gaze, 1989).

## THE 1984 LEGISLATION

In the event, the amendments to the Copyright Act extended its protection to computer software without any qualifications based on local suggestions or provisions in other countries. No distinction was made between indigenous and foreign software. The conventional term of protection was not limited. No registration or disclosure conditions were instituted. No special exceptions were made to copyright holders' rights, save to authorize acquirers to make one back-up copy of legally obtained software, though it was noted that the existing fair dealing provisions of the legislation would apply to software, as would allowances for photocopying for educational purposes where the programs were in a printed form. No provision was made for the compulsory licensing of other publishers, developers or users.

In the second reading speech to the Amendment Bill in the House of Representatives, the Minister for Science and Technology, Mr Barry Jones, gave several reasons why protection was essential (Commonwealth of Australia. House of Representatives, 1984a). The purpose of the Bill was to reduce uncertainty and enable the continued development of the software industry against a background of copyright protection. He stated (Commonwealth of Australia. House of Representatives, 1984a: 3144):

> The efficiency and competitiveness of Australian industry and commerce are in part dependent upon the availability of appropriate computer systems. Australia can best ensure this by fostering a strong capability for systems development. This capability needs to be able effectively to integrate locally developed, as well as imported, hardware and software to provide systems best suited to our requirements and which have the potential to be marketed overseas.

Later in the speech he added:

> Copyright protection will stimulate innovation and further growth of Australia's software industry and, to the extent that international copyright conventions apply, ensure protection for exported software. Protection also has important consequences for users. There are risks of a withdrawal or limitation on the availability of imported software in the absence of copyright protection. Such a limitation would seriously jeopardise the viability of most local computer manufacturers since many obtain their systems' software under licence from overseas suppliers.

## THE COVERAGE OF THE LEGISLATION

The commonwealth government's 1984 amendments extended the definition of a literary work to make it clear that computer programs and compilations of computer programs were to be protected as literary works. (They also extended the definition to ensure that computerized data bases could be treated as literary works, but this question will not be pursued here). A literary work was redefined to include: (a) a table or compilation, expressed in words, figures or symbols (whether or not in a visible form); or (b) a computer program or a compilation of computer programs. A computer program was defined to mean an expression, in any language, code, or notation, of a set of instructions (whether with or without related information) intended, either directly, or after either or both of (a) conversion to another language, code or notation, or (b) reproduction in a different material form, to cause a device having digital information process capabilities to perform a particular function. The explanatory memorandum accompanying the *Copyright (Computer Software) Amendment Bill* stated that the reference to an expression in the definition was intended to make clear that it was not the abstract idea, algorithm, or mathematical principle which was to be protected but rather the particular expression of that abstraction (Commonwealth of Australia. Senate, 1984). Subsequent provisions in the Bill may, however, have undermined this distinction. Commentators subsequently suggested that the amendments were broad enough to amount to protection for the ideas and logical structures which underlie programs (Stern, 1986).

The explanatory memorandum went on to say that reference to the phrase 'in any language, code or notation' was intended to ensure that copyright subsisted not only in high-level (generally human intelligible) but also low-level (generally only machine intelligible) and intermediate-level means of expression. Thus it would cover a computer language such as FORTRAN, assembly language, and compiled or assembled machine or object code. In addition, the words 'either directly . . . material form' were intended to make it clear that a program need not necessarily be capable of execution in its existing form but may need first to be translated into another language or converted into a suitable machine-readable form. The material form was defined in the amendments to include, in relation to work or an adaption of the work, such methods of fixation as storage or reproduction on magnetic tape, read-only or random-access computer memory, magnetic or laser disks, bubble memories and other forms of storage which will doubtless be developed.

Conventionally, the exclusive rights of the copyright holder include the right not only to reproduce the work but also to adapt it. The definition of adaptation in relation to computer programs was to be a version of the work (whether or not in the language, code or notation in which the work was originally expressed) not being a reproduction of the work. This definition of adaptation was intended to cover translation. Again, according to the explanatory memorandum, the new definition was intended to cover translation moving either way between the various so-called high-level program languages in which the programs may be written by humans, and languages, codes and notations which are actually computer operations, often called object codes. The memorandum stated:

> It is also possible for a program to be converted from object code into source code, or between different languages of similar level. In some circumstances this process will result largely in a substantial reproduction of the original program. In other cases, however, such as compilation followed by decompilation, the differences may be so substantial that one cannot speak of the reproduction although the final product is clearly derived from the original. The new definition of adaptation is intended to cover such situations. (Commonwealth of Australia. Senate, 1984: 6)

The amendments made it clear, then, that a reproduction of such an adaptation of the program would be an infringing copy where the making of the reproduction would infringe copyright in the original work.

## THE PERMANENCY OF THE LEGISLATION

In introducing the amendments, the Minister made it clear, however, that they represented only a short-term measure to enable a comprehensive review of the long-term policy to be conducted (Commonwealth of Australia. House of Representatives, 1984a). He suggested that the long-term policy should take account of a number of matters, including international developments, the concerns of educators and researchers, and the appropriateness of fully fledged copyright for industrial works. He noted a number of measures which might be considered to meet the possibility of the abuse of monopolies. They included compulsory licensing, the use of trade practices legislation, and a short term of protection. Public funding would also properly be an issue for long-term policy consideration. The Minister did not consider that copyright protection was incompatible with public funding, nonetheless he doubted that government officials would better anticipate the needs of users than the users themselves or entrepreneurs at large.

The Minister concluded by stating that the government was considering in what way the policy could best be reviewed and looking forward to the active co-operation of all interests. Nonetheless, the issue was not referred at that time to the government's Copyright Law Review Committee or to any other review body outside the Attorney-General's Department. The ensuing annual reports of the Attorney-General's Department were to indicate, however, that the legislation was being monitored. Notably, in a speech to the Copyright Society of Australia on 3 March 1987, the new Attorney-General, Lionel Bowen, stated

> Copyright is perhaps not a perfect solution. It is difficult to see why protection should last for the life of the software writer plus fifty years, for example. Software is, after all an industrial product and novel inventions are only protected for sixteen years under the Patents Act. On the other hand, at the moment the amendments seem to be working reasonably well, and to be generally acceptable to both software producers and users. We will continue to monitor the situation, including developments overseas. But I think the 1984 Amendment Act has to be viewed as the first example of this Government's commitment to providing adequate and effective protection for appropriate products of intellectual endeavour. (Bowen, 1987: 2)

On 19 October 1988, the Attorney-General charged the Copyright Law Review Committee to report on whether the Copyright Act adequately and appropriately protects computer programs in human and machine-readable forms, works created by or with the assistance of computer programs, and works stored in computer memory. The committee invited submissions and circulated an issues paper before informal meetings with major interest groups. The issues paper was cautiously non-committal, though the terms of reference of the committee and the flavour of the paper's discussion did not suggest that any radical changes in policy were anticipated (Commonwealth of Australia. Copyright Law Review Committee, 1990). The paper recognized there might be gaps which needed remedying in the Act's coverage of protected software technology. At the same time, it identified some concerns with the impact of protection. It noted the particular problems associated with the restrictions placed on the personal uses to which a legitimate purchaser might put a program, including the act of copying programs in the course of ordinary use and adaptation of a program to facilitate and improve its use. More significantly, perhaps, the paper mentioned the idea–expression problem and the possibility of merger. It also considered authorization for reverse engineering undertaken to promote compatibility between programs and referred to the provision in the recent Australian semiconductor chip legislation (the *Circuit Layouts Act 1989*) to permit reverse engineering for the purpose of developing futher new chip layouts (see also McKeogh, 1986). However, overall, the paper was still most respectful of the need to protect the first producer's investment in the formulation of his or her program.

## INTERNATIONAL DEVELOPMENTS

This section notes the continuing absence of a multilateral accord on copyright protection. It reports, however, on the emergence of bilateral initiatives, especially by the United States, to ensure that countries around the world adopt the fully fledged copyright model.

As it transpired, Australia was to be a pioneer in software copyright legislation. According to F.J. Smith, former Commissioner of Patents and one of the experts to make a presentation to the Copyright Symposium (Commonwealth of Australia. Attorney-General's Department, 1984), only the United States, the Federal Republic of Germany and probably the United Kingdom then had clear judicial guidance that computer software was protected under copyright laws. According to Smith, only about ten of the 120 odd members of the three major intellectual property conventions had indicated any firm position on computer software protection. A number of Third World countries were opposed to protection. The United States had by this time enacted legislation giving explicit protection to software. And other countries soon followed suit, notably such Western European countries as the United Kingdom, France and West Germany in 1985, and Japan in 1986. The spread of copyright was not however to be a multilateral process, the intellectual property conventions remained mute on the subject. Rather, the application of copyright has been the result of unilateral action or bilateral engagement. In this respect, the United States has been an active lobby.

### MULTILATERAL FORUMS

Smith was of the opinion that, 'it cannot be said with any degree of confidence that international protection for computer software is authorized under either the Berne Convention or the UCC' (Commonwealth of Australia. Attorney-General's Department, 1984: 179). (The UCC is the UNESCO Universal Copyright Convention.) Certainly, none of these conventions made explicit acknowledgement of computer software technology. Furthermore, the 1978 WIPO model provisions were not adopted. Again, in 1983, it was considered premature to take a stand on the best form of protection. Meetings in 1985 were also to prove inconclusive. Recently, WIPO was reported to be considering a protocol on software for addition to the Berne Convention (Styrcula, 1991). Perhaps WIPO will one day be able to seize the initiative, but to date it reflects its many members' differences on this important issue.

The general intellectual property conventions are not, however, without impact. It appears that if a signatory country chooses to place software protection within the ambit of such a convention, in particular by assimilating software to the Berne Convention's concept of literary works, then its domestic law may be required to meet the standards of this convention (Soltysinski, 1990; Ricketson, 1991). Some options, such as a deposit requirement or compulsory licensing powers, might then be off limits (Brazil, 1987). The signatory country engages the convention's principles of national treatment and independent protection. This means that it must afford the same protection to the works of foreign nationals as it does to locals, even if that level of protection is not available in the foreigner's home country. Nonetheless, with no explicit mention of software being made by the intellectual property conventions, it seems that a member country remains free to choose not to institute any protection at all. Protection may instead be obtained on a bilateral basis through the working of the principle of reciprocity or comity between nations. This avenue was to become the United States' main strategy. It is worth noting that up until a couple of years ago the United States was not a signatory to the Berne Convention.

In the eighties, as the United States seem to be slipping in the high technology stakes, domestic concern grew about the losses which local producers were suffering as a result of counterfeiting and other unfair trade practices in export markets (Dohlman, 1988). Official commissions were assigned the task of estimating the size of the problem and industry lobbies formed to seek action (Turnbull, 1989). Government and industry forces combined to place pressure on other countries to enact and enforce adequate intellectual property protection for United States products. As we noted in chapter 3, this campaign spilt over into the meetings of GATT, where intellectual property protection has been raised as a trade-related issue. Software copyright protection was to be one of the United States trade related intellectual property (TRIPs) agenda items. But the GATT offensive was to meet with obstacles, in part because the intellectual property proposals were tied to progress on other fronts, such as agricultural subsidies and trade in services. In part also, however, the proposals encountered the sentiment that WIPO was the proper forum for consideration of intellectual property standards, a sentiment, incidentally, which Australia was said to share (Commonwealth of Australia. Attorney-General's Department, 1988). Australia declared its trade interests in intellectual property rights in a 1990 publication by the Department of Foreign Affairs and Trade (Commonwealth of Australia, 1990).

BILATERAL INITIATIVES

Yet it remains the case that the United States has much at stake in the software market. It is estimated that the United States itself comprises around 50 per cent of the world market for software; its own products have been said to account for 70 per cent of total sales (Styrcula, 1991). With copyright chosen as the appropriate form of protection at home, the United States is encouraging other countries to reciprocate (Nimmer, 1991). Its campaign has involved the institution of the 'special 301' provision (Stuckey-Clarke, 1990). The special 301 provision requires action by the United States Trade Representative if a foreign trading practice denies rights under international trade agreements or is unjustifiable and burdens or restricts United States trade. Action may be taken if the practices are unreasonable or discriminatory and burden or restrict United States commerce. Practices are to be regarded as unjustifiable if they are in violation of the international legal rights of United States persons, including the denial of national or most favoured nation treatment or the right of establishment or intellectual property rights. Practices are to be regarded as unreasonable if they deny fair and equitable opportunities for the establishment of an enterprise, the provision of adequate and effective protection of intellectual property rights or market access opportunities, or if they involve export targeting or unfair labour practices.

At the same time, the existing section 337 provision was strengthened. Section 337 empowers action against unfair methods of competition and unfair acts in the importation of articles which threaten to destroy or substantially injure an industry or to prevent the establishment of an industry (Adams, 1990). Unfair acts include the importation of articles which infringe United States patents, copyright, trademarks or 'mask works' protection. Action may include exclusion orders and 'cease and desist' orders. Ironically, section 337 was to run into trouble with a GATT panel because it provided remedies to domestic producers that were not available to foreign producers (Brand, 1990).

Under 301, the United States Trade Representative may suspend the benefits of trade agreements, impose duties or other import restrictions, negotiate agreements with foreign countries, eliminate the burdens or provide United States persons with compensatory trade benefits. Sanctions under these provisions have been threatened against a series of countries that were placed on a 'priority watch list' by the United States Government. The threat is said to have been influential in obtaining the enactment of copyright laws in such countries as Brazil, Singapore, Taiwan and South Korea (Jehoram, 1989). Now, of course, many more countries have enacted protection (see Commonwealth of Australia. Copyright Law Review Committee, 1990). The Eastern European countries may be the next object of attention.

The United States was also influential in persuading Japan to adopt a copyright regime. As McNab pointed out at the Australian Copyright Symposium, Japan's MITI had proposed a limited *sui generis* form of protection (Attorney-General's Department, 1984). The United States threatened retaliatory action against Japanese imports if this proposal were adopted. United States producers were said to be concerned in particular about the prospect that the proposed registration procedure would reveal their vital source codes to potential Japanese competitors. Japan subsequently adopted a conventional copyright model (Karjala, 1988). Again, United States interests lobbied during the formulation of the EC directive on the legal protection of computer programs. The United States is said to supply 65 to 85 per cent of Europe's systems software and 55 per cent of its applications software (Styrcula, 1991). The EC's green paper argued the need to ensure effective uniform protection for software in order to promote the development of an increasingly important technical resource. The first draft directive extended protection but at the same time, mindful of the dangers of abuse of the property power and receptive to a local industry lobby, it sought to except interfaces from coverage and to allow reverse engineering. The second draft directive made no such exception, however, and the allowance for reverse engineering was limited (subject to several stringent conditions) to the purpose of creating and operating interoperative programs, so confining it to the standardization consideration (Waters and Leonard, 1991).

This movement away from the traditional multilateral intellectual property forums highlights the strategic use of intellectual property arguments. It is worth noting that the United States was also active in seeking bilateral reciprocal protection for semiconductor chip designs. Agreement in particular was reached with Japan. Australia has also come to the party (Gaze, 1989). This protection, however, was to be *sui generis* and most notably it was to allow for reverse engineering and the use of results of this process if it led to another original work. Japan was, of course, by this time much more of a leader in the semiconductor chip field than the United States.

## CONCLUSIONS

Software has helped to push the intellectual property form of copyright into the realm of industrial processes and products. Protection is thus extended to technologies that diverge markedly (in their sources of production, conditions of supply and circumstances of use) from the traditional subjects of copyright such as literary and other artistic works. Reservations have been expressed about the policy of settling this kind of protection on such a novel subject matter. In software production, ideas are not readily separated from their form of expression. And publication of the work cannot necessarily be expected. While one source of disquiet has been the impact of this policy upon the institution of copyright, concerns have also been expressed about the effect on the progression and diffusion of software and related computer technology innovation.

Given its traditional cultural preoccupations, the general copyright regime could not be expected to be attuned purposively to the conditions of software production. Of course the software work has had to meet the general criteria which apply to all candidates for copyright. But the legislators have not accepted the contention that computer software is so qualitatively different from the literary works with which it is being assimilated by copyright protection that it requires specially tailored provisions to secure the proper balance between the interests of producers and the opportunities available to subsequent developers and users. In particular, they have rejected the suggestion that some sort of scheme akin to the patent scheme, the finely tuned form of intellectual property traditionally associated with industrial techniques, should be preferred. Little is therefore required in the way of novelty and inventiveness before protection is available. The term of protection runs well beyond the life of the products. As well, deposit and registration requirements have not been instituted yet, except for some very limited facilities in the United States and Japan (Davis, 1985).

Writing in 1972, the former registrar of copyrights in the United States argued that we have reached the point where any new rights under copyright law cannot apparently be exclusive rights (Ringer, 1972). The pattern of legal adaptation to the new technologies is for claims to property to be met by opposition from other interests, such as institutional users and the sellers of copying technologies (Henry, 1975). Legislators resolve this conflict by conferring title upon the producers and then by providing for compulsory licensing of the works, at a fee fixed by the official tribunal if agreements cannot be reached privately. Such has been the response to the photocopying of books and the changing of performances in some countries.

By way of contrast, the response to the software question tends to confirm the resilience of the liberal form of private property. The state has not moved away from property rights into a scheme of collective administration and reward, where royalties, rather than rights to control access, are the ultimate recognition for producers. This response might cast some light on the reasons why property rights have been compromised in the mass consumer markets of books and records. As the Australian Attorney-General's Department (Commonwealth of Australia, 1986: 80) remarked: 'Particularly with the proliferation of new technologies, collective administration is often the only practical means for a copyright owner to receive renumeration for the use of his work'. In the case of software, producers seem still to hold out hope that they can enforce a property right. In part, a property rule may seem the kind of clear objective to be pursued across the many national jurisdictions traversed in an international economy. It is fair to say that software producers are not just concerned about the problem of copying for home use. They are interested in the powers of property rights to act as strategic weapons in their rivalry with commercial competitors in the struggle over the development of the software itself, as well as hardware, information services and related products.

Once copyright was enlisted for the protection of software, then perhaps the freedom to tailor its provisions to the particular technology was bound to be constrained. But why was copyright favoured? The debate was framed somewhat by the producers' initial attempts to bring software within the ambit of the general copyright schemes in place at the time. Copyright was an established and familiar body of intellectual property rights. Attractive, then, may have been the reassurance of a definite, if over-inclusive, rule of the law to settle uncertainty in the industry. Certainly, proposals to vary the grant of protection according to the merits of the individual case met with little sympathy (Karjala, 1987). Nonetheless, the complexities of the idea-expression distinction have left the scope of protection finally with the decisions of the courts. Despite the clear response of the legislative domain to economic pressures, the legal 'system' displays a lively unruliness. It is also to be noted that copyright protection has operated in an uneasy relationship with the continuing attractions of the patents regimes and the law of confidential information.

Australia's response has been very much in this mould. While, along with Court (1986), we should not ignore the influence of legal culture on the software response, economic considerations have been to the fore. The government has taken seriously the threats that foreign producers would withhold their advanced products from the Australian market. Additionally, it considered it important to provide protection to locally produced software, especially software being produced for export. It feared retaliation in foreign markets if protection was not made available in Australia. Yet the local software industry is very small. While there are some notable local successes, Australia is a net importer of software. For example, it has been estimated that around 90 per cent of software packages are imported from overseas (Commonwealth of Australia. Industries Assistance Commission, 1984). Local production concentrates upon specialized customized work which is likely to be protected by other means such as confidential agreements that can be formed with a limited number of customers. Software pirating means that local users can effectively gain access to overseas products without the permission of the copyright holders.

The Australian government showed some early signs of an original response. For instance it appears that the Attorney-General's Department argued for the virtues of a deposit system at the 1983 Paris Convention discussions on software protection (Commonwealth of Australia. Attorney-General's Department, 1984: 148). But Australia, like many other countries, has fallen into line with the United States which stood to gain the most from unqualified protection because its industry was the leader in this technology and best placed to take advantage of copyright. Yet the intellectual property conventions have not acknowledged computer software explicitly and it remains the case today that the idea of special protection has failed to gain acceptance in international intellectual property forums (Soltysinski, 1990).

CHAPTER 5

# *Information and Appropriation*

Moving beyond the specialist categories of patents and copyright, this chapter focuses on the drive to render appropriable the more diffuse intangible resource of information. It first considers features of the debate over a policy of legal appropriation, then looks in detail at the extent to which information has been rendered appropriable by the common law policy of protecting confidences. It notes legislative initiatives to settle protection on trade secrets. It then raises the prospect of the criminalization of the misappropriation of information.

The need to discuss law's policy towards the ownership and control of information, and specifically technical and commercial information, is recognition of the view that information is becoming a central feature of 'post-industrial' economies around the world (see, e.g. Commonwealth of Australia. House of Representatives Standing Committee on Long-term Strategies, 1991). However, before we commence, we should note that this view remains contested. In particular, the importance of the conditions of information supply to an understanding of the economy appears to be a bone of contention between the neo-classical and institutionalist schools of economic thought. Their debate is beyond the ken of this discussion, though we shall touch on some of the points they make in passing.

In its manifestations most relevant to this inquiry, information takes the form of particular formulae, patterns, methods and processes, and the research and processing know-how and organizational capability essential to the successful production of high technology inventions. Of course, if our treatment were to be exhaustive, we would not only consider the status in law of technical information and production know-how. As Kingston (1984) urged, we would also consider law's responses to efforts to control marketing and distribution advantages. In part, these advantages represent information (such as commercial information, especially about customers), but they also extend to other kinds of intangibles: goodwill, business reputation, the merchandizing power of character, and trade marks. Today, the law of intellectual 'property' expands as it seeks to grapple with these phenomena (McKeogh and Stewart, 1991). We cannot possibly deal with all these aspects. One of the reasons for curtailing the discussion is the need to be economical in the presentation of 'information' in this book, the economic constraints on the production of information being one of the hard facts of life which we (or rather our publishers) are beginning to appreciate only too well (Rescher, 1989).

## THE DEBATE OVER APPROPRIATION

This first section acknowledges the debate over the appropriation of information. It identifies arguments made for the provision of legal command over information holdings. It notes the concerns expressed about the impact on innovation of appropriability. It notes too concerns that appropriation may contribute to the uneven distribution of this increasingly important resource. It then considers some qualities of information which make it difficult to capture in discrete holdings. It also questions the importance to success in innovation of acquiring legal holdings.

## THE CASE FOR LEGAL RIGHTS

If information is claiming a vital place in the economy as a valuable factor or asset, the desire to capture and control its benefits might be anticipated. From an instrumental, economic point of view, appropriability can be justified as a way to exclude the free rider (the Jack Nicholson of economics) who avails himself of the information in order to take a short-cut to the introduction of a rival product. Certainly, in the high technology sector, we might expect to see attempts to take short-cuts to acquire the information of competitors, say by headhunting key employees and encouraging them to reveal secrets, or even by using techniques of industrial espionage, such as copying records, entering computer files and obtaining prototypes. Without the prospect of protection, creators, producers and investors would be discouraged from spending their time, effort and money on information production (Kitch, 1980).

There would be an undersupply of information relative to what would obtain if the returns on supply were fully appropriable (Newman, 1976). Similar arguments have of course been advanced for the more pointed protection afforded by patents and copyright regimes (see chapters 3 and 4).

Where they see value deriving, producers may wish to contain the disclosure and use of technical or commercial information, at least until such time as they have had an opportunity to exploit its advantage by being first into a market with the product. In some instances, for example in relation to a versatile production or marketing technique, or even a very popular single product (such as Coca Cola), they may wish to limit access to that information for a considerable time. Yet, as innovation takes on more of a collective aspect inside the firm and a collaborative dimension beyond the firm, producers may perceive the need to share such information. They will nevertheless try to limit the purposes for which they do so, or the range of persons to which it is exposed. Legal rights might therefore appeal as a secure basis on which to expose the information to scrutiny for assessment and enhancement by potential collaborators and perhaps subsequently to license it out for combination with other expertises and for application to the manufacture of an end product (OECD, 1989).

At the same time, extra-legal control strategies may not always prove effective. They may certainly generate costs of their own. Let us now take the example of physical measures of protection. We shall turn to various kinds of relational and organizational means to capture the benefits of information later in the chapter. It is clear that physical security measures can be burdensome to maintain. The same computer and communications technologies which so enhance the generation, analysis and retrieval of information also provide opportunities for outsiders to gain access without permission. Adelstein and Peretz (1985) argue that the ability to internalize the economic benefits of intellectual production and to create exclusionary barriers to free riders depends a great deal on the inviolability of the host technology used to store and transmit the information. If the free riders can themselves inexpensively use technology to unlock the information, they will not need to purchase it from the seller. Theoretically, legal controls might be sought over access to the host technology rather than the information itself, but aligned against this approach there are often interests, such as the producers of the free-riding technologies – the now pervasive cassette recorders, photocopiers and personal computers (Henry, 1975). So too, the physical measures may be counter-productive. While it does restrict access, a strategy of standing alone, segregating and compartmentalizing the facets of the research or production process, may not be the most creative and efficient way to proceed, especially in the early and uncharted stages of the product cycle (see below).

Yet the traditional categories of intellectual property (patents and copyright) might carry limited appeal as a means legally to protect such information. Being refined bodies of law (especially in the case of patents) they are concerned with rights over the use of 'information' of quite specific kinds, with novel industrial techniques and original creative works, respectively. In any case, it is likely – even if these intellectual property rights are applicable – that producers will wish to obtain other means of protection for the information. Most obviously, they may wish to preserve the exclusivity of the information until such time as the relevant intellectual property protection is obtained. However, even after protection has been obtained, they may also wish to continue to control the surrounding protocols, manuals and codes that must often accompany the invention or work if it is to be used effectively.

## THE CONCERNS FOR INNOVATION

The claims for appropriability of information meet opposition on economic grounds. Such opposition is often a variation on the themes of the debate over patents and copyrights. Critics fear that the commodification of information within a liberal regime of private property rights will provide the means to lock up a crucial resource. At best, commodification will have a restrictive effect upon availability by empowering those who acquire ownership to charge a price for access to the information. As a result, a naturally public good will be rendered artificially scarce. Such concerns like to stress information's quality of indivisibility. Information can be enjoyed by several people at the same time without any one being deprived of possession or access to it. Furthermore, it is the case that information does not deteriorate with use but can be used over and over again without the need for renewal. The cost of producing information is independent of the scale on which it is used

(Commonwealth of Australia. House of Representatives Standing Committee on Long-term Strategies, 1991).

If innovation benefits from protection for its products, it also benefits from the diffusion of its insights, the conduct of further inquiry and analysis, and the consequent enhancement and improvement of the stock of industrial knowledge (Weinrib, 1988). Appropriability is said to place too great an emphasis on the creation and generation of information. As such activity carries costs, it is possible that a protective policy will stimulate over-investment in the production of information (Hammond, 1981). In any case, the possession of information does not necessarily signify either the command of knowledge or the capability to exploit it. In a concern for successful innovation, as much emphasis ought to be given to encouraging those persons and organizations who can make effective use of information (Lamberton, 1990). In this vein, Rosegger (1991) underlines the fact that innovative firms succeed not just by producing their own information but also by drawing on the information resources of other firms, either competitively or cooperatively, and on the wealth of knowledge which is available in the public domain. Frame (1983) reminds us that some companies and nations may find their most realistic strategy to be one of feeding off new technologies from the leading producers and improving them through improvements and refinements. Undue restrictions on the circulation of information lead to the expenditure of resources on the independent discovery of the same information or the diversion of effort into the circumvention of the restrictions. A good example is provided by the role which small start-up firms play in innovation. To what extent should the law constrain employees and contractors from breaking away from large organizations and setting up in competition on their own?

A related criticism attaches to the impact of appropriability on the norms of scientific research and discourse (Eisenberg, 1987). Concerns have been raised about the impact of commercial considerations on the free communication and dissemination of new scientific knowledge. Secrecy runs counter to the traditional ethic of the open publication of results and the free exchange of materials within the academic scientific community. Recent experience suggests that scientists do become more guarded in their dealings with their colleagues as the prospects for commercialization increase (Nelkin, 1984). Even the public research institutions now press their scientists to preserve exclusivity as part of their efforts to earn funds by selling intellectual property to the private sector. Certainly, industrial collaborators and customers will want academics to maintain secrecy, at least until such time as they obtain the commercial advantage of being first to make use of the discovery. Academics also encounter strictures of confidentiality when they act as contractors or consultants to government agencies, because of the industrial, military or political sensitivity of the information involved (Wilson, 1987).

## THE DISTRIBUTION OF INFORMATION RESOURCES

These objections to appropriability range beyond the immediate concerns with its microeconomic effects to the macrosocial implications of subordinating information activities to the private marketplace. For the critics, the drive to privatize the creation and dissemination of information will skew information resources to the needs of those industrial and financial sectors which enjoy the capacity to pay for expensive information technologies (Schiller, 1981). A particular concern is expressed about the tendency of governments, as a result of financial pressures or possibly ideological imperatives, to privatize public information activities. A fitting test would be the conditions under which the legal information of the statutes and judicial decisions of the land are provided on line and on disk. Some see the danger of a new gap opening in society between the information rich and the information poor. Again, this distributional inequality may assume a global pattern, the Third World in particular being unable to find the wherewithal to purchase the new information commodities (de Sola Pool, 1990). Ironically, some of these commodities might constitute information drawn from the Third World's own natural resources, such as the herbal medicines which are sold back to it as proprietary products.

A related cultural concern surrounds the possible concentration of information resources in the hands of transnational corporations. Some regional and national interests fear that local cultural traditions and diversities will be overshadowed or crowded out by the seductive attractions of Western information commodities (Mattelart, 1979). Other sovereignty concerns include the suspicion that private international information networks will effectively remove decision-making, say in financial transactions, from the scrutiny of national regulatory bodies (such as tax agencies). A more material concern, now that information services are a lucrative and strategic sector of the economy, is that business and trade will be moved offshore at the expense of local industry and national capability (OECD, 1983). In this regard, a policy dilemma is whether to apply any national controls to trans-border data flows (OECD, 1983). We have already noted that the powerful computer and communications technologies make such regulation increasingly difficult to maintain on a practical level. As we shall see, at an international level regulatory movements also run up against strong free transit and free trade sentiments.

Such concerns remind us that the challenges of technologically sophisticated information systems go far beyond the immediate question of intellectual property. Intellectual property may not necessarily turn out to be the dividing line on many of these issues of information power. Instead, the debate must move onto a broader plane concerned, for example, with the role to be played by public policies in placing information resources, and the means of creating and utilizing them, within the reach of the information poor. The 'electronic estate' makes more pointed the resolution of the issues of the funding and accessibility of research, educational, reference and news resources. A key issue now is the design and distribution of the computer, telecommunications and broadcasting technologies (Nora and Minc 1980; Reinecke, 1985; Barr, 1985). While a proliferation of the technologies is not necessarily to be equated with the attainment of information richness, it can serve as a tool for liberation from centralized and standardized information channels. A testimony to this potential is the alternative uses to which video recorders, personal computers and fax machines have sometimes been put.

## THE ELUSIVE NATURE OF INFORMATION

Ultimately, attempts to contain information flows for proprietary or indeed other sectional purposes may founder because of the very nature of information itself. There are all sorts of problems in getting markets in information to work. In almost evangelical terms, information liberationists point out how arbitrary and perhaps illusory it is to expect to be able to fix, retain or rely on holding specific technical information as a means of economic control. Their points are worth exploring in this context. In the first place, there seems doubt that it is possible to take pieces of information and freeze and transfix them in time for the purpose of settling a holding upon them. Any such isolation of lumps of information would at the best be an arbitrary decision. Know-how is often of such a tacit, complex and idiosyncratic nature that it cannot readily be hived off into discrete, codified lumps of information separate from the persons and organizations who develop and apply it (Pavitt, 1984). For example, much of the knowledge which is applied by industry is not of a general nature and easily reproduced, but instead pertains to specific applications, firms and occupations. While attempts will always be made to do so, it may not even be possible to encapsulate it in a written text or program it into a computer.

Furthermore, contrary perhaps to the assumptions of mainstream economics, information resources cannot be treated as a given factor or endowment. Information is to be likened more to a cybernetic process. Often incomplete and imperfect, it is only enhanced by the force of a continuous cycle of interaction and application. Certainly, we know that innovation is much less of a serial activity. The clear distinctions between research, development, production and marketing do not hold up. Thus, so much of successful innovation today is a collective effort that requires the combination of different talents and different kinds of expertise, not only in the research and engineering departments, but also on the shop floors of industrial firms (Freeman, 1987). As we have noted, the speed, sophistication and convergence of recent technological innovations have also driven firms beyond their four walls in the search for complementary specialties. Again, moving the analysis up to a broader level, it can be said that successful innovation is often the outcome of an incremental and accumulative intellectual process, each advance in learning building upon the developments in the art which have gone before it. In the high technology sectors, much of this base is funded by the taxpayer through the public sector or has otherwise found its way into the public domain (Pugh, 1984; Kenney, 1986). For some, this fountain of ideas represents the common heritage of humanity itself (Hammond, 1981).

In such circumstances, it would also seem difficult to isolate and contain bodies of information. Information can be slippery stuff. Purchasers will not want to buy information until they have had a chance to inspect it. But once others have been exposed to information they have had the benefit of it, and it is not possible to require them to hand it back. In this way, information has a natural tendency to act as a public good. An endeavour may of course be made to limit the purposes and uses for which the information is disclosed. But such information can easily become mixed up with other information which the recipient already possesses, including information from the public domain, and subsequent use of it may even be merely unconscious. Its injection into collective operations, joint ventures and firm networks brings more people into contact with the information. It increases the risk that the information will spill out into the public arena, possibly through some accidental release or innocent finding. And, once realized in an end product that is intended for the mass market, the information may have to be declared in order to make the product user-friendly; certainly the opportunity arises for reverse engineering of its secrets. Indeed, the new technologies provide ingenious ways to gain access at the earliest stages of its development (Adelstein and Peretz, 1985).

## THE LIMITED VALUE OF INFORMATION

Finally, we should revive the point that the possession of technical information cannot guarantee success in innovation. The struggle to command more and more information may provide diminishing returns. For example, Rosegger (1991: 17) reaches the conclusion that: 'accelerated transfers of technical knowledge *per se* have done little to eradicate interfirm differences in organisational capabilities, in the qualities of managements, and the speed and the effects of learning'. These latter qualities are (as we observed earlier) crucial to eventual success in innovation (Teece, 1987). A simple point, often overlooked, is that any recipient must also have the capacity to understand and use such information. In characteristically wry fashion, Kitch (1980: 711) remarks: 'The point should not be unfamiliar to a teacher who has had the experience of teaching a course and then discovering that many of the students did not understand most of the subject matter'. The sophistication of the technologies and their underlying sciences are likely to provide natural barriers to entry into these fields. In a sense, information protects itself from misappropriation.

It follows that, if information is often embodied in a person or a firm, if skill and learning are tacit and amorphous qualities, and if specialized assets need to be combined, then the emphasis in industry is likely to shift to the construction of relational and organizational forms of command. Command will be sought through the structures of employment, joint venture and merger arrangements, arrangements in which collaboration and internalization are emphasized, and obligations of fidelity, trust and non-competition are realized. Yet we should not be surprised if the search to find ways to render appropriable the intangible resources of information, know-how and skill continues (Rosegger, 1991). So if the law is called upon to assist with appropriation, we should ask whether its doctrinal responses are likely to reflect the kinds of problems we have identified in the nature of information. At the same time, how does the law bring to bear its own concerns on the demands which are made of it? In particular, does it respond by trying to settle its traditional property rights on this resource, or does it offer some other (perhaps more limited) means of protection against unauthorized disclosure, dissemination and use of information? Has the law placed qualifications or conditions upon the protection it is prepared to offer, perhaps in the cause of optimizing the conditions for innovation? By what process has it settled on its policy?

## THE LAW OF CONFIDENCES

This section examines the construction by the courts of a law to protect confidences. It identifies the important elements of this common law category of protection. The first element is the quality of confidentiality which the information should possess. The second is the nature of the circumstances which give rise to the obligation to respect a confidence. Here, the section considers in particular the extent to which obligations have been extended beyond the relational form so that we may speak of a true property right over confidential information. The section then looks at the limits to the kind of information which may be the object of a confidence and especially the extent to which know-how is so captured.

### THE CONFIDENTIAL NATURE OF THE INFORMATION

The common law of confidential information is said to require three conditions to be made out if it is to recognize a 'cause of action' for protection on the part of the complainant. The information in question must have the necessary quality of confidentiality; it must be imparted in circumstances that give rise to an obligation on the part of the defendant to respect that confidentiality; and there must be a breach of that confidence by an unauthorized disclosure or use of the information (Gurry, 1984). The first element, confidentiality, is a good indicator of the extent to which judicial policy bears on technological innovation. How is confidential information to be distinguished from other information? In the British Commonwealth jurisdictions it has been said that the information need not be novel in the sense that a patentable invention is required to be, nor original in the sense of copyrightable work (Kearney, 1985). Neither need it be of objective economic value or in some other way significant if it is to attract recognition. However, we shall see that such features can influence the exercise of the courts' discretion, once a cause of action has been established, in deciding both whether to grant an injunction to restrain the offender from disclosing or using the information and the kind of monetary compensation to award for any breach.

At the same time, the law does not protect information which is of common or public knowledge. Thus, the information must in some way be inaccessible or unavailable to the public. This requirement does not deny any exposure of the information. As it is concerned with information that is imparted in confidence, some disclosure is to be expected, but it must be disclosure within a limited range. So, for example, if it is done in circumstances that signify its confidentiality, the information may be circulated within a firm or between contractors. This criterion of inaccessibility or unavailability does lend support to the kinds of technical information and trade secrets which reflect creative effort (Kearney, 1985). So, the courts have explained that it is the kind of information which the public could not acquire or duplicate independently without the expenditure of time, effort and money (Gurry, 1984). Someone is therefore likely to have added value by expending such resources in order to develop the information – interpreting data or reworking facts, for example, if not making new discoveries or producing new ideas. Confidentiality provides a competitive advantage to the controller: the ability to exploit the information exclusively or charge a price for access to it. In addition, the quality of confidentiality is evidenced by the efforts committed to maintaining its inaccessibility, such as the physical security measures which are put in place.

Such circumstances are meant only to constitute the kind of evidence that confirms the confidential nature of the information. However, some courts show a tendency to formalize these sorts of indicators, so that, in some of the cases, it looks as if the courts are levelling protection directly on certain worthy types of information *per se*. On the other hand, the classic formulation stresses that the law is to protect confidences rather than information as such (Gurry, 1985). In this regard, it is to be remembered that the law has also upheld confidences in all sorts of personal, subjective and possibly unmeritorious information. The elevation of these kinds of indicators to a definition of protection is strongest in those jurisdictions, such as the United States, which have formulated a specialist body of trade secret law (see below). In the British Commonwealth, the tendency is by no means as advanced. Nonetheless, it is interesting now to see use being made of the United States trade secrets law in some of the Australian courts (see for example, the judgment in Secton Pty Ltd and another v. Delawood Pty Ltd and others [1991] 33 Australian Industrial Law Reports #202) and the learned discussion of the law of trade secrets. Dean (1990: 4) enters a necessary caution but is still inclined to characterize his own comprehensive local work as a work on the law of trade secrets.

It does follow from the fundamental criterion that if the information finds its way into the public domain then it loses its quality of confidentiality, and thus any further protection under this head of law. This qualification remains a fundamental limitation on the reach of the common law's protection for interests in information. At the same time, it should be noted that legal action can still be taken against a person who has breached the confidence and realized the information, if that person would then gain a 'springboard' to get ahead of potential competitors as a result of his or her improper dealings with the information (this would apply, for example, to an employee or contractor of the confider who starts up on his or her own).

## THE BASIS OF THE OBLIGATION TO RESPECT THE CONFIDENCE

The second of the three elements defines the circumstances that give rise to the obligation to respect such confidentiality. The delineation of these circumstances by the courts is also crucial to the reach of the legal protection. Most clearly, the obligation arises out of a contract or some other kind of direct relationship between the confider and the confidant. Yet, it is a cause of action which may be made out against persons other than the confidant, in particular against some third person to whom the information is communicated in breach of the confidence (for example, the company which hires away an employee) or, significantly, who gains access to the information by some surreptitious means (for example, the company which spies on a competitor). As we shall see, the law of equity has struggled to provide a rationale for this extension, but ultimately we might have to ask whether, in extending recourse beyond the disrespectful confidant, the courts are establishing a new subject of property – that is, property in information itself. For this purpose, property might be defined as a right enforced specifically by the law to exclude the world from access to or use of the confidential information. Of course, such a right might be used to bargain for the purchase or the licensing of the information but, legally, this choice lies with the holder.

## CONTRACT

It is clear that the obligation to respect confidentiality of information may be created by making a contract. Contract may give expression to a term that employees, subcontractors or co-venturers, for instance, shall not disclose, or use for any purpose other than the business of the enterprise, the information which the confider wishes to preserve. It is but one instance of the difficulties of fit between the courts' conceptualization of this obligation and the practices in industry that the courts speak of confiders and confidants. The claimant may in fact be seeking to capture information that an employee has, for example, generated himself or acquired from outside the firm. The contract may therefore seek explicitly to settle the fact that the employer is to have the benefit of the confidential information, even to assert to say that such information is its property. To support this obligation, employees may also be required to report to the employer any such information they generate or discover, and to make all necessary efforts to preserve its confidentiality.

These contractual obligations are often created in tandem with obligations to report any inventions that might be patentable, to assign rights in them to the employer, and to support the employer's efforts to secure those rights. It is worth noting that patents legislation recognizes inventors, but liberally permits the assignment of rights through contract to other persons such as the inventor's employer, even in anticipation of an invention (McKeogh and Stewart, 1991). In some countries the legislation limits the kinds of employee inventions which may belong to the employer and prescribes compensation for assignments that do occur (Saxby, 1981). Copyright legislation in Australia makes the author the first owner of the copyright in a work, but, significantly, provides an exception in the case of works made in pursuance of the terms of a contract of employment. In this situation, the employer is deemed the owner (McKeogh and Stewart, 1991). (This attribution of the copyright to the employer may, at least in theory, be countermanded by the terms of a particular contract.)

In his American survey, Neumeyer (1971) found that the larger industrial companies routinely obtained such employment invention and confidential information agreements from their employees. The practice is likely to be much the same in Australia. McKeogh and Stewart (1991: 57) are of the view that: 'Such clauses will almost inevitably be found, for instance, in service agreements involving managerial employees, consultancy agreements, agreements to license technology, and arrangements designed to facilitate information disclosure during joint venture negotiations'.

In the absence of an express provision, the obligation to respect confidentiality may arise in several other ways. Indeed, it seems from judicial decisions that an express provision will not exclude the possibility of another underlying obligation which extends beyond the terms of that provision, say in the time it runs (Gurry, 1984). This willingness to supplement the contract provides an interesting variation on the idea of freedom of contract. For example, because of the way they construe the nature of the employment relationship, the courts are inclined to read into contracts of employment an implied obligation to respect the employer's confidential information (McComas et al., 1981). This protection for the employer's information is bolstered by the presence of another duty imported into the contract of employment by the courts: the employee's obligation of fidelity to the employer (Macken et al., 1978). In part, this obligation militates against competition with the employer during the period of employment (Creighton and Stewart, 1990).

## EQUITY

The obligation to respect a confidence may indeed arise independently of any contract through the operation of what lawyers call 'the jurisdiction of equity'. The equity jurisdiction is said to have developed in sixteenth-century England as a reaction to the rigidities and harshness of the common law of the day. While it retains elements of discretion and flexibility today, it is itself now a complex and weighty body of law. Furthermore, the equitable jurisdiction is no longer exercised by separate courts, the jurisdictions being mixed together as the courts endeavour to fashion effective protection for confidential information.

The courts have said that the equitable obligation may be sourced in a relationship which is inherently confidential, such a professional relationship, employment relationship or a joint venture. Or it may arise from the particular circumstances in which information is communicated and imparted. What justifies the imposition of such obligation if it is not the need to honour a contractual undertaking? The rationale of the equitable obligation has variously been styled as being a matter of good faith, conscionable conduct, ethical behaviour or business morality for the recipient of the confidence to respect the confidence. The obligation has connections with other concepts in equity such as the fiduciary obligations of company directors and senior officers, which also suggest that they should not use any (confidential) information in a way that conflicts with the interests of their company, say to compete with the company or profit at its expense (Finn, 1977; Austin, 1987).

Equity extends the reach of protection for confidential information to those circumstances in which no contract exists. An important instance is, in fact, the negotiations in which the confider might reveal information for the confidant's appraisal prior to forming a contract. It also extends the law to 'rope in' the third person who knowingly participates in a breach of the confidence by receiving information from a confidant and then using it to his or her own advantage.

The subjectivity of the rationale underlying the protection of equity leaves the scope of the law in some doubt. The courts have been presented with situations in which the value of the information is threatened but it is hard to fit the threatening behaviour within a rubric of bad faith. What for example of the confidant who subconsciously uses confidential information? Leaving aside the question of the validity of Freud's theories, can we call such use of information an act of bad faith (Weinrib, 1988)? So too, an action seems to lie against a third party who receives the information innocently, who for instance did not know and ought not to have known that it was confidential. In the drive to protect such information, the cases reflect an unsurprising tendency to make liability strict in the sense of being independent of any culpability.

## THE THIRD PERSON STRANGER

The position of third parties is the greatest challenge to the coherence of the equitable doctrine. Where a cause of action is founded against the third party, it is difficult to see how the protection remains one that is based upon the breach of a relation with the holder of the information. Perhaps, as those who seek a rationale to the law suggest, the innocent third person's liability may be built upon the confidant's relation with the holder if the third person knowingly participates in the breach of the confidence; otherwise he or she might be drawn into the confidence by being put on notice that information innocently received is in fact confidential. (After all, the remedies awarded by the court can be adjusted to take account of the extent of the defendant's culpability.)

Here, the real test of judicial policy is the case of the third person who directly obtains information by means of some sort of espionage. Much is now made of the decision in the Queensland case of Franklin v. Giddins ([1978] Queensland Reports 72), where the court found against a defendant who had surreptitiously taken wood cuttings from the plaintiff's orchard in order that he might examine the genetic structure of his trees and replicate his enhanced variety of nectarine. The trial judge was moved to say that he could not find that: 'a thief who steals a trade secret . . . is less unconscionable than a traitorous servant' (p. 80). Yet it is clear from the circumstances of this case that no confidential relationship had been formed between the plaintiff and the defendant; neither then had any confidence been breached. We can agree perhaps that the behaviour was unconscionable in the sense that the defendant stole the budwood from the plaintiff's orchard. But what if a lawful means were used to gain access to the information, say by taking photographs from a distance (Hodkinson, 1988)? Even so, one can see why the courts might wish to advance protection if the plaintiff has invested ingenuity and effort into developing the innovation, as the Law Commission for England and Wales suggested when it perceived the gap in the protection for information in 1981 (Law Commission for England and Wales, 1981).

As we shall see in the case of computer resident information, one response to the gap in the law is to render unlawful the surreptitious means of access to the information. Another is to ask if the defendant is competing 'unfairly' by drawing on the plaintiff's prior work, or 'reaping without sowing', as one learned commentator has put it (Ricketson, 1984d). Such an approach has a recurring fascination for those students of the field who see inconsistencies in legal policy. As a principle for extending protection, it has not found favour with British Commonwealth courts. A common reaction is to suggest that such a principle would throw the law open to the unpredictabilities of the differing senses of virtue and fairness that each court might employ (McKeogh and Stewart, 1991). It is hard to see, however, that good faith and good conscience are much less subjective standards.

## PROPERTY?

An alternative response is to treat information as property. We recall that property is a right against all the world – against strangers as well as those 'related' to the holder. The attraction of this approach is that it enlists an established concept with strong associations (Michalowski and Pfuhl, 1991). It evokes an elaborated body of law which can assist with the disposition of the novel and often 'hard' cases which the infinite variety of human behaviour can always throw up (Hammond, 1984). It promotes a rule-based response where consequences follow by deduction from the body of law rather than from an investigation into the ethical proprieties of every individual case.

Nonetheless, to return to one of our original points in this debate, the property approach may still be confounded by the character of information itself. It is hard to see how property can extend to all information, for what then would be the basis on which the courts could determine the rightful owner of information at large? Academics seemed fond of quoting a comment by Latham CJ in the case of Federal Commissioner of Taxation v. the United Aircraft Corporation ([1943] 68 Commonwealth Law Reports 525, at 534):

> Knowledge is valuable, but knowledge is neither real nor personal property. A man with a richly stored mind is not for that reason a man

of property . . . Either all knowledge is property, so that the teaching of, for example, mathematics, involves a transfer of property, or only some knowledge is property. If only some knowledge is property then it must be possible to state a criterion which will distinguish between that knowledge which is property and that knowledge which is not property. The only criterion which has been suggested is the secrecy of the knowledge – it is said that the fact that knowledge is secret in some way creates a proprietary right in that knowledge. I confess myself completely unable to appreciate this proposition as a legal statement.

If property rights were to attach only to information that was confidential, how would this approach differ from that of equity? A quote from a sympathetic judge in a Victorian case might indicate how this approach might not really advance the issue. In Deta Nominees Pty Ltd v. Viscount Plastic Products Pty Ltd ([1979] Victorian Reports 167, at p. 193), Fullagar J put the question this way: 'Would a person of ordinary intelligence, in all the circumstances of the case, including, *inter alia*, the relationship of the parties and the nature of the information and the circumstances of its communication, recognise this information to be the property of the other person and not his own to do as he likes with?'

## PROGRESS TOWARDS PROPERTY?

Nonetheless, the designation of property continues to be applied in a proportion of the judicial decisions made in this area. Perhaps this practice suggests that the concept of property is being used metaphorically (Gurry, 1984) or rhetorically (Palmer, 1990) in these cases. Such a flourish is an unusual practice for cautious judges who are meant to be declaring law with some precision. Instead, we might attribute substance to their assertions that information is property. Indeed, some of the developments do point to the appropriateness of a property characterization (Ricketson, 1977). We have mentioned the (tentative) extension of the cause of action to third person strangers. Significant also is the willingness to exercise judicial discretion in favour of specific relief, that is to enjoin disclosure or use of the information and to require the transgressor to account for any profits made. Anton Piller orders have also been granted as a way of making the cause of action effective. It is true that the grant of such coercive remedies is discretionary and the court may consider in exercising its discretion whether, for instance, monetary damages would act as an adequate remedy and whether (on balance) greater hardship would be caused to the defendant. Yet, the courts have clearly resisted the idea that the remedy should be confined to the payment of damages. They recognize that this policy would afford the defendants a unilateral taking or compulsory licensing of the information on the payment of a judicially fixed tariff (Kearney, 1985).

On the other hand, the extent of the protection against third parties is not settled. The confidentiality of certain information may be 'broken' by reverse engineering a product in which the information is expressed, provided of course that the product has been obtained lawfully. In comparison with the patent, it is also permissible to use the 'same' information if it has been generated independently. Consequently, it is not yet clear that the interest is one which is truly maintainable against all the world. Perhaps it is accurate to say that the law with regard to confidential information displays some of the consequences of a property classification but not all of them. It is fashionable to say these days that the law of confidential information is developing into a *sui generis* body of law (McKeogh and Stewart, 1991). It may well be the answer at this time is to say that law is reaching a point where it will be prepared to protect information which is held secretly, whether or not a confidence is broken, at least in the case of technical and commercial information (Thompson, 1990).

## THE OBJECT OF THE CONFIDENCE

Finally, before we leave the civil law, it is worth asking how the courts identify the 'information' which may qualify as the object of a protected confidence. In particular, given the kinds of attributes we identified above, how do the courts deal with the argument that a piece of information is not distinguishable from a wider body of knowledge, many aspects of which are not the subject of confidence and may in fact be at large within the public domain? This question causes particular heartache in the realm of employment, where an employee, for instance, may accumulate information gradually and subtly in the course of her or his work, or where the information forms part of the stock of general knowledge, skill and experience the employee needs to obtain a livelihood (Harris, 1985).

## Know-how

In some circumstances, the information is sufficiently discrete and identifiable to be separable from such generalized bodies of knowledge. It helps, for instance, if the information is held in a material form and then physically taken or copied by the transgressor. But the courts say that information does not have to be in such a form to attract protection: theoretically it might be observed and then stored in the defendant's mind. Need it have some element of concreteness? It seems that ideas, concepts and discoveries, as well as more down-to-earth practical information, such as chemical formulae and engineering processes, are not precluded from protection under this head. But a question most relevant to the interest here in innovation is whether the information must be sufficiently well developed to be capable of realization (Archibald, 1984). By way of contrast, patent law will only recognize scientific knowledge which has practical utility. It seems that the untested or unproven concept might still claim confidentiality. For strategic reasons, the originator may want to keep news of the lines of research inquiry being undertaken from competitors.

The limit is likely to be found in the need to distinguish the information, with sufficient particularity and specificity, from the general stock of common knowledge in the industry (Kutten, 1986). Potentially a general issue, it seems to crop up most frequently in disputes between employers and employees where the courts have been mindful of the fact that a restraint might deprive the worker of the opportunity to practise his or her trade or livelihood (Gurry, 1984). Such a restraint might also deprive the public of the full benefit of the worker's service. The dilemma most pointedly arises after the employment has ended. During employment, the employee is restricted in the use of such knowledge by the obligation of fidelity to the employer. It is agreed that, if the information is separable, an obligation of confidence may extend beyond the bounds of employment to restrain the worker. But if the information is inseparable from the skill and knowledge which is either accumulated in order to be able to pursue a calling or is acquired inevitably and naturally in the course of employment, the courts are reluctant to give effect to the confidentiality protection (Stewart, 1988). In an early case, Herbert Morris v. Saxelby ([1916] Appeal Court [Reports] 688, at p. 714) an English judge remarked: 'a man's aptitudes, his skill, his dexterity, his manual or mental ability . . . ought not to be relinquished by a servant; they are not his master's property, they are his own property; they are himself.' Recent cases indicate that such a reservation goes beyond the kind of trade know-how to which the judge was referring.

## Restrictive Covenants

As a result of these limitations, employers must double their strategies to control the competitive use of such subjective, embodied knowledge. It is now common for employers to obtain from employees an agreement not to compete with the employer's business after the employment has ended. Staff movements between organizations are more volatile in some sectors and in some countries, notably in the United States (Soma, 1983), but the issue is likely to arise everywhere. These restrictive covenants have been upheld by the courts as a means of containing the use of confidential information which is inseparable from the employee's other knowledge. Yet the courts have also insisted that such covenants should not amount to what is regarded as an unreasonable restraint on trade (Dean, 1990). The courts have shown some reluctance to enforce these 'trailing clauses' because of their effect on the employee's capacity to earn a livelihood and, indeed, upon freedom of trade generally. To survive scrutiny, such clauses will need to be reasonable in scope as to the time, area and activity they embrace. The courts' concern with restraint of trade might be viewed as a mild common law version of the competition policy which now finds form in legislative schemes in many countries (Trebilcock, 1986). We might also expect these competition law schemes to become increasingly interested in such control strategies as refusals to deal in know-how, or restrictive know-how licensing practices. We can, of course, regard the control of person-specific knowledge as only one of a number of anti-competitive innovation strategies. If we remember that know-how can also be specific to organizations, then restrictive arrangements within multi-firm consortia and mergers will also be relevant to the control of know-how.

## Defences?

Given the restrictions which the cause of action places on the free circulation of information, do the courts recognize any departures from the obligation of confidence? The courts have allowed for breach of confidence where disclosure is in the 'public interest' (Ricketson, 1979). Classically, it is in the public interest for criminal or other iniquitous behaviour to be revealed. It does not seem that innovation maximization considerations have found their way into these specific defences to an action for breach of confidence (Finn, 1984).

Disclosure may also be justified by some overriding legal duty, such as the need to answer an order from a court to reveal information which is required to try a case. An interesting issue of recent years, has been the onus on government under freedom of information legislation to disclose information (of value to its own enterprises) to its business partners or ordinary citizens. There is an understandable public interest in the ways in which public universities, for instance, are spending tax-payers' money on different kinds of research; as there is also in the real health and environment hazards of industrial technologies that come under official regulatory scrutiny (Nelkin, 1984). But freedom of information legislation has also been seen as an opportunity to obtain information about the strategies and operations of competitors (Dean, 1990). In Australia, such legislation is likely to exempt trade secrets and other commercially valuable information, indeed confidential information generally, from freedom of information requirements (Bayne, 1984). Most intriguing is the status of information generated by the public instrumentalities themselves. Its treatment is another manifestation of the ambivalence of the law towards the commercial activities of such organizations and their challenge to the public-private divide which liberal law attempts to maintain. We shall consider this broad question in chapter 11.

Another possible way the ownership of information may be qualified is through the various special purpose legislative requirements for disclosure. Their purpose is to overcome asymmetries in information and promote informed decisions. They are represented unevenly in the legal obligations of employers to workers, sellers to consumers, and companies to shareholders. Teubner (1989) sees these requirements as a good illustration of the newly emerging reflexive form of law (see chapter 12). It remains to be seen, however, whether such requirements make much inroad into information strongholds.

## LEGISLATIVE PROTECTIONS

This section points to legislative developments that have taken the question of appropriation beyond the indirect attention it receives in the common law of confidences. It refers first to the tendency in some overseas jurisdictions to afford protection to a specialist category of trade secrets as a matter of both civil and of criminal law. It notes also the faltering way that the criminal law affords more general protection to information resources, especially through the tendency to criminalize unauthorized access to information-bearing technology.

### TRADE SECRETS LEGISLATION

#### Civil Law Protection

As we have identified in our earlier discussions, the judge-made law of confidential information overlaps with the legal recognition of 'trade secrets'. But some jurisdictions, notably in the United States and Western Europe, have legislated specific protection for trade secrets. In part, this legislation has the effect of eliminating the need for the protection of information to be based on breaches of confidences or other relational harms. In the United States, the law received a boost in 1939 with the influential first restatement of the law of torts, which endeavoured to tie together the strands of this body of the common law in a coherent doctrine. The commentary to the restatement defined a trade secret as a formula, pattern, device or compilation of information which is for continuing use in business and which provides an opportunity to gain a competitive advantage over those who do not know or use it (Kutten, 1986). In 1979, another codifying body drafted a uniform trade secrets act for recommendation to state legislatures. Its definition of trade secrets covered information, including the formula, pattern, compilation, program, device, method, technique or process which derives independent economic value from information not generally known and readily ascertainable by proper means, and which is subject to reasonable efforts to maintain its secrecy. This legislation was adopted by some of the American states.

The restatement of the law of torts indicated several factors which ought to be considered when assessing whether a piece of information qualifies for protection. These factors are: the extent to which the information is known outside the business; the extent to which it is known by employees and others involved in the business; the accessibility of the information and the ease or difficulty with which this information can be independently acquired or duplicated by others; the costs in time, money and human resources incurred in developing the information; the methods undertaken to maintain the secrecy of the information; the degree to which these methods are enforced or implemented; and, finally, the value of the information to its owner or its owner's competitors. The primary consideration is the fact that the information is not generally known or readily ascertainable outside the business (Milgrom, 1985). However, efforts must also be made to keep the information secret.

As trade secrets move into the sights of the legislatures, does the law take on any of the innovation policy themes of intellectual property? A recent commentary on the law noted that:

> its protection is not based on a policy of rewarding or otherwise encouraging the development of secret processes or devices. The protection is merely against breach of faith and reprehensible means of learning another's secret. (Milgrom, 1985: 2-12)

Milgrom (1985) takes the view that the information which is within the ambit of the trade secrets legislation need not be original, novel or inventive except to the extent that any of these features are necessary to distinguish it from general or public knowledge. Nevertheless, the statutory definitions do suggest that the information needs to be sufficiently tested and tried for it to afford competitive advantage or to constitute independent economic value. At the same time, the prevailing view in the United States is that trade secrets represent a form of property. Protection will lie not only against those who are in breach of a confidence but also against those third parties who use some reprehensible means to obtain confidential information, such as luring away, tricking or intimidating the owner's employees or spying on, tapping into or breaking into the owner's premises (Kutten, 1986).

Japan makes an interesting comparison. Commentators have noted that trade secrets have not achieved the status of a recognized legal interest outside of obligations established by contract (such as employment contracts) or some specialist bodies of law such as the duties of company directors (Dosi, 1980). One reason might be that Japanese employees do not tend to move between companies

(Karjala, 1990). However, foreign firms contemplating licensing or practising know-how in Japan have expressed some concern about this lack of protection. Recently, the United States has been pressing Japan to amend its unfair competition prevention law, and injunctive relief is now available against the appropriation of trade secrets by such means as fraud, theft and extortion (Powers, 1991). A trade secret is here defined as production formulae, methods of sale or other technical or commercial information not known to the public and treated as secret.

In some Western European countries (for example Germany, Switzerland, the Netherlands, France and Sweden), trade secrets have attracted a similar sort of protection under the provisions of unfair competition laws (OECD, 1986a). By contrast, a proposal for legislative protection from the Law Commission for England and Wales (1981) failed to attract government support. The Australian Law Reform Commission (1983) declined to recommend legislation of this kind in the context of a wide-ranging report into the question of privacy. But of course, unlike the countries of Western Europe, England and Australia have a strong common law tradition of protection for confidences.

## Criminal Offences

Commencing with legislation in New York in 1964 and New Jersey in 1965, a notable development in the United States is the criminalization of the 'appropriation of trade secrets'. New York extends the protection of the criminal law to a category of secret scientific material which is misappropriated for use. New Jersey (a model for a number of other states) forbids the stealing or copying of articles which represent trade secrets with the intention to deprive or withhold from the owner the control of the trade secret, or to appropriate it to one's own use or the use of another. Fetterley (1970) suggests that these laws were a response to the failure of the civil law and especially to the difficulties private complainants encountered in effecting judgments against foreigners. In the United States, a technologically advanced nation, the mood had become more mercantilist again.

In some countries of Western Europe, misappropriation also attracts the displeasure of the criminal law (see Wise, 1981). For instance, Switzerland's criminal code contains a series of offences for industrial espionage such as spying out industrial or commercial secrets in order to make them available to a foreign public authority, foreign organization or private enterprise; it also proscribes abuse of trade secrets, such as betraying secrets. It is not difficult to imagine why Switzerland's economic specialities provide an impetus for this kind of protection. In contrast, Japan's penal code has given no explicit protection to trade secrets, though Wise (1981) notes several judicial decisions that have given creative interpretations to general offences such as larceny and embezzlement in order to sanction disloyal employees.

### International Trade Secrets Protection

In the past, trade secrets have not received the same consideration by international bodies as the mainstream categories of intellectual property. There are signs that their growing significance will spur efforts at this level. The protection of trade secrets was one of the objectives of the United States proposals to the Uruguay round of GATT (Stuckey-Clarke, 1990). The United States sought protection for undisclosed valuable business, commercial, technical or other proprietory data, as well as technical information (Raghavan, 1990). Consensus at a multilateral level is, however, likely to be difficult to achieve. Bilateral pressures are a more promising strategy. We have already noted initiatives by the United States in respect of Japan. It appears also that unfair use of American trade secrets has become a cause for the invocation of sanctions procedures under the provisions of the United States trade legislation (Milgrom, 1985). For example, misappropriation of a trade secret has been treated under section 337 as an unfair act in several cases (McGovern, 1986). The United States is concerned about the lack of protection for trade secrets in a number of developing countries (Gadbar and Richards, 1988). In the past, this concern has extended to regulatory requirements that United States investors seeking entry into the economy form associations with locals or permit them to hold equity.

As more and more sensitive information flows along international electronic 'highways', the security of information-bearing high technology may also become more of an international issue. Ample precedents for this interest exist in the conventions regarding the security of mail and telephone messages (OECD, 1983). At the same time, we must expect further pressures to break down any government regulatory resistance to the free flow of private information across national borders (Kirby, 1990). An early initiative was the OECD's Declaration on Transborder Data Flows. We know that UNESCO has encountered the wrath of Western nations for supporting certain Third World proposals to screen information (de Sola Pool, 1990). Information flows are rapidly becoming a trade issue, for the matter of liberalized international trade in services is in many ways about the transnational processing of information. We pick this theme up again in our discussion of telecommunications in chapter 10.

## THE CRIMINAL LAW

### The Misappropriation of Information?

Information is often manipulated, falsified or destroyed in order that goods, services or monies can be misappropriated. In these situations, information is the medium or the device for the perpetration of the crime. In recent years, legislatures have often been concerned to modernize the traditional offences of the criminal law so that they can catch these practices where the financial information (for instance) is present in computer and communications technologies. Here the objects of misappropriation are familiar and there is no problem with the notion of property. Rather, the discontinuity lies in the absence, for example, of written documents to falsify, human actors to deceive, or physical premises to enter (Brown, 1983).

If we move from the realm of familiar criminal practices which simply adopt a new guise, the issue becomes the protection from 'misappropriation' which criminal law extends to information itself. Where the offence is the abstraction of incorporeal information, conceptual problems associated with the application of traditional criminal offences assume greater proportions (Sullivan, 1988). This point is illustrated by the English case of Oxford v. Moss, in which the court held that it was not theft of property for a student surreptitiously to remove, read and replace a copy of an examination paper before the examination took place. The characteristics of information make it difficult to fit such activities to the requirements of the classic offences. For example, theft conventionally requires a taking or carrying away of property with the intention permanently to deprive the owner. It is difficult to see how such elements are met if information is merely perused or copied. Finally, the legislators have to face the issue of whether the information is to be treated as property for the purpose of such offences; the piece of paper which is taken or the computer terminal which is damaged is hardly the point. Should any information qualify, or do such potentially serious consequences of criminalization require a distinction to be made between different levels or qualities of information? Tettenborn (1985) is able to argue, for instance, that industrial and commercial information is now so important an economic asset that no objection lies to making their abstraction criminal. On the other, Mawhood (1987) recommends that information should attract protection only if it is in some way value-added by the holder. Criminalization seems a serious step, especially if the civil law remains ambivalent about the idea of property.

In 1986, an OECD survey reported that a clear consensus was lacking at the international and national levels about the appropriate roles for the civil, criminal or administrative law in this area (OECD, 1986a). The OECD's own experts went on to argue that the succour of static property theory should be denied to the protection of intellectual values. Instead, protection should continue to act on relational harms, such as breach of confidence, unfair competition and unjust enrichment. While the trend to trade secret protection should be encouraged, it should be based not on natural rights to property but rather on a purposive approach more discriminatingly concerned with encouraging research and investment (for example). As we have noted above, some such special purpose protection already invokes the criminal law.

## Unauthorized Access to Computer-Held Information

Of a more general nature, a notable development of the criminal law in the last decade has been the proscription of unauthorized access to computer systems. This initiative is analogous to the earlier prohibition of interference with telecommunications (Dean, 1990). After some initial hesitation, the tide has turned very much in favour of criminalization. Most states in the United States have enacted such laws (Hollinger and Lanza-Kaduce, 1988), and many European countries, including the United Kingdom, now have such offences (Cooke, 1991). In Australia, the commonwealth and most states have also moved to this position (Hughes, 1991).

In this context, we must ask whether this incursion is an attempt to circumvent the problem surrounding the application of property offences by striking directly at the means of misappropriation. Producers might seek to keep the enhanced information exclusive and inviolate by proscribing interference with the new housing for that information. In an interpretation of the United States experience, Michalowski and Pfuhl (1991) argue that the new laws are an attempt to incorporate within the established discourse of property a new form of value which is to be found in computer-resident information. It is not likely that this legislative push is concerned only with economic interests. Michalowski and Pfuhl suggest that the novelty of the technology creates a threat to the control of information systems, as they represent sources of power and authority in contemporary society. They cite the example of military systems. We can also see these concerns expressed in the recent controls placed on the export of advanced technology to certain proscribed countries under COCOM (MacDonald, 1990).

## CONCLUSIONS

In many respects the appropriability of information must read like a guide through the musings of various thoughtful judges. It lacks the high-powered cut and thrust of recent struggles over the reach of the patents and copyright regimes. However, the seeming formlessness of the common law conceals a vital issue. Appropriation of information implicates a far broader and functionally more important resource than the subjects of patents and copyright. The response to claims for legal command over information remains unsettled. The protection of confidences has developed strongly over the last century, especially in recent years. It threatens to break down boundaries and to extend the law's embrace to certain kinds of economically sensitive information *per se*, most notably in the crystallization of the idea of 'trade secrets', which are, after all, directly protected in some jurisdictions outside Australia. But the Australian law hesitates on the brink; the extension of redress to catch the third person stranger is the most characteristic reservation about property rights in the present policy of the law.

Opponents find comfort in the view that the very nature of information militates against the capture and coordination of such a vital resource. Information is slippery stuff. It proves difficult to transfix, contain and rely upon as a means of economic advantage.

Perhaps inarticulately, the present law is a realistic recognition of this limitation, especially in its disinclination to control the use of information once it has entered the public domain or merged with generalized bodies of knowledge. However would a property right over information at large be enforced? Yet we should not lightly dismiss the impact of the common law. The kinds of technical information which producers seek to keep close can often satisfy the law's requirements. The preparedness to litigate attests to that fact. It is more the outer limits of the law which one must set against the most intense apprehensions about the commodification of information.

The nature of the legal system is also a limitation upon appropriation. The fact that protection has been left to the incremental and decentralized decision-making of the ordinary courts undermines the effectiveness of information capture. The judicial process has its staunch adherents, especially among academic lawyers and equity barristers, revealing evidence of a self-confident and possibly self-referential legal culture. The equitable principles of good faith and their kin are roundly praised for their flexibility and pragmatism (Kearney, 1985). We should note that equity has been enjoying quite a resurgence within the consciousness of the law-making judges (Finn, 1989). Its standards of honour and chivalry are said to be tempering the consequences of the free market, where those with superior resources are able to strike and enforce hard bargains. One cannot but admire the desire of equity's erudite champions to see it as a brake on the domineering demands of economic rationalism. However, in terms of impact, it is hard to see after the experience of the eighties that its standards of procedural conduct are robust enough to control the contemporary marketplace. In focusing on the micro-morality of face-to-face transactions, these standards display a tendency to beg the important questions. For example, we might ask why it should be characterized as a matter of fidelity or loyalty that an employee not be able to use in a competitive way the information which the employer has claimed for her- or himself as a 'confidence' – information that the employee might well have had a large hand in generating. Such standards can after all be invested with all sorts of moral meanings, depending upon the standpoint of the judge (Lucke, 1987).

Indeed, the standards tend to nibble at the edges of the grand and powerful sweep of economic life, when we are faced with substantive decisions to make about the basic market structures which so condition the course of individual transactions and determine the distribution of vital economic resources. In particular, we might inquire about the grounds, as a matter of policy, on which any group should have the benefit of property or property-like power over information, even if their exercise of this power is tempered by some regard for others. The courts, after all, are also contributing to the construction of that property power. Specifically, we might ask here whether innovation is served by advancing property rights over information.

These questions point up the policy-making limitations of this area of law, the *ad hoc* and even erratic decisions which must congeal in an intelligible legal doctrine. Recently, Hunt (1978) noted that the English common law in some respects constituted an exception to Max Weber's observation that the substantive purposive rationality of capitalism was complemented by the logically formal rationality of modern legal thought. It is conceded that equity's ascendance will involve some diminution in the level of general certainty and finality to be associated with commercial dealings (Finn, 1989). Therefore, it is surprising, perhaps, that there has not been greater pressure to settle the operation of legal protection for interests in information, presumably by way of legislative intervention to create a statutory scheme. Among its effects, the uncertain state of the law can be exploited tactically by resourceful players (Hammond, 1981). How often can employees and small firms contest trade secrets litigation by large companies, even if ultimately the court might have decided in their favour?

If the lack of legislative intervention is a deliberate abstention, it may represent a view that the common law has little impact on the economy in general and innovation in particular. It relies on the elusive nature of information to check the dangers of appropriation. But the thrust of the law, especially the stress on confidentiality, can run counter to the kind of information sharing and clustering that is now seen as vital to effective participation in the high technology world. The common law category threatens to 'end run', even to cut across, the more finely tuned statutory regimes of patents and copyrights (Hammond, 1990).

As the OECD experts counselled, a more purposive approach is desirable (OECD, 1986a). There are growing signs of rationalization now. Trade secrets legislation has been instituted in some parts of the United States and Western Europe. Trade secrets protection has not formed a natural part of the international intellectual property agenda, but it now joins the United States TRIPs proposals at GATT, as trade secrets are exposed to foreign firms that are in a position to capitalize on them. But we have seen that this legislation still fails to make any more concession to the interest in innovation diffusion than does the common law. The collateral push of the criminal law into the protection of information-bearing technology seems even less apprised of the dangers of exclusivity. It also underscores the crucial point that information equity will depend as much upon access to (to use an old fashioned term) the means of production of information. That access goes beyond that to mere machines, to encompass access to educational and cultural opportunities.

Yet, in closing, we should acknowledge some practical limitations on appropriation. It is true that, in certain ways, such information is already treated as if it were property. It is often the subject of trade in know-how agreements and purchased as part of the assets of a business. But it remains the case that confidential information is most likely to survive in those close working relationships in which the information can be kept in-house and access to it limited. Nor can this law readily afford command over the kind of cumulative, inchoate know-how which is difficult to isolate as the subject of a discrete, identifiable holding – this characteristic has complicated the courts' task of demarcating the trade secrets to which the employer lays claim from the employee's general knowledge and skill. In other words, unless the interest can become one which is truly maintainable against all the world, then perhaps the hold over information remains a contractual or otherwise relational rather than a property form of assurance. It assumes its greatest practical significance when it is combined with the effort to internalize potential competitors and imitators through the media of employment, joint venture or merger arrangements. This conclusion leads us neatly into the following chapters. They are concerned with the policy of competition and foreign investment law on the kinds of restrictions on information-sharing to which untrammelled market forces can lead. While internationalists so eloquently argue the futility of small nation states resisting the embellishments of the new information-bearing technology, we cannot assume that the delivery system favoured by the private market is necessarily going to be a liberating one.

# PART III
*Competition and Trade*

CHAPTER 6

# *Competition Law*

This chapter examines the competition law approach to the strategies employed by producers in the high technology industries to capture the benefits of innovation. It considers first the developments in the content and style of competition policies in the major producer economies of the United States, Europe and Japan. In the light of these developments, it then evaluates the provisions and administration of the Australian trade practices scheme.

In the examination of competition law, we remain with the liberal legal framework for innovation strategies to be pursued in the market and private organizations. Competition law is quintessentially the layer of rule-based regulation applied by the state to the exercise of intellectual property and other kinds of market powers, not to supplant the workings of the market but to make it work better, to live up to its competitive promise. With the scaling down of direct substantive regulation, at least in some sectors, competition law becomes all the more important as a possible counterweight to the private rights which the state also supports. The Chairman of the Australian Trade Practices Commission recently emphasized this point (Commonwealth of Australia. CCH, 1991). Moreover, in the Commonwealth Government's major industry statement of 12 March 1991, 'building a competitive Australia', the Prime Minister stated: 'The Trade Practices Act is our principal legislative weapon to ensure consumers get the best deal from competition' (Commonwealth of Australia. House of Representatives, 1991: 1766).

Yet, competition law itself encounters the strength of the changed configurations and uses of the liberal form we identified in the opening chapter – the concentrations of economic power in industrial networks and integrations, with their instrumental and ideological arguments for size, control and collaboration as means to successful innovation. We must not only consider the responses which develop through the concessions made to existing industry structures in the body of the competition provisions, but also examine the approaches taken to administration and compliance in order to rationalize the conflicting demands made on the schemes and to achieve some realistic return for public policy.

## COMPETITION POLICY GENERALLY

This first section begins with a brief note of the industry structures which set the scene for anti-competitive practices to be pursued effectively. It then considers three significant kinds of restrictive practices in the high technology industries. These practices are: 'stand-alone' companies' use of product differentiation to discourage potential competition, the imposition of restrictions in patent licences on competition by licensees, and the control of competition between producers who combine in research and development consortia. The section examines the policies being adopted towards these practices in the leading producer jurisdictions. It discerns a tendency to depart from a policy of competition *per se*, partly through the use of rule-based exemptions and partly through provision for comparison of the costs and benefits of the practices (including for innovation) at the points of individual exemption and enforcement within the administration of the schemes.

### INDUSTRY STRUCTURES

The structure of many high technology industries reveals significant concentration in the hands of a small number of corporations (Beardon, 1980). While small firms are often the most innovative in the early days of a new technology, as the shape of the technology begins to settle, the demands of innovation mean that a select number of major producers are likely to become dominant. Competitors largely contemplate partial entry, most notably to provide products and services compatible with the core technology (Kutten, 1985). These peripheral firms feed off the major producers and are greatly affected by their innovation and competition strategies. Some such firms have found successful niches in the market, but the major producers press to maintain and extend their positions. They may resort to various practices designed to squeeze the smaller firms out of the market, tie them into dependent contract relationships, or buy them up. While the large corporations can in some respects 'stand alone', the high technologies are still developing at such speed and sophistication that even these corporations must look outside for specialized complementary capacities (Chesnais, 1986). Firms must look beyond their own boundaries to 'strategic partnering' and integration with other firms if they are to obtain and maintain command over complementary assets. Relevant then to innovation are the strategies of vertical and horizontal integration expressed in intellectual property licensing, joint ventures, and mergers.

Software production provides a pertinent example of these practices. An OECD survey (1985a) reported attempts by the large computer hardware manufacturers to marginalize the smaller, independent software houses and drive them from the market. Recently, the manufacturers are said to have employed such anti-competitive practices as supplying software exclusively for their own hardware; resisting attempts to standardize interfaces and to move to open systems and software portability; withholding information about the interface requirements of their new hardware; and embedding the necessary software in their hardware as firmware. At the same time, the manufacturers have been putting more investment into in-house software development, raising the investment threshold for participation in the production of software packages and integrated systems. Where they continue to go outside for development, particularly for applications software, they select particular suppliers and enter into exclusive distribution agreements with them or buy them up. Cooperative research consortia have also been established among these manufacturers. To meet such challenges, the software houses have been involved in a growing number of mergers; in the United States, in particular, software houses with complementary specializations have entered into technological and marketing cooperation agreements. Governments have also been involved, deploying a range of incentives to encourage linkages and organize consortia.

The biotechnology field provides more relevant illustrations. In the United States, where biotechnology commercialization began, development was characterized by the proliferation of small, entrepreneurial, start-up firms. Often these firms were initiated by academics with the support of venture capitalists. The large drug, chemical and food-processing corporations from the United States, Europe and Japan bided their time, but now they are beginning to assert themselves (Wald, 1989). They are undertaking more product development in-house, taking advantage of complementary assets such as production capability, distribution networks, product packages, and their experience with the regulatory systems (Sharp, 1990). They are also contracting out research, taking assignments or licences of intellectual property, and buying up the small firms. Genentech, the most successful of the diagnostic and therapeutic technology firms, was recently bought out by Hoffman-La Roche. Seed, plant and animal breeding companies have been another popular target. The large corporations are also directly commissioning research from public institutions. While few consortia have been formed among the large corporations themselves, governments are active in trying to organize collaboration, especially between public institutions and private firms (Kenney, 1986). Downline, the corporations are strategically licensing their product distributors and users so that they can keep control of the benefits of the innovation – licensing to the farm sector provides a good example of this (Lawrence, 1989; Phillips, 1989).

## AUSTRALIAN IMPACT

The impact of the structure of these industries can differ from nation to nation. Firms in countries such as Australia usually assume a peripheral position, assembling and distributing technology products for foreign producers or providing specialized goods and services in market niches (Commonwealth of Australia. Industries Assistance Commission, 1984). It has been estimated that the overall ratio of technology imports to exports for Australia is around 6:1 (Morris, 1983). The Australian trade deficit for information products was recently put at $4 billion (the *Age*, 8 April 1991). Around 75 per cent of payments for technological know-how are made to overseas companies (Commonwealth of Australia. ASTEC, 1986a). Technology can, of course, be transferred in the form of finished products and turn-key systems. If it is transferred at an earlier stage, it seems that intra-company transfer to local subsidiaries of transnational corporations is favoured over external licensing of indigenous firms; some 77 per cent of payments for imported technology are made in this way (Grant, 1983). Local product development (much of it in the public sector, especially in biotechnology) often ends in outward licensing or joint ventures with foreign firms to scale up for commercialization and to penetrate overseas markets. Local companies have difficulties gaining access to markets in the leading producer nations (Commonwealth of Australia. Bureau of Industry Economics, 1989).

## RECENT THINKING IN COMPETITION POLICY

As we suggested in the opening chapters, the liberal legal forms (such as property, contract, joint venture, partnership and incorporation) play a role in constituting and controlling such high technology practices. Where these practices threaten innovation, instead of adjustment in the body of liberal law itself, concern may be expressed in correcting or compensating legal policies such as competition, investment and trade law. If property, contract and company law are largely indifferent to the use of their facilities in such ways, or cannot be expected to cope with the contradictions of the real business world, a common approach in Western economies is to institute a regulatory scheme for the resulting restrictive trade practices which exploit the liberal form with anti-competitive and possibly anti-innovative effects. Characteristically, such trade practices or anti-trust schemes start by proscribing a number of anti-competitive practices. Some practices, such as exclusive dealing arrangements, price fixing and secondary boycotts, are specifically identified. The schemes may also be concerned with mergers and other practices that can lead to market domination and the subsequent anti-competitive misuses of such market power, for example in the strategic creation of barriers to entry by rival firms.

While the pattern of 'proscribed' trade practices is well settled, the ultimate treatment of them within the regulatory scheme is often ambivalent. Concentrations of resources and measures to secure markets are by no means actively proscribed practices. In part, the ambivalence stems from the conflicting characterizations of many practices as either pro-competitive or anti-competitive. For example, aggressive practices may harm a rival but still be characterizable as a natural part of a vigorous, competitive economy because they merely represent a company making use of its superior resources. Much is said to depend upon the position which the company enjoys in the market (OECD, 1989). So too, competition may not be closed if the market is left to one firm, so long as its position is 'contestable' and entry is possible for rivals. The threat of takeover, or the existence of a market in corporate control, might be as important to efficiency.

In part, the ambivalence stems from the persistent arguments which are made about the superior efficiency of many of these restrictive trade practices. The 'Chicago School' has been influential in recent competition law thinking within the English-speaking countries, several leading protagonists having been made federal court judges in the United States (Corones, 1990). (Japan and the other European countries have never displayed quite the same tradition of anti-trust concern.) These arguments are made in favour of vertical integration, including the licensing of intellectual property, and even in favour of horizontal integration, such as joint ventures and mergers (McCarthy, 1985). The Chicago School has been inclined to argue that a policy of competition *per se* or of competition as a desirable process should give way to the superior goal of economic efficiency and wealth maximization. The concern should not be for the well-being of rival producers but for the impact on the price and availability of goods to the ultimate consumer. It is evident that free markets do not necessarily mean crowded markets.

Not all these reservations about a policy of competition *per se* originate in the Chicago School. Concern for technical innovation, especially of a local variety, can fuel support for qualification. So, for example, it is argued that research and development would be deterred if companies were not confident that the resulting intellectual property could be withheld from competitors or restrictively licensed (OECD, 1989). Exclusive dealing by producers and the tying together of goods and services may be considered necessary to ensure that the technical standards of new products are maintained. Joint ventures are accepted if collaboration and pooling are the price to be paid for the innovation proceeding (OECD, 1986). So too, mergers attract support as a means to achieve efficiencies not only of scale but also of scope, as firms need to combine complementary assets in converging technological fields (Veljanovski, 1987).

In part, such ambivalence may be attributable to an assessment by governments that they cannot otherwise cope with powerful international trends. The structure of the worldwide market has led governments in the larger, leading producer nations to allow, if not promote, cartelization in the high technology areas, so that local industry can match the power of international competitors. In countries such as Australia, this might be as much an acceptance that local industry must work within the structure of dominance of the foreign corporations (Commonwealth of Australia. ASTEC, 1986a). Joint ventures give local firms access to resources and opportunities they would not otherwise enjoy. Technology transfer from overseas would be discouraged if the foreign producers could not control their intellectual property. Mergers may be a necessary rationalization of local industry in the cause of international competitiveness. The value ascribed in much recent innovation policy to the creation of industrial clusters or *filières* also sows seeds of doubt about the undesirability of vertical integration (Marceau, 1990).

Yet it is clear that few of these claims are uncontroversial. Whether practices are viewed as economically beneficial or not, or even procompetitive or not, can vary with the notion of efficiency one wishes to pursue: whether it be allocative or productive efficiency, for example, or static or dynamic efficiency (see, e.g., OECD, 1989). So too, the persistent debate about the relationship between firm size, market structure and technological innovation colours the position adopted on anti-trust measures. One dimension of the debate is the optimum size of the firm for innovation (Scherer, 1980). Interest has also been revitalized recently in the question of the optimum number of firms in the industry (Patel and Pavitt, 1990). Perhaps the only stable feature of the policy field is the existence of competing discourses or theoretical disagreements among the experts in the now copious literature. Intellectual fashions tend to chop and change: the 1990 publication of Michael Porter's book on the competitive advantage of nations inspired greater scepticism in some quarters about the virtues of horizontal integration. Reporting in December 1991 on mergers, monopolies and acquisitions policy, the Australian Senate Standing Committee on Legal and Constitutional Affairs (the Cooney Committee) was to remark (Commonwealth of Australia. 1991: 48):

> The economic evidence that mergers actually yield productive efficiencies remains equivocal. Nor is it clear that such efficiencies as have occurred have in fact improved the international competitiveness of Australian firms, or resulted in demonstrable benefits to consumers. A growing body of economic theory now suggests that international competitiveness, both in large and small nations, is achieved not by encouraging industry leaders to merge, but by encouraging them to compete.

In such a volatile intellectual climate, is competition law likely to represent an example of the liberal approach, with a regime of clear proscriptive rules and their general invocation against unwonted practices? Generalized, rule-based anti-trust proscriptions might appear in such an environment too unsubtle an approach to achieve the desired mix between competition and efficiency, say, or innovation. Other policy concerns are accommodated through changes to the proscriptions in the body of the law, but, also and importantly, by procedures for the exemption and authorization of anti-competitive practices on cost-benefit grounds. It has also been facilitated by the exercise of discretion at the enforcement stage over priorities for action among the categories of offences and the kind of action to be taken against offenders. These schemes develop a fascinating administrative lore of guidelines for producers (including lists of black, grey and white practices) concerning legal interpretations and cost-benefit criteria, voluntary codes of conduct, case-by-case exemptions or clearances, letters of comfort, declarations of administrative objectives and priorities, negotiated compliances and strategic enforcements. An acknowledgement of the kinds of arguments we have just mentioned increases the cognitive load and the value controversy with which the schemes must cope. How easy is it in constructing a competition policy to predict the restrictive impact of different kinds of practices, let alone to project their economic and social consequences? So much can turn on the particular circumstances, which leads Hopt (1987) to remark acutely that, like moving targets, the practices remove themselves from a well-ordered application of the law. There is pressure to contextualize the administration of the law and tailor enforcement to the merits of the individual case (OECD, 1989).

Yet, in noting this tendency, we should not lose sight of the overall trajectory of competition law. On a longer view, competition law represents a gradual expansion in regulation, a 'juridification' of business practices. In its concerns, it has moved from the prescription of specific market conduct rules to the control of market power and the scrutiny of market structure through merger provisions. It has shown growth in other ways too. It is extending its coverage into additional areas as wide-ranging as the licensing of know-how, dealings inside corporate groups, the privatized sectors, and trade across national boundaries. Its standards are being adopted in more countries as they seek to emulate the Western market economy model. For example, competition law provisions are becoming a condition of association with the EC (Horowitz, 1991).

The United States has made demands of Japan, most recently as part of the 'structural impediments initiative', that it strengthen its competition laws and apply them more vigorously (the *Age*, 8 April 1991). One concern has been, as the EC has also recently recognized in its own jurisdiction, that the discretionary deployment of the law does not discriminate against foreign firms seeking to enter the domestic market.

Competition law is also receiving a boost at the international level, most notably in the influential committees and directorates of the OECD. Efforts are being made to harmonize national schemes, beginning with provision for coordination of responses between countries as business practices such as mergers reach beyond territorial jurisdictions. One unifying theme is the idea that governments should seek to employ the provisions of general competition policy to deal with the unfair trading practices of foreign competitors and move away from the use of specific regulatory devices and retaliatory measures aimed at foreign trade and investment as such (OECD, 1984).

In the body of the law also, while one possible response to the complexity is to increase the room to move at the administrative level, another is to limit the inquiry by insisting on adherence to rules. We can see that the openings for the authorities are still circumscribed by the specifications in the legislation of the kinds of conduct that can be pursued and the grounds on which exemptions and authorizations can be made. Even some of the recent departures from a policy of competition *per se* have been in the form of rule-based categorical exemptions. In addition, the authorities perennially come under pressure to declare and regularize their administrative policies, for example through the publication of guidelines. They may also be required to open their proceedings to public scrutiny. Overall, this approach provides both the administering authorities and the regulated industries with a modicum of certainty about the legal consequences of the practices in question (Clarke, 1989). Concern is expressed, in a tactful way, about the use of competition provisions and the intrusion of political considerations into decisions on whether to investigate or prosecute.

Equally, a response to the difficulties of enforcement faced by the schemes may be to raise the penalties for non-compliance, increase the agencies' powers and vote them additional resources. Furthermore, in some jurisdictions, such as the United States and Australia, a placatory approach by the authorities can be counteracted by aggrieved private parties taking action in the courts on the breaches themselves. In the United States, anti-trust litigation has been an important strategy for competitors in the computer and telecommunications markets (see now the *Age*, 18 February 1992).

### STAND-ALONE TACTICS

Let us now examine the play between the approaches by looking at responses to three common kinds of anti-competitive practices in the high technology industries. Before turning to Australia, we shall look at the trends in three systems, those of the United States, the EC and Japan. Each system has a different way 'in' to the eventual decision on how to treat the individual instance of anti-competitive conduct. The United States system is the oldest and purest of the anti-trust schemes. The approach of the legislation (the Sherman Act) is to proscribe certain practices as anti-competitive *per se*. But the authorities (the Federal Trade Commission, the Department of Justice and the courts) have found room within the proscriptions for the operation of a 'rule of reason'. Practices will not be regarded as contraventions unless they unreasonably restrain competition. This reading permits the authorities some scope to vary their attitudes to different practices. They also vary in the processes by which they examine individual cases, the United States being on the whole the most open and judicial-like in its approach (Hawk, 1988). The EC legislation (articles 85 and 86 of the Treaty) again proscribes certain practices as anti-competitive *per se*, but block exemptions have been legislated for some versions of these practices, and, in addition, the European Commission is empowered to grant exemption for individual instances according to a public benefit test. In Japan, the anti-monopoly legislation is modelled on the United States provisions, however exemptions have been established by subsequent legislation, and the administering agency, the Fair Trade Commission, may also grant individual exemptions.

Firms strong enough to stand alone in the market can employ their technological leadership and other advantages to pursue practices which keep innovations in-house, inhibit market entry by competitors and lock in customers (Parry, 1984). The most graphic examples in this field are provided by the practices of the computer giant, IBM. In particular, the United States government, and some of IBM's competitors at the time, alleged that IBM adopted the practice of 'bundling' its technology, a practice which made it difficult for other producer firms such as plug-compatible producers to compete (Soma, 1976). IBM, for instance, tied the sale of its mainframe hardware, which occupied a central place in the market, to the sale of its software and peripheral equipment, either directly or through price discounting. Bundling or packaging has also been tried by other major companies, such as Data General in the mini-computer area and Apple in the micro-computer field.

For a variety of reasons, including the anti-trust suits it encountered in the fifties and sixties, IBM largely unbundled (Soma, 1983). More recently, IBM has been accused of employing other strategies to exploit its central position, such as foreshadowing new models to 'knock' customers off alternative hardware producers, and unilateral changes in product specifications, particularly interfaces, to frustrate peripheral producers (Sorbel, 1981). The role of interface differentiation in the information technology industries is a notably ambiguous one. While standardization, certainly in the early stages of the development of the technology, carries certain risks, industry-wide standards that facilitate open systems and ready connectivity provide greater options for users and hence greater opportunities for competitors. With the rapid development of new computer products and the convergence of computer and communications technologies, the compatibility and connectivity of the different elements of an information-processing system have become key considerations for users. It is now one of the major concerns in the information and communications sectors (Ferne, 1990). Of concern then may be the technical specifications for interfaces and exchanges between (for instance) mainframes and peripherals; mainframes and distributed processors such as mini and micro-computers; hardware and software; systems and applications software; and computers and communication controllers.

## PRODUCT DIFFERENTIATION

On the other hand, the use of proprietary 'standards' generates continued uncertainty about the further compatibility of different products and encourages conservatism in the market (Delamarter, 1988). IBM has recently experienced pressure to standardize its interfaces, both within its own product lines and with the product lines of its competitors. In the case of software compatibility, it has responded with the development of a proprietary standard called systems application architecture (SAA). This standard differs from the semi-open Unix industry standard for software portability, which is being promoted by other producers in the Unix International group, and IBM has been involved in organizing another industry group, the Open Software Foundation, to promote a different version of Unix (the *Age*, 10 May 1990). Other versions have also been developed.

Outside the United States, competition law has had some impact on these strategies (Wilson, Ashton and Egan, 1980). Anti-trust litigation has been brought with the aim of compelling companies to provide information about core technology and, in some cases, to license it out non-exclusively at reasonable charges after allowing the companies a period of time to recover their investment. Orders have been made to release the technology in order that other firms can enter the market by producing peripherals or developing enhancements. In the kind of negotiated settlement of anti-trust violations which has become common, IBM agreed with the European Commission in 1984 to release, in a timely fashion, adequate information about both its hardware–software interfaces and its systems network architecture (SNA) – the connections between hardware in distributed systems – so that its competitors could be in a realistic position to market plug–compatible equipment. It also undertook to endeavour to match its systems network architecture with the open standard for network connectivity, OSI (Raines, 1985).

However, the product differentiation issue is by no means dead. In part, the approach of the regulatory authorities is complicated by the fact that, without special exemptions, industry collaboration on product standards may itself run foul of the competition requirements (Vollmer, 1986). In any case, the EC agreement has to be counterbalanced with the Reagan government's unconditional withdrawal in 1982 of the thirteen-year-long anti-trust suit against IBM in the United States. Much of the progress on standards is likely to come from pressure from producers and users (including government consumers) in the market. But competition law could contribute to the creation of conducive market conditions. For example, in return for its requirement that AT&T divest its holdings in the telecommunications market, the 1982 anti-trust consent decree gave it the go-ahead to enter the computers market. AT&T is now a driving force behind the System V Unix International standard.

## LICENSING PRACTICES

We have suggested that the core producers are not always strong enough to stand alone, and that the demands of innovation in the high technology industries are encouraging various forms of licensing and collaborative practices (Chesnais, 1986). But where such corporations do establish links with other producers, restrictions may be imposed on competitive innovation. The large core producers can often deploy intellectual property rights to constrain potential competitors (Pengilley, 1977). The power of intellectual property can be employed, not only in stand-alone tactics but also within technology transfers to subsidiaries, exclusive licensing agreements with outsiders, pooling in consortia and joint ventures, and acquisition and merger bids. Core producers practise strategic transfer policies controlling the degree, timing, and conditions of release of technology to their local subsidiaries and licensees (Gee, 1981). If licenses to inspect and exploit the technology are granted by the core producers, they may be confined to exclusive licences for local subsidiaries (Long, 1981). Licences to outsiders might also involve several kinds of restrictions. The licensing policies have an impact not only upon the accessibility, appropriateness and price of the technology which becomes available for use, but also upon the opportunities for local innovation in research, development, enhancement and commercialization.

## IN-HOUSE TRANSFERS

While external licensing might be increasing, the predominant form of technology transfer is still through local subsidiaries (Johnston, 1983). Keeping the technology in-house provides the producer with reassurances about control of the technology and thus encourages the producer to transfer the technology overseas. But it can involve local restrictions on competitive innovation. Because these internal innovation policies are not systematically screened, information is incomplete. One concern, nonetheless, is the impact on the diffusion of technology to the host country. Among the allegations against the core companies is the charge that prices paid by local subsidiaries for the technology may be inflated so that profits can be repatriated home. Furthermore, while there is some evidence that the lag is declining with shorter product cycles, the speed of transfer to local subsidiaries has been questionable; new technology is generally first released onto the company's home market. The restrictions of opportunities for local innovation can be more direct. Internal policies may inhibit the ability of the subsidiary to engage in competition with the parent company. For example, the local subsidiary can be denied a 'product mandate', including the ability to develop and market improvements which compete with the parent company's own products (Morris, 1983). Certainly, it appears that the levels of research and development in subsidiaries of transnational corporations are no more than average, despite their resources, and that most of their research and development is devoted to adapting technology to local conditions (Lewis and Mangan, 1987).

## EXTERNAL LICENSING

External licenses can also contain restrictions on competitive innovation by the licensees. Studies have noted such restrictions in technology transfer agreements by foreign companies licensing local firms in Australia (Mandeville, 1982). Consolidating this information, the Australian Science and Technology Council (ASTEC) cited figures for the important engineering sector. According to ASTEC (Commonwealth of Australia, 1986a: 25), the evidence revealed the presence of conditions on licensees: (1) not to make similar products for specified periods (36 per cent); (2) not to modify products and to observe quality control (35 per cent); (3) not to dispute patents (32 per cent); (4) not to export from Australia (30 per cent); (5) to restrict their market to parts of Australia (24 per cent); (6) to limit the quantity or output produced under licence (22 per cent); (7) to purchase certain parts or tools from the licensor (18 per cent); and (8) to sell the product produced under licence at a price specified in the agreement (13 per cent). Generally speaking, other common restrictions can include limitations on competitive research and development by the licensee and the requirement that licensees grant back intellectual property to any further inventions and know-how.

## PATENT LICENCES

The traditional approach to these restrictions has been to accept the presence of intellectual property as a limited monopoly within the framework of competition policy and to except from the operation of competition requirements certain restrictions imposed upon the transfer of the intellectual property. Such an approach has not, however, afforded a blanket exemption from the operation of the competition provisions to the various uses of intellectual property power (such as patents). Restrictive practices have generally been allowed to the extent that they are necessary to safeguard the subject matter of the intellectual property, an example being technical requirements imposed by the licensor in order to protect the quality of the product made by the licensee. But other restrictions may be regarded by the authorities, to use the example of the intellectual property of most interest to competition authorities, as improper attempts to extend the patent's reach and use it as part of a general anti-competitive strategy. The conventional formula is to allow the restrictive arrangements, provided they fall within the 'scope of the patent' (Venit, 1987). Of course, the restrictions that fall on either side of such a line are not necessarily easy to identify. Moreover, it is possible to argue that the benefits which flow from the intellectual property and its safeguards outweigh the anti-competitive costs of the restrictive arrangements.

## UNITED STATES POLICY

In the seventies, in the key jurisdiction of the United States, the Department of Justice sought to ameliorate these issues by ordering its policy according to 'guidelines' which indicated to industry its view of the practices which would fall either inside or outside the scope of the patent. The list of nine unacceptable practices included tie-ins, grant-backs, compulsory package licensing, and the charging of unreasonable royalties. However, in the eighties, commentators detected a further shift in the policy of the authorities (Ewing, 1982). For example, in an article wistfully linking the study of patent licensing with windsurfing (actually the name of a legal case), Venit (1987) suggests that the authorities appear to be relaxing their traditional distrust of the patent power and emphasizing its value as a support for the necessary commercialization of inventions. Grant-backs and cross-licensing arrangements were among the practices receiving more sympathetic treatment. Overall, as evidenced by the 1988 Department of Justice Antitrust Enforcement Guidelines for International Operations, the authorities are moving away from a *per se* approach to the treatment of various licensing arrangements and a focus on the 'scope of the patent' towards the 'rule of reason' approach which discriminates between kinds of restrictions, particularly on the basis of whether the economic benefits outweigh the costs of the anti-competitive conditions (Davidow, 1989). (It is perhaps poetic licence to call this a 'rule' of reason, given the kinds of judgements which must be made. But it is one based on a reading of the anti-trust sections, for the United States legislation does not provide for individual exemptions or authorizations at the administrative level.)

## EC POLICY

In the then European Economic Community, the authorities had sought to settle the status of licensing arrangements with the 1984 passing of a regulation that listed restrictions deemed either to come or not to come within the scope of a patent (Korah, 1985). The blacklist included no-challenge clauses, non-competition clauses, quantity and customer restrictions, exclusive grant-backs by the licensee of new or improvement patents, and unwanted product tie-ins that were not necessary to the technically correct exploitation of the licensed invention. The white list included tying requirements to ensure technical standards, field of use restrictions, confidentiality conditions, restrictions on sub-licensing, and the disclosure and non-exclusive licensing back of new or improved patents.

These regulations suggest a leaning away from a policy of competition *per se* that seems consistent with the European Commission's general approach of using competition policy to promote the higher goals of EC industry and technological development. That they still represent a rule-based approach, it has been suggested, may be partly because the administering agency, the European Commission, has lacked the resources to process a large number of individual applications for exemptions on their merits (Corones, 1990). The EC has also provided block exemptions for other kinds of restrictive arrangements, such as know-how agreements (Winn, 1990). Latterly, commentators have detected a further softening of attitude towards patent licences, especially to territorially limited licences, as the European Commission becomes aware that an overly strict approach to technology transfer arrangements may have a negative net effect on the competitiveness of European industry (Venit, 1987). Recent individualized decisions seem to bear this reading out – an example being the favourable view taken by the commission of the collaboration and licensing agreements between Fujitsu and ICL in the field of computer components (European Commission, 1988).

## JAPANESE POLICY

In Japan, traditionally, much of the concern has been with the conditions on which foreigners transfer technology to the local market, but in 1989 guidelines were developed within its competition law framework to regulate generally unfair practices with respect to patent and know-how licensing agreements (Abell, 1990). The guidelines identify in considerable detail instances of black, grey and white clauses. The six black clauses include restrictions on research and development by the licensee him- or herself or jointly with a third person in relation to the licensed patent or its competing technology, as well as requirements to grant back exclusively improved or applied inventions. The twelve grey clauses include know-how grant-backs, tying requirements, no-challenge conditions, and restrictions on export by the licensee (with some exceptions). The seventeen white clauses include disclosure of know-how gained by the licensee, the granting of non-exclusive licences for improvements and applications, quality control requirements, best efforts requirements to exploit the licensed patent, and duties of confidentiality regarding secret know-how. The administering agency, the Fair Trade Commission, offers further guidance regarding the status of individual clauses within an informal clearance system.

## RESEARCH AND DEVELOPMENT CONSORTIA

Our earlier remarks noted the fact that even the large companies in the computer and biotechnology fields are looking outside for specialized complementary capacities. Of course, part of this strategy is the familiar drive to secure supplies and outlets by vertical integration. The companies are also involved in horizontal integration as they endeavour to acquire specialized, creative expertise in converging fields by buying into small firms. But the technology is often of such a range and complexity that the large companies also seek to combine resources in quasi-integrative research and development consortia.

While these relationships may make more efficient use of resources, they can also restrict access to and exploitation of the resulting innovation, especially as they involve the larger companies and the core technologies. Such ventures often involve the pooling or cross licensing of intellectual property. The terms of these ventures may reduce competition between the venturers, also promoting the parties' overall domination of the market by restricting the diffusion of the innovations to those outside the venture (OECD, 1986).

Such relationships can also have a differential impact on an international scale. Chesnais suggests that technology exchanges

> principally take place between firms of similar technological sophistication, possibly as part of loosely knit international oligopolies. Unless they offer very specialized and unique assets, small firms experience great difficulty in becoming parties and more generally in gaining access to licences. (Chesnais, 1986: 107)

Recently, ASTEC expressed concern that moves to intensify research and development collaboration between independent and often competing firms might have a significant impact on the free availability of technology. Furthermore, it was concerned about the consequences of the cooperative research and development programs which governments were sponsoring in the major economies (for example, the Strategic Defence Initiative of the United States and the Eureka project in the European Community) (ASTEC, 1986a).

## UNITED STATES POLICY

The anti-competitive implications of such ventures have not prevented the authorities from giving support to them in recent years. In 1984, the United States Congress modified its relatively pure anti-trust regime by enacting the National Cooperative Research Act and providing some relief for research and development joint ventures. The Act provides that research and development joint ventures which meet certain qualifying criteria shall not be considered anti-competitive *per se* but will be subject to scrutiny according to the rule of reason, looking to efficiencies such as economies of scale, risk spreading, and the benefits of research and licensing (McDonald, 1988). In addition, notification of such agreements to the Federal Trade Commission and the Department of Justice frees the agreements from judicial review on the government's initiative, exposing them only to private suit for the actual economic loss suffered by competitors and others, rather than punitive damages at three times the actual loss. Notable early products of this approach were the Semiconductor Research Corporation and the Microelectronics and Computer Technology Corporation (Arnold and Guy, 1986).

Essentially, the agreements qualify for exemption if they do not involve production, marketing or unnecessary ancillary restraints, and if they do not function as collusive devices (McInerney, 1987). Thus, the legislation seeks to maintain the distinction between pre-competitive research and production or marketing cartels, but the challenge from the Japanese, especially in the semiconductor market, is moving some to support local production consortia as well. Interestingly though, amendments to allow exemption of joint production consortia have met with resistance in Congress.

## EC POLICY

In 1984, the European Commission introduced a regulation that provides a block exemption from anti-trust scrutiny for defined research and development joint ventures (Frazer, 1987). Such ventures are ventures amongst competitors holding a combined share of less than 20 per cent of the relevant market, provided that these ventures do not involve certain blacklisted restrictions on competition, such as agreements curbing independent research by the venturers in fields unconnected with the joint venture research (Korah, 1988). Joint ventures which do not qualify under the block exemption provision may still seek individual exemption after notification to the commission.

The EC's legislative framework allows for exemption of restrictive agreements if they contribute to improving the production or distribution of goods or to promoting technical or economic progress, while allowing consumers a fair share of the resulting benefits. They should also not impose on the parties restrictions that are not indispensable to the attainment of the agreement's objectives or which afford them the possibility of eliminating competition in respect of a substantial part of the products in question. In applying this formula, a number of factors have been seen to contribute to the efficacy of joint ventures in promoting technical progress, such as economies of scale, increased production and profit, rationalization, risk sharing (for instance in research and development) and improved supply (Claydon, 1986).

EC competition policy is generally subjected to the higher goal of integrating and improving the member countries' smaller economies. In particular, competition policy may be attuned to overcoming the obstacles local firms face from regional fragmentation of markets and from small firm size in pursuing high technology innovation strategies. While reducing competition between European firms, joint ventures may strengthen the position of EC business against the power of large competitors from non-Community countries such as the United States and Japan.

In a recent review of European Commission decisions on joint ventures, Claydon (1986) finds that enhanced development of a new area of high technology has been considered a good ground on which to exempt individual joint ventures. Claydon takes the view that the commission has tended to overlook the long-term anti-competitive effects of such ventures in its desire to stimulate high technology development amongst EC firms, especially in oligopolist markets. Commonly these joint venture agreements contain clauses regulating the use of intellectual property and know-how, and Claydon feels that the European Commission should consider more strictly how necessary to the success of these ventures the intellectual property restrictions are. It is worth noting that in 1992 the European Commission issued fresh draft guidelines on cooperative joint ventures which extended the potential for exemptions (the *Australian*, 6 May 1992).

## JAPANESE POLICY

Such developments bring competition policy towards consortia in the large Western economies closer to the position of Japan. Japan has a familiar set of anti-trust and unfair trade practices provisions, enacted at the insistence of the American authorities at the end of the war. Its anti-monopoly law has, however, not been considered an obstacle to the realization of concerted industrial policies by government bureaucracies such as MITI acting in concert with major corporations. Not only is there allowance in the anti-monopoly law itself for exemptions to be granted by the administering authority, the Fair Trade Commission, but in recent years the enactment of bypassing statutes to authorize restructuring in specific industries has strengthened the hand of agencies like MITI (Yoshikawa, 1983).

In addition, these agencies use the informal contacts and administrative guidance for which Japanese industrial policy is renowned to promote capital investment coordination and production rationalization. A pertinent example is the formation of the Japanese Electric Computer Corporation in the seventies. While there is some question about the strict legal capacity of these industry agencies acting administratively to order consortia and cartels and override the anti-monopoly law, the practice of consulting and incorporating key corporations in the policy formulation process, combined with threats to withdraw government favours if they do not coooperate, often means that the 'guidance' encounters little objection (Upham, 1987).

## THE AUSTRALIAN TRADE PRACTICES LAW

This section examines the legislative and administrative policy of the Australian trade practices scheme. As the Australian legislation has not directly addressed practices in the high technology industries, we must also consider its application somewhat in terms of its own categories. The section considers the categories dealing with the presence of exclusionary arrangements, the misuse of market power and market-dominating mergers. It notes the interpretation of these legislative provisions as they bear on the relevant practices. It also notes the exemptions in the body of the legislation for certain kinds of relevant conduct, such as intellectual property related conduct. It considers the policy of the administrative agency (the Trade Practices Commission) in the light of the provision for authorization of anti-competitive practices and the exercise of discretion over enforcement. In particular, it considers the extent to which policy is attuned to the promotion of innovation.

The trade practices legislation was first enacted by the Commonwealth Parliament only in 1965. As Professor Brunt (1986) points out, the initial Act was tentative and experimental. The first comprehensive piece of legislation, the *Trade Practices Act*, was enacted in 1974 by the then Labor government. The object of this Act was to promote and regulate competition between business firms. Surviving essentially today, the Act is concerned with the protection of consumers as well as the control of anti-competitive business practices (see also Hopkins, 1978). Part Four of the Act reflects elements of both the United States and EC models. Most practices are only proscribed if they display an anti-competitive purpose or effect in the particular instance. Some kinds of anti-competitive conduct receive special exemption in the Act itself. In addition, the Trade Practices Commission (TPC) is empowered to 'authorize' many of the proscribed practices on a case-by-case basis, using a public benefit test like that of the European Commission. The TPC is a specialist agency established by the Act to administer and enforce the provisions. Its authorization decisions are subject to appeal to the Trade Practices Tribunal, a body made up of judges and experts such as economists. Pecuniary penalties and other coercive remedies for contravention are within the jurisdiction of the Federal Court and other courts.

### EXCLUSIVE DEALING AND RELATED PRACTICES

To begin with the most specific provisions of the legislation, section 47 contains proscriptions against exclusive dealing. Essentially, the practice of exclusive dealing for the purposes of the Act involves agreements to engage in exclusive dealing and refusals to deal with those who will not agree to engage in exclusive dealing (CCH, 1991). The types of exclusive dealings which are covered by the provisions include solace and requirements contracts. Such contracts confine distributors to the goods and services of a particular supplier and prohibit them from dealing with the supplier's competitors. They also include contracts that restrict distributors from resupplying the goods and services in certain markets defined by place or person, that is with territorial or customer restrictions. Also covered are tying practices, where customers may only obtain certain goods or services if they agree also to take other specified goods or services from the same supplier.

The practices caught by section 47 are not prohibited unless the conduct has the purpose or the effect of substantially lessening competition in a relevant market. An exception to this qualification is made in the case of a practice called 'third line forcing', which is illegal *per se*. The prohibition against exclusive dealing does not apply, however, to any conduct engaged in by a body corporate by way of restricting dealings with another body corporate if those bodies corporate are related to each other. This prohibition would appear to exclude to some extent the regulation of intra-group activities, such as in the internal allocation policies of the transnational corporations (OECD, 1986).

Section 47 is backed by a broad section 45 that proscribes contracts, arrangements and understandings containing an exclusionary provision or a provision which has the purpose or would have the effect of substantially lessening competition. Exclusionary provisions are defined in section 4D of the Act as provisions made between competitors for the purpose of preventing, restricting or limiting the supply or acquisition of goods or services from particular persons. Subsequent specific provisions proscribe practices like price-fixing arrangements (including resale price maintenance) and collective or secondary boycotts. Again, an exception is made to these provisions in the case of related bodies corporate.

## Commission Policy

Have these provisions application to practices in the high technology industries? It might be expected that the provisions of section 47 would deter the most extreme of the early bundling and tying practices in the high technology industries. Such practices are not unknown (see Gaze, 1989). There have been very few judicial decisions concerning exclusive dealing in Australia. It seems that the Trade Practices Commission authorizes various kinds of exclusive dealing arrangements each year (Commonwealth of Australia. TPC, 1985). Exclusive dealing practices can also be notified to the TPC and obtain exemption from the Act unless the commission makes a positive determination that this should not be the case. This procedure places the onus on the commission to take objection to the practices. The Act provides that the test for authorization (as for a determination) is whether the conduct results in a public benefit that outweighs any public detriment constituted by the lessening of competition.

Recently, the Trade Practices Commission has targeted these kinds of practices in the computer hardware retail market, saying at one point that breaches of the Act were rampant (TPC Bulletin, 1990). Hardware producers are concerned to control distribution outlets for their products and to discourage what is called grey marketing – or parallel importing. Allied attempts at resale price maintenance have also been pursued by the commission. At the same time, the commission has taken action (under other provisions) against retailers who engage in the practice of 'passing off' hardware as brand name products and in other misleading or deceptive retailing practices (CCH, 1991). While this intervention is important to ordinary consumers, it really is at the end of the line regarding product innovation.

The scope of sections 45 and the subsequent provisions in section 45A–45E are potentially wide-ranging. They could call into question a number of the anti-competitive practices noted in the high technology areas, such as restrictive licence conditions, cross-licensing, joint ventures, product standardization agreements and market sharing arrangements (Pengilley, 1980). For example, joint ventures might seem a likely candidate for attention under section 45, but the TPC has adopted a generally favourable attitude to them (Corones, 1990). No joint ventures have been taken to court. Joint ventures have received authorizations from the commission. The Act provides that arrangements that substantially lessen competition or contain exclusionary clauses may be authorized by the commission. The arrangements may be authorized if the commission is satisfied that the public benefits will outweigh the detriment to the public constituted by the lessening of competition. The exclusionary provisions may be authorized if the conduct results in such a benefit to the public that it should be allowed to take place.

## THE MISUSE OF MARKET POWER

Perhaps a more germane provision is the one dealing with misuse of market power: section 46. It provides that a corporation that has a substantial degree of power in a market for goods or services shall not take advantage of that power for the purposes of: (a) eliminating or substantially damaging its competitor or the competitor of a related body corporate; (b) preventing the entry of a person into any market; or (c) deterring or preventing competitive conduct in any market.

The misuse of market power provision is aimed at the exploitation of existing market power rather than the attainment of market power by restrictive practices; it is limited to concern with corporations which already have market power. This concern is particularly pertinent to the high technology fields.

### Markets

The definition of the relevant market is crucial to the identification of such corporations. The more narrowly the market is defined, the more likely a substantial degree of power resides in a particular corporation. In the United States, the definition of the market has presented problems in the high technology fields where corporations occupy central positions but there are different functional products. The product market increases with the range of products which are competitive or substitutable. In the computer field, for example, the law must then determine the extent to which hardware, software, peripherals and so on form the same markets. Indeed, given the central position occupied by the technology of companies such as IBM, it has been argued that brand name markets are formed for certain products (Soma, 1983). The convergence between computer and telecommunications technology muddies the waters still further (Janisch and Irwin, 1982). It has been suggested, for instance, that this convergence has already rendered obsolete the lines of competition drawn in the 1982 consent decree that saw the telecommunications giant AT&T broken up into separate companies, but allowed entry at the same time to the computer market.

Markets may also be defined geographically. For the purposes of the Trade Practices Act, 'markets' means markets in Australia and not overseas, but they may be more limited than the national market.

## Market Power

The measure of a substantial degree of market power is also crucial to the identification of such corporations. As a result of an amendment to the Act in 1986, the current test no longer requires a corporation to control or dominate a market (Corones, 1987). Oligopolist companies as well as monopolies are thus within the scope of section 46. The test requires the Trade Practices Commission to consider the extent to which the corporation can free itself from the discipline of the market (the constraints of competitors, suppliers and customers) in determining its production and distribution policies. Hence, such factors as the number and size of competitors, especially their market shares, the height of barriers to entry by new firms, and the degree of vertical integration are relevant to the identification of market power (TPC, 1990). Barriers to entry can include capital costs and economic scale or the incumbent's control of raw materials, technology or essential facilities.

The barriers might be institutional barriers, such as intellectual property rights or government regulation. As the explanatory memorandum to the amending Bill acknowledged, government controls on competition may afford a corporation market power (Commonwealth of Australia. House of Representatives, 1985). On this basis, action was once taken against the Australian Telecommunications Commission (Telecom) for breach of section 46. The litigant alleged that Telecom's power substantially to control the market for premium telephones in Australia was founded not only on Telecom's economic resources, such as its access to capital and its nationwide distribution organization, but also on its statutory monopoly to operate the telephone network and to regulate attachments to it (Corones, 1987).

## Taking Advantage

To contravene section 46, the corporation must take advantage of its market power. While a number of factors can contribute to market power, they are not necessarily involved in the exercise of that market power in an anti-competitive way. The corporation must be taking advantage of its power for one or more of the three proscribed purposes (see above). Indeed, it is said that it should be using the power in a way that can only be made possible by the absence of competitive conditions (TPC, 1990). To the contrary, it is possible to characterize some aggressive market tactics as highly competitive practices. In effect, the duality of many practices affords the authorities an opportunity to balance concern about concentration with other objectives. In this way, a corporation's action might be seen to have a legitimate business justification; for example it might simply be regarded as exploiting its superior performance or responding to competition from others. The TPC has suggested that whether firms compete is a matter not only of the structure of the market but also of the conduct and performance of firms (Commonwealth of Australia. TPC, 1976). Many of the commission's criteria work in favour of the market leaders, particularly where they continue to innovate. The commission might be concerned that the proscription of such practices would deter further investment in these beneficial strategies. For instance, proscription of the practice of refusing to license intellectual property rights might discourage further research and development (CCH, 1991). It is to be kept in mind that conduct contrary to section 46 cannot be authorized by the TPC.

Where contravention of section 46 occurs, the TPC may seek pecuniary penalties or an injunction from the courts, but cannot ask for divestiture.

## Commission Policy

Has the misuse of the market power provision application to practices in the high technology industries? It is here we might expect the greatest concern to be shown about the stand-alone and licensing practices of the core producers. If they are based upon a substantial degree of market power, as they might be if the corporation is oligopolist, the purposes of a number of practices, such as refusals to deal, under-cutting, product differentiation, bundling, exclusive licensing, restrictive licensing and cross licensing, might conceivably be called into question under section 46.

In keeping with the style of policy development outside Australia, the TPC has recently issued a set of guidelines for the edification of industry concerning its interpretation of section 46, together with an extensive background paper (Commonwealth of Australia. TPC, 1990). The guidelines categorize various relevant practices as black, grey or white. A black list indicates the practices the commission regards as generally restrictive of competition; these include tie-ins and similar practices (though not as a result of product design or for safety reasons rather than contractual restrictions), exclusive dealing arrangements and requirements contracts, lease-only policies and the withdrawal of supply to customers who deal with competitors or fail to follow price guidelines. A grey list of conduct that may be restrictive of competition includes intellectual property licensing arrangements where they are a form of leverage to obtain advantages outside the statutory monopoly of the property right, such as tie-ins, grant-backs and no-challenge arrangements may be. The grey list also includes denial of access to essential facilities, refusal to deal or failure to allow reasonable access to spare parts, manuals and the like, and the raising of rivals' costs and the strategic creation of barriers to entry (such as the creation of a new product might be). A white list includes research and development leading to the introduction of a new product. It also includes refusal to license intellectual property rights or disclose confidential information, though practices such as the accumulation of intellectual property to make entry more difficult or the initiation of frivolous or intimidatory infringement proceedings might still constitute a misuse of market power.

## MERGERS

If section 46 deals with the exploitation of substantial market power, section 50 is concerned with the acquisition of the power to dominate a market through merger. A merger is proscribed if it would result in a corporation being in a position to dominate a market for goods or services or, if it is already in such a position, if it would substantially strengthen its power to dominate the market. Merger involves the acquisition of shares either directly or indirectly in a corporation; in certain circumstances joint ventures may also be treated as mergers under the Act. Section 50 applies to the acquisition in Australia of local corporations by foreign companies. In 1986, section 50A was inserted to provide some control over the acquisition overseas of companies which have subsidiaries in Australia.

### Domination

Whether a corporation will be in a position to dominate a market after a merger involves a test akin to the test employed to determine substantial market power under section 46. The degree of power involved is, however, higher than that of substantial market power, though still less than the power to control or monopolize a market. This higher threshold for the activation of the section was installed in the Act in 1977 by the Coalition government. While take-over activity was intensifying at the time, the Labor government's 1986 amendments did not seek to alter it. What is the effect of this threshold? The TPC's 1985-1986 Report (Commonwealth of Australia. TPC, 1986: 15) states:

> Section 50 will usually not apply when there are, after the merger:
> - at least two competitors in the market; or
> - if there is only one major local competitor, there remain:
>   - a number of other viable local competitors with the opportunity to develop; or
>   - effective import competition.

The threshold was to be a specific concern for the inquiry of the House of Representatives Standing Committee on Legal and Constitutional Affairs (the Griffiths Committee) (Commonwealth of

Australia, 1989) into the adequacy of existing controls on takeovers, acquisitions and mergers. The Griffiths Committee received several submissions on the point. Notably, the Treasury took a Chicago School approach, arguing that competition should be subordinated to the goal of business efficiency (Corones, 1990). While also not in favour of any legislative change, the Department of Industry, Technology and Commerce (DITC) sought an approach which would balance the benefits of rationalization with the value of competition. The Law Council of Australia, the Attorney-General's Department and the Trade Practices Commission itself favoured a rule of law approach, opposing any change to the threshold on the basis that a change would give rise to too much uncertainty in the business community and the courts. Ultimately, the Griffiths Committee proposed no change to the threshold.

At the end of 1991, however, the Senate Standing Committee on Legal and Constitutional Affairs (the Cooney Committee) (Commonwealth of Australia, 1991) concluded a similar inquiry by recommending that the threshold be lowered again. It also called for a pre-merger notification requirement. But the government, like the opposition coalition parties, remained opposed to a change in the threshold. However, in February 1992, the government announced another review of the Trade Practices Act (the *Australian*, 25 February 1992). In May, the Attorney-General was reported to be pursuing a return to the threshold which applied before 1977 (the *Age*, 26 May 1992). A pre-merger notification procedure was also scheduled for introduction. At the same time, the provision for authorizations of anti-competitive mergers remained.

## TPC Merger Policy

A merger under sections 50 or 50A may be authorized by the Trade Practices Commission if it would result in such a benefit to the public that the acquisition should be allowed to take place. In recent years, the TPC has placed more emphasis on the authorization process in relation to mergers after a proposal for a pre-notification procedure was rejected by the government. The commission has also opened up the authorization process to increase the opportunity for public scrutiny and accountability of takeovers.

We have already noted how the commission offers its own view of conduct which is likely to contravene the Act. The commission also gives indications from time to time of its view of the public benefits which outweigh the anti-competitive effects of proscribed conduct. Of course the definition of the public interest is to be found primarily in the authorization decisions of the commission and the Trade Practices Tribunal. Nevertheless, the TPC has proffered guidelines concerning its approach to merger activity. New merger guidelines were promised for 1991. The then current (1986) merger guidelines ventured the view (CCH, 1991: 60,668):

> The range of public benefits which might be considered appropriate to authorise a merger is very wide. In general, however, the Commission has consistently recognised that mergers which effect a beneficial rationalisation of industry by resulting in greater efficiency and better allocation of resources confer a public benefit if the likelihood (the probability) of the resultant efficiencies can be demonstrated.
> 
> It also recognises that the attainment of international competitiveness (whether on Australian domestic markets against imports or in the export field) may be a public benefit.
> 
> Others which might be mentioned are;
> - a higher contribution to significant research and development activities
> - infrastructure development in regional areas
> - enhanced ability to absorb cost increases and/or contain price increases; and
> - substantial stability and enhancement of employment

Where contraventions of sections 50 or 50A occur, the TPC may apply to the courts for an injunction. It may also seek an order for divestiture of the acquired corporation, but this remedy has not so far been invoked.

Has the merger provision application to the high technology industries? In the light of our understanding of the provision, perhaps we should not expect it to have much purchase in these industries. After all, depending of course on how broadly the relevant markets are defined, they are not likely to approach monopolization. We have noted already that the Act is not concerned to promote competition *per se*. In any case, the speculative takeover activity of the eighties has centred concern on the indifference of the general companies and financial markets regulation to the interests of small shareholders and creditors. The deleterious impact of this takeover activity on competitive innovation is less clearcut. In the early days, it was fiercely argued that the activity would shake up complacent management. Now, some are saying that the activity diverted attention away from the long haul of product development. This kind of takeover activity was not focused on the high technology industries, though some of the companies involved might have become contributors if they had not been preoccupied with corporate raiders – the food companies for instance in relation to biotechnology and the broadcasting companies with communications technology.

## EXEMPTIONS

We should next note that the Act grants exemptions for certain classes of conduct that, *prima facie*, contravene the provisions. For example, a product standardization agreement does not attract liability under section 45 (for exclusive dealing) if it represents a provision requiring a person to comply with or apply standards of dimension, design, quality or performance prepared or approved by the Standards Association of Australia or by a prescribed association or body.

The most important exceptions are provided by section 51 of the Act. These exceptions include any act or thing that is of a kind specifically authorized or approved by, or by regulations under, a Commonwealth or State Act or Territory Ordinance. This exception is potentially wide-ranging, but the government is now engaged in eliminating some of these authorized immunities. In its 1989–1990 annual report, the TPC welcomed the elimination of some such authorizations (for instance in the case of Telecom), but argued that many government bodies were still insulated from the Act because they enjoyed the shield of the Crown or the protection of specific legislation (TPC, 1990). However, in its industry statement of 12 March 1991, the government signalled its intention to remove most of the remaining protections (Commonwealth of Australia. House of Representatives, 1991). Some, however, reside in State law.

## INTELLECTUAL PROPERTY

The most significant exception in section 51 relates to intellectual property. According to section 51, a contravention is not committed by the imposing of or giving effect to a condition of a licence granted by the proprietor, licensee or owner of a patent, registered design or copyright, or by an applicant for such, or of an assignment of a patent, registered design or copyright or the right to apply for such.

This exception only applies, however, to the extent that the condition relates to: (1) the invention to which the patent or application for a patent relates, or articles made by the use of that invention; (2) goods in respect of which the design is, or is proposed to be, registered and to which it is applied; or (3) the work or other subject matter in which the copyright subsists. The scope of this exception would thus appear to be limited (Ricketson, 1984b). The exception relates not to the intellectual property itself, then, but to the subject of the property. In this way, an agreement not to challenge property right would not be covered by the exception, and neither would an agreement not to sublicense or reassign the property right. Again, the exemption relates to the subject which has intellectual property recognition and not to related subjects. In this way, conditions requiring licensees to grant back intellectual property over improvements or other related developments, or conditions requiring licensees to buy other goods and services from the supplier, would not be covered by the exception.

The position of know-how protections seems less privileged. Except where the know-how is the subject of a patent, registered trade mark or copyright, the section 51 exception does not take in conditions designed to protect know-how, such as confidentiality agreements. Section 4M also provides that the Act does not affect the operation of the general law of the land relating to 'restraint of trade', insofar as that law is capable of operating concurrently with the Act. Nonetheless, we should note that, at the same time, the Act 'saves' the law relating to breaches of confidence. In addition, section 51 specifically excepts an important category of restrictive arrangements. In its own words, it excepts provisions regarding the conditions of employment of employees, or provisions to accept restrictions as to the work (whether as an employee or otherwise) which may be engaged in either during or after the termination of a contract of service or for services.

It should be remembered that the section 51 exceptions do not operate in the case of contraventions of section 46 (misuse of market power) or section 48 (resale price maintenance).

### IPAC RECOMMENDATIONS

The role of section 51 was considered in the Industrial Property Advisory Committee's (IPAC's) report on the patents system

(Commonwealth of Australia. IPAC, 1984). Indeed, the thrust of IPAC's report was that the anti-innovative uses of the patents power be countered with a stricter competition policy. In particular, IPAC recommended that, with a view to proscribing patent-related conduct which has the purpose or effect of substantially lessening competition: (1) the exemptions in section 51(3) be removed, (2) the operation of sections 45(1)(a) and 4D (relating to exclusionary practices), section 45A (horizontal price-fixing) and section 47(6) and (7) (third-party tying) be amended so as to apply to patent-related conduct (though subject to a lessening of competition test rather than a *per se* prohibition); and (3) authorization then be available under the Act for patent-related conduct.

The government chose not to take up IPAC's recommendations (Lamberton, 1987). In its response, the government said that, in order to promote innovation, a balance had to be struck between granting exclusive property rights and avoiding anti-competitive effects. IPAC had not provided evidence of a substantial problem or established a case for policy change. Furthermore, some of the recommendations would have the effect of softening the thrust of the Act's *per se* prohibitions. In addition, the recommendations raised technical problems of distinguishing patent-related conduct from other conduct. To pursue the recommendations, it would be necessary to consider similar issues in relation to other intellectual property rights. (As we noted in earlier chapters, the government had a different committee to advise it on copyright matters and indeed a different department was responsible for this.)

The government did propose that compulsory licensing powers be introduced into the *Trade Practices Act* to provide an additional competition law remedy where patent-related conduct contravened the existing provisions of the Act. (Compulsory licensing powers are also part of the Patents Act.) IPAC's recommendation that the licensing power be extended to related know-how was, however, rejected on the basis that such a power would be unworkable.

## ENFORCEMENT

At the moment, jurisdiction is given primarily to the Federal Court to hear actions for breach of the Act, with appeals by leave to the High Court. The Act empowers private parties to bring civil actions to court based on contraventions of the provisions. This avenue lifts some of the burden (both financial and political) off the TPC for the enforcement of the Act (Freiberg and O'Malley, 1984). But the private right provides no guarantee to the commission that action will be taken, and the litigant must decide whether its resources, and any remaining goodwill it enjoys with the contravening corporation, can withstand the initiation and pursuit of proceedings (Goldring, 1990). While most of the actions under the Act have in fact been brought by private parties, the number of actions overall have not been great (Brunt, 1990).

While the private right of action places the application of the Act somewhat outside the control of the administration, the practice of the TPC remains crucial to the shape and thrust of the scheme. The authorization power of the TPC has been noted. Contravening conduct that is authorized by the commission cannot be litigated, though persons with a sufficient interest can seek a review of the authorization itself by the Trade Practices Tribunal. In practical terms, the resources which a government agency might enjoy to sustain a case in the courts can also prove significant, though the TPC still complains periodically of inadequate resources. In addition, some of the Act's remedies for breach are available to the commission but not to private parties.

## TPC Compliance Policy

The TPC may, but is not obliged, to institute proceedings to enforce the proscriptions of the Act, and it may reach settlement with the defendant before or after instituting proceedings (Pengilley, 1984). In the analysis of the operations of the trade practices law, considerable store is therefore placed on the commission's working rules. We have noted above some of the TPC's policy statements concerning both the interpretation of the legislative provisions and the authorization criteria. The commission has also developed an internal policy regarding the categories of offence within the Act which it will pursue as a matter of priority. A recent statement of objectives and priorities identified mergers and serious breaches of section 46 as priorities for the commission (Commonwealth of Australia. CCH, 1991). Under a new, more pro-active chairman, Professor Bob Baxt, the commission also targeted practices in certain selected industries that were the subject of micro-economic reform and reduction in substantive regulation. Telecommunications was included, along with the likes of domestic aviation, financial services and the waterfront.

## Compliance Strategy

Allied to this selection of priorities is the discrimination in the manner in which the TPC will proceed against possible contraventions of the Act. Early indications can be obtained from the Summary of Operating Policy which has been attached to the commission's instructions to staff on the investigation of contraventions of the Act (CCH, 1991: 60,445). This policy provided a graduated set of actions appropriate to categories of practice such as restrictive agreements, exclusive dealing, monopolization and mergers. The staff instructions also contained a statement about the general circumstances which warranted administrative rather than court action and the types of administrative action which might be considered. These instructions placed stress on the efficient use of the TPC's resources, the seriousness of the offence, and the attitude of the corporation in question. Types of administrative action proposed included warnings to offending firms and the seeking of undertakings from offending firms. Again, in recent years, the compliance strategy was firmly articulated. The commission stated (Commonwealth of Australia. CCH, 1991: 32,053):

> Some have suggested that the Commission should confine itself to a traditional 'policeman' style law enforcement role – detecting and litigating individual breaches of the Act as its primary means of achieving compliance with the law. However, the Commission believes that more profound and lasting compliance can be achieved – at lower ultimate cost to the taxpayer and business – by working with the industry in question to negotiate broad-based changes to the way it operates so that breaches of the law are prevented rather than litigated.

While vigorously prosecuting some breaches of the Act, the TPC also experimented with a wider range of compliance-oriented measures, including guidelines, industry codes of conduct, informal clearance procedures, and corporate education programs (Commonwealth of Australia. CCH, 1991). Another reason given for this approach was that court actions were often not cost-effective. Nevertheless, it should be acknowledged that the TPC has been prepared to litigate the provisions in certain circumstances (Grabosky and Braithwaite, 1986). While the provisions of the Act are by no means enforced as a matter of course, in recent years the TPC's overall litigation rate has increased. The outgoing chairman has called for increased penalties for offences (Commonwealth of Australia. CCH, 1991) and the government is likely to enact them (the *Age*, 23 August 1991).

## THE AUSTRALIAN HIGH TECHNOLOGY SECTOR

Nonetheless, in summing up the Australian position, it is fair to say that there is little evidence of a concerted approach by the local trade practices authorities directed specifically to anti-competitive tendencies in the high technology industries. Yet, the central position of the key producers, their use of intellectual property and other strategies, does mean that industry practices at both the research and the production stages of innovation can be anti-competitive. The low level of anti-trust action locally may be due to the fact that the major strategic decisions in the high technology industries are being made overseas. Australian authorities may defer to the anti-trust policies of the 'home' governments of these companies. We have noted the tendency in these policies to accommodate some kinds of restrictive licensing and collaborative practices. Should Australia accept that trend? It might be argued that in Australia, a small economy importing much of its high technology and trying to find product niches, the focus is on somewhat different issues from those in the large home markets (ASTEC, 1986a).

It is to be appreciated that the Australian trade practices offences are not single-mindedly pro-competitive. The law respects the liberal form in the sense that it accepts that the 'natural' workings of the market lead to concentration. The schemes are built onto the imperfections of existing industry structures. In most cases, the thresholds for their activation concede a certain amount of market power to corporations. And the high technology industries are not monopolistic or even duopolistic, even if core producers wield considerable market power. In these circumstances, the most immediate issue for the scheme is the policy adopted towards attempts by the central companies to dominate the subsidiary areas of the market through the use of more direct trade practices such as product differentiation, restrictive licensing, and cross licensing (Pengilley, 1980). There is little evidence of vigorous use of the trade practices provisions against these practices. It is possible of course to surmise that the provisions have some deterrent effect, and the extension of such provisions to the key telecommunications sector might also result in more competition. To some extent, too, the core producers have had market reasons for allowing peripheral and specialist firms to operate. Yet, these firms continue to operate in a climate of uncertainty about the future magnanimity of the large companies. It must be the case that the authorities do not think that their practices necessarily work (perhaps on a percentage basis) against innovation, whatever their other effects.

## CONCLUSIONS

We have seen how the trade practices schemes, both in Australia and elsewhere, depart from the model of a regime of absolute rules for the enforcement of competitive conditions. But we have also noted that the engagement of the discretionary administrative approach within the regulatory heartland of competition law is bound to experience some checks. This byplay helps us understand the ambivalent nature of competition policy. In sum, the trade practices scheme is a weak gloss on the liberal form. The provisions for administrative flexibility represent a regulatory system trying to operate on top of the edifice of a liberal form that facilitates the concentration of private power in complex patterns of integration, collaboration and dependency. Within a framework of basic rules which exclude many practices from scrutiny, provision is also made for exceptions and authorizations of anti-competitive conduct, and discretion is permitted to discount certain kinds of breach and to settle for substitutional undertakings (Pengilley, 1984). The regulatory approach provides a little space for the authorities to negotiate with corporations for cooperation according to a mixed bag of competition and other criteria. The question now is whether governments like Australia's will use this space to push harder for concessions from the large producers. Even if the need to accommodate market concentrations is conceded, there might be scope for a well resourced and politically reinforced agency to do so. The Trade Practices Commission has given recent indications in other fields that this is possible.

CHAPTER 7

*Foreign Trade and Investment*

This chapter focuses on the policies regulating trade in goods and direct investment across national borders. It identifies the international context in which national trade policies are formed, in particular the GATT and OECD provisions regarding foreign investment review. It then examines Australia's foreign investment review policy. As high technology industry increasingly becomes a global activity, the trade policies of firms and governments are critical to the prospects for innovation. Yet neither the goals of policy nor their mode of implementation can be said to be unproblematic. Free trade is a rallying point today but it must not be forgotten that, while free trade might increase the sum total of innovation worldwide, countries are just as intent on securing a place for their local industry in the high technology economies and appropriating some of the benefits for their own regions.

FREE TRADE AND NEO-MERCANTILISM

This section identifies the free trade and neo-mercantilist currents running through contemporary trade policies. It considers their implications for the policies adopted towards both trade in goods and direct foreign investment.

GOVERNMENT POLICIES

We should begin by briefly elaborating these tensions in policy. National governments pursue strategies aimed at aiding high technology innovators to break into markets overseas, especially of course the lucrative large markets of the United States, the EC and Japan, but also the growing markets of the smaller industrialized and developing countries. This strategy may involve the pursuit on a multilateral or bilateral basis of open, liberal markets for goods, services and capital. But they may also be involved in providing advantage to domestic producers in different ways, for instance by supporting export cartels or providing subsidies to exports. On the other hand, they may be willing to open up local markets in order to encourage advanced technology transfer from sophisticated producers overseas. But they may seek to extract conditions in return for the grant of such rights of access or establishment, in order to ensure that the technology transfer and other spin-offs to the local industry really do occur. In fact, they may be tempted to place barriers in the way of foreign imports or foreign direct investment as a way of sheltering domestic producers from the full rigours of foreign competition and even of reserving pockets of the market for them so as to build up national capability.

So, trade policy, both at the national and international levels, is likely to afford expression to principled stances, yet the rhetoric also displays a tendency to be deployed strategically and inconsistently as different interests vie for the support of the policy makers. Indeed, the stance may shift as the advantage to be gained by any one interest varies with the context in which the principles are to be applied. Gaisford and McLachlan (1990: 99) comment on the Uruguay round of GATT: 'The approach of individual negotiating countries, both industrialized and developing, has been to press for trade liberalization in areas where their own comparative advantages are strongest, and to resist liberalization in areas where they are less competitive and fear that imports would replace domestic production'.

Interestingly, the argument rages not just about the extent to which trade should be unrestricted, but also about which regulatory measures are to be characterized as trade-related. A notable feature of GATT's Uruguay round is the drive by the larger industrialized countries to expand the category of national regulatory policies which come within the rubric of trade-related policies, while still keeping some areas outside the boundaries of such scrutiny as part of the given framework in which trade is to be conducted. For example, the lack of adequate and effective enforcement of intellectual property rights is to be treated as a trade-related matter, while the potentially restrictive effect of extending appropriability to new technologies is not (Raghavan, 1990).

Government structures are also in contest. Roughly speaking, the contending goals of free trade and neo-mercantilist policies can be associated, respectively, with the competition for ascendancy (here at the international as well as the national level) of our initial two legal types: the rule-based liberal regime and the conduct of closer, corporatist or administrative relationships between industry and government. In this regard, most engrossing in recent times have been the tensions between the multilateral rule-based disciplines of the GATT codes and the bilateral initiatives of individual governments, both industrialized and developing. Even if the Uruguay round of GATT fails to produce any new agreements, it will have been significant for symbolizing the kinds of choices governments must at some point make in their trade policies. The analysis should also make reference to the movements in other international forums such as the OECD and the United Nations Conference on Trade and Development (UNCTAD).

While the emphasis in debate is conventionally placed upon the positions which national governments adopt on these matters, we must not forget the important role that the private companies, and especially the transnational corporations, play. If the transnationals, like the small domestic firms, sometimes strike alliances with the governments in their 'home' countries as part of outward-looking economically nationalist stances, they also see advantage in transcending the restrictions at the national level by appeals for freedom of trade directly to the more remote and detached international forums (Peterson, 1991). Yet the transnationals themselves now play a major role in regulating international trade 'privately' on a global scale (Bercusson, 1988). The Third World countries in particular have been persistent in arguing that the international forums must be prepared to act on the trade distorting and restricting practices of the corporations' technology transfer and production strategies if the regulatory policies of national governments are to come under scrutiny (Raghavan, 1990). This debate offers a a good illustration of the public–private divide at work. Raghavan (1990: 157) quotes the South Commission's statement on the Uruguay round:

> Equal attention must be paid to those aspects of the behaviour of the TNCs – restrictive business practices, restrictions on freer flow of technology, market-sharing arrangements, etc. . . . Any equitable multilateral arrangements must then also include acceptance by TNCs and the governments of developed countries of their own responsibilities to curb restrictive practices of TNCs and to facilitate the freer transfer of technology to the Third World.

## THE TARGETS OF TRADE POLICY

Trade policy conventionally bears most directly on the supply across borders through imports and exports of finished goods. Obviously tariffs have been the main focus here. With the diminution (if not the disappearance) of tariffs, attention has turned to the question of non-tariff barriers. The ingenuity with which governments have devised non-tariff barriers has long been recognized (Gaisford and McLachlan, 1991). These barriers include differential technical requirements, opaque licensing procedures, purchasing preference in government procurement, and bounties for local production. Also increasingly under scrutiny are the aids governments offer to assist domestic producers in export markets – such as straight subsidies, credit retention facilities, and technical services. Increasingly, governments may also take defensive measures in reaction to the trade practices of foreign suppliers by imposing countervailing and anti-dumping duties or negotiating voluntary export restraints (VERs) and orderly marketing arrangements.

Many of these measures are engaged in the obviously fraught area of trade in agricultural products and foodstuffs, especially through the provision of production and export subsidies. High technology industries are less of a battleground for these types of trade weapons, though the alleged dumping of micro-electronic products and semiconductor chips recently became a flashpoint in United States–Japan trade relations. Countries nevertheless do institute tariff and non-tariff barriers. Australia is no exception. On the recommendation of the Industries Assistance Commission (Commonwealth of Australia, 1984), Australia recently reduced tariff protection for computerware while at the same time establishing, under the *Bounty (Computers) Act 1984*, a scheme to encourage the local production of computer hardware, sub-assemblies and micro-circuits (Commonwealth of Australia. Bureau of Industry Economics, 1990).

Innovation is also greatly affected by the policy adopted towards direct foreign investment in the high technology industries, such as the acquisition of local firms and the establishment of local businesses by foreign companies. The foreign company might of course have a variety of reasons for seeking the right to establish locally, such as access to raw materials, the supply of cheap and skilled labour, or closeness to new markets (Lall, 1985). One reason historically has been to avoid the tariff barriers placed before imported products. But the foreign company might baulk at the conditions which government seeks to place on its presence. Governments require foreign subsidiaries to make or purchase a proportion of their components locally rather than import from overseas suppliers in their corporate group. They may further be required to use the subsidiary as a platform for exports onto the world market. Out of a concern specifically with technology transfer and the build-up of local capability, the requirements might extend to licensing on reasonable terms, especially external licensing, and joint ventures or equity participation for local firms. Recognition of the importance of industrial clusters or *filières* leads governments to focus policy on creating such linkages (Porter, 1990).

Such investment policies may be characterized as trade-related. Indeed, one of the revolutionary effects of innovation in technologies is to upset the demarcations between trade in products and direct investment. Especially in the case of services markets, foreign suppliers may be more interested in the free flow of information across national borders than in rights to establish a local operation. With the aid of 'telematics', services may increasingly be performed offshore (de Sola Pool, 1990). The lowering of tariff barriers also reduces the attraction of a local establishment. Yet, at the same time, the laying of those electronic highways may be enhanced by a right to establish a presence in the local telecommunications market, creating pressure to break down the old public and private monopolies and permit competitors to connect with the core carriers (Cheeah, 1991). More generally, joint ventures, strategic alliances and local integration are spurred by the necessity for even the largest companies to go outside to obtain the specialized complementary assets required for entry into burgeoning high technology fields.

## THE INTERNATIONAL CONTEXT

This section identifies the international context in which national policies are pursued. It focuses first on the GATT framework, noting its provisions for exceptions to free trade principles and its position regarding non-tariff barriers and state subsidies, before turning to direct foreign investment. The section notes the kinds of regulatory schemes which governments have instituted in order to screen foreign investment proposals. It looks then at attempts to formulate an international code regarding foreign investment practices.

Have the kinds of pressures we have just described led to the institution of liberal, rule-based, free trade regimes? The GATT example is a timely one. The General Agreement on Trade and Tariffs was reached in 1949. As its name suggests, GATT cannot strictly be likened to a legislative body. Its adherents are styled as 'contracting parties' and there are now some ninety-eight such parties to the core agreement (Jackson, 1989). Amendments to the agreement have been made during subsequent negotiating rounds, but some matters, especially as a result of the Tokyo round in the early eighties, have produced side codes to which not all the contracting parties have chosen to accede. As is the case with most processes of international law, the GATT raises interesting constitutional and institutional issues. The niceties of international 'law' must unfortunately escape us here, yet they do represent one dimension of the questions which interest us, such as the extent to which the GATT is to be regarded as a rule-making institution rather than just a facility to air issues, negotiate deals and settle disputes.

## THE GATT FREE TRADE FRAMEWORK

The GATT endeavours to lay down some general principles regarding the permissible regulation of trade by participating countries, especially in regard to tariffs. The agreement attacks discrimination in regulation as much as restrictions on trade *per se*. A fundamental principle, the most favoured nation principle, provides that a party should not discriminate between foreign countries in its application of tariffs and basic commercial policy rules. A further principle is the principle of non-discrimination or national treatment, which requires that a contracting party's regulation should not favour locally produced goods at the expense of foreign produced goods.

## EXCEPTIONS

At the same time, the GATT itself provides for exceptions to the observance of these principles (McGovern, 1986). The GATT lore is a complex body of jurisprudence and it cannot all be assimilated here. But to give a few examples, in order that we may convey the character of the GATT framework, we should note that preferential treatment to developing countries is in part accommodated.

Recognition is also given to the special arrangements made within regional free trade areas and customs unions.

A notable escape clause concerns the 'safeguards' that a party may institute to deal with deleterious imports. Article XIX of the GATT allows parties to modify their concessions or suspend their obligations if a product is being imported in such increased quantities or under such conditions as to cause or threaten serious injury to domestic producers. It is here that the so-called grey area measures, such as VERs, have proved problematic. A related issue is the legitimate role of the countervailing and anti-dumping duties which the GATT also contemplates. Article VI provides that these duties may be imposed in part if it is determined that the subsidies provided to imports or the dumping of imports causes or threatens material injury to an established industry or is such as to retard materially the establishment of a domestic industry.

General exceptions include restrictions for national security purposes. The United States has invoked this exception through its export controls legislation and its participation with Western European and other countries (including Australia) in the Co-ordinating Committee on Multilateral Strategic Export Controls (COCOM). Another exception concerns intellectual property protection. Article XX permits parties to take measures necessary to secure compliance with laws and regulations, such as the protection of patents, trademarks and copyrights and the prevention of deceptive practices (McGovern, 1986). This exception provides a basis for the use by the United States of section 337 of its trade legislation (see chapters 3 and 4).

It is perhaps to be expected that the vigorous ways in which individual parties have availed themselves of these exceptions to take unilateral action against imports would create tension within the multilateral framework of the GATT. The negotiation of VERs and orderly marketing arrangements with individual countries is one questionable practice; the readiness to invoke anti-dumping procedures is another. The retaliatory measures themselves involve a kind of selective discrimination between trading countries (Golt, 1989). The measures which have caused perhaps the most alarm are those embodied in section 301 of the United States trade legislation. As we noted in the discussion of intellectual property, after several strengthening amendments, '301' is now a major weapon empowering the United States Trade Representative to take action against the imports of particular countries that place unreasonable, unjustifiable or discriminatory burdens on United States commerce abroad. These burdens include the denial of fair and reasonable opportunities for the establishment of enterprises, adequate and effective protection for intellectual property rights, and market opportunities for goods. Sanctions have been activated against countries placed on a priority list, including Brazil, India and Japan, and other countries have been placed on a watchlist. Australia reportedly has been placed on the list because its local content rules for television programming restrict access by United States products to the market. The United States also wants to see Australia drop its offsets requirements (see chapter 9) and sign the GATT Procurement Code (the *Age*, 1 April 1992).

Despite the GATT prescriptions regarding legitimate exceptions, not all the United States retaliatory provisions require actual injury to be proven before their sanctions are activated. The United States takes advantage of another GATT Article that saves those inconsistent provisions of national law which were in place before the GATT was concluded (Jackson, 1989). In any case, the United States operates a later-in-time policy which means that federal legislation enacted after the conclusion of GATT may still override it. This policy reminds us that, for some countries at least, international laws do not apply automatically at the domestic level but instead require local enactment to have the force of law. The need for this enactment can give rise to political problems in the acceding governments' own legislatures (Adams, 1990).

The GATT offers its own dispute resolution procedures. If bilateral consultation between the countries at odds fails, a party may refer the matter to the contracting parties in concert. The response generally is to establish an expert panel to make a report to the GATT Council, which may recommend the suspension of trade concessions and the other obligations of the aggrieved party. The extent to which countries defer to the GATT procedures varies, however. For example, in 1981 the EC instituted its own processes for responding to illicit commercial practices against its external trade but cast them in such a way that the GATT procedures took priority. The extent to which countries respect the decisions of GATT panels also varies. In all this, Jackson (1989) perceives a tension between a rule-based central regime and the use by individual countries of power-oriented techniques such as unilateral import restrictions, bilateral negotiations, strategic foreign aid, and military manoeuvres (such as the threat of withdrawal from NATO).

## NON-TARIFF BARRIERS TO TRADE

GATT has also been urged in recent years to take action on various kinds of non-tariff barriers to trade. The Tokyo round produced side codes rather than amendments to the original agreement on such issues as technical barriers, import licensing procedures and government procurement. Their status as codes means that they bind their signatories only, and not all the contracting parties to the general agreement – except perhaps to the extent they reach back and engage the principles of that agreement (Jackson, 1989). Let us briefly examine one of the codes. The Agreement on Government Procurement came into effect in 1981. It has so far been accepted by the United States, the EC and around ten other countries (McGovern, 1986). Its aim is to expand world trade by liberalizing government markets for goods. It exhorts parties not to use government procurement to afford protection to local suppliers or products or to discriminate between different foreign suppliers and products. Much of the code is concerned with establishing transparent and regular procedures for seeking and determining tenders for government purchases.

The code illustrates many of the limitations of the GATT regime. A review of the code's implementation was concerned with its lack of impact (Frignani, 1986). Not only were the signatories limited, but those signing excluded areas such as telecommunications and certain defence products from their adherence to the code. The code on its own terms did not apply to the purchasing policies of regional and local governments, a significant omission in some countries. In passing, it should be noted that government procurement is problematic for other free trade associations too. For example, local content rules are now an issue for the 'second generation' agreements which the EC is striking with the EFTA European countries which are destined soon to be members of the community (Horowitz, 1991).

## STATE SUBSIDIES

The other side of this strategic trade coin is the subsidies which governments provide to local producers especially to advantage them in export markets. These subsidies take all manner of forms, such as regional assistance, tax relief and aid to small business. As we know, subsidies to agricultural producers have been a major stumbling block to overall progress in the Uruguay round. GATT restrictions on subsidies are to be found in the general agreement and the corresponding provisions of the subsidies code negotiated during the Tokyo round (McGovern, 1986). These strictures again include an obligation to declare and make transparent their subsidies. In terms of the parties' substantive obligations, distinctions are made between primary and non-primary products and between export and non-export subsidies (Gaisford and McLachlan, 1990). For instance, in relation to non-export subsidies, signatories undertake not to use subsidies which cause injury to the domestic industry of another signatory. Yet, at the same time, the code permits the use of non-export subsidies in the pursuit of domestic social and economic policies such as industry restructuring and encouraging research and development.

Again, state aids are also a productive source of tension in more localized regional free trade associations. For example, the Treaty of Rome seeks to regulate aids granted by member states which distort competition by favouring certain undertakings or the production of certain goods, so far as this distortion affects trade between the member states (Harden, 1990). Social democratic governments, such as that in France of recent times, have reserved the right to provide subsidies to their industrial undertakings, especially in time of crisis. The EC policy does make exceptions of its own for activities such as research and development assistance (Schina, 1987).

State ownership of trading corporations provides a particular problem in the case of both non-tariff barriers and subsidies. State monopolies might be treated by foreign suppliers as barriers to free trade and, in particular, as trade in services reaches the agenda of the free trade bodies, telecommunications monopolies come under attack. Even state control of trading corporations might be characterized as a distortion of free trade. The financing, purchasing and sales policies of these corporations all come under scrutiny (McGovern, 1986). Once again, regional trade associations such as the EC have also taken up this issue (Papparlardo, 1991).

## DIRECT FOREIGN INVESTMENT

If the Tokyo round of the GATT advanced the cause of free trade, especially in connection with non-tariff barriers, it was still concerned with trade in goods. The Uruguay round has raised the prospect that the free trade ethos will be spread further, most significantly to trade in services (Golt, 1989). Another field under consideration, and the one we shall now discuss here, is direct foreign investment. We can readily concede the attraction, especially to the smaller and less industrialized countries, of direct foreign investment as a means for local industry to share in the benefits of scale and scope through resource rationalization, research and development sophistication, technology transfer and access to overseas markets. However, those same countries might be wary of the impact of unrestricted foreign presence, ownership and control on the development of an indigenous local industry if the foreigner's operations are to be the subject of global rationalization strategies in which local innovation is rendered subservient to the requirements of the corporate group and resources are repatriated to the home base (Commonwealth of Australia. Bureau of Industry Economics, 1989).

As we saw in chapter 6, an immediate concern may be the transnationals' use of restrictive business practices to organize production and order markets. Such practices could include limited licensing arrangements with outsiders, the takeover and integration of competitors and suppliers, and the exercise of controls on internal technology transfer, production and pricing (Frame, 1983).

## NATIONAL REGULATION

In response to these practices, national governments may seek to attach a number of conditions and controls to foreign participation in the domestic economy (Raghavan, 1990). Foreign companies buying in or setting up might be required to meet local content quotas when they purchase or manufacture goods; they also may be required to set export targets. A more direct concern for local innovation seizes upon the level of research and development activity and the extent of technology transfer which the parent company permits the foreign subsidiary. Opportunities for small, indigenous firms will also be in the government's sights. This concern may lead governments to regulate licensing practices, and even require joint ventures with locals or local equity participation. Certain of Australia's South-east Asian neighbours do just that (the *Australian Financial Review*, 6 May 1992). In the extreme, governments may seek to restrict or prohibit foreign entry in strategically sensitive sectors, at least until an indigenous capability has been established. Cabanellas (1984) identifies several of the objectives of such foreign investment policies. Governments may wish to increase the bargaining power of local suppliers, increase the flow of technical and commercial information to local industry, improve the quality and assimilation of foreign technology, and protect local innovation from harsh competition.

What form do these regulatory policies assume? Such investment review schemes are often constructed on a broad discretionary and informal basis to allow the agencies to balance the competing objectives of capital investment from overseas with the development of national technological sovereignty and capability. Their enabling legislation does little more than nominate the level of investment proposals which must be submitted to the agencies for review. The notification requirements are used as a means to establish a relationship to bargain over the conditions on which the transnationals are to participate in the local economy (Grant, 1983).

In his study of the legal aspects of technology transfer to the developing countries, Blakeney (1989) notes the features of these schemes. A good example is provided by the provisions of the Andean Code, struck by concerned South American countries. The schemes are likely to create a category of examinable agreements, then require relevant documents to be submitted to the executive or administrative agency empowered to evaluate and register the agreements. Agreements that fail to measure up to expectations may, if modifications cannot be obtained, be denied. The schemes may also entail follow-up monitoring of actual performance on the transnationals' commitments to technology transfer, local training, and research and development activity. Governments involved in such schemes may also invoke the threat of withdrawal of favours such as tax relief or government patronage to encourage compliance.

Despite their subscription to liberal international investment policies, many of the larger producer nations have been among the countries screening direct foreign participation in their own economies. Perhaps the most notable example again is the recent strengthening in the United States of the provision for federal screening of foreign investment proposals, spurred it seems by a concern about Japanese investment and particularly the proposed purchase of the Fairchild Corporation by Fujitsu (Davidow and Stevens, 1990). The Trade and Competitiveness Act of 1988 empowers the United States president to review acquisitions, mergers and takeovers which could result in foreign control. Transactions may be suspended or prohibited to ensure that 'national security' is not impaired. National security is not defined in the legislation, but factors nominated as relevant include: domestic production for projected national defense requirements; the capability and capacity of domestic industry to meet those requirements; and the control of domestic industry and commercial activity by foreigners as it affects that capability and capacity. Given that technological superiority and commercial strength have traditionally been identified with national security in the United States, the scope for review is potentially broad. Under the scheme, the president's decisions are not meant to be subject to judicial review on their merits.

A contrast with Japan might again be useful. Japan invokes through its Foreign Exchange and Foreign Trade Control Law a notification and screening system for certain foreign investment proposals, such as acquisitions by foreigners of shares in Japanese companies and the establishment of local businesses and the importation of technology through agreements with locals (Grice, 1988). In line with exceptions that are allowed under the OECD codes concerning the liberalization of capital movements and invisible transactions, the relevant ministries may withhold approval if the transaction poses a threat to national security; approval may also be withheld if it threatens to affect adversely and materially the activities of Japanese business enterprises or the efficient performance of Japanese industry. While this system is less restrictive than its predecessor in the early post-war period, it still allows the relevant ministries considerable room to move (Adams, 1990).

INTERNATIONAL CODES

Such schemes meet of course with resistance. Certainly, smaller countries, with heavy dependence on foreign investment or little resolve to go it alone, can be threatened with broad resistance from core producers and trade sanctions from their home nations if they seek to restrict investment opportunities too severely or to insist on local participation (Gee, 1981). Brazil's experience with its strategy to build a domestic computer industry is instructive. Such countries may look for reinforcement in the collective strength of international bodies. The United Nations forums, where the lesser developed nations predominate numerically, are likely to reflect a more critical attitude to the practices of the transnationals. Accordingly, a number of codes of conduct for multinational enterprises have been developed, although the final stage of agreement to a binding text within such diverse forums has proved problematic. The drafts include a code developed by the United Nations Centre on Transnational Corporations.

Most pertinent to this study is the Code of Conduct for Technology Transfer drafted by the United Nations Conference on Trade and Development (UNCTAD) (Thompson, 1982). The draft itemized restrictive practices relating to technology transfer in some detail, as well as the measures suitable for dealing with them. The Group of seventy-seven non-aligned nations was prepared to adopt the code but the Western market economy countries would not on the whole agree to the code becoming compulsory. They expressed the view that it was not their role to control technology transfer by private enterprise. Accounts of the negotiations have also suggested that they were concerned about the code's emphasis on the conduct of multinational enterprises (Nixson, 1983). Instead, they took the view that developing the nation's economic and social objectives ought to be balanced with the transnational enterprises' interests in a return on their investment and proprietary knowledge (Dickson, 1984).

Perhaps the most influential international forum for the examination of issues common to the Western industrialized nations is the Organization for Economic Cooperation and· Development (OECD). One of the subjects of attention in the OECD's Guidelines for Multi-national Enterprises is the terms of technology transfer. As we shall see below, the Australian government's present policy on foreign investment directs the attention of foreign investors to the OECD guidelines (Commonwealth of Australia. Department of the Treasury, 1989). The policy states that the government has associated itself with the guidelines and seeks the cooperation of foreign companies operating in Australian in observing them.

## THE OECD GUIDELINES

The OECD guidelines cover a broad range of concerns, such as disclosure of information, trade practices, financing, taxation, and employment and industrial relations. Regarding science and technology, the guidelines provide that enterprises should generally give due consideration to the host country's aims and priorities in regard to the promotion of innovation and the transfer of technology. More specifically, they recommend that enterprises should endeavour to ensure that their activities fit satisfactorily into the scientific and technological policies and plans of the countries in which they operate, and contribute to the development of national scientific and technological capacities, including, as far as appropriate, the establishment of and improvement in their host countries' capacity to innovate. They should also, to the fullest extent practical, adopt in the course of their business activities practices which permit the rapid diffusion of technologies with due regard to the protection of industrial and intellectual property rights, and, when granting licences for the use of industrial property rights or when otherwise transferring technology, do so on reasonable terms and conditions.

The OECD guidelines form an attachment to an OECD declaration on international investment and multinational enterprises which was promulgated at the same time as three OECD decisions concerning the national treatment of multinational enterprises, international incentives and disincentives, and intergovernmental consultation procedures on the guidelines (Long, 1981). The thrust of these OECD acts was that member countries should afford foreign enterprises treatment no less favourable than the treatment afforded to domestic enterprises. It should make official incentives and disincentives to international direct investment as transparent as possible. These particular OECD acts do not, however, deal with the member countries' right to regulate the entry of foreign investment or the conditions of establishment of foreign enterprises but are concerned instead with the subsequent activity of such enterprises and their treatment by the host countries. The Australian government is, however, associated with the OECD codes of liberalization of capital movements and liberalization of invisible transactions, which do bear on the question of entry policy (OECD, 1986b).

To implement this regime of investment acts, the OECD has established a set of monitoring committees. As part of its responsibilities under these acts, the Australian government has notified these committees of several local policies which discriminate in favour of companies incorporated in Australia – the industrial research and development incentives scheme (see chapter 8) is an example of such a policy. These OECD committees have also recently taken up the examination of conflicting legal requirements placed upon multinational enterprises by member countries, following an OECD Council agreement on conflicting requirements in 1984.

The OECD guidelines are a cautious expression of concern about certain of the multinational enterprises' international trade and business practices. At the same time they reflect the interest of the Western industrialized nations (the bulk of the membership of the OECD) and especially of the large net exporting countries in the liberalization of government restrictions and discriminations in the conduct of trade and business with foreign companies.

## THE GATT TRIMS AGENDA

In the Uruguay round of GATT, foreign investment policy has also been raised as a possible trade-related issue. Setting the scene for the negotiations, the *Punta del Este* ministerial declaration was non-committal regarding the direction that work should take, calling only for an examination of the operation of GATT articles relating to the trade-restrictive and distorting effects of investment measures, following which negotiations would elaborate, as appropriate, further provisions that might be necessary to avoid adverse effects on trade (Golt, 1989). Progress was slow, and it was likely that the Uruguay round would do no more than legitimize the continuing discussion of 'TRIMs'. One bone of contention was the fact that the TRIMs agenda focused almost exclusively on government regulatory measures (Raghavan, 1990). But the United States, backed to some extent by Japan and the EC, pushed the issue hard to reduce or eliminate any artificial or trade-distorting government barriers to the expansion of foreign direct investment. The United States has targeted such measures as production and sales arrangements (including local content requirements), equity shares, technology commercialization practices, incentive policies and licensing arrangements. Interestingly, as it loses its lead in certain high technology sectors to countries such as Japan, the United States also wants access to licensing arrangements, joint ventures and research and development consortia in those countries, especially those which are government sponsored.

In recent times, one approach has been to encourage governments to replace trade-related regulatory measures with an even-handed application of competition laws. Competition policy has the potential to strike at unilateral trade practices, such as the predatory pricing involved in some dumping practices and collusive arrangements like export cartels, without discriminating between domestic and foreign producers (OECD, 1984). Competition policy might also target government efforts to advantage domestic producers 'unfairly' by guaranteeing markets. We have seen in chapter 6 how competition policy is relevant to licensing practices, the formation of consortia and mergers.

Yet, competition policy can itself hinder the attainment of free trade objectives. We also noted in chapter 6 how some governments have taken the view that a relaxed policy towards collaborative arrangements will strengthen the position of domestic producers. There is a possibility that competition policy will be manipulated to favour local industry. So too, lack of clarity and consistency in the administration of the policy can present barriers to foreign entrants (Horowitz, 1991). One response to this prospect is to encourage more countries to adopt the legal model of competition policy advanced (though not always practised) by the leading market economies (Hopt, 1987). Another is to establish mechanisms at the supranational level to overcome national differences. The United States, which for some time forcefully asserted the extraterritorial jurisdiction of its own laws, reached bilateral agreements with countries such as West Germany and Australia. The OECD has also been active promoting cooperation procedures, for example on the issue of international mergers.

## AUSTRALIA'S FOREIGN INVESTMENT POLICY

This section examines the Australian government's policy. It characterizes first the legal structure favoured for the implementation of the policy. It looks at the changing internal criteria for review. It endeavours to place Australia's position in the international context.

Turning now to foreign investment policy in Australia, it should first be said that the review processes are potentially very important, because so much of Australia's technology is sourced overseas. Direct foreign investment comes under the scrutiny of the Commonwealth Department of the Treasury. (Some Australian states also operate policies, primarily in relation to key local sectors, such as minerals and resources, and urban real estate.) The Commonwealth Treasurer's powers to screen foreign investment proposals are sourced in a number of legislative enactments – notably in the *Foreign Takeovers and Acquisitions Act 1975*, the *Banking Act 1959* and the *Customs Act 1901*, and in regulations made under these Acts (Flint, 1985).

## THE LEGAL BASIS OF THE POLICY

Australian foreign investment policy is almost purely a creature of executive act, and individual decisions are highly discretionary. Some expectations are created about decision-making by the promulgation of policy. The policy, however, is most rule-like on the matter of which proposals do not receive scrutiny. The criteria for assessing the merits of the proposals are increasingly unstructured, signifying perhaps a move towards a more accommodating view of foreign investment activity. The structure of the scheme leaves room for negotiation with investors on a direct basis and many proposals are approved by the Treasury subject to conditions.

The *Foreign Takeovers and Acquisitions Act* empowers the Treasurer to make orders prohibiting the acquisition of Australian businesses by foreign interests where the Treasurer is satisfied that the acquisition is contrary to the national interest. The Act contains detailed provisions defining the types of investments which are subject to review. For example, the acquisition of shares is reviewable if it would result in, increase, or alter the foreign ownership of a substantial interest in a corporation that carries on an Australian business. Acquisition by purchase of the assets of an Australian business is also covered. Arrangements relating to the granting of rights to use the assets of an Australian business or to participate in the management or the profits of an Australian business are also encompassed. Conceivably then, under this ambit, the outward licensing of intellectual property rights to foreign companies could be examined, but inward technology licensing would not be reviewable except as part of a proposal to acquire or establish a business.

The review of foreign investment proposals is also based on foreign exchange control powers. The Banking Act gives the Reserve Bank absolute discretion over grants of authority for foreign exchange currency dealings in and out of Australia, subject to any directions provided by the Treasurer. Exchange control, such that it is today, is concerned largely, of course, with other objectives of macro-economic policy such as monetary and taxation policy. Other powers, such as the powers of various authorities to issue export and import licences, may also be invoked in certain circumstances to control foreign investment projects.

Government policy has been to review only those acquisitions of shareholdings of 15 per cent or more involving Australian corporations with total assets of five million dollars or more (Commonwealth of Australia. Department of the Treasury, 1989). In addition, proposals by foreign interests to establish new businesses in Australia are subject to review if the investment involved is $10 million or more. In early 1992, the government signalled that it was going to raise these thresholds considerably to exclude more proposals from review (the *Age*, 22 February 1992). Proposals in certain sectors would, however, continue to receive closer attention. These include all investment proposals in the media and civil aviation industries, certain real estate proposals, direct investments by foreign governments, and primary industry projects such as mining projects.

Approvals for foreign investment proposals are given by the Treasurer on the advice of the Foreign Investment Review Board (FIRB). Approvals are to be made in line with a government investment policy which is promulgated from time to time through statements of policy by the Treasurer and encapsulated in publications of the Treasury. The amalgam of these pronouncements is treated as the 'foreign investment policy guidelines'. This choice of form for the policy is of interest. In the opening chapter to the government's guide to investors, the Treasury (Commonwealth of Australia, 1989: v) states:

> The Government's policy is therefore to encourage direct foreign investment consistent with the needs of the Australian community, including the expansion of private investment, the development of internationally competitive and export-oriented industries and the creation of employment opportunities.
>
> Administration of the policy is based on guidelines rather than inflexible rules: it is practical and non-discriminatory. It is consistent with the Government's other policy objectives and plays its part in micro reform of the economy . . .
>
> Investors can expect that approval will not be withheld from proposals on national interest grounds other than in unusual circumstances affecting Australia's vital interests and development . . .
>
> The Board may recommend to the Government that any proposals which do not comply fully with foreign investment policy be allowed to proceed subject to the parties meeting certain conditions. This practice provides investors with a degree of flexibility in meeting the requirements of the policy.

The Foreign Investment Review Board does not appear to enjoy any statutory recognition, and the procedure for review is not legislatively elaborated, except for some notification requirements to alert the Treasury to acquisition proposals. In a past annual report, the board outlined the operative foreign investment review procedures within the board and the Treasury (FIRB, 1982). As noted, the board is prepared to discuss proposals with investors before formal notification. Once notified, proposals are examined within the executive of the board. The extent of examination depends upon the size and category of the investment proposal. Authority to approve certain types of proposals which do not involve issues of significance have been delegated to the executive member of the board. Proposals which are of significance are reported to the board. Following examination of the report, the board puts forward a recommendation to the Treasurer. If the proposal raises important considerations or impinges on other ministerial responsibilities, the Treasurer might consult other ministers or refer the matter to Cabinet (Flint, 1985). Decisions by the Treasurer to approve or reject foreign investment proposals are not subject to judicial review on their merits.

## THE REVIEW CRITERIA

The policy developed under the most recent government displays its ambivalence in economic policy. In 1982, the then coalition government Treasurer elaborated criteria by which proposals for the acquisition and establishment of businesses were to be assessed. The criteria included:

(a) whether, against the background of existing circumstances in the relevant industry, the proposal would produce, either directly or indirectly, net economic benefits to Australia in relation to the following matters:
  1. competition, price levels and efficiency;
  2. introduction of technology or managerial or work force skills into Australia;
  3. improvement of the industrial or the commercial structure of the economy and the quality and variety of goods and services available in Australia; and
  4. development of or access to new export markets.

The criteria went on to state that if a proposal was judged not to be contrary to the national interest on the basis of the above

criteria, the following additional criteria were to be taken into account:
(b) whether the business or project could be expected to be conducted in a manner consistent with Australia's best interests, such as:
   1. local processing of materials and the utilization of Australian components and services;
   2. involvement of Australians on policy-making boards of businesses;
   3. research and development;
   4. royalty, licensing and patent arrangements; and
   5. industrial relations and employment opportunities.

There were four other criteria, including the extent to which Australian equity had been sought for the project and the level of Australian management and control following implementation of the proposal (Flint, 1985). In 1983, a new Labor Treasurer added three more considerations to the criteria. These were:
(c) the extent to which commercial opportunities are provided for Australian contractors and consultants who participate in any construction work;
(d) the contribution the proposal would make to the improved utilization of resources, or the expansion of productive capacity arising from the introduction and diffusion of new technology and other skills, including managerial and workforce, new to Australia; and
(e) the benefits and cost to Australia of any export franchise limitations.

These criteria were included in a guide to investors which was issued in 1985 (Commonwealth of Australia. Department of the Treasury, 1985). In its prologue, the 1985 guide stated that the examination of proposals against these criteria would take into account economic, social and other national interest considerations. It went on to say that proposals by foreign interests for the establishment of new businesses which involved a total investment of $10 million or more were expected to provide for significant economic benefits to Australia and/or significant Australian equity participation. Proposals by foreign interests to acquire Australian businesses were to offer benefits in terms of the criteria sufficient to outweigh any costs, including those associated with the reduction of Australian ownership and control.

In July 1985, the Treasurer announced a new policy for foreign investment. In part, the new policy provided that in the manufacturing and services sector, proposals for the establishment of new businesses involving a total investment of $10 million or more and proposals for the acquisition of existing businesses were to be examined without the need to demonstrate economic benefits or to provide for Australian equity participation. They were to be approved unless judged by the government to be contrary to the national interest. The detailed assessment criteria which have just been recounted were omitted from the guide to investors put out in May 1987 (Commonwealth of Australia. Department of the Treasury, 1987). Combined with the new monetary thresholds for reviewable proposals, which leave small businesses exposed, the policy would now seem to be more liberal than before (Commonwealth of Australia. FIRB, 1988).

In any case, most proposals are approved. In the manufacturing sector, in the year 1985-1986, a total of 268 proposals for investment were reviewed (Commonwealth of Australia. FIRB, 1986). Of these, one was withdrawn, 264 were either approved outright or with conditions, and three were rejected. Most of the conditions concerned taxation obligations. The benefits included the introduction into Australia of technology and know-how, while foreign investors were also well placed to market Australian goods through their overseas networks. In 1989-1990, a total of 106 proposals were reviewed and all but one were approved. The Foreign Investment Review Board stated that benefits for industry restructuring and potential for exports were claimed in a number of these proposals (Commonwealth of Australia. FIRB, 1991).

## AUSTRALIA'S INTERNATIONAL STANCE

It is sometimes difficult for countries such as Australia, which share some of the characteristics both of the industrialized producer nations and of the Third World nations, to find an appropriate position in international forums. Australia, however, has been a longstanding member of the key international organizations and has displayed a commitment to international resolution. Its representatives are respected for their practical contributions and its officials find places in the secretariats of the organizations. Without a strong local technological base, it cannot in the short term afford to act as independently in high technology policy as European countries like France and the Scandinavian countries. Less tangibly, it does not enjoy the buffer of a strong cultural distance from the United States in particular, nor does it enjoy a tradition (despite the special early colonial circumstances) of a socialist or even statist approach to the organization of national economic development.

Australia, then, makes a contribution to the work of the international organizations while generally accepting the intellectual property and liberal trade stances promoted by the leading Western nations. Its work on the OECD's policy regarding restrictive business practices and on UNCTAD's principles for the control of restrictive business practices are cited by the government as evidence of its profile at this level (Commonwealth of Australia. Attorney-General's Department, 1987). It has again played an active role in advancing free trade issues in the Uruguay round of GATT (Golt, 1989). It has been very supportive of the free trade in services idea, but it is worth noting the caution it has expressed on the matter of TRIMs. The Department of Foreign Affairs and Trade (Commonwealth of Australia, 1991: 79) reported that: 'In the negotiations on TRIMs, Australia sought to ensure that new rules to address any adverse effects of investment measures were balanced and recognised the importance of the use of some measures as tools of positive structural adjustment leading to reduction in overall levels of industry protection'.

The conventions adopted in the international organizations often leave room for member countries to pursue their own objectives and interests. The leading producer countries have, in certain circumstances, found ways around the injunctions of the intellectual property and free trade conventions. With international competition intensifying, the leading nations are likely to be preoccupied with their own positions – the United States and Japan endeavouring to reach some understanding, and the European countries turning inwards. Australia is appreciating that it must fend for itself in international markets. In this context, it has been suggested on the example of the South-east Asian nations that Australia could bargain harder with foreign investors, or on the example of the Scandinavian countries and Japan that Australia could promote local capability in a more concerted fashion (Morris, 1983). But others doubt Australia's capacity to bargain unilaterally. Especially now, with Australia's orientation towards export markets, they suggest Australia's best hope lies with establishing a truly open international system on a multilateral basis.

Without detailed information about the conditions which the Foreign Investment Review Board imposes, the extent to which the terms of technology transfer in proposals above the threshold are reviewed cannot be properly assessed. Theoretically, the procedures provide one of the few opportunities for the government to review the terms of in-house transfer between foreign companies and local subsidiaries. The choice by a foreign investor between transfer to local subsidiaries and transfer to Australian firms as licensees could also be monitored. The current focus on the acquisition and establishment of businesses by foreign interests does not, however, provide much occasion to examine the terms of licensing agreements. The foreign exchange control powers would augment the powers to do so. But notification requirements for exchange transactions have of course been relaxed considerably since the decision to float the dollar in late 1983.

## CONCLUSIONS

Foreign trade and investment policy provides a very good illustration of the tension which develops between the inclination to further the close corporatist and administrative relationships between government and industry (here with a neo-mercantilist bent) and the continuing pull of rule-based free market liberalism. Through the unilateral incursions of national governments and large corporations, as well as the multilateral proceedings in the international forums, it moves the dance in time between these two approaches onto the world stage.

It is important to note that this performance is acted out as much in the private sphere of global industrial groups and networks as in government circles. Industry not only lobbies its 'home' governments for appropriate assistance in the circumstances but also structures its own internal domains of research, production and marketing to suit its interests, so a comprehensive account of the regulatory matrix includes the business practices of the private sector, especially the transnational high technology producers.

The tension is well represented in the structures and deliberations of the international trade bodies – most prominently in recent times the GATT, but also such other bodies as the OECD and UNCTAD. The

Uruguay round of the GATT reflects on the one hand the drive towards the formation of multilateral free trade rules. These rules are to apply predominantly to the regulatory policies of national governments. We are reminded that the liberal position does not necessarily involve the enforcement of open competitive markets but rather may defer uncritically to the anti-competitive and integrative tendencies of untrammelled market forces. The regulatory policies which endow corporations with the property power they bring to the market are treated as a given or are assumed to be trade and competition enhancing. Other international bodies, for instance the OECD and UNCTAD, have addressed the question of restrictive business practices, though with limited success, it must be said.

The formats, and, perhaps more tellingly, the purchase of these multilateral accords reveals the strategic manoeuvres by both the developed and developing countries to shore up domestic industry in the high technology sectors and to position it advantageously in overseas markets. The body of international principles admits to exceptions – such as national security and development policy – of which the participating member countries are ready to avail themselves. In particular, spurred on by local business interests, the member countries take unilateral action in defence of their domestic industries against imports from other countries. These measures are most successful where the country enjoys a power advantage over the target nation or corporation.

We can discern these tensions in play in the case of tariffs, non-tariff barriers, subsidies, countervailing measures and direct foreign investment review policy. In the context of high technology, the case of foreign investment policy is a worthwhile focus. National governments want local companies to have access to investment opportunities in overseas economies and may also want to encourage foreign investment in their own economies, but at the same time they may see the need to attach conditions that protect national sovereignty and industrial capability. These competing considerations send them in search of government structures that can flexibly attune investment policy to the particular case. Schemes are constructed with permissive legislative frameworks, essentially to enable the executive and administrative agencies to create bargaining relationships with major foreign investors. Governments endeavour to carve out a little space in which to exert influence upon the conditions under which foreign participation is to take place. More powerful nations may be somewhat more assertive than others.

Such review processes sit uneasily with the expectations of free trade liberalism. The transnational corporations may, for instance, threaten to place their investments elsewhere if conditions become disadvantageous. The national schemes also run up against the prescriptions of the liberal trade and investment regimes being fashioned in the international forums, such as the GATT and the OECD, which recommend free movement of capital and no less favourable treatment for foreign enterprises. At the least, such forums urge governments to articulate their review policies, minimize the grounds for scrutiny, and act with consistency on proposals.

Australia's case is perhaps a perfect microcosm of these ambivalences in play. Its current foreign investment review policy assumes very much the appearance of a flexible, discretionary administrative process. It avoids the straitjacket of substantive and procedural rules. But the government is at pains to stress that foreign investment is welcome and should expect no bar. It is doubtful whether in practice, in the manufacturing sector at least, the scheme is used to bargain purposefully over technology transfer and local participation in innovative activity. On the international stage, the government rightly has reservations about the insertion of free trade demands into the governance of investment measures (the *Age*, 23 November 1990). But it is unsure of its strength to break ranks with the free trade ideology and push unilaterally for concessions. It is persuaded its best strategy is to accept, even to promote, the whole package of free trade liberalizations in the expectation that the ensuing reciprocity will be of net benefit to the country.

PART IV

# Government Sponsorship and Entrepreneurship

CHAPTER 8

# *Direct Grants and Tax Concessions*

In the opening chapters, we identified some of the reasons why governments in many countries have been drawn into direct and discriminating relations of support and collaboration with industrial firms. Yet we noted that this approach continues to face problems, both in being effective instrumentally and in maintaining legitimacy. This last part of the book examines the experience with several recent Australian versions of government participation in the high technology industries – both as a sponsor and as an entrepreneur. Part IV pursues three case studies: (a) direct grants and tax concessions for research and development, (b) procurement preference and offsets, and (c) exclusive telecommunications licences. In this chapter, we begin by noting the take-up of this approach in Australia, before moving to the first of the three case studies.

## THE VEHICLES FOR SPONSORSHIP AND ENTREPRENEURSHIP

In recent years, Australian innovation policy has intensified the use of 'positive adjustment measures'. We might commence by reiterating that, despite the apparent adaptability of the liberal legal approach to different roles, both state and national governments in Australia have reached the view that it can be too indirect, obtuse and uncertain an approach to promote their innovation policies. In order to encourage the kind of local foundation of knowledge, skills and networks which the country needs in order to be able to participate in the benefits of the worldwide revolution in technology, government has turned away from the traditional use of negative defensive measures, most significantly by substantially scaling down tariff barriers. The emphasis has shifted to the use of such positive adjustment measures as research and development grants, tax concessions, production and export bounties, loan guarantees, equity investments, procurement purchases, favourably priced government services, and exclusive licences. Government has deployed these measures not only to pass off assistance to the private sector but, on occasions, actively to encourage industry restructuring by fostering linkages between public and private sector enterprises, indigenous and foreign companies, small and large firms, and producers and users.

Today, in Australia, as in many other countries, government appears to be retracting from this approach as it privatizes many of the public vehicles for this kind of participation. This retraction is evidence of the continuing pull of the liberal approach. Yet, we should note that the privatization programs remain partial. And the privatization which does occur can present fresh opportunities for the provision of subsidies to favoured private firms, especially where public assets are undervalued at sale or sold off uncompetitively. The conditions of sale, such as any requirements for indigenous private participation, also remain relevant. Sometimes, government itself retains a share in the privatized corporation or guarantees it custom, so that the public–private distinction is once again blurred. Full-scale public ownership may also of course be replaced by a regulatory relationship between government and industry. In the fields of telecommunications and broadcasting, for example, government may continue to control market entry and protect favoured firms from competition by issuing a limited number of licences. Licences may conceivably be used, then, to further local industry development, if not in the choice of local licensees at least in placing obligations on foreign licensees to out-source equipment, services and other requirements in the local industry.

## RECENT POSITIVE ADJUSTMENT MEASURES

Why have the positive adjustment measures proved attractive? Several of the measures have been enlisted to the cause of innovation policy as a result of gaps being identified in the private sector's commitment to innovation. One such gap is the failure of indigenous firms (with notable exceptions) to become involved in research and development, coupled with the failure of foreign corporations to locate a share of their research and development in Australia through their subsidiaries and contractors. In this respect, a great deal of importance has been attached to the reorientation of research in the public research institutes and universities and to the commercialization of this research through links forged with the private sector. As we shall see in a moment, another strategy has been the provision of incentives and inducements to sections of the private sector to engage and invest in local research and development. A further gap often identified is the failure of the private market to provide capital for the kinds of local start-up ventures that develop scientific ideas through the intermediate business stages towards their ultimate commercialization (Victorian Government Technology Statement, 1986). Shortcomings in the local venture capital market led not only to a tax concession scheme at the federal level but also to equity investment by government development corporations in high technology enterprises. The least successful of these government development corporations was the Victorian Economic Development Corporation. Others, such as the Australian Industry Development Corporation, have enjoyed more success.

As we move away from research and development into production and marketing, the measures of support do not necessarily abate. A variety of incentives have been made available to encourage investment in new plant and equipment, especially plant and equipment that is locally sourced. Bounties have been provided for the local production of high technology, such as computer ware. More recently, attention has been given over to the provision of subsidies and services to assist with export drives. In closer collaboration, the Australian government has reached special-purpose agreements with mining, refining, manufacturing and construction companies in order to settle such matters as permission for development, contributions from public works and patronage, the level of taxes, royalties and public rates, and provision for local sub-contracting opportunities (Head, 1986). The federal Labor government also crafted industry plans with employers and unions in established manufacturing industries (e.g. steel) which combined government assistance such as soft loans with efforts by the private sector parties to modernize production, especially through the exploitation of computer technology (Commonwealth of Australia. Department of Industry, Technology and Commerce, 1987). Perhaps the most ambitious combination of these techniques might eventually be realized in the construction of the 'multi-function polis' (Mouer and Sugimoto, 1990).

## THE OPERATIONAL RATIONALE FOR THE APPROACH

For practised social observers, little of this is news (Loveday, 1982). We shall therefore concentrate on the legal dimensions of these relationships. The styling of these measures also has an internal operational rationale that helps to explain the characteristic legal form which they assume and in particular their departure from constitutionality and legality. Of course, as we shall see from the three examples below, the measures vary somewhat along such lines as the discretion they afford the administrators, the closeness of their involvement with their subjects, and the demands they place upon their beneficiaries. Yet, the Australian experience confirms that many of these measures of support are legally sourced in broad permissive statutory frameworks or even in simple budgetary appropriations. Their real policy is developed in informal administrative structures, involving the use of ministerial directions, agency guidelines and other kinds of 'quasi-legislation' to structure the criteria by which the decisions are to be made (Ganz, 1987). Often they delegate authority to select the individual beneficiaries to specialist administrative agencies or all manner of hybrid commissions and councils that include business and other private sector representatives in their deliberations. In some cases, the administration of the particular support measure is given over to a joint venture, trading company, or other commercial association that operates only under the general private law standards of contract and business law. The result of these arrangements is to distance the support activity from the traditional forums of legal accountability, such as the courts and the legislatures.

Such an implementation structure provides simultaneously for greater scope for executive direction of the agencies' mission, the exercise of managerial discretion over the conduct of the agencies' work, and participation by private sector interests in the agencies' decision-making (Halligan and O'Grady, 1985). In the first place, the new 'managerialism' is intended to afford frontline managers and agency heads greater freedom to manage the day-to-day operations of the agencies. With corporatization, the agencies' own internal bureaucratic structures are relaxed. For example, management practice turns away from an emphasis on observing financial, regulatory and legal proprieties and towards the gearing of operations according to the objectives of strategy and business plans, through such techniques as program budgeting and performance evaluation (Howard, 1986; Carroll, 1986). At the same time, the managers operate within a framework of strategic control and internal accountability to the relevant ministry and the coordinating executive departments, such as prime minister and Cabinet or Treasury and Finance. The agencies may be subject to general obligations to heed government policy, supplemented by specific guidelines and particular directions from the ministries, and their strategic plans and financial targets (such as their borrowing levels) may require central approval. The construction of these relations can at times take on the language of the market, as agencies are asked to negotiate profiles, contract results and pay dividends to the central government.

Yet another simultaneous trend in public administration is the diffusion of decision-making through the use of advisory committees, consultative bodies, and specialist councils to government departments and statutory bodies. These hybrid bodies often include representatives of business and industry, and sometimes labour and consumer groups. The performance of functions is shifted further from the centre with the participation of public agencies in joint ventures, commercial companies and other private associations with business interests.

FREEDOM FROM REVIEW

Why might this kind of government structure seem suitable for the implementation of innovation policy? As we have noted, its most immediate attraction lies in overcoming the inflexibilities of the bureaucratic legal approach (Selznick, 1969). Exercising the government's financial powers through the medium of administrative schemes or contractual arrangements has the appeal of avoiding the complexity and rigidities of parliamentary legislation and judicial review (Daintith, 1979). Apart from the precise check of legislative supervision or judicial review, the implementing agencies may wish to avoid the political controversy of conferring favours by submerging them within the administrative and technical realms of government. In this vein, Krever (1985) suggests for example that tax concessions are attractive as a hidden form of assistance. Normally, they are not subject to scrutiny on a regular basis because they do not involve the act of dispensing money to beneficiaries but only result in revenue foregone to the Treasury. So too, we might say that the provision of assistance through property sales, government purchases, or debt and equity financing privatizes the act of conferring public benefits on particular economic interests. Government agencies purport to operate as ordinary players in the market, attributing their decisions to routine commercial considerations that are not susceptible to the conventional standards of public scrutiny (Aubert, 1985).

## THE INCORPORATION OF PRIVATE INTERESTS

The approach can also serve as a means of obtaining the private participation and cooperation which the agencies consider crucial to the success of their programs. Commenting on recent experience with this practice in Western Australia, Harman (1986: 250) suggested three major influences:

> some incentive has undoubtedly come from the Government's desire to find additional significant sources of revenue. The second inspiration has been the desire to expand and reshape the economy by using the public enterprise to supply new sources of finance or market access. The third rationale has been the desire to bring business practice into the management of government itself.

The quest for additional revenue cannot be underestimated as a motivation for the approach today, especially for governments desperate to overcome declining revenues and rising debts. As we shall see, the desire to offload the debt incurred in launching Australia's communications satellite was quite possibly a reason for providing a licence to a private company to compete with the country's core telecommunications carrier. Various agencies, such as the higher education institutions, have been driven to seek further funding in the private sector as their public sources constricted. So too, the wish to emulate the organizational structures and methods of successful private firms appears to be a motivating factor. Australian governments have attempted to reshape public organizations so that they resemble the modern corporation. Standards of economy and efficiency are emphasized, perhaps at the expense of other objectives (Taggart, 1991). The reforms also have the effect of staffing the agencies with managers more sympathetic to the outlooks and goals of private companies (Pusey, 1991).

## THE EFFICACY OF THE APPROACH

What of the government's attempts to reshape the economy by these means? The transnational corporations' mobility in a world economy seems to indicate that they can often play off competing nation states or regional provinces for the support they desire. Governments must endeavour to negotiate with their incentives and assurances in order to influence the corporations' locational decisions. The desire to incubate creative but rather fragile local firms proves no less difficult to achieve. Such firms appear to require more than a one-off vote of assistance if they are to survive in the tough high technology environments. Often, they seek continuing assistance with problems of credit, management, facilities and marketing that draws them into extended working relations with their public supporters. Let us see at least if these observations hold true in the three case studies.

## DIRECT GRANTS

This chapter now presents the case study of direct grants and tax concessions for research and development expenditure. It analyses first the grants for industrial research and development scheme (GIRD). It notes the criticisms which such grants schemes have encountered. The chapter turns next to the tax concession for research and development expenditure, identifying the terms of this concession. It traces the experience of the scheme in attempting to deal with the claims made in relation to intragroup contracting over expenditure. It assesses the impact of the scheme and its efforts to come to grips with ingenious efforts to exploit its provisions at the margins.

## GIRD

As we have noted, much of the Australian government's expenditure on research has gone to the public sector, but it has also underwritten research in the private sector. Some of this assistance has been *ad hoc*. One early example of a more substantial scheme was the Australian industrial research and development incentives scheme (AIRDIS). Originating in 1967, and re-established under the *Industrial Research and Development Incentives Act 1976* (Cth), the scheme provided grants to research projects organized in the private sector.

In 1985, the scheme was subjected to several reviews that raised questions about the return the government was obtaining from the provision of assistance (generally see MacDonald, 1986). One review, for example, suggested that the grants were not stimulating new research projects even if they had improved the quality of the projects which were funded (Commonwealth of Australia. DITC, 1985a). In 1986, the *Industry Research and Development Act* was passed so that the AIRDIS could be phased out and replaced with a new grants for industrial research and development scheme (GIRD). The new legislation reflected a decision to harness the scheme to stimulate research amongst start-up companies and new ventures in targeted high technology areas of growth (DITC, 1987). Oversight of the scheme was transferred to the Department of Industry, Technology and Commerce (DITC). An Industry Research and Development Board (IRDB) was constituted along similar lines to the AIRDS Board. The new board was to be assisted by advisory committees appointed by the minister though, as a matter of practice, the onus would still fall on the competence of the staff of the board to assess the quality of individual applicant projects (see DITC, 1987b).

For the purposes of the Act, research and development activities were defined as systematic investigation or experimentation activities (a) that involve innovation, technology transfer into Australia or technical risk, (b) that are carried out in Australia, and (c) the object of which is new knowledge (with or without a specific practicable application) or new or improved materials, products, devices, processes or services.

*Discretionary Grants*

The Act established a scheme of discretionary, generic technology, and national interest grants. Discretionary grants are payable for industrial research and development in respect of eligible activities, including the manufacture of goods, mining operations, construction operations and software production, and also any activity declared eligible by the minister in the Government Gazette. Grants are also payable for the development of new systems and processes for any of these eligible activities. The board may fund up to 50 per cent of the total expenditure on the assisted project, and funds may be provided for a maximum of three years.

Subject to the Act and to any directions by the minister, the IRDB may at its discretion enter into an agreement on behalf of the federal government with an eligible company, or with a company carrying out research and development for an eligible company, to make a grant of financial assistance. Eligible companies are companies carrying out eligible activities in Australia, or other companies proposing to carry out eligible activities in Australia and declared by the board to be eligible companies for the purposes of the Act. The Minister has prescribed economic, technical and commercial criteria for the assessment of individual discretionary grant applications. In part, discretionary grants are payable where the applicant intends to exploit the project results on normal commercial terms and otherwise for the benefit of the Australian economy.

## *Generic Technology Grants*

Generic technology grants are payable at the IRDB's discretion in respect of expenditure on a project of research and development activities in a field of generic technology. Under the Act, the minister may, by way of notice in the Government Gazette, declare a field to be a field of generic technology. Initially, the minister declared three such fields: biotechnology, information technology and new materials technology. The board has subsequently targeted research in a number of areas within the declared generic fields. For example, the target areas identified for information technology in 1987 were software engineering, person-machine interaction, information management, computer networking, and device and system hardware technologies. Within the field of biotechnology, the areas were plant agriculture, animal production, human pharmaceutical-medical technologies, biotechnology support, food processing, agricultural surpluses, and water treatment, and, as they fell within the disciplines of genetic engineering, cell manipulation and culture, and enzyme application and fermentation technology. Such areas were said to represent technologies of fundamental significance to future industrial competitiveness. These technologies were regarded as unlikely to develop if left to market forces alone, because, for example, of the existence of high entry costs or the inability of firms readily to appropriate the benefits of the research.

Again, the board may enter into an agreement for the making of a generic technology grant with a researcher who is carrying out or who proposes to carry out a project of research and development activities in one of these areas of generic technology. A statutory limit is not placed on the monetary amount of the project funding. The category of researchers takes in persons that, in the opinion of the board, are capable of carrying out a project, and includes a department of state, a company and an approved research institute.

## Criticisms of the Grants Schemes

The initial AIRDIS scheme attracted considerable criticism from academic economists for the faulty theories which were said to underwrite its orientation (for example, Gannicott, 1980). Its orientation to research was criticized, for example, for failing to understand the nature of the whole innovation process. Its allocations were attacked for trying to 'pick winners' (MacDonald, 1986). Fundamentally, the scheme was said to be in error in assuming that it was market failure, rather than a sound appraisal by the market, that led to certain projects not being supported by the private sector. The scheme was also claimed to be likely to assist precisely those projects which would run in any case – those projects which were not especially uncertain or inappropriable, and therefore not particularly deserving of public subsidy. The recast criteria for the provision of assistance under GIRD reflect some of these concerns. There is evidence also from the IRDB's own reports that it was internalizing the insights of recent innovation policy studies. For example, recognizing that invention was only one component of innovation, its 1990-1991 report signalled an intent to support projects that were closer to the market and that had commercial participation from the early stages (IRDB, 1991). While noting that the grants had already encouraged linkages between industry and other research sectors, it recognized that they had not targeted innovation in the kinds of competitive clusters Porter (1990) has championed.

However, the administration of GIRD has come under fire. As late as 1989, the Commonwealth Auditor-General expressed doubts about whether the applications for discretionary grants under GIRD were being systematically screened to ensure that the projects were really being run by start-up companies which would not be eligible for the tax concession and would not be able to proceed without the grant (Commonwealth of Australia. Auditor-General, 1989). The Auditor-General was also critical of the level of the board's prescription, documentation and monitoring of the conduct of projects in the category of generic technology grants. In response, the board intensified its scrutiny, claiming for instance that it had found that 78 per cent of the projects receiving discretionary grants in 1989-1990 had been successfully completed by the middle of 1990 and that 34 per cent had already been successfully commercialized (Commonwealth of Australia. DITC, 1990). A review of the effectiveness of the generic technology grants indicated that they had increased the amount of collaborative research work. The board agreed nonetheless that further targeting was necessary, and the areas nominated for assistance have since come under review by its committees. Interestingly, GIRD has received less criticism from industry. In the early days of AIRDIS, the majority of applicants received some grant, but, as the number of applications grew, the legislation introduced more discretion into the allocations. AIRDIS decisions were subject to review in the Commonwealth Adminstrative Appeals Tribunal, but this avenue was not provided under GIRD. The Commonwealth Administrative Review Council (1988) recommended that review be permitted.

## TAX CONCESSION

A key initiative among the federal government's recent innovation policies has been the tax concession for expenditure on research and development activities. The research and development concession is by far the most pointed tax device in the armoury of the government's innovation policy. But it is to be remembered that the taxation system can contain a range of allowable deductions on expenditure that conceivably relate to innovation in products and processes. At its introduction, the tax concession was made applicable to expenditure incurred between 1 July 1985 and 30 June 1991. It was to be excluded in October 1987 from a general review of company and business taxes being conducted at the time and scheduled in the Treasurer's May 1988 Economic Statement for reduction from 150 per cent to 100 per cent in 1991 (the *Age*, 26 May 1989). However, in its March 1991 Industry Statement, the government extended the 150 per cent concession until June 1993 and the 125 per cent concession indefinitely thereafter. The opposition has said it will retain the concession when in government.

## THE NATURE OF THE CONCESSION

Essentially, the concession is obtainable as of right once the conditions of the enabling legislation, first created by the *Income Tax Assessment (Research and Development) Act 1986* and the *Industry Research and Development Act 1986* (but subsequently amended numerous times as we shall see), are met by the claimant company. The size of the tax concession is open-ended. Yet, from the government's point of view, the cost of the concession does not show up in the appropriations legislation at Budget time but takes the form of revenue foregone to the Treasury in any one year. As a result of the concession, the Department of Industry, Technology and Commerce (1987c) anticipated a reduction in taxation receipts of $100 million in 1986-1987 and $105 million in 1987-1988. By 1990-1991, the revenue foregone had risen to $230 million per year (Commonwealth of Australia. DITC, 1991). This compares with an allocation of $34.25 million to the GIRD Scheme in 1990-1991.

## CONCESSIONAL EXPENDITURE

The scheme has allowed companies to deduct up to 150 per cent of the various recognized categories of expenditure incurred on research and development activities against their assessable income in each tax year. The Department of Industry, Technology and Commerce has estimated that the net effect on the budgets of eligible companies is that they bear the cost of research and development expenditure at a rate of 41.5 cents in the dollar. The full 150 per cent concession applies only where annual research and development expenditure is $50,000 or more. The concession operates on a sliding scale from 100 to 150 per cent for expenditure between $20,000 and $50,000, though research and development contracted to certain research bodies has attracted the 150 per cent rate from $20,000.

Research and development activities are defined in the principal tax legislation, the *Income Tax Assessment Act*, to mean systematic, investigative or experimental activities that (1) are carried on in Australia or in an external territory; (2) involve innovation or technical risk; and (3) are carried on for the purpose of (a) acquiring new knowledge – whether or not that knowledge will have a specific practical application, or (b) creating new or improved materials, products, devices, processes or services. Also eligible are activities that

(1) are carried on in Australia or in an external territory; and (2) are carried out for a purpose directly related to the carrying on of activities of that kind referred to in the first category. Certain other activities are specifically excluded.

## CLAIMS FOR THE CONCESSION

Claims for the concession are made by lodging the company's income tax return with the Australian Taxation Office. Eligibility is determined by the Commissioner for Taxation. Nonetheless, for the purposes of making an assessment of a claim by a company, the Commissioner for Taxation is empowered to request the Industry Research and Development Board to determine whether particular activities qualify as research and development activities. Such a determination is binding upon the commissioner. The board's powers and procedures in such matters are regulated by the *Industry Research and Development Act 1986*. The board makes provisional determinations, and claimants are afforded an opportunity by the legislation to make representations and provide information to the board for reconsideration (see Commonwealth of Australia. DITC, 1990a).

The IRDB has several other important certifying roles. One concerns the requirement that research and development activities have an adequate Australian content. Another concerns the exploitation of the results of the research and development. Under the legislation, a deduction is not allowable if the board gives the commissioner a certificate stating that, in the opinion of the board, any of the results of the research and development activities are exploited on other than normal commercial terms or in a manner that is not for the benefit of the Australian economy. According to the legislation, exploitation shall be deemed not to be on normal commercial terms if, in the opinion of the board, it is not on terms that persons dealing with each other at arm's length and from positions of comparable bargaining power would have reached. Exploitation is considered not to be for the benefit of the Australian economy if, in the opinion of the board, the profits or gains accruing to Australian residents are not commensurate with the amount expended in carrying out that activity in Australia. A particular concern of these provisions is the arrangements which are made for the conduct, transfer and utilization of innovations between parent companies and their Australian subsidiaries within the transnational corporate groups (see Commonwealth of Australia. DITC, 1990a).

Initially, the scheme provided that only companies were eligible to claim the concession. Companies must register annually with the board in order to be eligible to claim deductions. By the middle of 1991, 1153 companies had registered (Commonwealth of Australia. DITC, 1991). Such a company must be incorporated under a law of the commonwealth or of a state or territory in order to be registerable.

## THE USE OF THE CONCESSION BY INDUSTRY

The private arrangements for funding industrial research and development enterprises can of course vary considerably. All the commitments might for instance be met in-house. A company might incur expenditure to outsiders for the plant, buildings, materials or services necessary for it to perform its own research and development. Or a company might contract out the performance of the research and development to another body, such as a private research firm or a public research institution. A company might set up a subsidiary company to perform the actual research and development or establish a research and development company as a joint venture with other companies and bodies. Where research and development is hived off in these fashions, several questions have arisen for the administrators of the scheme. For example, what part of the expenditure is concessional expenditure? How is the concessional expenditure to be apportioned between the separate entities?

## CONTRACTED EXPENDITURE

In this regard, a key provision by the legislation is the recognition that research and development may be contracted out by an eligible company. At the same time, it specifies that a deduction cannot be claimed by a company for expenditure incurred for the purpose of carrying on research and development activities on behalf of any other person. So any claim must be by the funder, and the agencies have had to determine which entity bears the risk of the activity and is entitled to the results. The legislation also provides that if a company incurs expenditure to another person, and the Commissioner is satisfied (1) having regard to the connection between the company and the person and to any relevant circumstances, that the company and the other person were not dealing at arm's length, and (2) that the expenditure would have been less if they had been dealing at arm's length, then the commissioner may reduce the allowable expenditure.

The scope of such provisions as they applied to intragroup arrangements was soon tested. For example, it emerged that several large companies were establishing subsidiary or 'captive' companies to perform their research and development work. The financial advantage of this arrangement was said to be that the costs attributable to research and development activity can be boosted by separating the activity from a company's other activities where research and development work might otherwise be supported from the company's general facilities and operations. The companies in question sought a ruling from the Commissioner of Taxation on the acceptability of expenditure in these research and development companies (*Australian Financial Review*, 4 June 1987). A more complicated arrangement was presented by the joint venture between a United States company, California Biotechnology, the Garvan Institute of Medical Research in Sydney, and the local MIC company, CP Ventures, to establish a research and development company, Pacific Biotechnology. The joint venturers wished to claim their equity investments in the new research and development company as concessional expenditure and sought a ruling from the commissioner (*Australian Financial Review*, 14 April 1987).

## THE COMMISSIONER'S RULINGS

In August and November 1987, the Taxation Office issued rulings on these and other questions which had arisen in the implementation of the scheme. According to the Department of Industry, Technology and Commerce report on these rulings, they would erase considerable uncertainty about the extent of deductibility under the scheme (*Australian Technology Magazine*, no. 3, October 1987). The commissioner made rulings on such matters as the scope of eligible expenditure generally and the eligibility of expenditure within corporate groups. In his rulings, the commissioner focused his criteria on the location of control over the conduct and results of the research and development work (see Gotterson, 1990).

Yet such rulings do not achieve the status of binding law, even if some professionals seem to regard them as incontrovertible

(Tomasic and Pentony, 1991). In late 1987, the Treasurer and the Minister for Industry, Technology and Commerce jointly announced an internal government review to identify any looseness in the legislative provisions of the scheme. They also announced that the government would be retrospectively amending the legislation in order to deal with potential abuses of the concession and to confirm the interpretations of its provisions (*Australian Technology Magazine*, no. 4, December 1987).

## REVISIONS TO THE CONCESSION

In 1988 and 1989, the government made amendments to the *Income Tax Assessment Act* and the *Research and Development Legislation Act* to implement the findings of its 'technical' review of the operation of the concession. Greater definition was given to the criteria for the appropriate exploitation of the research and development. The notion of 'contracted expenditure' was refined. Provision was made for joint registration by eligible collaborating companies. The concept of approved research institutes was replaced with a system of registered research agencies. A major change was to be the extension of eligibility to claim beyond the company form to partnerships (of eligible companies) and to public trading trusts. Further aspects of dealings over research and development expenditure were regulated, such as the apportionment of expenditure between contracting parties (Commonwealth of Australia. DITC, 1990).

By this time, considerable attention was being given over to the syndication provisions of the legislation. Syndication had been recognized in the legislation as a means to allow groups of eligible companies to form consortia (such as joint ventures or special purpose companies) so that they might undertake significant research and development projects which were beyond the resources of a single company or too risky for a single entity to assume. Syndication was said to have the advantage of spreading risks and encouraging collaboration (Commonwealth of Australia. DITC, 1990). Syndicates were able to seek registration with the board.

Still, according to the Department of Industry, Technology and Commerce, the board became concerned that the practice in some syndicates of guaranteeing returns to investors (such as portfolio investors) could be shifting the focus of investment away from the commercial viability of research and development projects.

Additional amendments were made through the *Tax Laws Amendment Act 1990*, in part to vary the level of the concession according to the risk of the investment. Syndication remained, however, a source of aggravation to the scheme, and discussions with the Taxation Office led to another taxation ruling being issued in May 1991 (DITC, 1991).

## THE IMPACT OF THE CONCESSION

### Industry Autonomy

While it displays characteristics of a purposive action approach, the concession still works very much indirectly and at arm's length from the private sector firms it seeks to stimulate. It relies on the decisions of private firms to respond to the inducement within the framework which the enabling legislation provides, especially in terms of eligibility criteria concerning such matters as the definition of research and development, the scope of concessional expenditure and the need for proper exploitation of results. It is precisely this openness and detachment which has attracted praise. The Department of Industry, Technology and Commerce (Commonwealth of Australia, 1987) has itself stressed the point that the concession places decision-making concerning research and development activity in the hands of industry. It allows commercial and other considerations to determine the distribution and level of research and development efforts. The concession is not targeted to particular technologies or industry sectors. Nor does it discriminate between foreign-owned subsidiaries and indigenous companies.

It is worth noting that tax concessions for research expenditure or capital investment have been employed in other countries, such as the United Kingdom (Hughes, 1988) and the United States (Bozeman and Link, 1984). Singapore is said to have adopted the Australian model recently (the *Australian*, 6 November 1991). In the United States, President Reagan increased the available tax breaks. Bozeman and Link (1984) treat the tax concession's popularity with business and government, even with conservative Republicans, as one of its attractions. In particular, they place weight on the political invisibility and stability it acquires from the fact that it does not require the annual scrutiny of the budgetary appropriations process.

The Australian Science and Technology Council (1983) also listed some of the limitations of a tax concession. These drawbacks include the fact that it favours firms which are already making a profit (though firms may be allowed to carry forward losses and thus enjoy the benefit of the concession in a subsequent year). The concession is therefore for those (often large) firms which wish to mediate their cash flows rather than those firms which are just starting up and do not yet have much income. Further, a tax incentive scheme, being a general and indirect assistance scheme, does not provide an opportunity for the government to influence the pattern of research and development in the specific directions identified by its innovation policy. Indeed, the concession may not improve the overall rate of research and development. A question here is whether the concession funds research and development that would not have been undertaken otherwise or whether it simply makes ongoing research and development less expensive. The quality and the destination of the work undertaken is another concern. To this concern we should add the note that political accountability can also be weak because the spending is 'off-budget'.

## The Return on the Concession

What has been the impact of the concession? The Department of Industry, Technology and Commerce (Commonwealth of Australia, 1987c) estimated that companies were investing about $575 million on research and development in 1985-1986, the first year of the scheme. This investment represented an increase in expenditure of around 25 per cent in real terms in 1984-1985. Increases on this figure of 29 per cent and 6 per cent were also identified in the following two years (Commonwealth of Australia. DITC, 1989). This position represented a marked improvement, though private sector research and development still lagged behind levels in comparable industrial countries, and the sharemarket crash of October 1987 raised concerns that private companies would contain their discretionary expenditure upon research and development as they adopted more conservative investment policies. The Bureau of Industry Economics' interim evaluation of the program found, however, that levels continued to rise, with perhaps a third of the rises attributable to the presence of the incentive (Commonwealth of Australia. Bureau of Industry

Economics, 1989). More important, according to many, was the influence of the concession on the level of local consciousness and experience concerning research and development activity. The Department of Industry, Technology and Commerce (Commonwealth of Australia, 1989) was able to cite the findings of a consultants' report that the incentive had resulted in business research and development being re-evaluated and redirected with a more commercial focus. Collaboration was also up.

The Bureau of Industry Economics entered the reservation nonetheless that the net benefit from the policy, after allowing for the revenue foregone and the costs of administration, remained to be determined. Of course, for some, part of that cost is the distortion of the 'neutral' tax system for ulterior purposes and the diversion of investment away from more effective or efficient allocations of resources (Gormly, 1989; generally see Grbich, 1984). As we know, some doubt for example whether Australia should invest in research and development at all. Certainly, there is a danger that locally funded inventions will be exploited overseas with little spin-off or return to Australian industry. A related concern is that the results of private research will be retained in-house and not diffused to the benefit of the overall economy. The scheme's criteria have been refined to try to avoid these outcomes.

## The Quality of Research and Development

Questions have also been raised about the pattern of the research and development which is being supported. A 1987 internal Department of Science study revealed that spending on research and development in high technology firms was lower in Australia, compared to other OECD countries, than local spending in medium and low technology firms (*Australian Financial Review*, 31 March 1987). Another commentary suggested that spending had increased more in those industries outside the manufacturing sector. Again, some controls have been built into the scheme in terms of the definition of research and development activities. Another issue has been expenditure on the acquisition of technology from outside. In any case, these differential impacts may or may not be a bad thing, depending on the view taken about the country's best prospects for finding a place in the international technological order (Jevons and

Saupin, 1991). Risky product innovation is important, but so too is the modernization of existing processes. The Department of Industry, Technology and Commerce (Commonwealth of Australia, 1990a) has said that the objective of the incentive is to make Australian companies more innovative and internationally competitive through improving innovative skills in Australian industry. This objective is to be achieved by increasing companies' investment in research and development; encouraging better use of Australia's existing research structure; improving conditions for the commercialization of new processes and product technologies developed by Australian companies; and developing a capacity for adoption of foreign technology.

Another concern has focused on the opportunities the concession has provided to exploit the fuzzier concepts in the legislation. The concession has attracted practices that are a familiar hazard for the taxation system: manipulation of the provisions at the margins and the artificial construction of eligible claims. The scheme has several devices built into it to screen claims, such as the requirement of registration with the Industry Research and Development Board, but these devices have relied heavily on the resources of the board and the Australian Taxation Office. This hazard was underlined in the report of the Auditor-General's efficiency audit which raised concerns about the level of assessment of individual claims (Commonwealth of Australia. Auditor-General, 1989). The Auditor-General found that, in the early days of the scheme, the board was unable to screen individually all applications for registration. The eligibility of expenditure had been verified by the Taxation Office in only about 2 per cent of claims.

The Department of Industry, Technology and Commerce (Commonwealth of Australia, 1989) has, however, been tenacious in defending the effectiveness of the scheme. In 1989, it countered public comment alleging abuse of the concession by citing the Australian Bureau of Statistics' view that the very large increase in research and development since its introduction was genuine. It suggested that companies were not prepared to misrepresent information to the Taxation Office for fear of being open to significant penalties and close scrutiny. In DITC's view, the stringent reporting requirements imposed on eligible companies, annual registration, Industry Research and Development Board assessment and the role of the Taxation Office all acted to deter abuse.

## CONTROLS OVER DECISION-MAKING

Nevertheless, the problems of creative accounting or financial engineering, along with some genuine ambiguities in the legislation, led the Commissioner of Taxation to issue several detailed rulings on aspects of entitlement. But the policy of the commissioner remained subject, at least in part, to review through appeals regarding individual claims to the Commonwealth Administrative Appeals Tribunal and the ordinary courts in the well established legal appeal structure of the taxation system. Indeed, the Commonwealth Administrative Review Council (Commonwealth of Australia, 1988) recommended to the government that several remaining areas of discretionary administrative decision-making be subjected to review on their merits in the tribunal, and the government responded with legislation in 1990–1991. As we have seen, the government was obliged to tighten up the provisions of the Act in 1988 and 1989, yet in 1990 it was again moved to close off loopholes. At this point, the minister commented that creative accounting and financial engineering were testing the bounds of reality (the *Age*, 11 August 1989).

The need for repeated amendments was, perhaps, affecting the stability of the scheme. Indeed, efforts to secure the purpose of the scheme did not lead merely to yearly changes to the legislation. The efforts led to more particular and discerning criteria that required greater judgement on the part of the administering agencies about the eligibility of the projects and, inevitably, required them to see through the formal legal corporate structures into the realities of their technical and economic operations.

CHAPTER 9

# Procurement Preference and Offsets

This chapter presents the case study of procurement preference and offsets policy. It notes first the power of the public purchasing market. It considers next the operation of the principle of preference for local content in the supply of goods and services, and notes the use of several more collaborative efforts to place local firms in a position to win contracts. It looks also at two important sectoral industry development programs. The chapter subsequently explores the shift in the strategic use of the procurement power to the eliciting of offsets from the large foreign suppliers. It plots the movement from direct offsets arrangements to the partnerships for development program.

In Australia, it is fair to say that a major role in the implementation of innovation policy could be assigned to the purchasing and procurement powers of government. It has been estimated that the federal government spends around $8 billion a year in purchases (Commonwealth of Australia. Bureau of Industry Economics, 1988a). In the year 1985–1986, $3.6 billion was spent on high technology, but about half of that technology was sourced overseas (DITC, 1987a). The major objects of this expenditure were information technology, industrial electronics and telecommunications equipment. Within this expenditure, individual purchases are so big as to be strategically significant in their own right. For example, in 1987, the Australian Taxation Office was planning to spend $700 million on the purchase of new information technology and the Defence Department $300 million in the same area.

## PURCHASING PREFERENCE

### THE PURCHASING ACTIVITIES OF THE PUBLIC SECTOR

Yet, governments in Australia have been accused of not doing enough with this considerable power to promote local industry (Stewart, 1989). Of course, government departments and authorities continually require goods and services for the execution of their many executive and legislative responsibilities, such as the defence of the nation, the operation of the telecommunications network and the support of health services. Government purchasing is largely, then, an activity incidental to or supportive of the discharge of each agency's primary responsibilities. Purchasing policies and decisions must thus be justifiable in terms of an agency's primary objectives. Industry development may not feature directly amongst these objectives, except in the case of agencies like the Department of Industry, Technology and Commerce. Yet, naturally, arguments can be made about the importance of a healthy local industry to the maintenance of an agency's main functions. For example, the Department of Defence takes the view that the promotion of some local capability in the production and maintenance of defence equipment is important if supplies and services are to be assured when Australia is cut off from other countries during an emergency (Commonwealth of Australia. Auditor-General, 1984).

Conventionally, purchasing is also subject to general financial standards concerning the price, quality and efficacy of the goods and services which are purchased, and particularly concerning the procedures which are to be followed in order to ensure efficiency, economy and value for money in purchasing. Competitive tendering and contractual undertakings by suppliers are common in this regard (Commonwealth of Australia. DITC, 1987a). In the case of the federal government, which shall be our focus, financial standards are based on the *Audit Act 1901* and are to be found largely in financial regulations promulgated by the Governor-General in Council. These regulations are supported by various kinds of internal instructions, directives and guidelines, such as the Department of Finance's finance manual, the Department of Administrative Services' purchasing manual and the handbooks of the purchasing agencies themselves. Purchasing is also subject to review by central executive agencies like the Department of Finance, and to assessment by the Auditor-General and parliamentary committees such as the Joint Committee of the Parliament on Public Accounts.

## THE LOCAL PREFERENCE PRINCIPLE

It should be readily apparent that policies designed to favour local industries may sit uneasily with the financial and technical standards required to be met in purchasing programs. Nevertheless, as a means of affording support to Australian industry, the government has pursued for many years a local preference principle in the purchase of goods and services. The principle has had broad coverage of public agencies, with exceptions for some but not all government business enterprises. The principle has operated in the case of purchases above $20,000. In choosing between tenders for such purchases, a local bid may be allowed a margin over its rivals equivalent to 20 per cent of the value of that part of the goods or services which are Australian or New Zealand sourced. If, after the margin has been allowed, this bid is still 10 per cent higher than a rival foreign bid, then the Minister for Administrative Services or his delegate may permit a discretionary preference to be given to the local content bid in accordance with supplementary criteria which have been laid down in guidelines issued by the minister. The guidelines state that these criteria are: (a) to assist in establishing or maintaining the defence strategic capabilities of the country; (b) to avoid significant additional disruptions in severely depressed labour markets in those industries which are reliant on government orders; and (c) to assist the development of competitive technology-intensive industries offering high growth potential. According to the Australian Science and Technology Council (Commonwealth of Australia, 1984) report on government purchasing and offset policies, this discretionary principle had not been invoked on many occasions.

In addition, certificates of exemption can be granted to absolve an agency from the need to seek competitive bids for a particular purchase. The certificates are issuable by the Secretary of the Department of Finance or his delegate in accordance with criteria laid down in the departmental purchasing manual. There is no evidence, however, that these certificates have been used to favour local industry.

## THE EXPERIENCE WITH THE PRINCIPLE

The preference principle has come under question in recent years and its future in Australia is not assured. In its evaluation of the policy, the Bureau of Industry Economics (Commonwealth of Australia, 1988) doubted its effectiveness as a stimulus to industry development. It found that the margin was only applied to about 0.1 per cent of federal government purchases. In the bureau's view, its cost exceeded its returns, at least in terms of the aid it rendered to firms to become internationally competitive. At the same time, it appeared to cut across objectives of product quality and commercial efficiency, so that the individual agencies were likely to show some resistance to its imprecations.

The Bureau of Industry Economics was also sensitive to the fact that the principle acted like a non-tariff barrier to free trade. Apart from its micro-economic implications, such a policy was likely to attract the displeasure of the international free trade movements we examined in chapter 7. The bureau suggested that most (comparable) countries had moved away from direct preference policies. Certainly, we can see tendencies within liberalized national and regional markets to relax local content rules (Horowitz, 1991). And, in the Tokyo round, as we noted, the GATT produced a multilateral government procurement code. Interestingly, Australia is not yet a signatory to the code, though the government has reported it is considering acceding to it (Commonwealth of Australia. DITC, 1991). Furthermore, at least two of the major overseas markets, the United States and Japan, still apply local preference. The United States has enacted a Buy American Act that does not, however, apply to signatories to the GATT code or to partners in special bilateral agreements (Tidwell, 1986). While the passage of its competition in contracting legislation is said to have opened its procurement process to foreign bidders in recent years, the United States government, for national security reasons, still makes reservations regarding the supply of advanced technology. Japan, of course, operates a strong local preference policy on a more informal basis (Boyd, 1987).

## THE NATIONAL DEVELOPMENT PROCUREMENT PROGRAM

The problems faced by Australian firms in competing relevent markets have also led to consideration being given to using government facilities and capacities to develop local products to a competitive stage. Notably, in 1986, on the instigation of the Department of Industry, Technology and Commerce, the government established a committee of review of government high technology purchasing arrangements. In its report, the 'Inglis Committee' cited several examples of government attempts to assist local industry to develop and trial potential products in order that they might be placed in a position to bid for government contracts or to sub-contract to overseas suppliers (Commonwealth of Australia. DITC, 1987a). It advanced the view that such assistance would help to fill the serious gap between invention and production in the local innovation process. Experimentation and proving of the technology might even take place in government facilities.

In the result, the government established in 1987 a national procurement development program with funds initially of $7 million a year to enable government agencies to trial innovative products from indigenous information technology firms (*Australian Technology Newsletter*, no. 2, September 1987). The program was to be administered by the Industry Research and Development Board (IRDB), though it would, in practice, be driven by a specially constituted committee combining relevant industry and government expertise. Criteria for project selections were promulgated in the form of ministerial directions (see Murley, 1990). In 1988, the IRDB called for joint applications from managers within government agencies and companies with relevant skills and experience in technology intensive industries to support the research and development, demonstration and trialling of promising internationally competitive products. By 1990-1991, eighty-five projects had received support, thirty-three of which totalled $6.3 million. A good example was the development by AMRAD, in conjunction with the Fairfield Infectious Diseases Hospital and the Red Cross Blood Bank in Victoria, of kits for the diagnosis of AIDS (Commonwealth of Australia. DITC, 1991). However, in 1992 the Bureau of Industry Economics was to recommend that the program be phased out (the *Age*, 16 May 1992).

The Inglis Committee also urged the government to extend its forward planning of purchases in order that potential suppliers might receive early notice of prospective government contracts so that they might gear up to compete for supply. The Department of Administrative Services had already been operating a pilot program, using future ADP requirements as a test case. The committee suggested that forward planning would also be enhanced by the use of consultative mechanisms between agencies and industry; and a number of key agencies – such as the Australian Telecommunications Commission – have already set up bodies for this purpose. It seems clear that forward planning would also be facilitated by the co-ordination or centralization of purchasing requirements in such areas as computer technology. Individual agencies, however, are inclined to guard their territories and little progress has been made with this form of planning.

## TWO MAJOR SECTORAL PROGRAMS

### DEFENCE PURCHASING

Given the limited impact of these generic initiatives, one could argue that many of the critical decisions regarding the thrust of procurement policy still lie with the major purchasing agencies. Three key agencies are the Australian Telecommunications Commission (which is discussed in chapter 10), the Department of Defence, and the Department of Health. Defence procurement is an area in which individual contracts may amount to significant policy decisions. For example, the competition over the contract to construct submarines for the Australian Navy involved intensive bidding and lobbying by rival consortia of overseas and local firms, with the strong support of the governments of the states in which the work might be done.

*Local Development*

The Australian Industry Involvement Program of the Department of Defence has two main facets. The first and most apposite is Defence Offsets, a program component run separately from the government's civil offsets arrangements (see below). In its departmental instructions, the Department of Defence has required, if expenditure on a contract is to be greater than $2.5 million and if the overseas content is to comprise at least 30 per cent of the contract value, that 30 per cent of the contract value be placed locally (Commonwealth of Australia. Auditor-General, 1984; see now Department of Defence, 1991). Offsets may take the form of purchases of local products, local training, local participation in collaborative projects and export from Australia (Murley, 1990). The second component is Defence Designated and Assisted Work, whereby work which is specially designated for strategic defence reasons must be manufactured, assembled or trialled locally. The policy behind these instructions is not so much to stimulate local industry as an end in itself but to ensure that there is some local support for the life of defence equipment, especially in the case of a war. Almost all major items of defence technology are designed and supplied from overseas, normally from the United States.

Indeed, the Department of Defence and the Department of Defence Support may be said to have resisted the application of their considerable purchasing resources to local industry development, given their desire to obtain the most sophisticated technology. For example, in June 1984, the Ministers for Defence and for Defence Support, in announcing a set of revisions to the participation program for Australian industry, again required support for local industry to be justified in strategic defence terms. They also expressed reservations about the cost premiums and technical limitations entailed in using both local public and private industry (Commonwealth of Australia. Auditor-General, 1984). In 1988, the prize one billion dollar computer contract was awarded to IBM, on the basis, it appears, that a number of local companies would be involved in supply as subcontractors (the *Australian*, 7 February 1988).

Any overall understanding of the relation between defence policies and technological innovation would of course require a great deal of analysis of practices outside Australia. Worldwide, defence spending accounts for a large proportion of the research and development budget, especially in the leader country, the United States, but also in other Western countries such as the United Kingdom and France. The military agencies have thus been major sponsors and shapers of the course of the new technologies (for example, Noble, 1979). Many of the major innovations in the computer and communications related areas have been funded and specified in their infancy by the United States military authorities (Pugh, 1984). It is said that United States spending in defence areas accounts for over half the country's research and development activity. Such spending has long shielded innovators from the economic pressures of the market and permitted them to work on large-scale and sophisticated development projects. It has also fostered a network of administrative relations between the military authorities, industrial contractors and university science faculties (Dickson, 1984). As the Strategic Defense Initiative indicates, the huge military research projects can spread the network of relations beyond the boundaries of any one state, exciting all sorts of industrial and national interests in the dispensing of patronage and the sharing of results (Lakoff and York, 1989).

## MEDICARE SUBSIDIES

### Health Expenditures

A second example of the role in innovation promotion of purchasing decisions by key agencies is the public healthcare system. In Australia, the provision of medical, hospital and pharmaceutical services is funded substantially out of public taxation revenue, and the decisions to schedule technology-intensive services for rebate under the Medicare system is a crucial one for the fate of new procedures and treatments. The use of new high technology diagnostic and remedial equipment, such as the kidney stone lithotripter, has created difficult resource allocation decisions for public hospitals and government health departments, not only because of the large capital costs of the equipment but also because of their high operating costs as medical procedures (Kirby, 1983). The issues raised by the new medical technology, and particularly the public choice implications, have been subject to considerable philosophical and policy analysis elsewhere (Fineberg, 1985). Of course, the use of these technologies goes beyond economic issues into moral and social questions concerning expert intervention in the natural processes of life and death.

Another dimension of the public healthcare system which will serve an example for the present study is the pharmaceutical benefits scheme. The purchase of the drugs and other medicinal preparations which are incorporated in the Pharmaceutical Benefits Schedule is subject to a federal government rebate at a prescribed level. In 1985-1986, the direct cost of the rebate scheme to the government was $615.8 million (Commonwealth of Australia. Department of Health, 1986). It has been estimated that, through the scheme, the government buys around 75 to 80 per cent of the pharmaceutical industry's output of scheduled drugs.

## Factor F

In recent years, the government's procurement powers in this field have received attention from the point of view of their potential contribution to innovation policy. The Industries Assistance Commission's 1986 report on the local pharmaceutical industry in part recommended changes to the Pharmaceutical Benefits Scheme and the deregulation of the industry (Commonwealth of Australia. Industries Assistance Commission, 1986). In September 1987, the Minister for Community Services and Health and the Minister for Industry, Technology and Commerce put forward a joint strategy plan for the development of the industry (the *Australian*, 14 September 1987). In an effort to encourage local innovation and export, the government signalled that it would use its pricing and subsidy powers (and, in particular, the Dr Strangelove-like Factor 'F') under the Pharmaceutical Benefits Scheme to favour firms which researched, developed and manufactured drugs in Australia. The government would provide this support by allowing these firms to charge higher prices for their products under the rebate scheme. Decision-making under the new scheme would be moved out of the Department of Community Services and Health to a new authority comprising a chairman and four other members representing government, industry and consumer interests. (Ministerial authority over the scheme was subsequently assumed by the Minister for Industry, Technology and Commerce.)

By 1991, the Department of Industry, Technology and Commerce (1991) reported that nine major drug companies, including Glaxo, Faulding, Sigma, Beecham, and ICI Australia, had joined the scheme. The scheme had encouraged local links with other manufacturers, service industries and research institutes. Yet there was also criticism by the opposition in the parliament of the tension between the industry policy and the minister's regulatory responsibility for quality, safety and efficacy in the drug supply program.

## CIVILIAN OFFSETS

### THE OFFSETS POLICY

A distinctive shift in the use of the procurement power since 1970 has been the policy that overseas suppliers to the federal government should 'offset' the imported content of their contracts by agreeing to place work locally (Commonwealth of Australia. DITC, 1985). Some state governments have also operated offsets schemes. The strategy of an offsets policy is not to insist that a proportion of a particular contract need be sourced locally but rather that the overseas supplier should patronize local industry in various creative ways in order to compensate for the foreign content of a purchase. As a precondition for receiving major orders of purchases from the government, overseas suppliers must be prepared to provide Australian industry with significant commercial and technological opportunities. The offsets arrangements thus provide government with a more flexible approach to local industry development. Acknowledging both the limitations of the local firms and the roles of the foreign corporations, they seek in various ways to harness the foreigners' power to the 'up-skilling' of the local industry. These ways extend beyond the purchase of Australian goods and services into technology transfer, local training in research and development, co-production and collaboration in export marketing. Murray and Horwitz (1988) report that some eighty countries worldwide are engaged in offsets programs, ranging through counter-trade, technology transfer, and co-production to local equity investment.

The obligation to provide offsets business to Australian firms arises when overseas companies provide services or sell or lease goods produced outside Australia to federal or state government departments and authorities, and to some Australian companies associated with the federal government (*Australian Financial Review*, 1 March 1988). The offsets requirements have applied when the duty-free price of the purchase exceeds $2.5 million and the imported content exceeds 30 per cent of this price, though this threshold may be varied by the appropriate minister. The offsets obligation applies to both single and cumulative orders over a financial year. The supply of certain goods and services (such as second-hand goods) is excepted from the requirement, and a minister may exempt other goods or services.

## OFFSETS ARRANGEMENTS

The offsets policy has been subject to various modifications since its inception and, at the time of its most recent revision, the policy allowed for a range of arrangements to meet offsets obligations. These arrangements included: (a) offsets credits, in which the overseas supplier provides offsets in anticipation of future obligations; (b) contract-by-contract offsets, by which the discharge of obligation is tied to particular contracts; (c) cumulative order arrangements, by which the discharge of obligations is associated with total government purchases over a set period; (d) pre-qualified offsets supplier (PQSS) agreements, in which the good record of an overseas supplier entitles the supplier to accumulate and discharge offsets obligations progressively in a program spread over one to three years; and (e) partnerships for development, in which agreements are reached between the Australian government and transnational corporations to except the corporation from offsets obligations if it undertakes to develop and export products from Australia.

A variety of activities discharges the offsets obligation. Obligations may be met by contracting out assembly or other manufacturing work to local firms or by buying locally produced components, materials, services, equipment and so on. In contract-by-contract and cumulative order arrangements, offsets have to be provided at a level of 30 per cent of the imported content of the overseas purchase. Offsets must nonetheless meet certain threshold criteria, which include (a) the new work criterion, providing that offsets should be new-work motivated to meet the offsets requirement, not simply work that would have been placed otherwise through normal commercial arrangements; (b) the commercial viability criterion, providing that offsets should result in Australian activities which are competitive in process, quality and delivery, and whose viability is assured without government assistance; (c) the price criterion, providing that offsets should not incur a price premium; and (d) the technology criterion, providing that offsets should be at a level of technological sophistication not inferior to that of overseas goods or services (Liesch, 1986).

Especially since the change in the tenor of the policy in 1986, offsets obligations can also be discharged by activities that upgrade the technological capability of local industry. These obligations may be discharged by collaborative ventures between overseas and local companies, where the local company is involved in the concept, design, development and production stages. Furthermore, offsets may be satisfied through the transfer of technology to Australian firms. The transfer may involve technologically specialized knowledge for products or processes and be in the form of patents, licences, software, technical data, process instructions or access to expertise and know-how. Transfer may also take the form of training and skilling, where these are associated with the development of advanced technology and with production for export. Research and development work initiated and supported by the overseas supplier will also discharge offsets obligations. Expenditure incurred on training and skills transfer and on local research and development activity is credited towards an offsets obligation at three times its nominal value. Offsets may also be discharged through the overseas marketing of local production and the generation of export earnings.

## IMPACT OF THE OFFSETS SCHEME

As the various reviews of the policy have shown, the scheme has been affected by reporting and monitoring difficulties (for example, Commonwealth of Australia. Bureau of Industry Economics, 1987a). Any estimate of its impact is necessarily qualified. Nevertheless, it was estimated that, in the period 1970-1986, $1,250-1,500 million was committed by way of offsets in the civil sector, though by no means all of these commitments had been completed (Liesch, 1986). Defence work has accounted for around 50 per cent of total offsets; civil offsets have been predominantly in the areas of aerospace, computing and telecommunications technologies. Offsets became a major arm of the federal government's recently developed information industries and telecommunications equipment strategies; in late 1987 they were stressed again as a possible measure within a planned electronic components industry strategy. The Inglis Committee estimated that about 25 per cent of offsets were accounted for by contracting out production to local firms, 50 per cent by 'co-production' with the overseas supplier, and 10 per cent by technology and training transfer.

## NATURE OF THE OFFSETS OBLIGATION

The offsets scheme has not enjoyed legislative status. The policy and procedures are represented in ministerial guidelines for the various purchasing authorities, supervision by the Offsets Authority within the Department of Industry, Technology and Commerce, and agreements with the successful suppliers. The hold of the offsets program has depended largely upon the goodwill of the overseas suppliers, reinforced perhaps by the strength of the government's threat that suppliers will be viewed unfavourably in future tenders if offsets are not arranged and completed. Not all the successful suppliers to the government have honoured their offset obligations. The American corporation, General Dynamics, the sole supplier of many sophisticated military devices, was publicly upbraided in 1987 by the Minister for Defence for its failure to honour its offsets obligations (*Australian Financial Review*, 9 April 1987). The record suggests that little over a third of the offsets committed between 1970-1984 had been completed by 1987 (Liesch, 1986).

The legal status of the agreements between the government purchasing authorities and the supplier firms makes an interesting question, though it is not likely that specific enforcement by way of action for breach of contract would be a practical avenue. The government does, however, intend that supplier commitment to offsets be legally binding (*Australian Financial Review*, 1 March 1988). The arrangements made with suppliers for offsets are built into purchase contracts or embodied in separate deeds of arrangement. Among the sanctions listed by the government are the implementation of penalty clauses in contracts, the withholding of offsets clearance for future contracts, a moratorium on further payments under the purchase contract, and public disclosure of failure to meet agreements. The government retains the option of cancelling offsets arrangements and requiring new ones if the activities actually undertaken tend to deviate from and circumvent the intention of an agreement. Obligations can also be adjusted to take account of changes in circumstances and the Offsets Authority may agree to alternative offsets being substituted.

## THE QUALITY OF OFFSETS

The scheme has attracted other kinds of criticisms. Suggestions have also been made that the value of technology which is transferred under offsets has been overstated by the suppliers and that the work involved may in any case be given to local subsidiaries of foreign companies within Australia, so that the technology is kept in-house and competition with the parent company is contained (Commonwealth of Australia. Joint Parliamentary Committee of Public Accounts, 1987). One local company suggested, for example, that regular audits of the Australian content of the computer products tendered to the government were necessary (the *Age*, 5 February 1991).

The overseas suppliers must be able to find local firms which can perform the offsets at a technologically comparable level. Local firms have sometimes found the requirements of the work too demanding. In any case, it has been suggested that a small number of local firms obtain the bulk of such work (Commonwealth of Australia. Joint Parliamentary Committee of Public Accounts, 1987). There have been questions raised about whether government departments should act as sponsors or brokers for individual local firms in obtaining work from overseas companies and bolstering them against the rigours of international competition. The Department of Industry, Technology and Commerce has been providing assistance in various direct ways, such as providing information about technical requirements in order to make local firms more attractive to foreign contractors. Resistance may be encountered from the transnationals if they hold reservations about the locals' capability or if they do not wish to transfer technology outside their group (Murray and Horwitz, 1988). These concerns may surface at the international level and, as chapter 7 revealed, offsets are now receiving some attention from international free trade bodies such as the OECD and GATT.

## THE PARTNERSHIPS FOR DEVELOPMENT AGREEMENTS

In January 1986, the Minister for Industry, Technology and Commerce revised the scheme administratively in order to transform it from a general counter-trade activity into an instrument of the government's policy to promote a viable and competitive local high technology sector (Commonwealth of Australia. DITC, 1987). Since March 1986, greater emphasis has been placed upon offset arrangements that involve transfer by the overseas supplier of advanced technology and training to local firms, the local commissioning of research and development work, and participation by local enterprises in design and related work. Emphasis was also placed upon the generation of export earnings. The minister issued a press release outlining the change in policy, and later in 1986, departmental guidelines were published for the edification of interested firms (Commonwealth of Australia. DITC, 1986a). An offsets advisory committee was established, with business representation.

In 1987, the Minister for Industry, Technology and Commerce introduced an additional and different form of offsets arrangement

(*Australian Technology Magazine*, no. 2, September 1987). The new arrangement was to apply to large foreign suppliers that were prepared to enter into a corporate citizenship or partnership for development program (PDP) agreement with the government, by which the parties would settle on long-term plans to boost local high technology industry. Companies making these agreements would be relieved of their offset requirements if they made a commitment to the principles of the government's innovative strategy and agreed to endeavour to achieve nominated levels of performance in local research and development work and import–export ratios. Accompanied by senior departmental officials, the minister embarked upon a round of negotiations with key suppliers in the information technology sector, travelling to the headquarters of the transnational corporations in late 1987. A number of these companies intimated that they were willing to make agreements, including Honeywell-Bull, the Digital Equipment Corporation, Unisys, Wang, Telex Computer Products, and Cincom Systems. It is to be noted that a number of other information technology firms had already invested in local research and development as part of their offsets arrangements, including Hewlett-Packard, Ericsson and Rank Xerox.

Nonetheless, the requirements for corporate citizenship were demanding, particularly of the largest foreign companies operating within the Australian market. For example, Unisys Corporation, the result of a merger between Burroughs and Sperry Rand, announced in November 1987 that it was prepared to spend more than $100 million on software development in Australia during the next five years. This expenditure would more than meet a commitment of 5 per cent of turnover to research and development, but the company's exports would have to total around $50 million a year in order to achieve the export to import ratio of 50 per cent (the *Age*, 24 November 1987). The requirements were magnified in the case of IBM, whose operations are estimated to be as big as those of its next ten competitors combined (*Australian Financial Review*, 23 September 1987). Yet IBM signalled its preparedness to enter into an agreement despite the fact that most of its participation traditionally has been by way of local assembly and re-export (*Australian Financial Review*, 27 January, 1987). By 1991, twenty-one companies had joined the PDP program, representing aggregate commitments of $400 million in research and development and $1.8 billion in exports (Commonwealth of Australia. DITC, 1991).

The Minister for Industry, Technology and Commerce announced that the new policy was not to discriminate between indigenously and internationally owned firms. Product development and competitive export activity could be undertaken by foreign owned subsidiaries (as well as by Australian-owned firms) so long as the overseas corporate supplier facilitated the local activity. Still, the new policy was to attract criticism in some quarters of the local information industry. The criticism was to the effect that the government might be tempted to favour its new foreign partners in making future government purchases (the *Age*, 20 October, 1987). Furthermore, the foreign firms, seeking to perform the necessary research and development locally, would out-bid indigenous firms for research expertise or would move to acquire local firms, rather than placing work out to them. One computer industry association called for the individual partnership agreements to be submitted to federal cabinet for approval (*Computerworld*, 14 August, 1987).

Resistance was also encountered from some of the transnationals, notably the Japanese, and, in 1991, the government made PDP participation mandatory for offshore companies with public sector sales of information technology of over $40 million. At the same time, acceptable local activities were extended to initiatives in strategic infrastructure development, third party indigenous industry capability, and local manufacturing capability (Commonwealth of Australia. DITC, 1991).

CHAPTER 10

# *Telecommunications Licensing*

This chapter presents the case study of telecommunications licensing measures for industry development in Australia. It first reports on the conditions in the telecommunications industry generally and the equipment industry in particular. It acknowledges the recent initiatives to liberalize the telecommunications market. It then surveys the development of policy for the growth of the local equipment industry. It considers the opportunities for government to further such a policy within the new regulatory structure. It looks in particular at the commitments of the public (core) carrier and the second (private) carrier under the new licensing system. Finally, drawing on recent overseas experience, it projects the impact which privatization has on government's ability to influence industry development.

## INDUSTRY CONDITIONS

### THE SIGNIFICANCE OF THE TELECOMMUNICATIONS MARKET

The field of telecommunications is, of course, substantially larger than the question of local innovation suggests. It represents a huge field for the application of advances in technology to a variety of customer uses. Telecommunications technology is rightly regarded as an enabling or core technology (Houghton and Partridge, 1991). As a result especially of its convergences with computer and broadcasting technologies, it is opening up opportunities for new markets in facilities and services. Much of the recent focus of telecommunications policy has been on the means to encourage the provision of these new facilities and services to the potential customer. A major target in this respect is the business user. The new technology offers more powerful and sophisticated means to convey and coordinate information of a financial, commercial, legal, manufacturing or sales nature. The Australian Minister for Transport and Communications, Kim Beazley, acknowledged the increasing local demand for large-scale international private networks (Beazley, 1991). High volumes of information can be moved speedily over the international electronic highways, becoming available at geographically dispersed points in an organization. Particularly as a result of the development of digital systems, communications can be effected directly between technologies without the need for human voice or text mediation.

Such a novel, disembodied technology provides both a means and an impetus to override established national monopoly and regulatory structures. The enablement of the technology is one of the reasons why the liberalization of trade in services (such as information processing services) is now high on the agenda of bodies such as the GATT, as we saw in earlier chapters. Countries are now competing to become platforms or hubs for transnational information systems of various kinds (Thomas and Miles, 1988). More directly, huge pressures are now being applied to open access to the telecommunications markets themselves, especially to foreign participants, internationalizing such profitable sectors as the business-information-network-based services (Mansell, 1988). The United States in particular is prepared to push for this liberalization bilaterally, wielding the threat of the closure of its own considerable market (Oxley, 1991). An early response has been the opening of the customer premises equipment (such as private exchanges) and value-added services markets to competition. But the pressure extends to the deregulation of the basic carrier markets, especially along the lucrative trunk routes. In some countries, this deregulation is accompanied by the privatization of the core public carriers. While supporting the liberalization of trade in telecommunications goods and services at GATT, Australia has been opening up its own markets.

## AN INNOVATIVE LOCAL EQUIPMENT INDUSTRY?

These major structural changes have many implications. One issue beyond the scope of this inquiry is the access which ordinary household consumers are to gain to these enhanced facilities and services. Another of direct concern is the impact upon the future of the research and development in Australia of innovative telecommunications products. In one view, modernization may be best served by encouraging the importation of the most advanced and least expensive technology from overseas. Houghton and Partridge (1991: 24) put the familiar conundrum well:

> The free-market argument suggests that carriers in the deregulated services environment should not face the cost burden of supporting a local industry that is not internationally competitive. The more strategic or interventionist view is that the IT industries are an integral part of modern economies and involve core technologies. The ability to at least accomplish all stages of production in such key industries is increasingly important to delivering quality products that will sell in competitive world markets. Are these incompatible options, or is some compromise possible?

The local equipment market is said to be a large one in Australian terms, amounting to around $12 billion per year (Houghton and Partridge, 1991). It is likely to grow. Given the convergence of technologies, involvement in telecommunications equipment manufacture such as terminals creates linkages with related industries, such as software engineering and servicing and systems construction and operation. The argument we saw in chapter 1 about the cumulative effects of these linkages is stressed in this area. To participate at all competitively in the international technological revolution, it seems it is necessary to maintain a sound base of local knowledge, skill and capability in a cluster of core technology activities. Given the strategic importance of telecommunications, this argument takes on a defence as well as an industrial complexion.

Already, the Australian equipment industry is dominated by eight corporations, seven of which are foreign transnationals with local subsidiaries. While most of Telecom's equipment has been sourced locally, at least one-third represents indirect imports. And the equipment has rarely been researched and developed in Australia, as opposed to manufactured or assembled locally. Yet, if the state of the local industry is of concern, the policy options may still vary. One direction is to insist that the telecommunications providers give preference to equipment sourced locally, even to equipment supplied by indigenous companies. In particular, the carriers should build relationships with local manufacturers which provide them with a secure market for development, the core carrier itself perhaps jointly engaging in equipment production. More recently, another option has emerged. Under this option, the carriers accept more foreign supply, tariff barriers are lowered, and the preference for local suppliers is reduced. In return, the foreign suppliers are encouraged to locate some of their own important research and development and export activities locally. In part, these activities could be contracted out to local niche firms, the transnationals' global presence being used in return as a means of gaining access for local products to markets overseas.

## LIBERALIZATION OF THE TELECOMMUNICATIONS MARKET

### Early Initiatives

Before we identify the preferred approach to equipment development in Australia, we should first establish the major changes taking place in telecommunications markets. These structural changes have significant implications for the future of the equipment sector. In Australia, the pressures to erode the (public) monopoly over telecommunications began in earnest under the Fraser coalition government. Business interests argued before a public inquiry (the Davidson inquiry) that Telecom, through a combination of its marketing and regulatory powers, had been stifling opportunities for private enterprise in the telecommunications area, enterprise which would lead to greater innovation and diversity in goods and services (Reinecke and Schulz, 1983). In line with these arguments, the Davidson inquiry recommended a number of measures to relax Telecom's grip upon the market, providing opportunities for participation by private operators (Commonwealth of Australia. Committee of Inquiry into Telecommunications Services, 1982). In part, Davidson recommended that Telecom be obliged to operate a more liberal policy in regard to lines leased or dedicated to private groups and that these private lines be permitted to resell unused capacity. It proposed that the relevant minister rather than Telecom itself decide where private lines could be connected to the network. It also recommended that Telecom lose control over the regulation of equipment attachments. It proposed that private entry be allowed into the peripheral markets and that Telecom be restricted from participating in new markets, such as videotext. However, on the change of government in 1983, these recommendations were not implemented.

In addition, the Fraser government decided to make a major investment in a satellite communications system. The launching of the AUSSAT satellite, with its ability to transmit communications outside the telephone terrestrial network, raised the prospect that major users might in future be able to bypass Telecom. After the election in 1983, the Labor government decided to exclude private equity participation in the satellite's controlling body and allocated equity of 25 per cent to Telecom and 75 per cent to the public overseas telecommunications commission (the Overseas Telecommunications Commission or OTC), which enjoyed at the same time a monopoly on communications outside Australia. Nevertheless, in 1984, the Minister for Communications provided guidelines permitting AUSSAT to allocate the leases on the satellite's transponders to private users. The minister also provided authorization for private users to set up their own receiving earth stations so that they could take signals from AUSSAT or other satellites and transmit them to their own offices (Barr, 1985). AUSSAT's lack of commercial success was, however, to become a major burden to the government.

During the same period, Telecom began to move into new specialist markets, such as business data transmission and switching through its Austpac and digital data services. This was a strategy to compete with the alternative media, such as the satellites and private services on independent systems. At the time, it was suggested that Telecom was in a position to extend its operations and compete successfully in such growing markets because of its ability to offer whole systems complete with terminals, other computer technologies and the data bases themselves (Reinecke, 1985).

## The 1988 and 1990 Statements

These *ad hoc* developments were to come to a head with a major telecommunications policy statement by the Labor government in May 1988 (Armstrong, 1990). The government announced that Telecom's regulation of technical standards would be removed to a new authority (the Australian Telecommunications Authority or AUSTEL), while the government itself would assume greater responsibility for determining basic policy. Private competition would be permitted in certain peripheral sections of the market, such as the installation of small business systems, and an ongoing review would consider competition in first-phone installation and the provision of value-added services, such as two-way videotext services. The resulting (1989) amendments to the principal statute, the

*Telecommunications Act*, opened up opportunities for private firms to offer customer premises equipment and value-added services that connected with the Telecom carrier network. By the commencement of the legislation, AUSTEL had already designated a number of value-added services which were to be open to competition, such as computer bureau services, videotext services, electronic mail services, electronic data interchange services and EFT services.

In November 1990, the government announced that it would liberalize the market even further. It restructured the market generally so that licences would be available for entry into four defined sectors: general carriage, public mobile carriage, public access cordless telephone services, and services such as value-added services and private network operations. In this last category, it would now permit private firms to sell on unused carrier capacity which they had leased from Telecom or the second carrier (Armstrong, 1991). It would open up the core carrier network to one private competitor, thereby creating a duopoly. Bids were called from interested parties. The second carrier was to be guaranteed access to Telecom's infrastructure, know-how and customer information. In particular, if it chose not to build its own lines, it would be permitted to connect with Telecom's local area networks in the different cities. The peripheral private providers would also maintain the right to connect with the carriers' networks.

## EQUIPMENT INDUSTRY POLICY

What impact might this change in structure have on innovation in the telecommunications sector? Clearly one goal was to increase the range of advanced facilities and services available to the user. For the purposes of our inquiry, the question is whether the stimulation of local innovation in equipment was also a purpose of the policy. For many years after the Second World War, the Post-Master-General and, since the split between postal and telecommunications carriage, Australian Telecom favoured local manufacturers, providing them with long-term commitments and sharing work across the industry (Commonwealth of Australia. Industries Assistance Commission, 1984a). The public monopoly over procurement gave the government the opportunity to influence the conditions of supply, though some commentators still felt that Telecom could have done more to ensure that research and design work was performed locally (Reinecke,

1985). Telecom used its purchase contracts to monitor compliance by its preferred suppliers with local content and value-added requirements (Houghton and Partridge, 1991a).

## THE INDUSTRY DEVELOPMENT ARRANGEMENTS

In 1987, the Department of Industry, Technology and Commerce targeted telecommunications equipment for one of its concerted industry strategies. With the liberalization of the peripheral markets, the strategy was followed up in 1988 with the promulgation by the government of guidelines to institute industry development arrangements (Brown, 1990). Applying to the supply of customer premises equipment, such as first phones and PABXs, and small business systems, such as key systems and cellular mobile telephone handsets, these arrangements (the IBAs) required suppliers to meet specific targets for research and development, local production and content, and exports. A points system was instituted, and any supplier who failed to meet its target in a given year was to lose its permit to supply for one year. In the first year of operation, 1989-1990, thirty-six suppliers were endorsed. AUSTEL was charged with administering the arrangements. As the purchasers of this equipment now extended to private operators, the insistence on the arrangements were made a condition of AUSTEL's approvals for these operators to connect with Telecom's network. In their review of the IDA policy, Houghton and Partridge (1991) report that the arrangements worked well as an incentive for the transnationals' Australian subsidiaries to increase their exports. Nevertheless, some doubts were expressed in another quarter about the quality of the innovation involved in these offsets (Reinecke, 1991).

## THE SECOND CARRIER'S OBLIGATIONS

With the subsequent liberalization of the carriage market, were similar arrangements established for supply to the carriers of basic network equipment, such as customer access networks, switching systems, and transmission lines? A key consideration in the formation of any such policy might be the willingness of the second, private carrier to locate some of its innovative activity in Australia and to forge links with local equipment companies. In this regard, attention has been drawn to the nature of the commercial environment in which this carrier was to operate. The local environment would help determine the proportion of the market which the second carrier captured and hence the resources it would have available to spend on equipment. One determinant of its likely position was the number of competitors which the carrier would face in the mobile carrier and peripheral markets. Another, of course, was the conditions on which it would compete with Telecom and in particular the level at which the fee was to be struck for it to interconnect with Telecom's network. Also said to be relevant was the fact that the government had indicated that Telecom would be privatized in 1997 and the reserved core market opened up to further competition.

## THE LICENSING PROCESS

More directly, the licensing process might be regarded as a point at which the second carrier could be encouraged to play its part in boosting the international competitiveness of the local equipment industry. The industry development arrangements, which are in any case due to be phased out in 1993, were not designed to apply to the purchase of network equipment. It is to be noted that, in its bid for the second carrier licence, the key contender, Optus Communications, foreshadowed that it would assign some 70 per cent of its equipment budget to local content, together with commitments to investment in research and development projects, training for local partners, and some export activity (the *Australian*, 17 July 1991). It later announced that it had already forged links with four local companies (the *Age*, 23 November 1991).

Optus faced, however, only one rival for the licence, a rival badly wounded by the late withdrawal of some of its key backers. Optus was successful in gaining the licence from the government. In a joint statement, on 19 November 1991, the Minister for Industry, Technology and Commerce and the Minister for Transport and Communications declared themselves well pleased with the quality of the industry proposals from both the bidders (see Commonwealth of Australia. Minister for Industry, Technology and Commerce, 1991). Optus had indicated that the major transnational equipment suppliers were willing to undertake a range of partnerships for development-type activities in Australia. Long-term opportunities for the suppliers would be combined with a role for local industry, without limiting the carriers in their options for network development.

## LICENSING OUTCOME

In their statement, the Ministers for Industry, Technology and Commerce and for Transport and Communications foreshadowed a new framework for the development of Australia's telecommunications industry. This framework was to involve the setting of several major objectives enumerated in the ministers' statement, including: (a) the maintenance of a leading quality network, providing advanced services at affordable prices to users; (b) the promotion and maintenance of new and existing long-term strategic relationships between the carriers and the global equipment suppliers, which would involve world or regional mandates in switching, transmission and network management; (c) support for indigenous equipment suppliers in export markets, as part of a national marketing approach to telecommunications, within the overall government approach to support for innovation; and (d) support for the development of software and research and development skills in telecommunications within the overall government approach to support for innovation. The ministers announced that another body, the Telecommunications Industry Authority, would be established to advise on the extent to which the carriers and their suppliers met these industry 'undertakings'.

Yet, the precise force of these arrangements was left unclear. In particular, an expert policy institute, the Centre for International Research into Communications and Information Technologies (CIRCIT), decried the missed opportunity to build the requirements into the carrier licences (the *Age*, 26 November 1991). It remained to be seen if the commitments were anything more than the pledges which New Zealand Telecom had made to its government on the privatization of the carrier in that country (Taggart, 1991, also see below). However Optus' subsequent announcement of plans to use local firms to supply and build its optical fibre network gave some cause for optimism (the *Age*, 28 April 1992).

## TELECOM'S ROLE

### Telecom as Entrepreneur

Whatever Optus' future, for the foreseeable future Telecom is likely to remain the main purchaser of network equipment. It also of course participates in the CPE and VAS delivery markets. Indeed, Telecom could also be viewed as the most promising prospect for an Australian-based telecommunications multinational company. In the past, Telecom has been urged to take a more active approach to the commercialization of its own inventions (see, e.g., Australian Science and Technology Council, 1985). It has been suggested that opportunities have been missed. Two examples cited are the electronic switching device which Telecom put aside in favour of a model supplied by Ericsson for installation in the local network, and the digital radio concentrators which Telecom licensed through Japan's NEC for development in the international market. While Telecom could not be expected to realize all such innovations inhouse, its enabling legislation, the *Telecommunications Act 1975*, was amended to empower it to form, or participate with others in the formation of, companies to carry out various businesses related to telecommunications. In fact, joint venture companies were subsequently set up, some notably with the assistance of the Australian Industry Development Corporation. Telecom has indeed been successful in joint venture work overseas, for example in Thailand, Hong Kong and Pakistan. Industry commentators such as Reinecke (1991) have argued that these activities should extend to the promotion of large-scale collaborative innovations in systems development, like the development of infrastructure which the French mounted under their national plan.

Telecom's freedom to act in an entrepreneurial way has, however, been constrained by ministerial discretion. The Minister for Transport and Communications has reserved the right of veto over such joint ventures. In a notable development, the minister withheld approval for Telecom investment in a local project to develop digital mobile telephone services (the *Age*, 25 May 1991). In fact, in several ways, Telecom has found its relationship with executive government problematic. Government seems concerned that Telecom might take advantage of its established position in the market to steal a march on its new competitors. But other considerations also intrude upon its autonomy. Telecom has recently been required to pay corporate tax. It is also subject to the executive government's directions regarding its borrowing levels and the amount of revenue it may obtain for reinvestment after paying dividends. This control on capital raising has been a major source of friction between the central government and such instrumentalities in other countries too, in part because government often views the public sector borrowing requirement as an important instrument of macro-economic policy (Wiltshire, 1987).

## Telecom's Local Options

Telecom's commercial environment is also conditioned by the conditions on which the second carrier and the peripheral providers are permitted to connect with its network and in particular the compensation it receives through the interconnection fee for making its facilities available. Under the recent regime, determination of these conditions is taken out of Telecom's hands to be the subject largely of directions by the minister to AUSTEL. Again, it has been suggested that these conditions might be shaped not so much to open the market to vigorous competition as to confer public benefits on the favoured private entrants in order to ensure their viability (Morgan, 1991).

A consequence of these constraints is a concern that Telecom will no longer be able to maintain a supportive approach to the local equipment industry. In particular, it has been suggested that it will not be able to act as readily as an instrument of preference or offsets policy if these policies are not to be equally applicable to its rivals (Houghton and Partridge, 1991a). In April 1992, Telecom unveiled a purchasing program for the following five years that would give preference to Australian suppliers provided they could supply world best value products (the *Age*, 24 April 1992). It also afforded a small amount of money to aid local small firms with product development. But other pressures also militate in favour of Telecom looking abroad for suppliers. For example, if Telecom is to gain entry to export markets, it may need to form strategic alliances with the suppliers in these markets, partly as a result of their own governments' requirements. The national PTTs in Western Europe have been grappling with a similar dilemma (Grewlich, 1987).

In such circumstances, the conditions which are placed on Telecom's carrier licence within the new regime may be as important as those placed upon its rival, Optus. And this means of influencing the carrier's industry policy will become more crucial when Telecom is privatized, as the Labor government foreshadowed for 1997. (Privatization will in fact come much faster if the Conservative coalition wins the next election.) In many countries around the world where the core carriers have been public monopolies, government is now experiencing pressures to privatize. The most notable instances to date have occurred in the United Kingdom and Japan. New Zealand's Telecom was also recently sold off. Privatization is clearly gaining pace in several sectors of the Australian economy and it is worthwhile in this context, I think, to identify briefly the role which government retains when a major public instrumentality such as Telecom is transferred to the private sector.

## PRIVATIZATION

In the program of the 'new right', privatization represents a shift away from government involvement in the economy. Indeed, it may be regarded as the apostasy of industry policy. Yet, as recent experience indicates, it does not necessarily signify a complete abdication by government in favour of market forces. As a matter of course, privatization really only eliminates the option of deploying the instrument of public ownership as a means to further industry policy. As Prosser (1989) points out, public ownership was never itself automatically the flexible and positive instrument of policy for which governments hoped. The instrumentalities have a tendency to develop identities and interests that are difficult to control from the centre. Privatization certainly alters the nature of the legal relationship between government and industry, perhaps in the direction of a more arm's length and rule-based relationship, but it does not sever all connections. Indeed, the evidence suggests that government may retain a special relationship with privatized corporations, at least in the transitional phase, employing the 'soft' strategies such as licensing, shareholdings and contracts identified earlier in this chapter to influence the private corporations' behaviour (Graham and Prosser, 1987). The relationships often illustrate well what is awkwardly termed the com-penetration of the public and private sectors.

In this regard, we now have the experience of the evolving relationships in the United Kingdom, where privatization has made the most emphatic change in industry structure. As we know, in the eighties, the British government implemented an ambitious program of privatization of state-owned instrumentalities (Veljanovski, 1987). Its program raised fresh questions about the extent to and the means by which government would continue to promote innovation in the local industry. The telecommunications sector was a key target of this program. British Telecom was sold off to the private sector and the second company, Mercury, was allowed into the core carrier market.

## THE GOALS OF PRIVATIZATION

The United Kingdom experience reveals that privatization bears the burden of several, sometimes conflicting, aspirations. For instance, it may be seen as a source of revenue raising and a relief from heavy responsibilities by a straitened government. It may be regarded as a means by which to extend allegiance to private property, involving employees and ordinary citizens in share holding. Fuelled by the belief that private firms operate more efficiently than public monopolies, privatization may be designed to provide the consumer with a wider range of facilities and services, perhaps at cheaper prices. Of course, at the same time, it throws into question the practice of cross-subsidization and the support of community service obligations. On such a basis, it is concerned in a broad way with the nature of industry structure. However, it is less likely to be concerned with more sectional industry goals, such as the maintenance of an indigenous or local equipment manufacturing industry, though again, its adherents may be encouraged to think that a liberalized market will lead to more innovation.

Certainly, the program has the tendency to throw the industry open to the workings of global strategies, especially if the privatized carriers attract foreign ownership or control. They are likely then to have developed connections with suppliers at their home base. For such reasons, the issue of local sovereignty and capacity is likely to recur once privatization has been effected. For example, in the United Kingdom, the issue surfaced quickly in the matter of 'system X'. Here the government sought to persuade British Telecom to buy large digital switchboards from the GEC-Plessey company rather than from overseas (Wiltshire, 1987). British Telecom grudgingly agreed.

## GOVERNMENT-INDUSTRY RELATIONSHIPS UNDER PRIVATIZATION

### Arrangements for Competition

By what means, under privatization, is a government likely to seek to influence the behaviour of firms in such key sectors? With an avowed faith in the disciplines of the market, one might expect these sectors to be subjected to the workings of open and vigorous competition. In this vein, the Australian Minister for Transport and Communications, Kim Beazley, was to say that competition would provide the main source of regulation under the new regime in Australia. A logical feature of such a regime would seem to be the prescription and enforcement of general anti-trust safeguards. As we saw in chapter 6, Australia has such a generalist anti-trust or restrictive trade practices scheme in place. Anti-trust has certainly played an important role in shaping the industry structure in the United States, even though specialist communications regulators also operate at federal and state levels to determine such matters as the industry's rates of return. Anti-trust has been deployed in an endeavour to control the private monopoly carrier's influence upon the equipment manufacturing industry (Irwin, 1987).

In contrast, a characteristic of the British approach is to make the matter of competition essentially a concern for the specialist telecommunications scheme of regulation, providing only for reference of questions to the general competition law authorities (Prosser, 1989). Australia's new regulatory arrangements seem largely to be based on this model (Baxt, 1991). In any case, for the time being, the goal of competition is qualified by the government's retention of control over market entry through the licensing system. But even with the relaxation of this control, now in the United Kingdom, and at a later date in Australia, it is quite possible that 'natural' technical and economic conditions may still provide barriers to entry by new firms. Without the discipline of genuine competition, the danger is that deregulation leads to private monopolies which are even less accountable than the public instrumentalities they replace (Veljanovski, 1987). A prime concern of course is the impact of the carriers' control over essential core facilities on the ability of rival firms to compete in the provision of peripheral services such as VAS and CPE. In Western Europe, the national PTTs are for this very reason beginning to encounter anti-trust scrutiny from the European Commission (Mansell, Holmes and Morgan, 1990).

On the other hand, competition does not necessarily lead to the support of a locally innovative equipment industry. Indeed, the figures suggest that deregulation is accompanied by a deterioration in the balance of trade over equipment. In the United States, AT&T has sourced more of its equipment needs overseas since the divestiture, and a $1.1 billion surplus in 1978 had become a $1.98 billion deficit in 1989 (Houghton and Partridge, 1991). According to Wiltshire (1987), British Telecom is spending less on research and is looking overseas for supplies. In New Zealand, it is reported that local supply dropped from 50 to 10 per cent of the market within a year of privatization (Gosman, 1991).

## The Use of Dominium

If the promotion of local innovation remains an objective of telecommunications policy, we might expect the close and informal relationships between government and industry to continue in some form. How are they likely to be constructed? In this regard, the retention by government of a shareholding in the privatized corporation, the so-called 'golden share', seems more concerned with the desire to screen possible takeovers, especially by foreigners (Graham and Prosser, 1987). Licences do not seem to be used as a purposeful instrument to extract concessions for local industry. The obtaining of pledges from the carriers in the bidding process leading up to the grant of licences is, as Taggart (1991) so emphatically points out in the New Zealand context, no substitute for real influence. To a large extent, the future of particular government influence appears to rest with its procurement powers as a major consumer of telecommunications products. Another avenue of influence is the provision of government support for research and development. Intent on retaining a role for the local equipment industry, which has supplied most of their carriers' needs in the past, the Europeans made funds available for research and development through the ESPRIT and RACE programs (Grewlich, 1987). Again, these sorts of devices may in part be deployed to help foster collaborative relationships between different organizations such as local firms, research institutes and foreign corporations. Privatization need not alter the balance between local and foreign supply. In its usual enigmatic way, Japan has not permitted partial privatization of Nippon Telephone and Telegraph to open up the telecommunications procurement market to foreign firms (Boyd, 1987).

## Criticism of the Relationships

Yet, at the same time, these hybrid kinds of arrangements will encounter criticism from a constitutional point of view. Critics are often concerned about the absence of a set of rules that delineates the substantive and procedural standards by which government is to regulate the industry. In Australia's case, as we know, the telecommunications reforms did establish a new regulatory body, AUSTEL. But, as Armstrong and Anderson (1991) point out so clearly, the major policy decisions were still reserved to the prerogatives of the executive government and specifically the responsible minister. Under the *Telecommunications Act,* the responsible minister allocates the all-important general carrier and mobile carrier licences, attaching in the process any conditions they might be intended to express. AUSTEL does have the power to issue class licences for value-added services and private network systems. However, these licences are not apportioned to individual applicants but are more in the nature of delegated legislation, declaring and defining certain kinds of peripheral operations as open to market entry. AUSTEL also issues permits for the connection of customer equipment. Even in these regards, the exercise of its powers is subject to directions from the Minister for Transport and Communications. In many respects, its functions are essentially those of monitoring performance, reviewing issues and reporting to the minister. In any case, it is to be noted that AUSTEL's own proceedings are not on the whole legally structured to provide access to information, consultation procedures, or the holding of hearings. Nor are they subject to review in the Commonwealth Administrative Appeals Tribunal. Indeed, one former minister went so far as to say that the government was opposed to the abuse of appeals machinery to thwart AUSTEL's legitimate decision-making authority (see Armstrong, 1991a).

More significantly, the Act does not subject the minister's decision-making to any procedural ordering. The second carrier licence was awarded after an informal bidding process and a round of private negotiations. While AUSTEL's establishment as a statutory authority perhaps provides some scope for judicial review, the minister's discretionary powers are in many ways effectively insulated from the jurisdiction of the ordinary courts. Rather, it seems that any accountability is to lie in the force of the political and parliamentary processes, though Armstrong (1991a) again regards the minister's responsibility to parliament as largely formal and conventional.

Similar observations have been made about the arrangements in the United Kingdom (Prosser, 1989). They have added bite because of privatization. Australian Telecom remains a public statutory authority even if the second carrier and the additional peripheral operators are in the private sector. While it is true, in the United Kingdom, that the actions of the government and the regulatory body (the Office of Telecommunications) remain formally accountable because these bodies reside in the public sector, their particular decision-making is cast in a highly discretionary way by the enabling legislation. Some of their decisions are implemented solely through private law forms, such as contract and company law. At the same time, the privatization of the actual operators places more elements of the industry outside the realm of the public officials' responsibilities. For example, the Secretary of State is said to decline to answer questions in parliament about the carriers' operations on the basis that they are private bodies (Wiltshire, 1987). And of course, the operators themselves fall on the private side of the public–private divide, avoiding scrutiny, for example, by the Ombudsman and the National Audit Office.

## Proposals for Reworking the Relationships

It is perhaps not surprising that these developments have led to calls to legalize decision-making. In this regard, the foremost Australian legal expert, Mark Armstrong (1991a) cites with favour the North American model of the procedural ordering of government regulation. He supports the establishment of specialist regulatory commissions which are detached from executive government. Accountability is enhanced by administrative practices such as the public notification of plans to make policy, the provision of opportunities to put cases before the agencies, and the conduct of round-table proceedings to work through issues. Of course, such a model places a great deal of faith in the efficacy of a particular kind of legalized process, a point to which we shall return in the conclusion to this book. But it remains in question whether a government is likely to impose such obligations upon itself through the force of legislation. If government is unwilling so to do, can we look to the courts to attach these kinds of standards to regulatory proceedings? We shall also have something to say generally about the attitude of the courts to this kind of administrative decision-making in the critique which follows these case studies.

The hopes of the reformists are bold. In New Zealand, Taggart (1991) is especially concerned to see this kind of procedural ordering extended because of the fact that the government declined to institute any specialist regulatory oversight for the telecommunications sector. As a consequence, he identifies a need to break with the public–private law divide and to introduce public law standards of decision-making such as openness, fairness, participation, impartiality and rationality, into the appraisal, not only of the government's decision-making, but also of the decision-making of the large corporations which now wield great power in the private market to 'regulate' telecommunications.

CHAPTER 11

# The Positive Adjustment Measures in the Courts and Legislatures

Having characterized the form these measures assume, and illustrated the experience with their use in the three case studies, this chapter now draws out some of the sources of resistance they have met in Australia. It discusses first some of the limitations which the case studies reveal in their capacity to elicit the sort of innovative response they desire from the private sector. It then identifies the kinds of criticisms they attract and in particular the concerns about favouritism and capture by sectional interests, and the tensions which develop with the more established roles of government. The chapter considers particularly how opposition to the approach may find expression in the law, the attitude of the courts being treated as a litmus test for the possible reassertion of liberal legality over the policy space. It notes the opportunities the courts provide for review of the legality of administrative decisions, pursuing the example of the judicial review of the award of public contracts. It also looks at the claims made in the legislatures to render decision-making in the space accountable.

## LIMITATIONS AND OBJECTIONS

### LACK OF IMPACT

In the first place, we should note that the incentives offered by government in Australia have not necessarily been influential enough to bring about the desired changes in behaviour from their target groups. In terms of the overall operating costs of the firms concerned, even in the total round of government expenditures, the amounts given over to the positive adjustment measures have often seemed small. The offer of assistance relies for its success upon the decisions of the private firms to respond to the inducement and to apply themselves to the activity which government seeks to promote. Opening the gate to the private sector provides no guarantee that complementary investment will be forthcoming. The inducement may not seem large enough to overcome complacency or outweigh alternatives. Even the exclusive licences granted to the telecommunications carriers may fail to measure up in this way. Most dauntingly, the general settings of the economy (such as the availability and cost of credit and the attraction of alternative investment options) may loom larger in the calculations of private firms than the attractions of the specific incentives. Ironically, the same national government's fiscal and monetary policies may have contributed to these unsympathetic environmental conditions. Especially for those target firms which enjoy the luxury of a global strategy, broader economic considerations may overshadow the attractions of locating research and development in the host country. The proliferation of *dominium* often means that a number of smaller countries are vying to outbid each other for the patronage of transnational corporations, and, as the bids increase, the prospects of a net return on the government's outlay can soon decline. Notwithstanding the measures it has deployed, Australia is often said to offer fewer inducements to foreign investment than its South-east Asian neighbours, such as Singapore.

The task of fostering collaborative work between a number of producers proves to be especially difficult. While, logistically, it is easier for government to organize when it only has a few large oligopolist companies with which to deal, these companies may in fact be resourceful enough to contemplate going it alone. It was evident that the large Japanese computer companies proved hard to wed to the local offsets arrangements. So too, the foreign telecommunications companies are likely to retain loyalties to industry back home. In other sectors, organization proves difficult because of the fragmented and diverse nature of the firms involved. In particular, small firms may lack the necessary stability and maturity to deal effectively with the large corporations or, for that matter, their potential government sponsors. So some scepticism has been expressed for example about the ability of local firms to play their part in offsets arrangements. For different reasons, the public research institutions have sometimes resisted the imprecations of the grants and tax schemes to forge links with the private sector.

Furthermore, where the assistance is taken up, its impact may not necessarily be positive. Firms may avail themselves of the assistance to perform work which they would have undertaken in any case. This accusation was levelled both at the direct grants and at tax concessions for research and development expenditure. Also, on occasions, funds will go to support ventures that the market declines to support, not because of any market failure, but because their commercial viability has rightly been adjudged to be poor (Pavitt, 1979). Thus, the grants schemes were criticized for funding projects that lacked commercial input. The assistance might attract firms that are more interested in obtaining government favours than in cultivating the activity which government aims to promote. The tax concession encountered the familiar hazard which we see in the manipulation of eligibility provisions at the margins and the artificial construction of qualifying claims through the use of creative accounting and financial engineering.

## THE POWER OF PRESCRIPTION

Is there much that government can do to ensure a return on its provision of assistance? We have noted that the nature of innovation itself inclines the government to use soft measures such as financial incentives to stimulate activity. For enforcement, the agencies are more likely to rely upon the threat of withdrawing their goodwill than upon the strength of legally binding obligations to obtain returns on the investment of their resources. The unwillingness of the Australian government to use the new telecommunications licences to impose strict conditions on the core carriers is a good example. Given the nature of the activity, where undertakings are obtained, they are likely to be confined to good faith and best endeavours obligations. The economic measures of performance may be left so vague or indirect that it is difficult to assess compliance in any individual case (Ganz, 1977). Where agencies take equity in a commercial company, such conditions are not readily imposed, and the companies may be subject only to the accounting and reporting requirements of the general commercial and company law. Queries may therefore be raised about the yield from the measures. We saw how doubts were raised about the quality of the local research, development and technology transfers which have been arranged under the offsets program.

As they refine their innovation policies, governments appear to be becoming more pointed about the sectors and projects to which they will provide assistance. Care may be taken to build criteria into the schemes in order to ensure that the selection of beneficiaries is consistent with the policy. A common theme of Australian innovation assistance has been that it is only given to projects that involve the local commercialization of the innovation. The tax concession legislation does, for example, lay down some basic eligibility criteria, particularly in regard to the definition of research and development, the scope of concessional expenditure on this activity, and the need for research and development to be properly exploited to the benefit of the Australian economy. Yet, in their nature, the criteria often leave much of the real judgement about the promise of an individual beneficiary to the administering agency. As part of the drive towards administrative rationality, we might expect these agencies to regularize and intensify their internal procedures for screening and monitoring the beneficiaries. But the resource demands upon them, in terms of both labour and expertise, can be imposing. This hazard was underlined by the Auditor-General's recent efficiency audit, which raised concerns about the level of administrative assessment under the tax and grants schemes. Indeed, exploitation of the tax scheme also presented challenges to the legislators. So too, the monitoring of compliance with the offsets arrangements was cast into doubt.

## PERCEPTIONS OF FAVOURITISM AND CAPTURE

Nonetheless, the problems which the approach encounters are not explained simply by the instrumental difficulties which are faced in making rational decisions and producing positive responses. The Australian experience indicates that government policy is an important site of a struggle over the allocation of resources in the economy. It is therefore not surprising that any measures of support to particular sectors or ventures are likely to arouse some opposition from outside. They experience criticism of course from those in the target group who miss out on the award of favours. But the measures of assistance may also attract criticism from those who see them as conferring on their recipients an artificial advantage in the market, for example by allowing them to reduce their costs or boast of their viability. The brokerage facilities which government offered to favoured local firms as part of the offsets policy was a target of such criticism.

In Australia, this kind of criticism is afforded considerable intellectual respectability by the strong free market and new right movements. We have noted how they argue that selective intervention distorts the operation of vigorous market forces, diverts resources away from the more efficient sectors of the economy, requires politicians and administrators to pick winners, and engenders a dependence upon government support amongst the recipient groups. Particularly influential in elite circles has been the critique of government regulation (regulation in a broad sense) which originated with the Chicago School's producer interest theory (Stigler, 1972) and took full flight in contemporary public choice theory (e.g. Chandler, Trebilcock and Howse, 1990). These theories interpret all arguments for support as 'rent seeking' special pleading. Consequently, they are extremely sceptical that market controls or government assistance benefit anyone but the private groups and government officials who advocate them.

In Australia, such criticisms are given a receptive ear by the industry lobbies which distribute or consume technology coming from overseas. The criticism emanates not only from the powerful external lobbies on government but also from agencies within the state itself. For example, within the federal government in recent years, these sentiments have found a strong voice in the Treasury and its associated agencies. In its 1986-1987 annual report, the Australian Industries Assistance Commission (1987) took the opportunity roundly to criticize the government's innovation policy and specifically the grants for research and development, tax concessions, local preference policy, and the offsets scheme. In the past, one could expect counter-balancing views to emanate from the industry and trade agencies within the same government. But for the time being, the philosophies seem to dominate all the major parliamentary parties and the senior echelons of most government agencies (Pusey, 1991), even if there have been notable exceptions to this rule (e.g. Charles, 1990). Such a formative context does more than cast the onus upon the advocates of selective intervention to argue their case. It conditions the whole terms of the debate about the role of government in industry and, especially in recent times, it has privileged the framework of a particular school of thought within the discipline of economics. In a recent study, Joseph (1989) recounts how the advocates of selective intervention within the Labor government found it necessary to engage in expressive politics, recasting their position as a key technology strategy rather than a key industry strategy in order to overcome the legitimacy problems associated with the approach.

In such a climate, any 'failures' by firms which have received assistance from government are likely to be characterized as an abuse of public monies. Arguably, the recent investment failures by public agencies have received much harsher treatment than the corresponding failures of the private financial institutions and corporate entrepreneurs. But, as public agencies move into closer working relationships with particular private firms, they may do more than risk public monies. The favoured firms may also be afforded privileged access to intangible public resources. For example, firms seek a special relationship with a university department or centre not simply to acquire isolated pieces of intellectual property but also to gain a 'window' on the frontiers of the science and any specific ideas that might so materialize. Likewise, as a benefit of the licence granted by the Australian government to connect with the public carrier, the new private competitors have been given access to the body of technical knowledge which Telecom has built up over many years at considerable public expense. Similarly, at the pre-market price of a share, privatization allows purchasers to acquire command of infrastructure and expertise that are the result of sustained public investment and service. This kind of assistance attracts trenchant criticism from the left of politics, so, in a sense, the government finds it hard to please anyone.

It can also be suggested that the provision of selective support confers respectability on the ventures of the beneficiaries. For example, a manager of the Victorian Government's 'Nascent Technology Ventures Program' (a program like the National Procurement Development Program) was quoted as saying that:

> a major contribution of the programme to start-up firms is credibility. The link with an educational institution provides start-ups with an image of having broadly based and highly stable structures. These images help to attract bank funds and product orders. (Mathews, 1984: 31)

Consequently, government pays a higher price for firm failure than its mere financial outlays.

## TENSIONS WITH TRADITIONAL ROLES

Moreover, for public agencies to involve themselves in commercial ventures with private partners carries the risks of a conflict of interest between the agencies' public functions and their new-found commercial obligations. Tensions develop between the public and private roles where, for example, government agencies are involved in enterprises that are seeking contracts or other government support; that contravene regulatory requirements such as corporate duties or environmental provisions; or that cause losses to suppliers, investors, creditors or employees (Harman, 1986). These conflicts were eventually a major source of the concern over the Western Australian government's heavy involvement in large resource-development projects (Peachment, 1991). The agencies must discharge regulatory or other public responsibilities that come into conflict with their promotional objectives. In connection with a local preference policy, we noted for example the purchasing agencies' responsibility to obtain the most technically sound and reasonably priced equipment for government use. In the case of the telecommunications instrumentality, exposure to private competition intensifies the pressures to operate commercially and downgrade industry development and community service obligations. Both within government and amongst its various constituencies, concern may be expressed about the mix of promotional and other functions.

## JUDICIAL REVIEW

How, if at all, are these kinds of objections and criticisms translated into law? In this chapter, we shall now focus on their expression in the jurisdiction of the courts to review the legality of administrative action. We might first imagine that those supplicants who miss out on favours seek a legal avenue to check and correct the government's exercise of its financial powers. The most obvious avenue for an individual complainant is the review jurisdiction of the courts over the decisions of the executive and administration. It also the one which most emphatically reasserts the liberal legal approach.

If the individual has been granted a favour, such as a research contract, he or she may become the holder of a legal right, in the private law sense, that that person is then entitled to enforce through the courts. For several reasons, the government agencies, especially those within the shield of the crown, have been afforded immunities from complaints based on obligations in contract and the like (see Puri, 1978), but in recent years the courts have been less receptive to these arguments of *raison d'état* and more inclined to give claimants access to a legal remedy (Allars, 1989). What is now in more dispute is the jurisdiction of the courts to review decisions not to award favours (such as contracts) to a particular person, or to award them to another person on the basis that the agency has not met the decision-making standards expected of a body discharging public responsibilities.

## THE DEMAND FOR JUDICIAL REVIEW

As we may surmise from the discussion above about the opposition to these schemes, litigation might also be contemplated by competing firms, taxpayers or other external groups seeking to discredit and overturn the agencies' selections. Indeed, the opposition may take on a constitutional theme as the outsiders perceive a conflict between this approach to economic management and the maintenance of the rule of law (Bayne, 1989). For instance, the constitutionalist lobby may wish to see the standards for determining the allocation of favours to be articulated in proactive, open and clear enactments, preferably with the authority of parliament. In keeping with this, the powers conferred upon executive and administrative agencies should be measurable against such legal criteria in order to see whether they are being exercised for some improper purpose or according to some irrelevant consideration. Each decision about individual applications should be made correctly and consistently in accordance with these criteria. Agencies should be obliged to collect evidence in order to assess the merits of applications (this requirement might necessitate affording the applicants an opportunity to be heard) and to base their decisions on that evidence. Failure to do so should be answerable to the courts.

Pressures are therefore brought to bear on the courts to check the exercise of discretion by granting agencies, to measure administrative decisions by legal criteria, and to model administrative processes along due process lines. However, it is possible that, if they are benefiting regularly from their special relationship, those in the recipient class may not be at the forefront of these moves to legalize the handling of claims for government subsidies and services (Broekman, 1985). Judicial oversight might appeal to those groups which are concerned about the cosy relationships which develop between government agencies and certain private commercial interests. From this viewpoint, governments may be accused of neglecting their public responsibilities and indeed of compromising their political sovereignty by bypassing the usual rule-bound processes of decision-making and treating some companies as co-equal partners in a bargaining relationship over resources (Cameron and Midgeley, 1982). The Australian government's relationship with the two core telecommunications carriers has attracted this criticism. The major tax claimants' access to the Taxation Office is perhaps another instance. In this respect, the accessibility of the courts to claims from persons outside the class of beneficiaries also becomes important.

In the common law (and also to some extent in the legislation which now embodies the principles of the common law), a set of grounds has developed for checking administrative decisions. In this body of administrative law, the main ground for overturning administrative decisions is any excess or abuse of power. Courts are prepared to restrain a public agency that acts in excess or *ultra vires* its legal powers, whether those powers are to be found in the statute or in the inherent prerogatives of the crown. The court might find, for example, that the agency had exercised its statutorily structured discretion for some purpose or according to some consideration other than those allowed by the statute. Or the agency might be found not to have exercised its discretion at all. It might have committed itself in advance to an inflexible position, so prejudging the individual applications. Procedural unfairness has become the other main ground for review. Increasingly, the courts are also likely to remit decisions of government agencies that have not afforded the applicant and other affected parties an impartial hearing.

## THE SEARCH FOR DECISION-MAKING AUTONOMY

Yet, because the courts need to find a legal peg on which to hang their jurisdiction to review, government may be tempted to explore ways of avoiding their scrutiny. So, as we have seen, government may establish the authority of the agency with a broad permissive statute that provides little opportunity to derive criteria or procedures by which to constrain discretion (Ganz, 1987). The statute may do no more than authorize in one line the expenditure of monies on an item of assistance. Or the government may avoid legislation by relying on the powers which it enjoys, like an ordinary citizen, to: 'make promises, conclude contracts, acquire and dispose of property, acquire and disseminate information, make and receive gifts, form companies, set up committees and agencies and perform a wide variety of other functions within the policy process' (Daintith, 1985: 176).

In Australia, it seems that many of the technical obstacles which the law placed in the way of a grievant seeking review have now been jettisoned by the courts (Allars, 1990). The courts have been reasserting their constitutional role to restrain government action. In particular, the courts have relaxed the distinctions which were maintained between different kinds of decision-makers (crown representative, legislator, administrator or quasi-judicial body, for instance) in order to reduce immunity and widen access to review. In the face of the relaxation of these restrictions, it has been suggested that government might now attempt to recapture some of its decision-making autonomy and freedom of action by characterizing its activities as ones unsuited to moulding according to the judicial standards of public administrative law (Allars, 1989). One such tack is to characterize them as commercial or managerial activities, invoking the private–public divide. Taggart's account of developments in New Zealand is worth relating (Taggart, 1991: 86):

> Increasing justiciability is an explicit concern of the courts due to the removal of former obstacles to judicial review; private powers are no longer sacrosanct, the concept of jurisdiction has been collapsed into the flexible error of law standard, the administrative/judicial dichotomy has withered under the fairness sunlamp, even the immunity of 'legislative' action is under threat. Not to mention the liberalisation, some would say the obliteration, of standing requirements, or the supposed simplification of judicial review procedure. Rising phoenix-like from the ashes of these distinctions come new ones like the labelling of certain activities as commercial or purely managerial. Such labels render the decision immune from judicial review and place it on the private law side of the nebulous line that divides public and private law.

The field of administrative law is obviously a large and complex one. By way of illustration, let us look at the position of decisions concerning the award of public contracts. We might just as pertinently look at decisions about participation in companies or the disposition of property, but contracts are a good illustration, given their role in dispensing favours and effecting conditions. Are these decisions about contracts to be placed on the public or the private side of the divide? Unlike the United Kingdom, where procedural rules directly raise the question whether the decisions are of a public nature, Australian law requires the courts look for clues in the source and the subject matter of the power being exercised by the body in question. Specifically do these features indicate that the body is exercising a governmental power?

THE CASE OF PUBLIC CONTRACTS

## The Jurisdiction to Review

The most common inquiry becomes whether the contractual decision is being made pursuant to a statutory power. But, given the practice of assistance in this field, the question must arise on occasions: what if the organization is exercising a non-statutory power, indeed if the organization itself has no statutory status? Allars (1989) is of the opinion that decisions may be reviewable in the common law jurisdictions of the courts even if they are not statutorily based. But there are other serious obstacles to this jurisdiction. Of particular interest to grievants are the facilities of the *Administrative Decisions (Judicial Review) Act 1977* (Cth) which provides a sounder footing on which to obtain judicial review of the decisions of commonwealth government officers. The Act limits its facilities of review to decisions of 'an administrative character made, proposed to be made or required to be made under an enactment'. Some contract decisions, such as decisions in the tendering process, have been successfully challenged under this Act because the criteria or procedures to be followed are regulated by statute. But it appears that an exercise of the government's personal capacity to enter into contracts does not qualify as a decision made under an enactment (Allars, 1989).

Interestingly, in its recent consideration of the scope for expanding the review of government decisions under the Act, the Commonwealth Administrative Review Council (1989) considered the amenability to review of a number of decisions relevant to the administration of industry assistance, including contract and tender decisions, decisions within non-statutory schemes, and decisions of bodies established by executive order. On the whole, the council's response to submissions for the extension of judicial review was cautious. It only went as far as recommending that decisions of an administrative character made by an officer of the commonwealth under a non-statutory scheme or program should be reviewable decisions where their funds were authorized by a parliamentary appropriation.

## The Scope of Review

Critics query why such decisions should be free from review if what government is really seeking to do is to implement its policies (or possibly even to disguise their implementation) through the use of private law forms and techniques (Daintith, 1979; Harlow, 1980). These questions raise a fundamental dilemma. Should the courts seek to penetrate these forms and regulate such a subtle use of public power by administrative law standards or should such activities be left to the economic disciplines of the market and recourse to the remedies of private law (Taggart, 1991)? Yet, we can see how the provision of access to the courts might not greatly assist the grievant. On what basis would the courts be able to check the legality of decisions? We have noted that, if the power has a statutory backing, the enabling statute may be so broadly permissive that it will be difficult to argue that a particular decision was in excess of power (Harden, 1990).

According to Allars (1990), the better prospect is the implication of the requirement of procedural fairness. But the courts have said this implication also requires a legal peg, else how wide might the right to be heard be spread? The courts have said that, if the grievant does not have a legal right that is directly affected by the decision, then he or she should have a legitimate expectation to be treated fairly before a decision is made. This expectation might arise if the grievant's interests are being affected in a manner substantially different from those of other members of the public, for example because of the impact of the decision upon the grievant's financial interests. But such a requirement limits the range of complainants who can effectively gain a remedy. Allars (1989) takes the view that the contractor whose contract is not renewed would be entitled to claim this right; perhaps other unsuccessful tenderers might also be able to claim it if they had been put to considerable trouble and expense to tender. This sort of concern for a legitimate interest finds broader expression in the requirement of 'standing' to invoke the jurisdiction of the courts at all. While more accommodating than in the past, the requirement of standing is also likely to act as a barrier, if not to unsuccessful applicants, then to the business competitors of the beneficiaries, to taxpayers or to public-spirited groups, because they cannot be said to suffer as a result of a decision to any greater degree than an ordinary member of the public (Allars, 1989; Harden, 1990).

## The Impact of Review

Whatever the precise scope of their jurisdiction, we should also ask whether the courts are likely to make much impact on the conduct of policy if they do entertain review. In their definition of the issues to be decided, the courts have a tendency to translate broad collective questions of policy into issues of legality and the impact on individual rights (McAuslan, 1983). This inclination leads them to focus upon the interests of those whom the state burdens with financial impositions, regulatory standards or loss of liberty. In some circumstances it brings in those who miss out on a grant of government support. But the concerns of the surrounding community are unlikely to find expression in this way. Furthermore, their procedures are not adapted to handle problems in which an unusual degree of complexity in the issues to be addressed is accompanied by a lack of established principles for resolving them. The courts are not suited to deal with what have been called 'polycentric' disputes, where flexible solutions must be found to multifaceted and interdependent social problems (Fuller, 1960).

The remedies which the courts can effect are also limited. In the immediate dispute, their options are to check government action and remit the decision for reconsideration. The agency may be able to observe the legal proprieties and especially the procedural niceties without varying the outcome of its deliberations. While there are always wrong government decisions, which should be overturned, we should note that litigants also use the judicial avenue strategically: for example to inconvenience their competitors, to obtain publicity for their cause or to postpone their day of reckoning (Vogel, 1987). The intervention of the courts can contribute to the kind of economic uncertainty and social conflict which scares away potential investors. In particular, the added delay and expense may render projects unviable. Such effects have led to some questioning of the contribution the courts can make to policy formation (Harrington, 1988).

### OVERSEAS COMPARISONS

The opportunities for judicial intervention vary, of course, with the particular constitutional and other legal traditions of the country in question. In the United States, several constitutional factors have created a stronger base for judicial review of the administrative process. The political separation between the legislature and the executive often leads to a more prescriptive legislative style. The constitutional recognition of due process and other individual rights also affords an opening to the courts. In addition, the United States legal culture is notable for developing in administrative law a refined procedural jurisprudence which emphasizes the need for agencies to open their proceedings and hear those affected by their decisions. It also requires administrators to base their decisions on the record of the substantial evidence which is to be built up by these adversary proceedings.

The United States is one country in which the resort to litigation to contest government decisions has recently been questioned. However, these administrative law standards have perhaps had the most impact in the realm of safety, environmental and other social regulation. It is the use of the courts by 'third parties', such as public interest groups, that has come under most attack. A leading administrative lawyer still suggests that the courts have not on the whole been able to reformulate decisions to withhold subsidies and contractual opportunities in the necessary mould of wrongs actionable by individuals against the government. At the same time, he recognizes that the parties to economic regulation often reach a bargained accommodation in a spirit of mutual restraint (Stewart, 1985).

In the case of Japan, it is widely observed that the deployment of the government's powers of patronage to guide development into selected areas escapes legal control. The same government party has dominated the legislature for many years. While some genuine legal questions surround the authority of government agencies to use their powers for such purposes, compliance is often obtained merely by the threat to withdraw favours, so that the agencies do not actually make administrative dispositions which deny rights and provide aggrieved individuals with standing before the courts (Upham, 1987). Furthermore, litigation may be construed as signifying the breakdown in a cooperative relationship, a situation which firms with longstanding dealings with government may wish to avoid. In any case, the courts themselves are said to be inclined to afford a broad interpretation to the scope of the agencies' legislative authority, such as the purposes for which they may withhold approval. Interestingly, Abe (1990) finds that this judicial abstentionism (and the space so left free for the conduct of informal and reciprocal relations between government and industry) is a common theme of American explanations for the 'success' of Japan's industry policy.

## ALTERNATIVE TRIBUNALS

One reason why there has not been more pressure for judicial redress from discontented groups in Australia is the presence of the 'new administrative law' forums such as the Ombudsman. Perhaps the initiative with most impact has been the establishment of specialist administrative appeals tribunals which enjoy the power to inquire into the merits of administrative decisions and the policies which drive them (Kirby, 1981). Such tribunals may be staffed with expertise in their area of coverage. They may offer relaxed requirements of standing. These tribunals presently operate in the federal, Victorian and New South Wales jurisdictions. At the federal level, access to the Administrative Appeals Tribunal depends, however, upon the parliament specifically assigning jurisdiction over a particular area to the tribunal. The tribunal does have jurisdiction to review decisions in relation to certain aspects of patents, customs, tariffs, export assistance, bounties, taxation and telecommunications, but on the whole the real guts of these schemes have been shielded from the jurisdiction of the tribunal. Tax matters are the exception. As we noted, in 1988 the Commonwealth Administrative Review Council (1988) recommended to the government that several of the remaining areas of discretionary decision-making in the area of the industry research and development grants and tax concessions should be subjected to review on their merits in the tribunal. The council took the view that these decisions were amenable to review in such a tribunal, even though they involve making economic judgements. The government was to take up the council's recommendations. As we shall note below, in chapter 12, some commentators see such tribunals as the trail blazer for a new kind of responsive legal process (for example Carney, 1991). However, for the time being, we shall have to say that they share enough of the structural limitations and legalistic tendencies of the courts to raise doubts about their potential to be a real alternative.

## ACCOUNTABILITY TO THE LEGISLATURE

Whatever the reasons, the case studies do not give the impression that litigation has (yet) been a major source of opposition to the measures involved. While the courts and tribunals are likely to continue to play an important limiting role at the boundaries of administrative action, accountability for the overall programmic thrust of such policies is likely to depend upon the opportunities for their screening and monitoring within other public forums. In Australia, accountability for innovation support measures has at times been translated into the question of accountability to the parliament, its committees and offices. It is another matter of course whether these attempts to reassert representative democracy over the corporate state will prove successful. As we know, political science remains sceptical of the prospects for making ministers responsible to parliament for the conduct of affairs within their portfolios. The ministers may be able to use broad statutory frameworks and inherent powers to shield policy-making from scrutiny. As we have seen, hiving off activities into hybridized bodies is another way of distancing their administration from the traditional sites of accountability.

## LEGISLATIVE ENACTMENT

Parliamentary oversight begins with the legislative enactment of a program. Government's choice of the enactment form is crucial at this stage. In Australia, the presence of written constitutions ensures some necessity to source authority in legislation, but, as we know, the observance of convention also counts for much. In the United Kingdom, Daintith (1976) took the view that the oversight of industry assistance policy depended essentially upon the degree to which the criteria and procedures for awards were detailed in legislation or were otherwise accountable to parliament. Yet taxing and spending programs were often legislated on a broad categorical or aggregate basis. The opportunity for parliamentary control depended upon the observance of the constitutional convention that continuing expenditure programs were to be expressed in specific permanent legislation rather than in simple line items in the yearly appropriations legislation: 'The appropriations legislation in no way reflects the important issues and decisions regarding the quality and direction of public expenditure' (Daintith, 1976: 71). Indeed, if the scheme is to be administered from a government department, specific legislation may not be employed at all, and the department may call upon its ordinary legal capacities to form connections with private firms. It is worth noting that parliamentary opposition, especially in hostile upper houses, might give impetus to this strategy.

If policy is to be expressed in subordinate or delegated legislation, it must be made in line with the requirements of the principal enabling act. Customarily, such regulations must be reported to parliament; they are also required to be published. In some Australian jurisdictions, a notable recent reform is the provision for subordinate legislation to be assessed by parliamentary committees according to a range of constitutional provisions, civil liberties and economic criteria (Allars, 1990). The Victorian *Subordinate Legislation (Review and Revocation) Act 1984* is the most far reaching, requiring the proposing agency to prepare a regulatory impact statement along the lines of the 'cognitive reform' measures identified by McGarrity (1986) in his survey of recent regulatory reforms in the United States. Such requirements do not, however, usually apply to the plethora of directives, guidelines, circulars and the like which often embody the agency's working policy (Baldwin and Houghton, 1986). It is pertinent to note that the Commonwealth Administrative Review Council (1992) recently recommended that a new framework be created to regulate the making of all commonwealth instruments of a 'legislative character'. Within this framework, all substantive policy would have to be embodied in legislation. The making of delegated legislation would require public consultation, tabling before parliament and official publication.

## PERIODIC PROGRAM REVIEW

### Ad Hoc Review

Accountability can also be measured by the opportunities which are created for the periodic parliamentary review of programs when they are in operation. An opportunity for individual members is presented by the procedure for questions with or without notice. In Australia, and especially in Victoria, opposition members have also been heavy users of the general freedom of information legislation and have tested the exceptions to this legislation in the administrative appeals tribunals (the *Age*, 23 February 1989). Governments have on occasions claimed that the commercial sensitivity of information about their dealings with the private sector is a reason for invoking exemptions from the requirements of this legislation. In any case, not all states, it should be noted, have enacted such legislation. More systematically, the various standing and *ad hoc* committees of the parliaments have been a source of appraisal of innovation support measures. To its credit, the federal government has also been willing to refer a variety of its programs to the expert statutory bodies, such as the Industries Commission, the Bureau of Industry Economics and the Australian Science and Technology Council, often for critical evaluation.

## The Role of the Audit Offices

Thus, the effectiveness of such review depends in part upon the continuing preparedness of government to tolerate what is often an uncomfortable experience of examination. Experience with the innovation support measures reveals some ambivalence amongst governments on this score. Their attitudes to the increasingly important role of audit offices provides perhaps the most topical example. In Australia, both at the national and state levels, the Auditor-General's functions have been upgraded in recent years. For example, at the national level, since the 1979 reforms, the Auditor-General's responsibilities have been extended to the conduct of efficiency audits of the operation of many departments, authorities and organizations (Adams, 1986). While routine financial audits are concerned primarily with the observance of financial procedures, efficiency audits also assess the management and operational performance of the agency in efficiently using its financial and like resources. The federal Auditor-General has conducted a number of efficiency audits in areas related to innovation policy, such as the offsets policy, the industrial participation program with respect to overseas procurement, the export market development grant scheme, and the defence science and technology organization.

In relation to the deeper commercial dealings of government, particularly at the state level, the Auditors-General have expressed concern over their loss of jurisdiction to the authority of private auditors operating under general companies legislation, as the conduct of commercial affairs has become more distanced from the conventional core of government, such as the departments of the crown and the statutory authorities. An example of these concerns is provided by the remarks made by the New South Wales Auditor-General concerning the examination of the accounts of the subsidiary companies of government authorities, including the various university technology companies (New South Wales Auditor-General, 1989). Strengthening the role of the Auditor-General is also the theme of the discussion paper issued by the Western Australian Royal Commission (1991) into the recent commercial activities of government in that state.

One critical point of uncertainty is the dividing line between the audit of financial efficiency and the appraisal of government policy. The Victorian Auditor-General, who enjoyed a stormy relationship with the state Labor government, raised this issue in his special report on financial assistance to industry (Victorian Auditor-General, 1989). McEldowney (1991) notes a similar tension in the United Kingdom, where the National Audit Office has played an important role in overseeing the government's privatization program. He detects a tension between the assessment on the one hand of the economy and efficiency and on the other of the effectiveness of departmental decisions concerning the sales of public assets. He notes that the office is restricted by its charter from questioning the merits of government policy on privatization. But he also acknowledges that the office's own accounting mentality is likely to limit the features of programs which it chooses to assess (for Australia, see Howard, 1986). The refinement of social accounting techniques might offer more scope. The consideration of social objectives is curtailed, however, if the government's very brief to the administering agency is merely to realize a commercial dividend (Taggart, 1991). In relation to the British experience, McEldowney also raises a question of the post-privatization jurisdiction of the National Audit Office over the performance of the privatized instrumentalities and the agencies established to regulate them.

## CONCLUSIONS

### RELATIONS WITHIN THE SPACE

We have noted the tendencies to depart from the standards of liberal legality in the implementation of government innovation policy. We suggested that government seeks to create a space in which to deal with the key individual organizations in order to inspire and persuade them to apply their elusive assets to the cause of local innovation. Innovation promotion schemes are often structured in such a way as to permit administrators the opportunity, free of the strictures of the legislatures and the courts, to bargain with industry by offering inducements and exchanging benefits (Loveday, 1982).

Why is this approach adopted? We identified a search for a government structure that assists the state to promote its policies within the constraints of its environment. In particular, the strength of the liberal legal form provides producers with a source of independence from the specific administrations of the government of the day. As we saw in earlier chapters, the government, especially in smaller countries such as Australia, cannot readily ignore or override the claims of this law. Consequently, government seeks a means to induce the private sector to deploy its rights in the cause of innovation. It is inclined to turn to incentives and inducements rather than directives in order to achieve this end. In a global economy, resourceful foreign corporations may have a realistic option of locating their research and development activities elsewhere if they do not consider local conditions sufficiently favourable. The nature of innovation also seems to necessitate this approach. Small firms and creative individuals also play an important role in the success of innovation. These contributors are often of a fragile and fragmented nature. Government is led into close, ongoing relations designed to sustain these contributors in a harsh environment.

We have noted how these circumstances also create a risk that the government will be ineffective in selecting successful innovators and obtaining a return on its assistance. As a result, the purposive action approach becomes one with limited goals and achievements, employed not so much to direct or replace innovative activity as to create a bargaining and working relationship with industry in order to maximize the realistic prospects of 'getting things done' (Blankenburg, 1985). In Australia, despite the many criticisms we have acknowledged, the efforts of Senator John Button and his officers can be viewed as a partial success, making modest gains from careful instrument design.

## LIBERAL COUNTERS

Yet, the new schemes of inducement and collaboration will always operate in a complex interaction with the private world of property, contract and association – a relationship that has been characterized as a 'contradictory symbiosis' (Picciotto, 1983: 36). The approach encounters problems not just at the level of instrumental effectiveness but also at the level of political legitimacy. The institutions of government are placed under stress as the state moves from a legitimacy based on its role in upholding the liberal form of law to a legitimacy which is contingent upon its success in the particularized management of the economy. Government takes on full responsibility for private failures. Less tangibly, the approach engenders a loss of faith in the state's preparedness to guarantee the categorical and formally equivalent legal conditions for the conduct of private economic activity and to maintain the rule of law generally (Offe, 1984). The practice of this approach is likely to create a tension with the continuing claims of liberal legality. The state encounters a strong lobby, not only to prevent further encroachment into this sphere of private economic autonomy, but also to legalize claims to government subsidies and services, and indeed to privatize public assets (Broekman, 1985). We can detect movements in the courts and the legislatures to insist upon the observance of constitutionality and legality in the award of government aid and patronage. In Australia, despite the courts' preparedness to relax their technical barriers to access, it is interesting that this scrutiny has been more of a parliamentary nature.

## PRIVATIZATION

Yet, more so in some countries than others, the claims of liberal legality have a more final impact. The logical extension of these claims (one that appeals to governments unwilling to engage in the demanding task of economic management) is the movement of industry supports onto the private side of the liberal public–private divide. This shift does not signify the end of government involvement with industry, but it does locate it more squarely in the private world where, traditionally, different legal standards apply. Collective public interests are not necessarily enhanced by this retraction. The opportunities for external review are reduced, both at the point of the decision to privatize and in the operations of the instrumentalities after privatization. As Taggart (1991) remarks, almost all of the accountability mechanisms operating in relation to state-owned enterprises are stripped away. These controls are thought inappropriate to 'private enterprise'. The various avenues of public accountability are replaced by the disciplines of the market. But whether the change of ownership solves the problems of control is open to doubt. Government must rely more heavily on the efficacy of its conventional powers, both of *imperium* and, especially in recent times, of *dominium*. More to the point, as this study has endeavoured to show, the collective interest relies even more heavily on the efforts which governments put into designing and implementing the discerning property, competition and trade policies which condition so heavily how that reinvigorated 'private' economy works. In Australia, where privatization is still very much to run its course, these efforts will soon be strongly tested.

# Conclusions

## THE PROPERTY FRAMEWORK

With the collapse of the communist regimes in Eastern Europe and changes elsewhere, Fukuyama (1992) has written prominently of the 'end of history'. Veterans of social instability doubt the inevitability of this evolution, but, for the time being, capitalism in the guise of liberal democracy and market economics has everywhere triumphed. Yet this simple observation glosses over the multitude of arrangements possible within a liberal capitalist framework. Graham (1989: 210) comments:

> there is a tendency to assume markets are free, spontaneous growths. However, even in the classical *laissez-faire* model, the ground rules for the market are set by the minimal state. The selection of any one particular rule against another will create a different type of market. As Frug puts it: 'There is . . . not "a" market mechanism, but as many markets as there are possible rules to define them.' This leads to the final point, which is the paradox at the heart of the neo-classical view. It is a mistake to see the minimal state as a weak state. In order to guarantee the conditions that will allow markets to flourish the state must be strong and active.

In some sectors of the economy, those rules might seem settled. But innovation, now a global technological revolution, undermines, without determining, the existing monopolies of thought and interest in the structures of the economy and law. It is hoped that this study, especially in chapters 3 to 5, has demonstrated that innovation raises again the basic questions concerning the appropriation of important resources, and sometimes essential attributes, through the media of property and related private rights. As profound as they are, these questions are being determined in relatively quiet terms and select circles when they are compared to the agonizing taking place in cultures such as Australia over the appropriate role for government in regulating or replacing the resource allocations of the market. Yet, following Graham (1989), we should concede that the state has already 'intervened' when it decides to confer property rights, and conditions the power which individuals have to realize their preferences in the market. As Klare (1982) has remarked, the real debate ought not to be about the contrast between civil autonomy and state control but about the forms and content of 'intervention' at any particular juncture.

Such a *caveat* is not to deny that the case for offering the incentive of appropriation to spur innovation often has force. There is arguably more individual desert and social utility in encouraging innovative production than there is in protecting inheritance or rewarding speculation. Yet, as we have seen, the economic arguments do not always themselves point in the direction of state-sponsored exclusivity. And the capture in private hands of information technology and biotechnology has moral and social implications as well as economic consequences. Certainly, there is room for debate over the qualifications and conditions which are to be placed on the grant of property and related rights, partly in the cause of innovation continuing to the greatest possible extent.

If capitalism is all we have at the end of the century, then care should be exercised and imagination displayed in the design and tuning of its institutions when opportunities arise. After all, we might recall that Friedrich Hayek, while championing the free market, stressed the need to take great care with the design of its legal institutions (e.g. Hayek, 1960). One imperative is that property policy be explored in its industrial context. In this study, we have endeavoured to restate the point that property's social roles are transformed in a world of big science, planned production, and industrial integration. At points, this contextual sensibility informs us that property is not necessarily the key to successful innovation. Command over other assets assumes more significance. To some extent, the nature of innovation itself works against appropriation through the medium of property rights and sends producers in search of other strategies to capture its benefits. Certainly, it tells us that property is often used for purposes other than standing alone or for arm's length trade on the open market. It alerts us to the need to explore property policies in conjunction with the legal policies adopted towards the relational and organizational forms which the players also pursue to capture the benefits of innovation. These legal policies include competition, trade and investment policy.

Yet, the study suggests that the inclination is to reaffirm private property when innovation creates a gap in the legal protection of economic value. It is true that variations in national economic conditions, ideological debates and even legal cultures temper the response to some degree. But we can discern a tendency for the property question to be lifted out of the relatively politicized forums of the nation state. The movement towards the globalization of the economy is one about the internationalization of policy as much as the real spread of innovative activity. It is often a movement to argue that the nation state has no choice concerning the coverage and force of the property and related rights which are to obtain in a worldwide liberal trading regime.

These powerful unifying or harmonizing movements present a special challenge to the smaller developed nations. They confront a dilemma. Is their best strategy to seek access to world markets through the extension of the liberal regime multilaterally at the global level or should they take measures unilaterally or bilaterally at the national level to shore up their local industry in an inevitably imperfect market? Often, they cannot boast the locally based transnational corporations or industrial clusters which are said to provide the competitive advantage in such open markets. Yet their prevailing ideologies and cultural associations incline them in the direction of the liberalizing international movements. Their choice is not made any easier by the fact that the leading Western economies are often playing the policy game strategically, favouring free trade where it suits their strengths, practising neo-mercantilism where it does not. Again, a sense of the recent compromises of national competition and investment regulation, as well as the selective support of property rights, is valuable here.

## THE REGULATORY SPACE

What has the study told us about the experience with policy formation and implementation in the regulatory space? It reminds us that there are compelling reasons for government to try to carve out a space in which to deal more directly and discriminatingly with the firms it seeks to enlist to the cause of innovation. We considered some of the reasons why government might find the rule-based, market-oriented liberal approach at times too obtuse, indirect and uncertain an approach to further its purposes. Of course, some of those reasons were to be discovered in the nature of the field the government was seeking to change. The offer of property and related rights provides no guarantee that private capital will choose to invest its resources in innovative activities, especially those which are locally based. For instance, large transnational producers seem to require special inducements to locate parts of their core innovative functions outside their home bases. Small fragile firms seem dependent on favourable conditions to bolster their position in a tough industrial environment.

Given our interest in the nature of government structures, and especially legal frameworks, we also identified an internal operational rationale for the creation of a discretionary administrative space in which to particularize policy. Government seeks ways of insulating its practices from the judicial review and parliamentary oversight of public law standards. We began to see this at work in the reconstruction and operation of the trade practices and foreign investment schemes of regulation, Picciotto (1983) was able to conclude, for instance, that their administration has become a matter of corporatist consensus between the state agencies and the leaders of industrial and finance capital. Following Daintith (1985), we were inclined to see the approach in full flower where government deploys its powers of *dominium* rather than *imperium* to encourage innovation. In the final case studies, we examined the use of tax concessions and direct grants, government purchasing and exclusive licensing. Despite the apparent differences in their administrative traditions and political rhetoric, all the Western governments do practise sponsorship and entrepreneurship under one guise or another.

The study also endeavoured to assess the significance of government practices within the space to the overall course of innovation. The conclusion was that they had limited effect, especially in the Australian context. Consequently, they were coping strategies, with limited expectations, which were meant to deal with the policy problem of making government objectives effective (Blankenburg, 1985). Quite often, then, they meant that policies were actually negotiated with the target groups and applied adaptively, legal powers in particular being used to open up bargaining for cooperation rather than to impose controls or direction. Private interests were incorporated in the policy-making process.

What limited the effect of the government's approach? There were a variety of reasons why the approach had limited impact in an instrumental sense. Industry structure was one reason. For example, large transnational producers often enjoyed options elsewhere within their global operations. The nature of innovation was another. Successful innovation, especially amongst the small startup firms, was not something that could be readily programmed. Government measures did not always derive the quality of response from the private sector to which they aspired.

The approach also encountered legitimacy problems. A great concern, at least in the Anglo-American commentary on public policy, is the discrimination between firms or industries. We noted that the award of government favours to private players, or government involvement directly in production, may be characterized as a capture of public policy by sectional interests and a distortion of natural and even market forces. This concern acquires a political voice in the lobbies and forums that surround government and is indeed to be found within the various arms of government itself. Another outlet, and one of special interest to this study, was its expression in legal terms. Here it finds voice in the drive to reassert liberal legality over the conduct of administrative action in the space. Claims are made in the courts and legislatures to hold administrative agencies to legally circumscribed purposes and procedures when they decide whether to dispense patronage to particular favourites.

The study indicated that the drive is not wholly successful in controlling freedom to formulate policy within the space. In part, their own outlooks restrict what the courts or government offices (like the audit offices) can see and order. In part, too, the executive continues to explore ways of shielding administrative action from scrutiny. But a further drive is to cut back the space altogether, returning contested and perhaps lucrative functions to the private sector. It is clear that for some the answer is for government to withdraw from these areas of economic activity. Paradoxically, the criticism which government experiences when it engages in particularized economic management may encourage it along this road. It may seek to place some of its more complex and controversial activities back on the private side of the public–private divide. In some cases, the aim is to submerge the continued performance of its public functions within the privacy of private law forms; in others, it is an abidication of responsibilities for policy to the security of rules and deference to the market. The role government reserves for itself on the privatization of public instrumentalities is a good test of which objective is uppermost.

## FURTHER RESEARCH AND DISCUSSION

It is too late in the piece to advance any sort of reforms to remedy these unsatisfactory conditions for policy advancement. It would be an idealist exercise to do so in any case. Instead, perhaps, the mention of a recent reform proposal might help suggest some fruitful lines for the research and discussion which ought to be maintained in this field. For some, it is clear that the law should simply return to its role in liberal legality of guaranteeing the formally equivalent conditions for resource allocation through the market and the other autonomous domains of the private economy. Government's role itself would be contained by such rules. Fashioning an appropriate response to the problems of the administrative or corporatist approach seems to cause more heartburn to those on the left of politics. As we remarked in chapter 2, they seem caught between a wariness of the discordant and uneven impacts of liberal legality and a desire to rein back the corporate state with its potential for capture and closure. A good illustration is their ambivalence about an increased role for the ordinary courts in policy formation. How to control the arbitrariness and favouritism of the exceptional state without wholly obstructing the prosecution of public policy?

For those who have in a sense given up hope of attaining any coherence or commonality in the substantive reform of policy, one attractive diversion seems to be the beneficial effects of revitalized procedural ordering. Something of this inclination can be seen in the focus on the procedural reform of public sector administrative decision-making through the injection of values of openness, participation and fairness along North American lines. I do not think it stretching the point to discern this theme also in the law of equity's recent emphasis on good faith and honest dealings in the private law realm of contracts and other commercial dealings. Yet, it has its most articulate theoretical advocacy in the ideas of responsive law (Nonet and Selznick, 1978) or reflexive law (Teubner, 1983). These two overlapping ideas have enjoyed much intellectual currency in recent years.

For our limited purpose at this late stage, let us focus on reflexive law. As reflexive law, the law's role is to design and coordinate self-regulating systems through the prescription of norms of competence, organization and procedure (Teubner, 1984). Such law seeks to shape the structures of systems such as science or industry so that they are open to the messages of their environment. It requires the recognized stakeholding groups, for instance, to exchange information and negotiate issues. Yet it refrains from prescribing the substantive positions they ultimately adopt. Reflexive law's norms are meant to apply to decision-making in both the public and the private spheres, a valuable contribution at a time when the lines between the two are being blurred. Reflexive law places a great deal of faith in the role of communication and process to guide these social systems to suitably responsive outcomes (Teubner, 1988). Others, however, have doubts about the capacity of such procedures to discourage those with power from exploiting their position in their dealings within these systems (Fredman and Lee, 1986). The relative importance of substantive and procedural standards is again part of a grander debate in socio-legal studies (Eder, 1988). But it is not hard even at this point to suggest that any rights to be informed, consulted and heard, even if the agenda is broadly defined, might be satisfiable without a powerful interest having to concede substantive ground. In part, the proponents of reflexive law need to let us know whose position is to be upheld should its processes of inquiry and negotiation fail. Some initial scepticism is in order about the preparedness of the law to back procedures that have penalties for the powerful. The matter is complicated by the fact that the state itself will often be an interest directly implicated in those procedures (Carney, 1991). Can we expect the state to render itself more accountable?

Yet the point must be made that the state, despite its popular image in the writings of constitutional and administrative law, is not always the strong and overbearing player in these systems. Certainly, we can perceive, in the realm we currently term private, large corporations that wield a great deal of regulatory power, even at the expense of the nation state (Bercusson, 1988). Surely these power differences must affect the outcome of dealings within the systems (Howse, Pritchard and Trebilcock, 1990). This query returns us to our original point in this chapter about the importance of the property framework within which such procedures will have to operate. At present, the case for reflexive law remains vague about the nature of the boundaries which its law would place on these self-regulating systems. The law's choice of the norms of competence and organization for these systems (the interests which are to be included and canvassed within any one system) is critical to the outcomes of 'self-regulation'. We need to know who is to be in or out of these systems. We need also to know why some of those interests which are included will be able to bring power to these systems with its predictable impact on their outcomes (Kettler, 1987). Is the law likely to redefine and redistribute the boundaries in an innovative and expansive way?

The purpose of these remarks about reflexive law is to bring the chapter round to a point that is close to the heart of the long and now thankfully almost finished journey of this book. The reflexive law prospectuses are not alone in their need to make clear just to what extent they take for granted the framework of the traditional liberal institutions (Treiber, 1984). After all, the liberal legal approach is also often presented as a kind of content-free faith in the processes of the market to produce the right outcomes. Yet our point is that it is not possible to talk about the appropriate ordering of the space without thinking about the boundaries to it. Is, for example, property power to be something that is open to consideration and compromise or is it to be something which some participants bring to bear from outside on their dealings with others inside the process? If the conditions of property grants are to be among the issues, then which groups are to be part of the system which settles their fate?

The understandable concern to make process work more rationally and fairly inside the space should never be at the expense of the enduring questions we first identified about the framework of property and related rights. This evident concern about government practice in the space should not need to cripple the state's remaining potential to contribute to the advancement of public policy over sectional private interests. Somehow, a sense of proportion needs to be maintained, a kind of a balance achieved. It is not made any easier by the fact that much of the significant decision-making over innovation policy is now taking place at an international level rather than the simply national level where the focus of legal debate has hitherto largely resided.

# Bibliography

Abe, M. (1990) 'Review Essay: Japanese Industrial Policy in Perspective', *Law and Society Review* 24: 1071.
Abell, M. (1990) 'Japanese Anti-trust Law and Patent and Know-how Licensing', *European Intellectual Property Review* 1990: 413.
Acharya, R. (1991) 'Patenting of Biotechnology: GATT and the Erosion of the World's Biodiversity', *Journal of World Trade* 25(6): 71.
Adams, L. (1990) 'The Law of United States-Japan Trade Relations', *Journal of World Trade* 24(2): 37.
Adams, N. (1986) 'Efficiency Auditing in the Australian Audit Office', *Australian Journal of Public Administration* XLV: 189.
Adelstein, R. & S. Peretz (1985) 'The Competition of Technologies in Markets For Ideas: Copyright and Fair Use in Evolutionary Perspective', *International Review of Law and Economics* 5: 209.
Allars, M. (1989) 'Administrative Law, Government Contracts and the Level Playing Field', *University of New South Wales Law Journal* 12(1): 114.
 (1990) *Introduction to Australian Administrative Law*, Butterworths, Sydney.
Allen, S., S. Green, J. Friedman, B. Harrington & L. Johnson (1972) 'New Technology and the Law of Copyright: Reprography and Computers', in G. Bush (ed.), *Technology and Copyright: Annotated Bibliography and Source Materials*, Lomond Systems, Mt Airy, Maryland.
Anon. (1985) 'More on Copyright in Computer Programs – Reproduction in Terminal Works', *Copyright Reporter* 3(3): 11.
Archibald, A. (1984) 'The Law of Confidential Information: Quo Vadis?', *Law Institute Journal* 58: 511.
Armstrong, M. (ed.) (1990) *Telecommunications Laws: Australian Perspectives*, CIRCIT, Melbourne.
 (ed.) (1991) *New Telecommunications Laws: The 1991 Revolution*, CIRCIT, Melbourne.
 (1991a) 'Implementing Communications Policy: Who Makes the Decisions, and How', Policy Research Paper no. 14, CIRCIT, Melbourne.
Armstrong, M. & P. Anderson (1991) 'The Regulatory Process: Access, Participation, Information', in W. Melody (ed.), *Implementing*

*the New Telecommunications Policy: From Words to Deeds*, CIRCIT, Melbourne.
Arnold, E. & K. Guy (1986) *Parallel Convergence: National Strategies In Information Technology*, Frances Pinter, London.
Arnold, T. (1937) *The Folklore of Capitalism*, Yale University Press, New Haven.
Arrowsmith, S. (1990) 'Judicial Review and the Contractual Powers of Public Authorities', *Law Quarterly Review* 106: 277.
Arup, C. (1982) 'Genetic Engineering and Patent Law', *Legal Service Bulletin* 7: 9.
  (1983) 'Regulating Industrial Carcinogens: Dealing with Uncertainty and Risk', *University of New South Wales Law Journal* 6: 37.
  (1985) 'Intellectual Property in the Context of Research-Industry Collaboration', *Vestes – The Australian Universities Review* 28: 14.
  (1991) 'Labour Law, Production Strategies and Industrial Relations', *Law in Context* 9(1): 36.
Atiyah, P. (1979) *The Rise and Fall of the Freedom of Contract*, Clarendon Press, Oxford.
Aubert, V. (1985) 'The Rule of Law and the Promotional Function of Law in the Welfare State', in G. Teubner (ed.), *Dilemmas of Law in the Welfare State*, Walter de Gruyter, Berlin.
Austin, R. (1987) 'Fiduciary Accountability for Business Opportunities', in P. Finn (ed.), *Equity and Commercial Relationships*, Law Book, Sydney.
Baldwin, R. & J. Houghton (1986) 'Circular Arguments: The Status and Legitimacy of Administrative Rules', *Public Law* 1986: 239.
Bankowski, Z. & J. Mugham (1974) '"Warwick University Ltd." (Continued)', *British Journal of Law and Society* 1: 179.
Baranson, J. (1978) *Technology and the Multinationals*, Lexington Books, Lexington, Massachusetts.
Barr, T. (1985) *The Electronic Estate: New Communications Media and Australia*, Penguin, Melbourne.
Baxt, R. (1991) 'Enforcing Competition Policy', in W. Melody (ed.), *Implementing the New Telecommunications Policy: From Words to Deeds*, CIRCIT, Melbourne.
Bayne, P. (1984) *Freedom of Information*, Law Book, Sydney.
  (1989) 'Administrative Law and the New Managerialism in Public Administration', *Canberra Bulletin of Public Administration* 58: 39.
Beardon, C. (1980) 'The Political Economy of Computing in Australia', *Journal of Australian Political Economy* 7: 3.
Beazley, K. (1991) 'The Key Steps Towards Successful Implementation: A Progress Report and Current Assessment', in W. Melody (ed.), *Implementing the New Telecommunications Policy: From Words to Deeds*, CIRCIT, Melbourne.
Beier, F. & G. Shricker (eds) (1989) 'GATT or WIPO?: New Ways in the International Protection of Intellectual Property', IIC Studies in

Industrial Property and Copyright Law, Max Planck Institute, Munich.
Bercusson, B. (1988) 'Economic Policy: State and Private Ordering', in T. Daintith (ed.), *Law as an Instrument of Economic Policy: Comparative and Critical Approaches*, Walter de Gruyter, Berlin.
Bertin, G. & S. Wyatt (1988) *Multinationals and Industrial Property: The Control of the World's Technology*, Harvester Wheatsheaf, Hemel Hempstead, England.
Biddle, A. (1984) 'A Patent on Knowledge', *Harpers* 273(1574): 22.
Blakeney, M. (1989) *Legal Aspects of the Transfer of Technology to Developing Countries*, ESC Publishing, Oxford.
Blankenburg, E. (1984) 'The Poverty of Evolutionism: A Critique of Teubner's Case for "Reflexive Law" ', *Law and Society Review* 18: 273.
—— (1985) 'The Waning of Legality in the Concept of Policy Implementation', *Law and Policy* 7: 481.
Bowen, L. (1987) 'Keeping up with Copyright: Speech to the Copyright Society by the Attorney-General', *Copyright Reporter* 5(2): 1.
Boyd, R. (1987) 'Government-Industry Relations in Japan: Access, Communication and Competitive Collaboration', in S. Wilkes & M. Wright (eds), *Comparative Government–Industry Relations*, Clarendon Press, Oxford.
Bozeman, B. & A. Link (1984) 'Tax Incentives for R & D: A Critical Evaluation', *Research Policy* 13: 21.
Brand, A. (1982) 'Against Romanticism: Max Weber and the Historical School of Law', *Australian Journal of Law and Society* 1(1): 87.
Brand, R. (1990) 'Private Parties and GATT Dispute Resolution: Implications of the Panel Report on Section 337 of the US Tariff Act of 1930', *Journal of World Trade* 24(3): 5.
Brazil, P. (1987) 'Infringement of Copyright and the Problem of "Piracy" ', *Australian Law Journal* 61: 12.
Breyer, S. (1970) 'The Uneasy Case for Copyright: A Study of Copyright in Books, Photocopies and Computer Programs', *Harvard Law Review* 84: 281.
Broekman, J. (1985) 'Legal Subjectivity as a Precondition for the Intertwinement of Law and the Welfare State', in G. Teubner (ed.) *Dilemmas of Law in the Welfare State*, Walter de Gruyter, Berlin.
Brown, G. (1990) 'Regulation of The Telecommunications Equipment and Cabling Markets', in M. Armstrong (ed.), *Telecommunications Laws: Australian Perspectives*, CIRCIT, Melbourne.
Brown, R. (1983) 'Crime and Computers', *Criminal Law Journal* 7: 68.
Brunt, M. (1986) 'The Use of Economic Evidence in Antitrust Litigation in Australia', *Australian Business Law Review* 14: 261.
Brunt, M. (1990) 'The Role of Private Actions in Australian Restrictive Trade Practices Enforcement', *Melbourne University Law Review* 17: 582.

# Bibliography

Cabanellas, C. (1984) 'Antitrust and Direct Regulation of International Transfer of Technology Transactions', IIC Studies in Industrial Property and Copyright Law, Max Planck Institute, Munich.

Calabresi, G. & A. Melamed (1972) 'Property Rules, Liability Rules and Inalienability: One View of the Cathedral', *Harvard Law Review* 85: 1089.

Callinicos, A. (1989) *Against Postmodernism: A Marxist Critique*, Polity Press, London.

Cameron, P. & S. Midgeley (1982) 'Contract, the Rule of Law, and the Liberal-Democratic State: The Case of Britain and North Sea Oil', *International Journal of the Sociology of Law* 10: 239.

Carney, T. (1991) *Law at the Margins: Towards Social Participation?*, Oxford University Press, Melbourne.

Carroll, J. (1986) 'Background and Reasons for Proposed Policy Guidelines for Government Business Enterprises', *Australian Journal of Public Administration* XLV: 284.

CCH Australia (1991) *Australian Trade Practices Reporter*, CCH, Sydney.

Chandler, M., M. Trebilcock & R. Howse (1990) 'Trade Restrictive Policies and Democratic Politics: A Proposal for Reform', *Public Law Review* 1: 234.

Charles, D. (1990) 'Technological Innovation', *Australian Journal of Public Administration* 49: 332.

Cheeah, C. (1991) 'GATT and the Emerging International Framework', in W. Melody (ed.), *Implementing the New Telecommunications Policy: From Words to Deeds*, CIRCIT, Melbourne.

Chesnais, F. (1986) 'Science, Technology and Competitiveness', *STI Review* 1: 85.

Cicciotti, G., M. Cini & C. De Maria (1976) 'The Productivity of Science in Advanced Capitalist Society' in H. Rose & S. Rose, *The Political Economy of Science*, Macmillan, London.

Clark, S. (1981) 'Philosopher's Paradise: Should a Microorganism the Product of a Microbiologist be Patentable?', *Auckland University Law Review* 4: 129.

Clarke, A. (1986) 'Issues in Applying University-Based Research, in University of New South Wales, Science, Technology and the Economy – Papers from the Symposium', University of NSW Occasional Papers no. 11, Sydney.

Clarke, P. (1987) 'Monopolisation Without A Misuse of Market Power – A Lacuna in s.46?', *Australian Business Law Review* 15: 310.

(1989) 'Trade Practices Policy and the Role of the Trade Practices Commission', *Australian Business Law Review* 17: 291.

Claydon, J. (1986) 'Joint Ventures – An Analysis of Commission Decisions', *European Competition Law Review* 7: 151.

Collingridge, D. (1980) *The Social Control of Technology*, Open University Press, Milton Keynes, England.

Collins, H. (1982) 'Capitalist Discipline and Corporatist Law: Parts I and II', *Industrial Law Journal* 11: 78 & 170.
— (1986) 'Market Power, Bureaucratic Power and the Contract of Employment', *Industrial Law Journal* 15: 1.
— (1990) 'Ascription of Legal Responsibility to Groups in Complex Patterns of Economic Integration', *Modern Law Review* 53: 731.
Commons, J. (1924) *The Legal Foundations of Capitalism*, Macmillan, New York.
Commonwealth of Australia. Administrative Review Council (1988) 'Review of Decisions Under Industry Research and Development Legislation', Report no. 31, AGPS, Canberra.
— (1989) 'Report to the Attorney-General, General Review of the Administrative Decisions (Judicial Review) Act: The Ambit of the Act', AGPS, Canberra.
— (1992) 'Rule Making by Commonwealth Agencies', Report no. 35, AGPS, Canberra.
Commonwealth of Australia. Attorney-General, Minister for Home Affairs and Environment, and Minister for Employment and Industrial Relations (1984) 'The Trade Practices Act – Proposals for Change', Canberra.
Commonwealth of Australia. Attorney-General's Department (1984) 'National Symposium on Legal Protection of Computer Software', Canberra.
— (1986) *Annual Report 1985–86*, AGPS, Canberra.
— (1987) *Annual Report 1986–87*, AGPS, Canberra.
— (1988) 'Review of Developments in International Trade Law, in Attorney-General's Department', Fifteenth International Trade Law Conference, Papers, AGPS, Canberra.
— (1989) *Annual Report 1988–89*, AGPS, Canberra.
Commonwealth of Australia. Auditor-General (1984) 'Reports of the Auditor-General on Efficiency Audits: Administration of the Offsets Policy, Administration of the Australian Industry Participation Program in Relation to Overseas Procurement', AGPS, Canberra.
— (1989) 'Taxation Concessions and Grants for Industry Research and Development Schemes, Efficiency Audit Report', AGPS, Canberra.
Commonwealth of Australia. Australian Industrial Research and Development Incentives Board (1985) 'Future Government Incentives for Innovation: The Role and Relevance of Industrial Research and Development Incentives', AGPS, Canberra.
— (1985a) *Annual Report 1984–85*, AGPS, Canberra.
Commonwealth of Australia. Australian Research Grants Scheme (1985) 'Advice to Applicants', Canberra.
Commonwealth of Australia. Australian Science and Technology Council (1980) 'Industrial Research and Development: Proposals for Additional Incentives', AGPS, Canberra.

(1982) 'Biotechnology in Australia', AGPS, Canberra.
(1983) 'Incentives for Innovation in Australian Industry', AGPS, Canberra.
(1984) 'Government Purchasing and Offsets Policies in Industrial Innovation', AGPS, Canberra.
(1985) 'Telecommunications Research and Development in Australia', AGPS, Canberra.
(1986) 'The Defence Science and Technology Organization and National Objectives', AGPS, Canberra.
(1986a) 'Mechanisms for Technology Transfer Into Australia', AGPS, Canberra.
Commonwealth of Australia. Bureau of Industry Economics (1987) 'Studies in Industrial Development and Innovation Policy: Introduction and General Overview', AGPS, Canberra.
(1987a) 'Monitoring of the Offsets Program – First Report', Program Evaluation Report no. 3, AGPS, Canberra.
(1988) 'Importing Technology', Research Report no. 25, AGPS, Canberra.
(1988a) 'The Commonwealth Purchasing Preference Margin as an Industry Development Mechanism', AGPS, Canberra.
(1989) 'Globalisation: Implications for the Australian Information Technology Industry', AGPS, Canberra.
(1989a) 'The 150% Tax Concession for Research and Development Expenditure – Interim Report', Program Evaluation Report no. 7, AGPS, Canberra.
(1990) 'The Computer Bounty Scheme', Program Evaluation Report no. 8, AGPS, Canberra.
Commonwealth of Australia. Committee of Inquiry into Telecommunications Services in Australia (1982) *Report*, vols 1–3, AGPS, Canberra.
Commonwealth of Australia. Copyright Law Review Committee (1990) 'Issues Paper: Computer Software Protection', AGPS, Canberra.
Commonwealth of Australia. Department of Defence (1987) *Defence Report 1986–87*, AGPS, Canberra.
(1990) *Defence Report 1989–90*, AGPS, Canberra.
Commonwealth of Australia. Department of Foreign Affairs and Trade (1990) 'Intellectual Property Rights: A Guide to the GATT Uruguay Round', Canberra.
(1991) *Annual Report 1990–91*, AGPS, Canberra.
Commonwealth of Australia. Department of Health (1986) *Annual Report 1985–86*, AGPS, Canberra.
Commonwealth of Australia. Department of Industry, Technology and Commerce, *Australian Technology Magazine*, a newsletter issued periodically by the department.
(1985) 'Committee of Review on Offsets, Report', AGPS, Canberra.
(1985a) 'The Promotion of Indigenous IR&D in Australia and the Effectiveness of the Industrial Research and Development Incentives Scheme – A Summary Report', Price Waterhouse, Canberra.

(1986) *Annual Report 1985–86*, AGPS, Canberra.
(1986a) 'Australian Government Offsets Program – Guidelines for Participants', Canberra.
(1986b) 'Recombinant DNA Monitoring Committee, Monitoring Recombinant DNA Technology: A Five Year Review', AGPS, Canberra.
(1987) *Annual Report 1986–87*, AGPS, Canberra.
(1987a) 'Committee of Review on Government High Technology Purchasing Arrangements, Report', AGPS, Canberra.
(1987b) 'Mechanisms for Encouraging Tertiary Institution and Industry Interaction', Seminar, Record of Proceedings, Melbourne.
(1987c) *Budget 1987–88*, AGPS, Canberra.
(1989) *Annual Report 1988–89*, AGPS, Canberra.
(1990) *Annual Report 1989–90*, AGPS, Canberra.
(1990a) *150% Tax Concession: Guide to Benefits*, AGPS, Canberra.
(1991) *Annual Report 1990–91*, AGPS, Canberra.
Commonwealth of Australia. Department of Science and Technology (1982) 'Genetic Engineering: Commercial Opportunities in Australia', AGPS, Canberra.
Commonwealth of Australia. Department of the Treasury (1985) 'Australia's Foreign Investment Policy – A Guide for Investors', AGPS, Canberra.
(1987) 'Australia's Foreign Investment Policy – A Guide for Investors', AGPS, Canberra.
(1989) 'Australia's Foreign Investment Policy – A Guide for Investors', AGPS, Canberra.
Commonwealth of Australia. Foreign Investment Review Board (1982) *Report 1982*, AGPS, Canberra.
(1986) *Report 1985–86*, AGPS, Canberra.
(1988) *Report 1986–87*, AGPS, Canberra.
(1990) *Report 1989–90*, AGPS, Canberra.
Commonwealth of Australia. House of Representatives (1984) *Parliamentary Debates*, vol. H of R 136, page 895, 28 March 1984, Patents Amendment Bill.
(1984a) *Parliamentary Debates*, vol. H of R 137, page 3141, 7 June 1984, Copyright Amendment Bill.
(1985) *Trade Practices Amendment Bill 1985 – Explanatory Memorandum*, Canberra.
(1991), *Daily Hansard*, page 1760, 12 March 1991, Building a Competitive Australia.
Commonwealth of Australia. House of Representatives Standing Committee for Long-term Strategies (1991) 'Australia as an Information Society: Grasping New Paradigms', AGPS, Canberra.
Commonwealth of Australia. House of Representatives Standing Committee on Legal and Constitutional Affairs (1990) 'Mergers, Takeovers and Monopolies: Profiting from Competition', AGPS, Canberra (the Griffiths Committee).

Commonwealth of Australia. Industrial Property Advisory Committee (1981) 'The Economic Implications of Patents', AGPS, Canberra.
  (1984) 'Patents, Innovation and Competition in Australia', AGPS, Canberra.
Commonwealth of Australia. Industries Assistance Commission (1984) 'Computer Hardware and Software; Typewriters, Calculating and other Office Machines; Parts and Accessories; Recording Media', AGPS, Canberra.
  (1984a) 'Telecommunications and Related Equipment and Parts', AGPS, Canberra.
  (1986) 'Pharmaceutical Products', AGPS, Canberra.
  (1987) *Annual Report 1986-87*, AGPS, Canberra.
Commonwealth of Australia. Industry Research and Development Board (1987) 'Supporting Australian Innovation', Canberra.
  (1991) *Annual Report 1990-91*, AGPS, Canberra.
Commonwealth of Australia. Joint Parliamentary Committee of Public Accounts (1987) 'Implementation of the Offsets Program', Canberra.
Commonwealth of Australia. Law Reform Commission (1983) *Privacy*, Report no. 22, AGPS, Canberra.
Commonwealth of Australia. Minister for Industry, Technology and Commerce (1991) 'New Arrangements for the Telecommunications Industry', DITC, Canberra.
Commonwealth of Australia. Patents Office (1989) *Annual Report 1988-89*, AGPS, Canberra.
Commonwealth of Australia. Senate (1984) *Copyright Amendment Bill 1984 - Explanatory Memorandum*, Canberra.
  (1988) *Parliamentary Debates*, vol. S.130, page 3181, 30 November 1988, Questions Without Notice.
  (1990) *Weekly Hansard*, no. 7, page 2478, 17 September 1990, Patents Bill.
  (1990a) *Weekly Hansard*, no. 7, page 2654, 20 September 1990, Patents Bill.
  (1990b) *Weekly Hansard*, no. 4, page 1271, 29 May 1990, Patents Bill.
Commonwealth of Australia. Senate Standing Committee on Finance and Government Operations (1987) 'List of Commonwealth Bodies', AGPS, Canberra.
Commonwealth of Australia. Senate Standing Committee on Legal and Constitutional Affairs (1991) 'Mergers, Monopolies and Acquisitions: Adequacy of Existing Legislative Controls', AGPS, Canberra (the Cooney Committee).
Commonwealth of Australia. Senate Standing Committee on National Resources (1984) 'Plant Variety Rights', AGPS, Canberra.
Commonwealth of Australia. Trade Practices Commission (1976) *Second Annual Report 1975-76*, AGPS, Canberra.
  (1985) *Annual Report 1984-85*, AGPS, Canberra.
  (1986) *Annual Report 1985-86*, AGPS, Canberra.
  (1987) *Annual Report 1986-87*, AGPS, Canberra.

(1990) 'Background Paper on Section 46 of the Australian Trade Practices Act 1974', *European Competition Law Review* 11: 147.
Commonwealth of Australia. *Trade Practices Commission Bulletin* (1990), no. 54, a periodical published by the commission.
Considine, M. (1988) 'The Corporate Management Framework As Administrative Science: A Critique', *Australian Journal of Public Administration* XLVII: 4.
Cooke, P. (1991) 'Computer Misuse Bill', *Computer Law and Practice* 7: 5.
Corones, S. (1987) 'The New Threshold Test for the Application of Section 46 of the Trade Practices Act', *Australian Business Law Review* 15: 31.
(1990) *Competition Law and Policy in Australia*, Law Book, Sydney.
Cotterell, R. (1984) *The Sociology of Law: An Introduction*, Butterworths, London.
Court, J. (1986) 'The Politics of Copyright and the Problem of Home Taping', *Copyright Reporter* 4(2): 11.
Craig, P. (1987) 'The Monopolies and Mergers Commission: Competition and Administrative Rationality', in R. Baldwin & C. McCrudden (eds), *Regulation and Public Law*, Weidenfeld & Nicolson, London.
Creighton, B. & A. Stewart (1990) *Labour Law: An Introduction*, Federation Press, Sydney.
Crespi, R. (1986) 'Prospects for International Cooperation', in W. Lesser (ed.), *Animal Patents: The Legal, Economic and Social Issues*, Stockton Press, New York.
Daintith, T. (1976) 'The Functions of Law in the Field of Short-term Economic Policy', *Law Quarterly Review* 92: 62.
(1979) 'Regulation by Contract: The New Prerogative', *Current Legal Problems* 32: 41.
(1985) 'The Executive Power Today: Bargaining and Economic Control', in J. Jowell & D. Oliver (eds), *The Changing Constitution*, Clarendon Press, Oxford.
(1988) *Law as an Instrument of Economic Policy: Comparative and Critical Approaches*, Walter de Gruyter, Berlin.
Daintith, T. & G. Teubner (eds) (1986) *Contract and Organisation: Legal Analysis in the Light of Economic and Social Theory*, Walter de Gruyter, Berlin.
Davidow, J. (1989) 'US International Anti-trust Enforcement: Goals and Guidelines', in B. Hawk (ed.), *North American and Common Market Antitrust and Trade Laws, Annual Proceedings of the Fordham Corporate Law Institute*, Matthew Bender, New York.
Davidow, J. & P. Stevens (1990) 'Antitrust Merger Control and National Security Review of Foreign Acquisitions in the United States', *Journal of World Trade* 24(1): 39.
Davidson, D. (1983) 'Protecting Computer Software: A Comprehensive Analysis', *Jurimetrics Journal* 23: 337.

Davis, G. (1985) *Software Protection: Practical and Legal Steps to Protect and Market Computer Programs*, Van Nostrand Reinhold Company, New York.
de Miramon, J. (1990) 'The International Interest in Intellectual Property', *OECD Observer* 163: 4.
de Sola Pool, I. (1990) *Technologies without Boundaries: On Telecommunications in a Global Age*, Harvard University Press, Cambridge, Massachusetts.
de Sousa Santos, B. (1985) 'On Modes of Production of Law and Social Power', *International Journal of the Sociology of Law* 13: 299.
Dean, R. (1990) *The Law of Trade Secrets*, Law Book, Sydney.
Delamarter, R. (1988) *Big Blue: IBM's Use and Abuse of Power*, Pan Books, London.
Dharjee, R. & L. De Chazournes (1990) 'Trade Related Aspects of Intellectual Property Rights (TRIPS): Objectives, Approaches and Basic Principles of the GATT and of Intellectual Property Conventions', *Journal of World Trade* 24(5): 5.
Dickson, D. (1984) *The New Politics of Science*, Pantheon, New York.
Dohlman, E. (1988) 'International Piracy and Intellectual Property', *OECD Observer* 154: 33.
Dosi, T. (1980) *The Intellectual Property Law of Japan*, Sijthoff & Noordhoff, Alphen aan den Rijn, Netherlands.
Drahos, P. (1985) 'Law, Science and Reproductive Technology', *Bulletin of the Australian Society of Legal Philosophy* 9: 270.
Dresser, R. (1988) 'Ethical and Legal Issues in Patenting New Animal Life', *Jurimetrics Journal* 28: 399.
Dunford, R. (1986) 'Is the Development of Technology Helped or Hindered by Patent Law – Can Antitrust Laws Provide the Solution?', *University of New South Wales Law Journal* 9(1): 117.
Edelman, B. (1979) *Ownership of the Image: Elements for a Marxist Theory of Law*, translated by E. Kingdom, Routledge & Kegan Paul, London.
Eder, K. (1988) 'Critique of Habermas's Contribution to the Sociology of Law', *Law and Society Review* 22: 935.
Edgeworth, B. (1988) 'Post-Property? A Postmodern Conception of Private Property', *University of New South Wales Law Journal* 11(1): 87.
Edwards, R. (1979) *Contested Terrain: The Transformation of the Workplace in the Twentieth Century*, Basic Books, New York.
Eisenberg, R. (1987) 'Proprietary Rights, and the Norms of Science in Biotechnology Research', *Yale Law Journal* 97: 177.
— (1989) 'Patents and the Progress of Science: Exclusive Rights and Experimental Use', *University of Chicago Law Review* 56: 1017.
Eisinger, P. (1989) *The Rise of the Entrepreneurial State*, University of Wisconsin Press, Madison.

Elkington, J. (1985) *The Gene Factory: Inside the Biotechnology Business*, Century Publishing, London.
Ellinson, D. (1987) 'Patents and Micro-Organisms', *Law Institute Journal* 61: 1141.
Emerson, J. (1984) 'Computer Software: Detailed Enquiry Needed Before Legislation', *Law Institute Journal* 58: 514.
Etzkowitz, H. (1983) 'Entrepreneurs, Scientists and Entrepreneurial Universities in American Academic Science', *Minerva* 21: 198.
European Commission (1988) 'Document – Articles 85 and 86 EEC Treaty Applied to Agreements Relating to Distribution, Enterprise, Cooperation, Industrial Property Rights and Copyright', *International Review of Industrial Property and Copyright Law* 19: 346.
Ewing, K. (1982) 'Technology Transfers under U.S. Antitrust Law: A Private View', in B. Hawk (ed.), *Antitrust, Technology Transfers and Joint Ventures in International Trade*, Annual Proceedings of the Fordham Corporate Law Institute, Matthew Bender, New York.
Ezrahi, Y. (1980) 'Utopian and Pragmatic Rationalism: The Political Context of Scientific Advice', *Minerva* 18: 111.
Farrell, J. (1989) 'Standardization and Intellectual Property', *Jurimetrics Journal* 30: 35.
Ferne, G. (1990) 'The Economic Stakes in Computer Standardisation', *OECD Observer* 164: 9.
Fetterley, D. (1970) 'Historical Perspectives on Criminal Laws Relating to the Theft of Trade Secrets', *Business Lawyer* 25: 1535.
Fineberg, H. (1985) 'Irresistible Medical Technologies: Weighing the Costs and Benefits', *Prometheus* 3: 119.
Finn, P. (1977) *Fiduciary Obligations*, Law Book, Sydney.
Finn, P. (1984) 'Confidentiality and the "Public Interest" ', *Australian Law Journal* 58: 497.
 (1989) 'Commerce, the Common Law and Morality', *Melbourne University Law Review* 17: 87.
Flint, D. (1985) *Foreign Investment Law in Australia*, Law Book Company, Sydney.
Foy, N. (1974) *The IBM World*, Eyre Methuen, London.
Frame, J. (1983) *International Business and Global Technology*, Lexington Books, Lexington, Massachusetts.
Frazer, T. (1987) 'Competition Law: Mapping the Minefield', *Computer Law and Practice* 3: 199.
Fredman S. & S. Lee (1986) 'Natural Justice for Employees: The Unacceptable Faith of Proceduralism', *Industrial Law Journal* 15: 15.
Freeman, C. (1983) 'Technological Change and the New Economic Context', in S. Hill & R. Johnston (eds), *Future Tense? Technology in Australia*, University of Queensland Press, Brisbane.
 (1987) *The New Technology Gap: Lessons From Japan*, Frances Pinter, London.

Freeman, C. & B. Lundvall (eds) (1988) *Small Countries Facing the Technological Revolution*, Pinter Publishers, London.
Freiberg, A. & P. O'Malley (1984) 'State Intervention and the Civil Offence', *Law and Society Review* 18: 273.
Friedmann, W. (1971) *The State and the Rule of Law in a Mixed Economy*, Stevens, London.
Frignani, A. (1986) 'The GATT Agreement on Government Procurement', *Journal of World Trade Law* 20: 567.
Fukuyama, F. (1992) *The End of History and the Last Man*, Hamish Hamilton, New York.
Fuller, L. (1960) 'Adjudication and the Rule of Law', *Proceedings of the American Society of International Law* 54: 1.
Gadbar, R. & T. Richards (1988) *Intellectual Property Rights: Global Consensus, Global Conflict?*, Westview Press, Boulder, Colorado.
Gaisford, J. & D. McLachlan (1990) 'Domestic Subsidies and Countervail: The Treacherous Ground of the Level Playing Field', *Journal of World Trade* 24(4): 55.
Galbraith, J. (1974) *The New Industrial State*, Pelican Books, Harmondsworth, Middlesex, second edition.
Gamon, L. (1983) 'Patent Law in the Context of Corporate Research', *Journal of Corporation Law* 8: 497.
Gannicott, K. (1980) 'Research and Development Incentives', in Commonwealth of Australia, *Committee of Inquiry into Technological Change in Australia*, vol. 4, AGPS, Canberra.
Ganz, G. (1977) *Government and Industry: The Provision of Financial Assistance to Industry and Its Control*, Professional Books, Abingdon, United Kingdom.
 (1987) *Quasi-legislation: Recent Developments In Secondary Legislation*, Sweet & Maxwell, London.
Gardner, P. & R. Rothwell (1986) 'Innovation and Re-innovation: A Role for the User', *Journal of Marketing Management* 2: 109.
Gaze, B. (1989) *Copyright Protection of Computer Programs*, Federation Press, Sydney.
Gaze, E. (1985) 'The Anton Piller Order – A Review of its Development and Scope', *Australian Business Law Review* 13: 354.
Gee, S. (1981) *Technology Transfer, Innovation, and International Competitiveness*, John Wiley & Sons, New York.
Gesmer, L. (1986) 'Developments in the Law of Computer Software Copyright Infringement', *Jurimetrics Journal* 26: 224.
Gibbons, M. & B. Wittrock (eds) (1985) *Science as a Commodity: Threats to the Open Community of Scholars*, Longman, Harlow, Essex.
Glendon, M. (1981) *The New Family and the New Property*, Butterworths, Toronto.
Goldring, J. (1990) 'Privatising Regulation', *Australian Journal of Public Administration* 49: 419.

Golt, S. (1989) *The GATT Negotiations 1986–90: Origins, Issues and Prospects*, British-North American Committee, London.
Goodfield, J. (1977) *Playing God: Genetic Engineering and the Manipulation of Life*, Hutchinson, London.
Gordon, M. (1987) *Computer Software: Contracting for Development and Distribution*, Wiley Law Publications, New York.
Gordon, R. (1985) 'Macaulay, Macneil, and the Discovery of Solidarity and Power in Contract Law', *Wisconsin Law Review* 1985: 565.
Gormly, R. (1989) 'Using the Tax Act to Fund Research and Development', *Sydney Law Review* 12: 241.
Gosman, A. (1991) 'Issues for Manufacturing and Industry Development', in M. Armstrong (ed.), *New Telecommunications Laws: The 1991 Revolution*, CIRCIT, Melbourne.
Gottersen, A. (1990) 'Income Relief for R & D', in G. Hughes (ed.), *Essays on Computer Law*, Longman Professional, Melbourne.
Grabosky, P. & J. Braithwaite (1986) *Of Manners Gentle: Enforcement Strategies of Australian Business Regulatory Agencies*, Oxford University Press, Melbourne.
Graham, C. (1989) 'Regulating the Company', in L. Hancher & M. Moran (eds), *Capitalism, Culture and Economic Regulation*, Clarendon Press, Oxford.
Graham, C. & T. Prosser (1987) 'Privatising Nationalised Industries: Constitutional Issues and New Legal Techniques', *Modern Law Review* 50: 16.
Grant, P. (1983) 'Technological Sovereignty: Forgotten Factor in the "High-Tech" Razzamataz', *Prometheus* 1: 239.
Grant, W. (1982) *The Political Economy of Industrial Policy*, Butterworths, London.
Grbich, Y. (1984) 'Tax Expenditures As Regulatory Tools: Targeting Superannuation Dollars', in R. Tomasic (ed.), *Business Regulation in Australia*, George Allen & Unwin, Sydney.
Greif, S. (1982) 'The Compulsory Working of Patents: Economic Possibilities and Limits with Special Reference to the Developing Countries', *Law and State* 26: 75.
Grewlich, K. (1987) 'Telecommunications: A European Perspective', in S. Wilks & M. Wright (eds), *Comparative Government-Industry Relations*, Clarendon Press, Oxford.
Grice, R. (1988) 'Joint Ventures with Japanese Companies – Problems of Anti-Monopoly Law', in H. Oda & R. Grice (eds), *Japanese Banking, Securities and Anti-Monopoly Law*, Butterworths, London.
Gurry, F. (1984) *Breach of Confidence*, Clarendon Press, Oxford.
— (1985) 'Breach of Confidence', in P. Finn (ed.), *Essays in Equity*, Law Book, Sydney.
Habermas, J. (1985) 'Law as Medium and Law as Institution', in G. Teubner (ed.), *Dilemmas of Law in the Welfare State*, Walter de Gruyter, Berlin.

Halligan, J. & M. O'Grady (1985) 'Public Sector Reform: Exploring the Victorian Government Experience', *Australian Journal of Public Administration* XLIV: 34.
Hammond, R. (1981) 'Quantum Physics, Econometric Models and Property Rights to Information', *McGill Law Journal* 27: 47.
  (1984) 'Theft of Information', *Law Quarterly Review* 100: 252.
  (1990) 'The Legal Protection of Ideas', *Osgoode Hall Law Journal* 29: 93.
Hancher, L. (1988) 'The Public Sector as Object and Instrument of Economic Policy', in T. Daintith (ed.), *Law as an Instrument of Economic Policy: Comparative and Critical Approaches*, Walter de Gruyter, Berlin.
Hancher, L. & M. Moran (eds) (1989) *Capitalism, Culture and Economic Regulation*, Clarendon Press, Oxford.
Hancher, L. & M. Ruete (1987) 'Legal Culture, Product Licensing and the Drug Industry', in S. Wilks & M. Wright (eds), *Comparative Government–Industry Relations*, Clarendon Press, Oxford.
Harden, I. (1990) 'The Approach of English Law to State Aids to Enterprise', *European Competition Law Review* 11: 100.
Harden, I. & N. Lewis (1986) *The Noble Lie: The British Constitution and the Rule of Law*, Hutchinson Education, London.
Harding, H. & D. Anderson (1982) 'A Patent Dilemma: Plant Variety Rights Legislation for Australia', *Current Affairs Bulletin* 58(12): 4.
Harlow, C. (1980) ' "Public" and "Private" Law: Definition without Distinction', *Modern Law Review* 43: 241.
Harman, E. (1986) 'Government and Business in Western Australia 1983–1985: Legal and Political Aspects of the New Hybrid Enterprises', *Australian Journal of Public Administration* XLV: 247.
Harrington, C. (1988) 'Regulatory Reform: Creating Gaps and Making Markets', *Law and Policy* 10: 293.
Harris, J. (1985) 'A Market-Oriented Approach to the Use of Trade Secret or Copyright Protection (Or Both?) for Software', *Jurimetrics Journal* 25: 147.
Harris, L. (1985) 'Ownership of Employment Creations', *Osgoode Hall Law Journal* 23: 275.
Hausser, E. (1989) 'Intellectual Property Protection for Advanced Biotechnological Processes and Products', *Industrial Property* 28: 161.
Hawk, B. (1988) 'The American (Anti-trust) Revolution: Lessons for the EEC?', *European Competition Law Review* 9: 53.
Hayek, F. (1960) *The Constitution of Liberty*, University of Chicago Press, Chicago.
Head, B. (1986) 'Western Australia: The Pursuit of Growth', in B. Head (ed.), *The Politics of Development in Australia*, Allen & Unwin, Sydney.
Hedley, S. (1988) 'Contract, Tort and Restitution, or, On Cutting the Legal System Down to Size', *Legal Studies* 8: 137.
Heilbroner, R. (1970) *Between Capitalism and Socialism: Essays in Political Economics*, Random House, New York.

Henry, N. (1975) *Copyright, Information Technology and Public Policy*, Part I: 'Copyright - Public Policies' and Part II: 'Public Policies - Information Technology', Marcel Dekker Inc., New York.

Hersey, J. (1979) 'Dissent from CONTU's Software Recommendation', in G. Bush & R. Dreyfuss (eds), *Technology and Copyright: Sources and Materials*, Lomond Books, Mt Airy, Maryland.

Hill, S. (1983) 'Technology and Society', in S. Hill & R. Johnston (eds), *Future Tense? Technology in Australia*, University of Queensland Press, Brisbane.

(1988) *The Tragedy of Technology: Human Liberation Versus Domination in the Late Twentieth Century*, Pluto Press, London.

Hills, J. (1984) *Information Technology and Industrial Policy*, Croom Helm, London.

Hirsch, J. (1978) 'Elements of a Theory of the Bourgeois State', in J. Holloway & S. Picciotto (eds), *State and Capitalism: A Marxist Debate*, Edward Arnold, London.

Hirst, P. (1979) 'Introduction', in B. Edelman, *Ownership of the Image*, translated by E. Kingdom, Routledge & Kegan Paul, London.

Hodkinson, K. (1988) 'Spies, Braindrains and Allied Problems: Reflections on English Industrial Espionage Law', *International Journal of Technology Management* 3(1/2): 87.

Hollinger, R. & L. Lanza-Kaduce (1988) 'The Process of Criminalization: The Case of Computer Crime Laws', *Criminology* 26: 101.

Holloway, J. & S. Picciotto (eds) *State and Capitalism: A Marxist Debate*, Edward Arnold, London.

Hopkins, A. (1978) *Crime Law and Business: The Sociological Sources of Australian Monopoly Law*, Australian Institute of Criminology, Canberra.

Hopt, K. (1987) 'Restrictive Trade Practices and Juridification: A Comparative Law Study', in G. Teubner (ed.), *Juridification of Social Spheres: A Comparative Analysis in the Areas of Labor, Corporate, Antitrust, and Social Welfare Law*, Walter de Gruyter, Berlin.

Horowitz, D. (1991) 'The Impending "Second Generation" Agreements between the European Community and Eastern Europe - Some Practical Considerations', *Journal of World Trade* 25(2): 55.

Horwitz, M. (1977) *The Transformation of American Law 1780-1860*, Harvard University Press, Cambridge, Massachusetts.

Houghton, J. & S. Paltridge (1991) 'Telecommunications Equipment Manufacturing in Australia: Opportunities and Policy Options', Policy Research Paper no. 15, CIRCIT, Melbourne.

(1991a) 'Telecommunications Policy and Industry Policy: How Compatible?', in W. Melody (ed.), *Implementing the New Telecommunications Policy: From Words to Deeds*, CIRCIT, Melbourne.

Howard, J. (1986) 'Administrative Chronicle - Federal Government', *Australian Journal of Public Administration* XLV: 271.

## Bibliography

Howse, R., J. Prichard & M. Trebilcock (1990) 'New Perspectives on Instrument Choice: Smaller or Smarter Government?', *University of Toronto Law Journal* 40: 498.
Hughes, G. (1988) 'Australian Computer Law and the English Experience', *Australian Business Law Review* 16: 208.
  (1991) 'Recent Developments in Australian Computer Crime Regulation', *Computer Law and Practice* 7(3): 94.
Hughes, G. & M. Sharpe (1987) *Computer Contracts: Principles and Precedents*, Law Book, Sydney.
Hunt, A. (1978) *The Sociological Movement in Law*, Macmillan, London.
Hurst, J. (1977) *Law and Social Order in the United States*, Cornell University Press, Ithaca, New York.
Irwin, M. (1987) 'Telecommunications and Government: The US Experience', in S. Wilks & M. Wright (eds), *Comparative Government–Industry Relations*, Clarendon Press, Oxford.
Jackson, J. (1989) *The World Trading System*, MIT Press, Cambridge, Massachusetts.
Janisch, H. & M. Irwin (1982) 'Information Technology and Public Policy: Regulatory Implications for Canada', *Osgoode Hall Law Journal* 20: 610.
Jarass, H. (1988) 'Regulation as an Instrument of Policy', in T. Daintith (ed.), *Law as an Instrument of Economic Policy: Comparative and Critical Approaches*, Walter de Gruyter, Berlin.
Jasanoff, S. (1985) 'Technological Innovation in a Corporatist State: The Case of Biotechnology in the Federal Republic of Germany', *Research Policy* 14: 23.
Jehoram, H. (1989) 'Critical Reflections on the Economic Importance of Copyright', *International Review of Industrial Property and Copyright Law* 20: 485.
Jessop, B. (1982), *Theories of the Capitalist State*, Martin Robertson, Oxford.
Jevons, F. & M. Saupin (1991) 'Capturing Regional Benefits from Science and Technology: The Question of Regional Appropriability', *Prometheus* 9: 265.
Johnston, R. (1983) 'The Control of Technological Change in Australia', in S. Hill & R. Johnston (eds), *Future Tense? Technology in Australia*, University of Queensland Press, Brisbane.
Johnston R. & P. Gummett (eds) (1979) *Directing Technology: Policies for Promotion and Control*, St Martin's Press, New York.
Joseph, R. (1984) 'Recent Trends in Australian Government Policies for Technological Innovation', *Prometheus* 2: 93.
  (1989) 'The Politics of High Technology in Australia', *Prometheus* 7: 103.
Kahn-Freund, O. (1967) 'A Note on Status and Contract in British Labour Law', *Modern Law Review* 30: 635.
Kamenka, E. & A. Tay (1975) 'Beyond Bourgeois Individualism: The Contemporary Crisis in Law and Legal Ideology', in E. Kamenka

& R. Neale (eds), *Feudalism, Capitalism and Beyond*, Australian National University Press, Canberra.

Karjala, D. (1987) 'Copyright, Computer Software, and the New Protectionism', *Jurimetrics Journal* 28: 33.

(1988) 'The Protection of Operating Software Under Japanese Copyright Law', *Jurimetrics Journal* 29: 43.

(1990) 'Intellectual Property Rights in Japan and the Protection of Computer Software', in Rushing, F. & C. Brown (eds), *Intellectual Property Rights in Science, Technology, and Economic Performance*, Westview Press, Boulder, Colorado.

Kearney, J. (1985) *The Action for Breach of Confidence in Australia*, Legal Books, Sydney.

Keenoy, T. (1980) 'Industrial Relations and the Law: From the Webbs to Corporatism', in Z. Bankowski & T. Mungham (eds), *Essays in Law and Society*, Routledge & Kegan Paul, London.

Kenney, M. (1986) *Biotechnology: The University-Industrial Complex*, Yale University Press, New Haven.

Kettler, D. (1987) 'Legal Reconstitution of the Welfare State: A Latent Social Democratic Legacy', *Law and Society Review* 21: 9.

Kindermann, M. (1988) 'The International Copyright of Computer Software: History, Status and Developments', *Copyright* – Monthly Review of the World Intellectual Property Organization, April 1988, p. 201.

Kingston, W. (1984) *The Political Economy of Innovation*, Martinus Nijhoff, The Hague.

Kirby, M. (1981) 'Beyond Frontier Marked "Policy – Lawyers Keep Out" ', *Federal Law Review* 12: 121.

(1983) *Reform the Law*, Oxford University Press, Melbourne.

(1990) 'Legal Aspects of Informatics and Transborder Data Flows', in G. Hughes (ed.), *Essays on Computer Law*, Longman Professional, Melbourne.

Kitch, E. (1978) 'The Nature and Functions of the Patent System', *Journal of Law and Economics* 20: 265.

(1980) 'The Law and Economics of Rights in Valuable Information', *Journal of Legal Studies* 9: 683.

Klare, K. (1982) 'Critical Theory and Labour Relations Law', in D. Kairys (ed.), *The Politics of Law: A Progressive Critique*, Pantheon Books, New York.

Kloppenburg, J. & D. Kleinman (1987) 'Seed Wars: Common Heritage, Private Property and Political Strategy', *Socialist Review* 95: 7.

Korah, V. (1985) *Patent Licensing and EEC Competition Rules*, ESC Publishing, Oxford.

(1988) 'R & D Joint Ventures and the EC Competition Rules', *International Journal of Technology Management* 3(1/2): 7.

Koval, R. (1987) 'What Price The Sale of Reproductive Technology?', *Critical Social Policy* 7: 5.

Krever, R. (1985) 'Tax Expenditures: The Other Spending Program', *Legal Service Bulletin* 10: 63.
Krommenacker, R. (1986) 'The Impact of Information Technology on Trade Interdependence', *Journal of World Trade Law* 20: 381.
Krygier, M. (1987) 'Critical Legal Studies and Social Theory – A Response to Alan Hunt', *Oxford Journal of Legal Studies* 7: 26.
Kutten, J. (1985) 'Some Comments on the American Software Industry', *Computers and Law* 45: 14.
  (1986) 'An Overview of American Trade Secret Law', *Computers and Law* 47: 6.
Labonze, E. (1988) 'Automatic DNA Sequencing and the Human Genome Sequencing Project', *Impact of Science on Society* 38: 75.
Lahore, J., J. Dwyer & J. Garnsey (eds) (1980) *Intellectual Property in Australia: Patents, Designs, Trade Marks, Confidential Information, Unfair Competition*, Butterworths, Sydney, updated.
Lakoff, S. & H. York (1989) *A Shield in Space? Technology, Politics and the Strategic Defence Initiative*, University of California Press, Berkeley, California.
Lall, S. (1985) *Multinationals, Technology and Exports – Selected Papers*, Macmillan, London.
Lamberton, D. (1984) 'The Economics of Information and Organization', *Annual Review of Information Science and Technology* 19: 3.
  (1987) 'Patent Reform in Australia', *Prometheus* 5: 73.
  (1990) 'Information Economics: "Threatened Wreckage" or New Paradigm?', Working Paper 1990/1, CIRCIT, Melbourne.
Landes, D. (1969) *The Unbound Prometheus: Technological Change and Industrial Development in Western Europe from 1750 to the Present*, Cambridge University Press, Cambridge.
Lash, S. & J. Urry (1987) *The End of Organized Capitalism*, Polity Press, Cambridge.
Law Commission for England and Wales (1981) *Breach of Confidence*, HMSO, London.
Lawrence, G. (1984) 'Biotechnology: Sunrise or Sunset?', *Journal of Australian Political Economy* 17: 3.
  (1989) 'Genetic Engineering and Australian Agriculture: Agenda for Corporate Control', *Journal of Australian Political Economy* 25: 1.
Lewis, D. & J. Mangan (1987) 'Research and Development in Australia: The Role of Multinational Corporations', *Prometheus* 5: 368.
Liesch, P. (1986) 'The Australian Government Offsets Program', *Prometheus* 4: 306.
Llewellyn, H. (1981) 'The Use of Patents by Australian Industry', *Search* 12: 389.
Lockhardt, J. (1984) 'Copyright and Advancing Technology', *Copyright Reporter* 2(4): 9.
Locksley, G. (1986) 'Information Technology and Capitalist Development', *Capital and Class* 27: 81.

Long, F. (1981) *Restrictive Business Practices, Transnational Corporations, and Development: A Survey*, Martinus Nijhoff Publishing, Boston.
Loveday, P. (1982) *Promoting Industry*, University of Queensland Press, Brisbane.
Lowe, G. & R. McQueen (1985) 'Drawing Together a Sociology of Law in Australia: Law, Capitalism and Democracy by Pat O'Malley', *Australian Journal of Law and Society* 2(2): 84.
Lowe, J. & M. Atkins (1991) 'Australian, US and UK Technology Transactions', *Prometheus* 9: 138.
Lucke, H. (1987) 'Good Faith and Contractual Performance', in P. Finn (ed.), *Essays on Contract*, Law Book, Sydney.
Luhmann, N. (1982) *The Differentiation of Society*, translated by S. Holmes & C. Larmore, Columbia University Press, New York.
Macaulay, S. (1985) 'An Empirical View of Contract', *Wisconsin Law Review* 1985: 465.
MacDonald, S. (1983) 'High Technology Policy and the Silicon Valley Model: An Australian Perspective', *Prometheus* 1: 330.
(1986) 'Theoretically Sound: Practically Useless? Government Grants For Industrial R and D In Australia', *Research Policy* 15: 269.
MacDonald, S. (1990) *Technology and the Tyranny of Export Controls: Whisper Who Dares*, Macmillan, London.
Macken, J., C. Moloney & G. McCarry (1978) *The Common Law of Employment*, Law Book Company, Sydney.
MacLeod, C. (1988) *Inventing the Industrial Revolution: The English Patent System, 1660-1800*, Cambridge University Press, Cambridge.
Macneil, I. (1980), *The New Social Contract: An Inquiry into Modern Contractual Relations*, Yale University Press, New Haven.
Macpherson, C. (ed.) (1978) *Property: Mainstream and Critical Positions*, University of Toronto Press, Toronto.
MacPherson, C. (1975) 'Capitalism and the Changing Concept of Property', in E. Kamenka & R. Neale (eds), *Feudalism, Capitalism and Beyond*, Australian National University Press, Canberra.
Mandeville, T., D. Lamberton & E. Bishop (1982) *Economic Effects of the Australian Patent System: A Commissioned Report to the Industrial Property Advisory Committee*, AGPS, Canberra.
Mansell, R. (1988) 'Telecommunication Network-Based Services: Regulation and Market Structure In Transition', *Telecommunications Policy* 12: 243.
Mansell, R., P. Holmes & K. Morgan (1990) 'European Integration and Telecommunications: Restructuring Markets and Institutions', *Prometheus* 8: 50.
Mansfield, E. & L. Switzer (1985) 'The Effects of R and D Tax Credits and Allowances in Canada', *Research Policy* 14: 97.
Marceau, J. (1990) 'Neither Fish nor Fowl: Theorising Emerging Organisational Forms in a Small Open Industrial Economy (Australia)', Working Paper 1990/2, CIRCIT, Melbourne.

Markey, H. (1989) 'Patentability of Animals in the United States', *International Review of Industrial Property and Copyright Law* 20: 372.
Marks, C. (1987) 'Copyright Tribunal in Australia', *Copyright Reporter* 5(3): 11.
Mathews, J. (1987) 'Proposal to Establish a Victorian Technology Incubator Facility in the Western Suburbs with Links to Tertiary Educational Institutions', Background Paper and Consultancy Brief, Resources Coordination Division, Ministry of Education, Government of Victoria, March 1987.
— (1989) *Tools of Change: New Technology and the Democratisation of Work*, Pluto Press, Sydney.
Mattelart, A. (1979) *Multinational Corporations and the Control of Culture*, translated by M. Chanan, Harvester Press, Sussex.
Mawhood, J. (1987) 'Information, Equity and Entropy (Information Technology Law in England)', *Computer Law and Practice* 3: 186.
McAuslan, P. (1983) 'Administrative Law, Collective Consumption and Judicial Policy', *Modern Law Review* 46: 1.
McAuslan, P. & J. McEldowney (eds) (1985) *Law, Legitimacy and the Constitution: Essays Marking the Centenary of Dicey's Law of the Constitution*, Sweet & Maxwell, London.
McCarthy, T. (1985) 'Copyright Law and Antitrust Policy – Coexistence or Conflict? The American Experience', *Australian Business Law Review* 13: 198.
McComas, W., M. Davison & D. Gonski (1981) *The Protection of Trade Secrets*, Butterworths, Sydney.
McDonald, G. (1988) 'US Antitrust Law as it Relates to US r & d Joint Ventures', *International Journal of Technology Management* 3(1/2): 123.
McEldowney, J. (1991) 'The National Audit Office and Privatisation', *Modern Law Review* 54: 933.
McGarrity, T. (1986) 'Regulatory Reform and the Positive State: An Historical Overview', *Administrative Law Review* 38: 339.
McGovern, E. (1986) *International Trade Regulation: GATT, the United States and the European Community*, Globefield Press, Exeter, second edition.
McInerney, D. (1987) 'Antitrust Scrutiny of Joint R & D Ventures in the US and the EEC', in B. Hawk (ed.), *United States and Common Market Anti-Trust Policies*, Annual Proceedings of the Fordham Corporate Law Institute, Matthew Bender, New York.
McKenna, M. (1991) 'Dyason v. Autodesk Inc: Copyright Protection for Computer Software in the 1990's', *University of Western Australia Law Review* 21: 183.
McKeogh, J. (1986) 'Semi Conductor Chip Protection: Copyright or Sui Generis?', *University of New South Wales Law Journal* 9: 101.
McKeogh, J. & A. Stewart (1991) *Intellectual Property in Australia*, Butterworths, Sydney.

McQueen, R. (1980) 'Propagation of Growth: Agribusiness and the Seed Industry in Australia', *Journal of Australian Political Economy* 9: 59.
Mercer, D. (1987) *IBM: How the World's Most Successful Corporation Is Managed*, Kogan Page, London.
Michalowski, R. & E. Pfuhl (1991) 'Technology, Property and Law', *Crime, Law and Social Change* 15: 255.
Milgrom, R. (1985) *Milgrom on Trade Secrets*, Matthew Bender, New York.
Miller, R. (1974) *Legal Aspects of Technology Utilization*, Lexington Books, Lexington, Massachusetts.
Morgan, K. (1991) 'Structural Adjustment in the Labour Force', in W. Melody (ed.), *Implementing the New Telecommunications Policy: From Words to Deeds*, CIRCIT, Melbourne.
Morris, P. (1983) 'Australia's Dependence on Imported Technology – Some Issues for Discussion', *Prometheus* 1: 144.
Mouer, R. & Y. Sugimoto (eds) (1990) *The MFP Debate: A Background Reader*, La Trobe University Press, Melbourne.
Moufang, R. (1989) 'Patentability of Genetic Inventions in Animals', *International Review of Industrial Property and Copyright Law* 20: 823.
Murley, K. (1990) 'Government Assistance to the Software Industry', in G. Hughes (ed.), *Essays on Computer Law*, Longman Professional, Melbourne.
Murray, J. & F. Horwitz (1988) 'Technology Offsets: Structuring A New Strategy For Industrial Benefits", *International Journal of Technology Management* 3: 427.
Nelken, D. (1982) 'Is There A Crisis in Law and Legal Ideology?', *Journal of Law and Society* 9: 177.
Nelkin, D. (1984) *Science as Intellectual Property: Who Controls Scientific Research?*, Cornell/Macmillan, New York.
Neumeyer, F. (1971) *The Employed Inventor in United States: R & D Policies, Law and Practice*, MIT Press, Cambridge, Massachusetts.
New South Wales Auditor-General, *Auditor-General's Report for 1989*, vol. 1, Auditor-General's Office, Sydney.
Newman, E. (1976) 'An Institutional Perspective on Information', *International Social Sciences Journal* XXVIIII: 466.
Newman, O. (1981) *The Challenge of Corporatism*, Macmillan, London.
Niers, H. (1990) 'Patent Protection of Biotechnological Inventions – American Perspectives', *International Review of Industrial Property and Copyright* 21: 480.
Nimmer, R. (1991) 'Globalization of Law: Commercial and Intellectual Property Markets', mimeo, Law Center, University of Houston, Texas.
Nixson, F. (1983) 'Controlling the Transnationals? Political Economy and the United Nations Code of Conduct', *International Journal of the Sociology of Law* 11: 83.
Noble, D. (1977) *America By Design: Science, Technology and the Rise of Corporate Capitalism*, Oxford University Press, New York.

(1979) 'Social Choice in Machine Design: The Case of Numerically Controlled Machine Tools', in A. Zimbalist (ed.), *Case Studies on the Labour Process, Monthly Review*, Academic Press, New York.
Nogues, J. (1990) 'Patents and Pharmaceutical Products: Understanding the Pressures on Developing Countries', *Journal of World Trade* 24(6): 81.
Nonet, P. & P. Selznick (1978) *Law and Society in Transition*, Harper Colophon, New York.
Nora, S. & A. Minc (1980) *The Computerisation of Society*, MIT Press, Cambridge, Massachusetts.
O'Donnell, G. (1983) *A Short Note on Anti-Copyright*, Copyright Agency Limited, Sydney.
O'Hagan, T. (1984) *The End of Law?*, Basil Blackwell, Oxford.
O'Malley, P. (1983) *Law, Capitalism and Democracy*, George Allen & Unwin, Sydney.
O'Malley, P. (1984) 'Technocratic Justice in Australia', *Law in Context* 2: 31.
Offe, C. (1975) 'The Theory of the Capitalist State and the Problem of Policy Formation', in L. Lindberg (ed.), *Stress and Contradiction in Modern Capitalism: Public Policy and the Theory of the State*, Lexington Books, Lexington, Massachusetts.
Offe, C. (1984) *Contradictions of the Welfare State*, edited by J. Keane, Hutchinson, London.
Organization for Economic Cooperation and Development (1982) *Biotechnology: International Trends and Perspectives*, OECD, Paris.
(1983) *An Exploration of Legal Issues in Information and Communication Technologies*, OECD, Paris.
(1984) *Competition and Trade Policies: Their Interaction*, OECD, Paris.
(1985) *Biotechnology and Patent Protection: An International Review*, OECD, Paris.
(1985a) *Software: An Emerging Industry*, OECD, Paris.
(1986) *Competition Policy and Joint Ventures*, OECD, Paris.
(1986a) *Computer Related Crime: Analysis of Legal Policy*, OECD, Paris.
(1986b) *Liberalization of Trade and Investment in the Services Sector: The Role of the OECD Codes*, OECD Observer 136: 25.
(1988) *Biotechnology: The Changing Role of Government*, OECD, Paris.
(1989) *Competition Policy and Intellectual Property Rights*, OECD, Paris.
Orkin, N. (1981) 'The Legal Rights of the Employee Inventor in the United States: A Labor-Management Perspective', in J. Phillips (ed.), *Employee Inventions: A Comparative Perspective*, Fernsway Publications, London.
Oxley, A. (1991) 'International Trade in Telecommunications Services: The Pressure of Free Trade Paradigms', Policy Research Paper no. 12, CIRCIT, Melbourne.
Palmer, J. (1986) 'Copyright and Computer Software', *Research in Law and Economics* 8: 205.

Palmer, N. (1990) 'Information as Property', in L. Clarke (ed.), *Confidentiality and the Law*, Lloyds of London Press, London.
Panitch, L. (1980) 'Recent Theorizations of Corporatism: Reflections on a Growth Industry', *British Journal of Sociology* 31: 159.
Papparlardo, A. (1991) 'State Measures and Public Undertakings: Article 90 of the EEC Treaty Revisited', *European Competition Law Review* 12: 29.
Parry, T. (1984) 'International Technology Transfer: Emerging Corporate Strategies', *Prometheus* 2: 220.
Parsons, T. (1964) 'Evolutionary Universals in Society', *American Sociological Review* 29: 339.
Patel, P. & K. Pavitt (1990) 'The Nature, Determinants, and Implications of Uneven Technological Development', in J. de la Mothe & L. Ducharme (eds), *Science, Technology and Free Trade*, Pinter Publishers, London.
Pavitt, K. (1979) 'Governmental Support for Industrial Innovation: the Western European Experience', in R. Johnston & P. Gummett (eds), *Directing Technology: Policies for Promotion and Control*, Croom Helm, London.
Pavitt, K. (1984) 'Sectoral Patterns of Technical Change: Towards A Taxonomy and A Theory', *Research Policy* 13: 314.
Peachment, A. (ed.) (1991) *The Business of Government: Western Australia 1983-1990*, Federation Press, Sydney.
Pearson, H. (1984) *Computer Contracts: An International Guide to Agreements and Software Protection*, Kluwer, London.
(1987) 'Second Thoughts on "Look and Feel" Copyright Protection for Software', *Computer Law and Practice* 3: 157.
Pengilley, W. (1977) 'Patents and Trade Practices – Competition Policies in Conflict', *Australian Business Law Review* 5: 172.
(1980) 'Building An Australian Enterprise Based on Overseas Technology – Antitrust Considerations', *Antitrust Bulletin* XXV: 831.
(1984) 'Competition Policy and Law Enforcement', *Australian Journal of Law and Society* 2(1): 1.
Peterson, J. (1991) 'Technology Policy in Europe; Explaining the Framework Programme and Eureka in Theory and Practice', *Journal of Common Market Studies* XXIX: 269.
Phelps, B. (1990) 'Should We Tamper With Nature?', in Centre for Human Bioethics, Ethics and Intellectual Property – 'Should We Create and Commercialize New Life-forms?', papers for a one-day conference, 19 October 1990, Monash University, Melbourne.
Phillips, B. (1989) 'The Patent Paradox in Competition Policy', OECD *Observer* 159: 19.
Phillips, J. (1981) 'Employee Inventions: An Analysis of the Nature of the Subject', in J. Phillips (ed.), *Employee Inventions: A Comparative Study*, Fernsway Publications, London.

Phillips J. (ed.) (1985) *Patents in Perspective*, ESC Publishing Limited, Oxford.
Picciotto, S. (1979) 'The Theory of the State, Class Struggle, and the Rule of Law', in B. Fine & others (eds), *Capitalism and the Rule of Law*, Hutchinson, London.
— (1983) 'Jurisdictional Conflicts, International Law and the International State System', *International Journal of the Sociology of Law* 11: 11.
Poberezny, M. (1982) 'Plant Varietal Rights - The Case Against Plant Patenting', *Legal Service Bulletin* 7: 225.
Polfanders, J. (1989) 'The Idea/Expression Dichotomy', *Copyright Reporter* 7(5): 1.
Porter, M. (1990) *The Competitive Advantage of Nations*, The Free Press, New York.
Porter, V. (1989) 'The Copyright Designs and Patents Act 1988: The Triumph of Expediency over Principle', *Journal of Law and Society* 16: 340.
Posner, R. (1970) *Economic Analysis of Law*, Little Brown, Boston.
Powers, M. (1991) 'Japanese Intellectual Property Law', *Journal of Proprietary Rights* 3(3): 8.
Poynter, T. (1985) *Multinational Enterprises and Government Intervention*, Croom Helm, London.
Prosser, T. (1982) 'Towards A Critical Public Law', *Journal of Law and Society* 9: 1.
— (1989) 'Regulation of Privatised Enterprises: Institutions and Procedures', in L. Hancher & M. Moran (eds), *Capitalism, Culture and Economic Regulation*, Clarendon Press, Oxford.
Pugh, E. (1984) *Memories That Shaped An Industry: Decisions Leading to IBM System/360*, MIT Press, Cambridge, Massachusetts.
Puri K. (1978) *Australian Government Contracts: Law and Practice*, CCH, Sydney.
Pusey, M. (1991) *Economic Rationalism in Canberra: A Nation-Building State Changes its Mind*, Cambridge University Press, Sydney.
Raghavan, C. (1990) *Recolonization: GATT, The Uruguay Round and the Third World*, Zed Books, London.
Raines, J. (1985) 'Common Market Competition Policy: The EC-IBM Settlement', *Journal of Common Market Studies* XXIV: 137.
Reinecke, I. (1985) *Connecting You: Bridging the Communications Gap*, McPhee Gribble/Penguin Books, Melbourne.
— (1990) 'The Future of R & D and Innovation in Australia', in W. Melody (ed.), *Implementing the New Telecommunications Policy: From Words to Deeds*, CIRCIT, Melbourne.
Reinecke, I. & J. Schulz (1983) *The Phone Book: The Future of Australia's Communications on the Line*, Penguin, Melbourne.
Renner, K. (1949) *The Institutions of Private Law and Their Social Functions*, translated by A. Schwarzchild, Routledge & Kegan Paul, London.

Rescher, N. (1989) *Cognitive Economy: The Economic Dimension of the Theory of Knowledge*, University of Pittsburgh Press, Pittsburgh.
Ricketson, S. (1977) 'Confidential Information – A New Proprietary Interest?', *Melbourne University Law Review* 11: 223.
— (1979) 'The Public Interest and Breach of Confidence', *Melbourne University Law Review* 12: 176.
— (1984) 'The Patentability of Living Organisms', in D. Galligan (ed.), *Essays in Legal Theory*, Melbourne University Press, Melbourne.
— (1984a) 'The Concept of Industrial Property', *Law Institute Journal* 58: 499.
— (1984b) 'Copyright and the Trade Practices Act 1974', *Copyright Reporter* 2(2): 7.
— (1984c) *The Law of Intellectual Property*, Law Book Co., Sydney.
— (1984d) 'Reaping Without Sowing: Unfair Competition and Intellectual Property Rights in Anglo-American Law', *University of New South Wales Law Journal* 7: 1.
— (1991) 'New Wine in Old Bottles: Technological Change and Intellectual Property Rights', Working Paper 1991/5, CIRCIT, Melbourne.
— (1991a) 'The Concept of Originality in Anglo-American Copyright Law', *Copyright Reporter* 9(1): 1.
Rifkin, J. (1985) *Declaration of a Heretic*, Routledge & Kegan Paul, London.
Ringer, B. (1972) 'Copyright Law Revision: History and Prospects', in G. Bush (ed.), *Technology and Copyright: Annotated Bibliography and Source Materials*, Lomond Systems, Mt Airy, Maryland.
Rosegger, G. (1991) 'Advances in Information Technology and the Innovative Strategies of Firms', *Prometheus* 9: 5.
Rosenfeld, S. (1988) 'Sharing Research Results in a Federally Sponsored Gene Mapping Project', *Rutgers Computer and Technology Law Journal* 14: 311.
Roszak, T. (1986) *The Cult of Information; The Folklore of Computers and the True Art of Thinking*, Pantheon, New York.
Rothwell, R. & W. Zegveld (1981) *Industrial Innovation and Public Policy: Preparing for the 1980's and the 1990's*, Frances Pinter, London.
Ryan, N. (1989) 'The MIC Program and the Politics of Science Policy', *Prometheus* 7: 93.
Saxby, S. (1981) 'Employee Invention and English Law', in J. Phillips (ed.), *Employee Inventions: A Comparative Perspective*, Fernsway Publications, London.
Scherer, F. (1980) *Industrial Market Structure and Economic Performance*, Houghton Mifflin, Boston, second edition.
Schiller, H. (1981) *Who Knows: Information in the Age of the Fortune 500*, Ablex Publishing Corporation, Norwood, New Jersey.
Schina, D. (1987) *State Aids under the EEC Treaty: Articles 92 to 94*, ESC Publishing, Oxford.
Schumpeter, J. (1954) *Capitalism, Socialism and Democracy*, Unwin University Books, London, third edition.

Scott, J. (1979) *Corporations, Classes and Capitalism*, Hutchinson University Library, London.
Scott, R. (1981) *The Body as Property*, Allen Lane, London.
Selznick, P. (1969) *Law, Society and Industrial Justice*, Russell Sage Foundation, New York.
Sharp, M. (1987) 'National Policies Towards Biotechnology', *Technovation* 5: 281.
 (1990) 'David, Goliath, and the Biotechnology Business', OECD *Observer* 164: 22.
Sherman, B. (1990) 'Genentech and another v. Wellcome Foundation Ltd', *International Review of Industrial Property and Copyright Law* 21: 78.
Simiditis, S. (1986) 'The Juridification of Labour Relations', *Comparative Labour Law* 7: 93.
Simmie, J. (1981) *Power, Property and Corporatism: The Political Sociology of Planning*, Macmillan, London.
Slattery, J. (1989) 'Recent Patent Law Developments Affecting Biotechnology', *Law Institute Journal* 63: 485.
Slaughter, J. (1990) 'The GATT Intellectual Property Negotiations Approach Their Conclusion', *European Intellectual Property Review* 1990: 418.
Slazidits, C. (1965) 'The Structure and Divisions of the Law - The Civil Law', in *International Encyclopaedia of Comparative Law*, vol. 2, JCB Mohr, Tubingen (edited by R. David).
Smart, B. (1991) *Modern Conditions, Postmodern Controversies*, Routledge, London.
Smith, A. (1980) *Goodbye Gutenberg: The Newspaper Revolution of the 1980s*, Oxford University Press, New York.
 (1982) 'Information Technology and the Myth of Abundance', *Daedalus* 111: 1.
Soltysinski, S. (1990) 'Protection of Computer Programs: Comparative and International Aspects', *International Review of Industrial Property and Copyright Law* 21: 1.
Soma, J. (1976) *The Computer Industry: An Economic and Legal Analysis of Its Technology and Growth*, Lexington Books, Lexington, Massachussetts.
 (1983) *Computer Technology and the Law*, Shepards/McGraw Hill, Colorado Springs.
Sorbel, R. (1981) *IBM: Colossus in Transition*, Truman Talley, New York.
Sprowl, J. & J. Myrick (1982) 'Patent Law for Programmed Computers and Programmed Life Forms', *American Bar Foundation Research Journal* 68: 920.
Stern, S. (1986) 'Computer Software Protection After the 1984 Copyright Statutory Amendments', *Australian Law Journal* 60: 333.
Stewart, A. (1988) 'Confidentiality and the Employment Relationship', *Australian Journal of Labour Law* 1: 1.
Stewart, J. (1989) 'Industry Policy and Why Australia Needs One', *Canberra Bulletin of Public Administration* 59: 11.

Stewart, R. (1981) 'Regulation, Innovation, and Administrative Law: A Conceptual Framework', *California Law Review* 69: 1259.
— (1985) 'The Discontents of Legalism: Interest Group Relations in Administrative Regulation', *Wisconsin Law Review* 1985: 665.
— (1988) 'Regulation and the Crisis of Legalisation in the United States', in T. Daintith (ed.), *Law as an Instrument of Economic Policy: Comparative and Critical Approaches*, Walter de Gruyter, Berlin.
Stigler, G. (1971) 'The Theory of Economic Regulation', *Bell Journal of Economics and Management Science* 2: 3.
Storey, J. & K. Sissons (1990) 'Limits to Transformation: Human Resource Management in the British Context', *Industrial Relations Journal* 21: 60.
Stuckey-Clarke, J. (1990) 'GATT/TRIPS and the Loss of National Sovereignty', *Copyright Reporter* 8(3): 23.
Styrcula, K. (1991) 'The Adequacy of Copyright Protection for Computer Software in the European Community 1992: A Critical Analysis of the EC's Draft Directive', *Jurimetrics Journal* 31: 329.
Sugarman, D. (1983) 'Law, Economy and the State in England, 1750-1914: Some Major Issues', in D. Sugarman (ed.), *Legality, Ideology and the State*, Academic Press, London.
Sugarman, D. & G. Teubner (eds) (1990) *Regulating Corporate Groups in Europe*, Nomos Verlagsgesellschaft, Baden Baden.
Sullivan, C. (1988) 'The Response of the Criminal Law in Australia to Computer Abuse', *Criminal Law Journal* 12: 228.
Szabo, G. (1990) 'Patent Protection of Biotechnological Inventions – European Perspectives', *International Review of Industrial Property and Copyright* 21: 468.
Taggart, M. (1991) 'Corporatisation, Privatisation and Public Law', *Public Law Review* 2: 77.
Taggart, W. (ed.) (1987) *Computer Law in Australia: A Collection of Essays*, Legal Books, Sydney.
Tapper, C. (1978) *Computer Law*, Longman, London.
Taylor, C. & Z. Silberston (1973) *The Economic Impact of the Patent System: A Study of the British Experience*, Cambridge University Press, Cambridge.
Teece, D. (1987) 'Capturing Value From Technological Innovation: Integration, Strategic Partnering, and Licensing Decisions', in B. Guile & H. Brooks (eds), *Technology and Global Industry: Companies and Nations in the World Economy*, National Academy of Engineering Press, Washington.
Teitelman, R. (1989) *Gene Dreams: Wall Street, Academia, and the Rise of Biotechnology*, Basic Books, New York.
Teso, B. & S. Wald (1984) 'Government Policy and Biotechnology: Four Key Issues', *OECD Observer* 131: 16.
Tettenborn, A. (1985) 'Computer Crime in the Commonwealth', *Computers and Law* 46: 24.

Teubner, G. (1984) 'Substantive and Reflexive Elements in Modern Law', *Law and Society Review* 17: 239.
— (1984) 'After Legal Instrumentalism: Strategic Models of Post-regulatory Law', *International Journal of the Sociology of Law* 12: 375.
— (1989) 'How the Law Thinks: Toward a Constructivist Epistemology of Law', *Law and Society Review* 23: 727.
Teubner, G. (ed.) (1988) *Autopoietic Law: A New Approach to Law and Society*, Walter de Gruyter, Berlin.
Thomas, G. & I. Miles (1988) *The Emergence of the New Interactive Services in the United Kingdom, A Report to the Leverhulme Trust*, Science Policy Research Unit, University of Sussex, Brighton.
Thomas, P. (1982) 'Patents for Genetic Engineering Inventions', in Commonwealth of Australia, Department of Science and Technology, *Genetic Engineering: Commercial Opportunities in Australia*, AGPS, Canberra.
— (1983) 'Patents and Biotechnology in Australia: A Race Between Industrial Development and the Law', A Paper Presented to the Australasian Universities Law Schools Association Conference, Auckland, New Zealand, August 1983.
Thompson, D. (1982) 'The UNCTAD Code on Transfer of Technology', *Journal of World Trade Law* 16: 311.
Thompson, M. (1990) 'Breach of Confidence and Privacy', in L. Clarke (ed.), *Confidentiality and the Law*, Lloyds of London Press, London.
Thurow, L. (1992) *Head to Head: The Coming Economic Battle among Japan, Europe and America*, Morrow, New York.
Tidwell, R. (1986) 'United States Defence Procurement', *International Journal of Technology Management* 1(3/4): 541.
Tisdell, C. (1974) 'Patenting and Licensing of Government Inventions – General Issues Raised by Government Policy', *Australian Economic Papers* 13: 188.
Tomasic, R. & B. Pentony (1991) 'Tax Compliance and the Rule of Law: From Legalism to Administrative Procedure?', *Australian Tax Forum* 8: 85.
Trebilcock, M. (1986) *The Common Law of Restraint of Trade: A Legal and Economic Analysis*, Carswell, Toronto.
Treiber, H. (1985) 'Crisis in Regulatory Policy? Remarks on a Topical Theme, or Reflexive Rationality in the Shadow of Codified Law', *Contemporary Crises* 9: 255.
Tribe, L. (1973) *Channelling Technology Through Law*, Bracton Press, Chicago.
Turnbull, B. (1989) 'Intellectual Property and GATT', *Journal of Proprietary Rights* 1(3): 9.
Unger, R. (1976) *Law in Modern Society*, The Free Press, New York.
— (1986) *False Necessity: Anti-necessitarian Social Theory in the Service of Radical Democracy*, Cambridge University Press, New York.
Upham, F. (1987) *Law and Social Change in Postwar Japan*, Harvard University Press, Cambridge, Massachusetts.

Van Zyl Smit, D. (1985) ' "Professional" Patent Agents and the Development of the English Patent System', *International Journal of the Sociology of Law* 13: 79.
Vandevelde, K. (1980) 'The New Property of the Nineteenth Century: The Development of the Modern Concept of Property', *Buffalo Law Review* 29: 325.
Vaver, D. (1990) 'Intellectual Property Today: Of Myths and Paradoxes', *Canadian Bar Review* 69: 98.
Veljanovski, C. (1987) *Selling the State*, Weidenfeld & Nicolson, London.
Venit, J. (1987) 'In the Wake of "Windsurfing": Patent Licensing in the Common Market', in B. Hawk (ed.), *United States and Common Market Anti-Trust Policies, Annual Proceedings of the Fordham Corporate Law Institute*, Matthew Bender, New York.
Victorian Auditor-General, 'Financial Assistance to Industry', Special Report no. 11, Government Printer, Melbourne.
Victorian Department of Industry, Technology and Resources, *Link-Melbourne*, a new technology communication produced periodically by the department.
*Victorian Government Technology Statement* (1986) Government Printer, Melbourne.
Vogel, D. (1987) 'Government–Industry Relations in the United States: An Overview', in S. Wilks & M. Wright (eds), *Comparative Government-Industry Relations*, Clarendon Press, Oxford.
Vollmer, A. (1986) 'Product and Technical Standardization Under Article 85', *European Competition Law Review* 7: 388.
Vossius, V. (1990) 'Patent Protection for Animals: Onco-mouse/Harvard', *European Intellectual Property Review* 1990: 250.
Wakiyama, T. (1987) 'The Implementation and Effectiveness of MITI's Administrative Guidance', in S. Wilks & M. Wright (eds), *Comparative Government-Industry Relations*, Clarendon Press, Oxford.
Wald, S. (1985) 'Biotechnology: How to Improve Patent Protection', *OECD Observer* 136: 15.
Wald, S. (1989) 'The Biotechnological Revolution', *OECD Observer* 156: 16.
Wallerstein, M. (1991) 'Controlling Dual-Use Technologies in the New World Order', *Issues in Science and Technology* VII(4): 70.
Waters, P. & P. Leonard (1991) 'The Lessons of Recent EC and US Developments for the Protection of Computer Software under Australian Law', *European Intellectual Property Review* 1991: 124.
Weber, M. (1954) *On Law in Economy and Society*, translated by E. Shils & M. Rheinstein, Harvard University Press, Cambridge, Massachusetts.
Weeramantry, C. (1983) *The Slumbering Sentinels*, Penguin, Melbourne.
Weinrib, A. (1988) *Information and Property*, University of Toronto Law Journal 38: 117.
Western Australian Royal Commission into Commercial Activities of Government and Other Matters (1991) Discussion Paper, Perth.

Whaite, R. & N. Jones (1989) 'Biotechnological Patents in Europe - The Draft Directive', *European Intellectual Property Review* 1989: 145.
Whalan, D. & K. Kaney (1986) 'Biotechnology and the Law: Co-Operation Nationally and Internationally', *Federal Law Review* 16: 99.
Wilks, S. & M. Wright (eds) (1987) *Comparative Government-Industry Relations*, Clarendon Press, Oxford.
Williams, R. (1973) *European Technology: The Politics of Collaboration*, Croom Helm, London.
Williamson, O. (1981) 'Contract Analysis: The Transaction Cost Approach', in P. Burrows & C. Veljanovski (eds), *The Economic Approach to Law*, Butterworths, London.
Wilson, D. (1987) 'Federal Control of Information in Academic Science', *Jurimetrics Journal* 27: 283.
Wilson, R., P. Ashton & T. Egan (1980) *Innovation, Competition and Government Policy in the Semiconductor Industry*, Lexington Books, Lexington, Massachusetts.
Wiltshire, K. (1987) *Privatisation: The British Experience - An Australian Perspective*, Longman Cheshire, Melbourne.
Wineberg, A. (1988) 'The Japanese Patent System: A Non-Tariff Barrier to Foreign Business?', *Journal of World Trade Law* 22: 11.
Winkler, J. (1975) 'Law, State and Economy: The Industry Act 1975 in Context', *British Journal of Law and Society* 2: 103.
    (1977) 'The Corporatist Economy: Theory and Administration', in R. Scase (ed.), *Industrial Society: Class, Cleavage and Control*, St Martin's Press, New York.
Winn, D. (1990) 'Commission Know-how Regulation 556/89: Innovation and Territorial Exclusivity, Improvements and the *Quid Pro Quo*', *European Competition Law Review* 11: 130.
Winner, L. (1977) *Autonomous Technology: Technics-out-of-Control as a Theme in Political Thought*, MIT Press, Cambridge, Massachusetts.
Winter, G. (1985) 'Bartering Rationality in Regulation', *Law and Society Review* 19: 219.
Wise, A. (1981) *Trade Secrets and Know-how Throughout the World*, Clark Boardman, New York.
Yachinski, S. (1985) *Setting Genes to Work: The Industrial Era of Biotechnology*, Penguin Books, Harmondsworth, Middlesex.
Yoshikawa, S. (1983) 'Fair Trade Commission v. MITI: History of the Conflicts between the Antimonopoly Policy and the Industrial Policy in the Post War Period of Japan', *Case Western Reserve Journal of International Law* 15: 489.
Yoxen, E. (1981) 'Life as a Productive Force: Capitalising the Science and Technology of Molecular Biology', in L. Levidow & R. Young (eds), *Science, Technology and the Labour Process: Marxist Studies*, volume 1, CSE Books, London.
Yoxen, E. (1983) *The Gene Business: Who Should Control Biotechnology?*, Pan Books, London.

# Index

administrative law
  audit offices in, 295-6
  grants for research and development and, 233
  liberalism and, 31, 55
  positive adjustment measures and, 56, 226-8, 284-92, 304
  private regulation and, 31, 277, 298-9
  proceduralism in, 289-90, 305
  public/private divide and, 49, 58
  rule-making and, 226, 294
  tax concessions for research and development and, 242, 243, 292
  telecommunications licensing and, 275-6
Australian government
  competition law, 157, 177-8, 185, 189, 192
  foreign investment review, 210-17
  GATT and, 117, 216, 219, 247, 261
  grants for research and development, 229-33
  local purchasing preference, 245-9, 252
  offsets, 252-9
  patents policy, 73, 76, 90-92
  software copyright, 108, 110-15, 122
  tax concessions for research and development, 233-43
  telecommunications markets and, 263-5
  telecommunications equipment industry and, 265-71
  trade secrets, 147, 153

company law
  competition and, 161
  corporatism and, 47-9
  functions, 43, 46
  public enterprise and, 226, 295
competiton law
  Australian scheme, 177-8
  biotechnology sector and, 71-3, 159-60, 166-8
  computer industry and, 99-101, 158-9
  common law and, 143
  enforcement policy (Australia), 189-93
  exclusive dealing (Australia), 178-80
  foreign trade and, 165, 209-10
  intellectual property licensing practices, 169-73, 179-80, 182-4, 187-9
  intellectual property exceptions for Australia, 187-9
  mergers (Australia), 184-7
  misuse of market power (Australia), 180-4
  nature of, 163-7
  policy towards, 16, 33, 53, 161-3
  research and development consortia, 173-7
  stand-alone tactics, 166-8
  telecommunications industry, 166, 181, 182, 187, 272-4
contract
  confidential information and, 135-6
  competition and, 161
  corporatism and, 47-9
  functions, 15, 43-6
  public purchasing and, 256, 288-9
  significance of, 43-4
copyright of software
  Australian legislation, 110-15
  Australian policy, 108, 110-15, 122
  compulsory licensing, 103-4, 120-21
  criticisms of, 101-3, 110
  derivation and, 97, 99-101
  economic attractions, 98, 108-10
  idea/expression distinction, 96, 101-3, 105
  international developments, 115-19
  piracy, 98-9
corporatism
  competition law and, 163-4, 193
  copyright and, 120
  efficacy, 26-33, 55, 229, 297, 303-4
  nature, 17-19, 50-54

operational rationale, 226-8, 303
patent law and, 95
proceduralism and, 276, 289, 292, 305-7
quasi-legislation in, 226, 294
public/private divide in, 55, 60, 196, 276-7, 287, 295-6, 304
rule of law and, 31, 55-6, 60, 285-6
trade law and, 196, 217-19

developing nations
 foreign investment regulation, 204-5
 GATT and, 200
 globalization and, 26-7, 31-2, 302
 industry development in, 22-4

EC
 competition law, 164, 166, 168, 172-3, 175-6
 copyrighting of software, 118-19
 local content rules and, 247
 patenting of living organisms, 88-9
 positive adjustment measures, 22, 28, 203
 telecommunications industry regulation, 269, 270, 271, 273, 275
 trade secrets, 147-8

free market thought, 30-32, 282

GATT
 foreign investment measures and, 209, 218
 framework of, 198-202
 intellectual property and, 66, 75, 89-90, 117
 liberalism and, 31-2
 public purchasing and, 202, 247
 trade in services, 261
 trade secrets and, 148
globalization
 law of, 31-2, 302
 nation states and, 26-7, 31, 307
grants for research and development
 Australia, 229-33
 EC, 22, 203
 US, 21

information, appropriation of
 confidences law of, 132-44
 criminal law and, 149-51
 contract and, 135-6
 criticisms of, 126-9
 economic attractions, 15, 124-6
 efficacy, 13, 15, 43, 129-31, 151-2
 equity and, 137-9, 152-3
 international developments, 148-9
 know-how and, 142-3

property, as, 44, 135, 139-41, 153
trade secrets and, 134, 145-8, 152-3
innovation
 appropriability importance of, 12-15, 39, 66-71, 98-101, 124-6, 129-32
 competition and, 158-60, 162-3
 complementary assets importance to, 8, 27, 68-9
 industrial clusters and, 9-11
 know-how and, 8, 15, 27
 nature of, 7-11
 opposition to, 32-3, 73-5
 positive adjustment measures and, 20-24, 224-5
 significance of, 1, 7, 26-7
 technocracy and, 24-5

Japan
 copyrighting of software, 115, 118, 120
 competition law, 166, 173, 176-7
 courts, role of, 291-2
 foreign investment regulation, 206
 local purchasing preference, 247
 patenting of living organisms, 88
 positive adjustment measures, 21
 telecommunications industry, 274
 trade secrets, 146-8

liberalism
 competition law and, 164-6, 193
 copyright law and, 120-21
 continuing claims of, 26-32, 57-60, 298, 300
 corporatism, relationship with, 25-33, 56-60, 296-8, 303-5
 nature, 12, 36-49
 patent law and, 95
 private regulation in, 44-6, 196, 217
 privatization and, 276
 trade law and, 196, 199, 217-19

OECD
 competition law and, 165, 209-10
 guidelines for multinational enterprises, 207-9, 210
 information appropriation and, 149, 150
 patent policy, 88
offsets
 around the world, 253
 Australian arrangements for, 252-5
 impacts, 255-7
 partnerships for development program (Australia), 257-9
 telecommunications equipment industry in, 266-71

patents
  administration, 64-5, 68
  Australian policy towards, 76, 90-92
  competition law and, 169-73, 187-9
  compulsory licensing of, 78-9
  conditions on, 78-9
  criteria for grant, 76-8
  criticisms of, 71-5
  deposit procedures, 92-3
  gene shears and, 86
  Harvard mouse and, 87
  industrial significance, 66-71
  international developments, 65-6, 75, 89-90
  living organisms and, 79-89
positive adjustment measures
  Australia and, 223-5
  courts in, 56, 275, 284-92
  EC and, 22
  effectiveness problems of, 26-9, 278-81
  Japan and, 21
  legal nature, 19, 53-4, 226-7
  legislatures and, 56, 292-6
  legitimacy problems of, 29-31, 56, 281-4, 298
  public/private divide and, 227-9
  United States and, 21-2
  use of, 20-24, 53-4, 223-5
post-modernism, 33
privatization
  accountability for, 298
  audit offices and, 276
  government/industry relationships on, 224, 271-7, 283
  telecommunications industry, 271-7
proceduralism
  faith in, 58, 276, 305-7
  public contracts and, 289
  telecommunications licensing in, 276
  tribunals and, 292
procurement preference
  Australian principle, 246-7
  defence purchasing, 249-51
  health care purchasing, 251-2
  national development procurement program, 247-9
  power of, 244-6
  United States, 21-2, 247
property
  confidential information as, 139-41
  copyright, 96-122
  functions, 14-15, 36, 44-6, 301
  innovation and, 12-15, 40-41
  patents, 63-95
  policy towards, 19-20, 23, 39-44, 302
  state intervention as, 36-8, 300-01
  trade secrets as, 146

tax concessions for research and development
  around the world, 239
  eligible activities (Australia), 235-7
  impact of, 240-42
  regulation problems of, 237-9, 243
  syndicates and, 238-9
telecommunications licensing
  Australia Telecom, 268-71
  competition law and, 166, 181, 182, 187, 272-4
  equipment industry development and, 261-3, 265-71, 273-4
  market liberalization, 260-61, 263-5
  regulatory framework Australia, 274-7
  United Kingdom, in, 271-7
  uses of, 266-71, 273-6
trade and investment, foreign
  Australian legislation, 210-13
  Australian policy, 213-17, 219
  developing nations and, 196, 199, 205, 206-7
  direct foreign investment, 198, 204-19
  GATT agenda, 209
  GATT framework, 198-203
  national policies, 16, 19, 23, 53, 194-8, 204-6, 218-19
  OECD guidelines, 207-9
  UNCTAD draft code, 207

United States
  competition law, 162, 165, 166, 168, 171-2, 174-5
  copyrighting of software, 115
  courts, role of, 291
  defence spending, 21-2, 250-51
  foreign investment regulation, 205-06, 209
  patenting of living organisms, 88
  positive adjustment measures, 21-2
  purchasing preference, 247
  structural impediments initiative, 52, 165
  trade secrets, 145-51
  trade sanctions and intellectual property, 88-90, 116-19, 200-01
UNCTAD, 207, 218

WIPO, 65, 89, 116

For EU product safety concerns, contact us at Calle de José Abascal, 56–1°,
28003 Madrid, Spain or eugpsr@cambridge.org.

www.ingramcontent.com/pod-product-compliance
Ingram Content Group UK Ltd.
Pitfield, Milton Keynes, MK11 3LW, UK
UKHW020352060825
461487UK00008B/628